WITHDRAWN

THE MARINES' WAR

An Account of the Struggle for the Pacific from Both American and Japanese Sources

Other Books by

FLETCHER PRATT

HAIL, CAESAR!

ROAD TO EMPIRE

EMPIRE AND THE SEA

NAVY: A HISTORY

NAVY'S WAR

The Marines' War

An Account of the Struggle for the Pacific
from Both American and Japanese Sources

FLETCHER PRATT

WILLIAM SLOANE ASSOCIATES, INC.
Publishers   New York

COPYRIGHT, 1948, BY
FLETCHER PRATT

First Printing

PRINTED IN THE UNITED STATES OF AMERICA

940.54
P914m

To the men with the World and Anchor Badge,
who are always the first in a war and the last
out of it.

5987

A considerable portion of this book has appeared serially in the *Marine Corps Gazette,* to which publication thanks are due.

Contents

Foreword

IN CONNECTION WITH WORKS OF THIS TYPE CONCERNING WORLD War II, it seems to have become customary to issue a disclaimer of official character. If such a disclaimer is necessary in the present case, it is hereby offered; but the fact ought to be obvious without the disclaimer.

A great many official records were placed at the author's disposal, and where the records seemed inadequate or inaccurate, he was allowed to interview eyewitnesses to his heart's content, often subjecting them to highly personal forms of cross-examination. Officers have read the manuscript in various stages and checked it for accuracy as to statement of event; but no one has checked it for opinion, or has attempted to do so. This was the arrangement made when the book was undertaken, and it seemed so incredible to a former war correspondent that any organization would permit such a thing that in the first version of some of the earlier chapters he deliberately introduced some criticisms that were pretty harsh and more than a little unfair—just to see what would happen.

Nothing happened. The Marines to whom they were submitted blinked and took it like the good soldiers they were, even when the points made concerned them personally. The test passages were, of course, removed later, since they were only for test; but they proved to the author's satisfaction that such a book could be produced without benefit of censorship. The point is that when the end of the war was reached the Marine Corps felt pretty proud of its record—proud enough so that it could afford to admit whatever errors had been made, to submit a completely straight record.

That record has been made as thorough as the size of such a book will permit. There are one or two gaps which might be worth mentioning. No account is offered of the doings of the old 4th Regiment on Bataan, nor of the heroic defense of Wake Island. This is a history, not of Marine operations alone, but of Marine operations as integrated into the general strategy of the war—of how they affected and were affected by that strategy. Wake Island was one of the finest exhibitions of combined courage and skill in the whole war, but the full story involves considerations that do not properly belong in this book; and it is the same with Bataan.

Another gap is with regard to Marine air operations, especially on Guadalcanal, and it is a gap that probably never will be filled. The Marine fliers who operated from that beleaguered island were so desperately beset that they kept almost no records (for one thing, they had an actual physical lack of paper on which to keep them), and so many were killed in action that it is almost impossible to recapture their story.

It should also be noted that a full account of Marine influence on the war would say something about the African and European landings. There were no Marines in them except the normal guards aboard the warships, but all the landings were, to a very large degree, the result of Marine training and research. The corps had been discussing the question of amphibious operations ever since World War I, and in 1934 it staged with the fleet a series of exercises in landing on Culebra Island, off Puerto Rico—probably the first of the kind in the world. It is to be noted that most officers of foreign services believed at this time that amphibious operations were impossible on any scale above a raid (they had Gallipoli to back them) and that the Marines had to invent most of their own equipment, including the famous Higgins boat and the amphitrac, LVT.

It is probably too much to say that the Casablanca landing in November, 1942, could not have been a success without the experience of Guadalcanal behind it, though that helped; but it can be maintained that without the Marine background down through the years that crucial African operation would have been something far different than the quick, low-cost victory it was.

So many individuals have been so helpful in the preparation of this book that the thanks due would cover several pages, and are therefore offered to the Marine Corps in general. But especial gratitude is due to Brigadier General O. P. Smith; to Colonel M. B. Twining; to Lieutenant Colonels Clare W. Shisler and V. H. Krulak; and to Miss (ex-Captain) Eugenia Lejeune.

Chapter 1

Guadalcanal: The Planning Phase

T HE PLAN WAS DESIGNATED AS "LONE WOLF." IT CALLED for the 1st Marine Division to be assembled in New Zealand and there to undergo a period of intensive training in amphibious war, looking toward employment in action about January 1, 1943. Behind Lone Wolf lay the easily reached decision at the Joint Chiefs of Staff level that in this war the Marines would be used exclusively in the Pacific.

During the twenty-year peace, when so much of the theory of our military establishment was worked out, the reasons for the existence of the corps had come under consideration. It was clear that the Marines could be justified neither as small-arms men aboard warships nor as elite storm-troop infantry, their employment in World War I. There had accordingly been a steady orientation of Marine thought and training toward specialization for beachhead work. A statement of naval policy in the middle twenties places the Fleet Marine Force highest among the functions of the corps—in the sense of service afloat with interludes of landing on what amounted to police duty. A similar statement of 1940 mentions prominently, and indeed almost exclusively, the far more serious task of winning beachheads under the guns of the Navy and holding them till the arrival of the Army. The area where the Pacific war was being fought consists largely of beachheads beyond which there is so little territory that once they were gained there would be no use for the Army men. It was the obvious theater for Marine activity; but they were primarily an offensive outfit and in those early months of the war it seemed altogether unlikely that we would have the

3

naval means of conducting an offensive anywhere before the turn of the year.

Hence Lone Wolf, and hence Major General Alexander A. Vandegrift, commanding the division, arriving at Wellington, New Zealand, on June 14, 1942, with his new headquarters staff to set up housekeeping and the prospects of six months' intensive training ahead. The time was needed. In the first place, the division was full of new enlistees who were aware of the tradition that Marine is a very tough individual, but who did not quite know how to be tough themselves. They were particularly in need of physical conditioning after the long voyage out aboard transports so thoroughly loaded there was not much opportunity even for calisthenics. In the second place, the organization of the division as such was still far from complete or smoothly functioning. It was the 1st Marine Division not only in designation but also in actuality, the first in Marine Corps history. There had never before been enough Marines to make a division, since beachheading on the scale this war eventually demanded had not even been contemplated.

Various officers had been to the Command and General Staff School, but there was no reserve of experience in handling divisional problems and the lessons of Army experience were not altogether applicable. An Army division is one of infantry, armored troops, mountain fighters, or some other specialists, to which other specialized formations are attached to form a corps which can conduct the type of operation demanded by the terrain. A Marine division approaches far more nearly the old divisional ideal of being a little self-contained army. All the special formations—tanks, for example—are here within the organization, and so are some the Army never has, such as an amphibious tractor command made necessary by the special problem of moving across beaches into battle. Moreover and very important, all these specialists of whatever character have to be trained by the Marine Corps as combat infantry; there are no rear areas in beachhead fighting. For that matter nobody had a really clear idea of what beachhead work would be like, how best to handle such an apparently minor detail as the question of whose message should have priority on the few radio sets accompanying the first wave.

Six months was none too much if details like this and questions like the field performance of the new Reising sub-machine gun were to be settled without the far costlier process of battle experience. For that matter there were a good many unsettled details within the organization of the division itself. General Vandegrift had never seen his men assembled in a single place, and many of the officers, even in the higher ranks, he did not know. Of the three combat teams into which the division was separated, only one had come with the convoy. While the divisional organization was still in progress, back in the States, one team—and that the most nearly trained —had been shipped to Samoa when there was every expectation that the Japanese drive to the southwest would carry them into that island group. The third combat team was just leaving San Francisco for New Zealand when on 26 June General Vandegrift was called to Auckland for an interview with Vice-Admiral Ghormley.

That officer was then commander of the South Pacific Area, which marched with the Southwest Pacific Area commanded by General MacArthur along a line that gave Ghormley authority in New Zealand, New Caledonia, and the islands up to a somewhat ill-defined point near the equator, beyond which it did not matter since the only authority that ran was Japanese. The Admiral was a big man, genial as to temperament, secretive as to disposition, regarded by a good many in his own service as the best brain it had. He handed the Marine general an order from Washington: The Lone Wolf plan was off in favor of a new operation designated "Pestilence." It was to be an attack on the Japanese in the Guadal-canal-Tulagi region at the southern tip of the Solomon Islands chain. The Japanese had occupied the place in May and were believed to be building an airfield. (This fell within the MacArthur area and the fact was to cause some bickering later until the boundaries were redrawn, but at present it did not matter.) The date would be 1 August. The forces assigned were the two available combat teams of Vandegrift's own division (Samoa to keep its allotment), a combat team of the 2nd Marine Division now at San Diego; with the 1st Marine Raider Battalion (now at New Caledonia) and the 3rd Marine Defense Battalion (now at Pearl Harbor).

Rear Admiral Richmond Kelly Turner, the brilliant dynamic (and difficult) planner, would come on from Washington to be over-all commander of the attack forces; Rear Admiral V. A. C.

Crutchley of the Australian Navy with some of his ships from the MacArthur area would lead the screening force of surface vessels. Rear Admiral Frank J. Fletcher, who had done so well at Coral Sea, was coming down from Pearl with three carriers as the nucleus of his support force. Simultaneously the British would make a heavy carrier strike at Timor or in that area, the MacArthur command would turn on the heat in New Guinea, and there would be a raid by Marines landed from submarines among the islands to the north, the whole making up a pattern of energetic simultaneous attack which should leave the Japanese in considerable confusion as to the true objective. It was America's first offensive movement in the war, the first time we would fight the enemy on our terms, not theirs.

II

General Vandegrift's face expressed nothing but interest and enthusiasm; the staff were no little shaken and, talking it over later, developed among themselves, as the only adequate explanation why Washington had been willing to embark on so mad a project, the theory that the Japanese were about to attack the Russians in Siberia and that the Soviet had warned us to do something to distract them by 1 August or else.

The troops were half trained, incompletely equipped, and scattered; so were the commanders. D day was 37 days away and Admiral Ghormley had set the concentration area at Koro in the Fijis, which meant two voyages of approximately a week each (Wellington-Koro, Koro-Solomons) and left a little over twenty days for all other processes. Out of this had to be squeezed a certain amount of time for training in beachhead landings, about which even the combat team present knew very little. The supplies for the expedition must be embarked at once; if for no other reason, to clear the limited docking space for the second echelon, which would come in ships that must be returned to the States. But the loading of supply ships, which items went in first and came out last, depended upon the plan of operations, the tactics adopted in the face of the enemy during the crucial first hours. But the decision on these was the business of the attack commander, Admiral Turner, who would have under him both ships and troops till the latter reached a foothold ashore

6

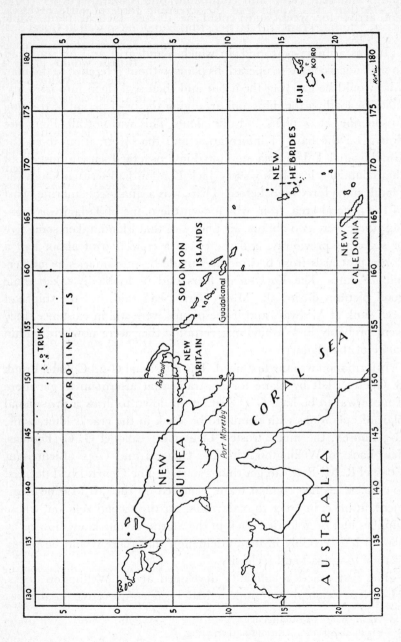

7

and Vandegrift came into command. But Admiral Turner could not arrive for weeks, nor could he discuss tactical plans while traveling.

It was a merry-go-round, in which Vandegrift and his staff had to make decisions as to operations plans without reference to the man who would be carrying them out and then seal them into irrevocability by loading the ships and arranging the brief period of training to suit one set of plans and one alone. This was not all. Plans are drawn on the basis of information and the information about the Guadalcanal-Tulagi area amounted in a practical sense to just about that contained in a funny story Jack London had written about the islands some forty years before. There was a small-scale marine chart of the general area, from which even the name of Tulagi was missing; there were two oblique air photos of that island, taken some five or six years previously, and there was a collection of about half a dozen postcards from bad pictures made by missionaries at indeterminate dates. The *Yorktown*'s fliers had undoubtedly taken some good pictures during the May (Coral Sea) raid, but the ship had been sunk at Midway, and if the photos were still in existence, they were probably in Washington; certainly they were nowhere within range of the planners.

Information was the first need. The divisional G-2,[1] Colonel Frank B. Goettge, left by plane for Australia that afternoon to get more if more was to be had. G-3[2] Section sat down to draw a provisional plan of operations with details to be stuck in the cracks later, while G-3 himself, the much trusted Lieutenant Colonel G. C. Thomas, flew back to Wellington with the General and G-4[3] (Lieutenant Colonel R. M. Pate) to get things started. The General had decided to embark his first combat team, centered on the 5th Marine Regiment, at once, in order to make room for the second echelon, whose supplies had been loaded back in the States, no one knew how or by whom, but certainly in the anticipation that there would be plenty of time to unload and reclassify.

The first practical difficulty developed at the Wellington docks. The New Zealand government had been co-operative to the last

[1] G-2 is in charge of Intelligence.
[2] G-3 is in charge of operations and training.
[3] G-4 is in charge of logistics.

8

degree, turning over to us the big Aotea Quay of five-ship capacity. But the docks themselves were in the hands of a longshoremen's group of extreme left political thinking, whom nothing could induce to move faster than a slow crawl ("Why kill a good job when you have it?") as had been discovered when the troops landed. It was decided to let the Marines do their own loading. Colonel Pate was new to the division and had been appointed to G-4 to develop a logistic service of divisional character. Supervisory help had to be borrowed from G-3. Pate worked out the labor problem by setting up shifts right around the clock, each unit handling the unloading and loading of its own supplies, an arrangement which at least guaranteed a certain amount of interest in the task.

It was the New Zealand winter and across Aotea Quay under the glaring lights there pelted almost horizontally the continual driving rain of that clime. The stores were mainly naval dry stores, which means that most of them were packed in the light cardboard boxes so convenient for use aboard ship, but which simply melt on exposure to weather in the field or on a New Zealand dock. Within twenty-four hours the quay was ankle-deep in toasted corn flakes and water-logged cigarettes which the wind piled into sopping drifts. It did not matter at the moment—there are few items a Marine would rather not eat than toasted corn flakes and it had already been discovered that shipping space permitted taking supplies for only sixty days instead of the ninety demanded by Marine Corps standing operating procedures. The men already embarked upon the ships lying out in the stream were bored. It was no fun on the weather decks, so they organized black-face war dances in the hold and sang endlessly, including the new "Bless 'Em All," which some had picked up in New Zealand.

III

Colonel Goettge did not reach Melbourne until 1 July, but the results of his researches began to appear at once after that date in the form of a string of singular individuals—ex-missionaries, planters, schoonermen, and a giant with a scarred face named Mather who had been a blackbirder among the Solomons. Each had some scrap or patch of information to contribute to the gradually growing dossier on the islands and eight of the candidates revealed

9

so much knowledge that they were made petty officers of the Australian forces and taken along as pilots.

The process presented difficulties, however. The first was that Goettge had organized his section as a one-man show with nobody below him but inexperienced lieutenants, and in his absence these juniors were not too well aware of the process involved in extracting information from people who do not know what they ought to tell. "Certainly you can get across the Tenaru River," said the manager of the coconut plantation on Guadalcanal and it was not till an hour of relaxation over a drink some time later that he reminisced about the last time he had seen the place—"Went down there to shoot a couple of cows that couldn't get out." There were lifted eyebrows, glances passed, and then a few more questions. Oh, yes, the way you crossed the Tenaru was by means of the sandstrip at its mouth; upstream it was unfordable, flowing between banks eight feet high and precipitous. That little item alone meant taking along bridging equipment (since the Tenaru was in the projected line of advance) and redistributing the whole load of at least one cargo carrier to make room for it.

Volumes like the *Pacific Island Yearbook* and the British colonial reports were laid under contribution, but as material accumulated an evident over-all defect in information developed. It was background stuff, almost nothing about changes the Japs had made in the landscape and how many of them were there, for military purposes precisely the most important features. The Australians turned over to Colonel Goettge their estimate of enemy forces as drawn from the coast-watcher system but warned that, though it was fairly accurate as to Tulagi and the minor islands, it could not be relied upon for Guadalcanal, where the system had run into difficulties.

The Australians had made the coast-watcher setup at the beginning of the war in 1939 to keep tabs on German surface raiders, spies, and submarines—composing it from residents of the islands who knew the natives and were provided with radio sets. When the Japs swooped down most of them were pulled out; those who remained took to the bush for one of the most romantic, perilous, and thankless jobs of the war, moving from place to place and concealed by the islanders, who became increasingly anti-Japanese as the meaning of the Greater East Asia Co-Prosperity Sphere was

10

borne in upon them. Guadalcanal had four such watchers—a lazy Frenchman, an apathetic German, a missionary who did not know how to ask the right kind of questions, and the later famous Martin Clemens, captain in His Majesty's Solomon Islands Police of the colonial service, one of the very best coast-watchers of all.

Unfortunately he had sprained his ankle badly just at this juncture and an order had gone out that he was not to broadcast for the time being—the Japs would surely put the radio locators on him and it wouldn't do to have him hopping through the jungle on a bad gam with them on his tail. "Moon" Mumma, the famous submarine skipper, offered to take his boat in and land a party to contact Clemens, but this was vetoed as risking a tip-off of the whole expedition. As next best thing to a report from Clemens two operations officers, Lieutenant Colonel M. B. Twining and Major William B. McKean, were flown to Australia, then to Moresby, where they picked up a B-17 and went out to Guadal for visual and photographic reconnaissance.

Of course, they had to pick a clear day and three float Zeros came up at the plane from Tulagi harbor. The B-17 took what is probably understated as "violent evasive action" and shot down two of the Zeros. The third made off and so did our plane—without enough gas to take it home, but fortunately it caught a tail wind and rode in on it. At Townsville on the way back Twining and McKean picked up some more photos, the result of various flights over the area. The pictures were not pieced together for a long time (nobody seemed to be responsible) but from what maps could be had and from visual observation it was pretty clear that the Japs had no defenses along most of the many northern beaches of Guadalcanal. Their installations seemed to be concentrated at Lunga point, north and slightly west of the airfield they were building, where the Lunga River flows through several mouths into the lagoon. The best estimate was that including labor troops, they had 5,000 men on the island, a reinforced infantry regiment with an antiaircraft battalion. There would be some 1,500 on Tulagi and Gavutu.

These facts determined the plan of operation. It called for practically simultaneous attacks on Tulagi, Gavutu, and Guadalcanal. The first two islands were the tough ones because of their construction and the fact that surrounding coral in the water limited the

11

avenues of approach. Edson's Raider battalion, the best-trained outfit in the show, would take Tulagi with an infantry battalion in support. The parachutists, also in a high degree of training, were to hit Gavutu (from boats of course, not from the air). The remainder of the division would not be too many men for the bigger island and the heavier Japanese forces there. They would land at a place denominated "Beach Red," 6,000 yards east of the airfield, where the Ilu River would cover their flank against attack from the Jap positions during the delicate business of getting ashore. From the beachhead, resistance permitting them, one wing would strike along the shore toward Lunga Point, the other somewhat inland

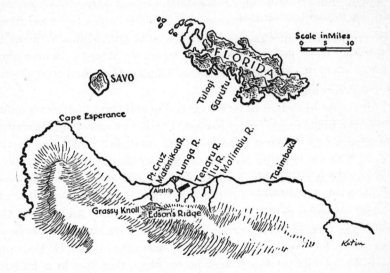

toward a great flat-topped hill called "Grassy Knoll" west of the upper course of the Lunga River which, the planters said, dominated the whole area down to and including the airfield. With speed of movement a double envelopment might be achieved, and in any case the Japs should be swept from the area down to the mouths of the Lunga.

There were two "combat groups" in the Guadalcanal attack, under Colonel Leroy P. Hunt and Colonel Clifton B. Cates respectively. It is worth giving the organization of one as indicating a pattern that was followed with a fair degree of consistency throughout the remainder of the war. The infantry component of Hunt's

12

combat group consisted of the 5th Marine Regiment; it was reinforced by a battalion of the 11th Marines, an artillery regiment; a company of tanks; a platoon of a transportation company; a medical company; a company of amphibious tractors (whose name was soon shortened to "amphitracs"); a scout platoon—212 officers, 4,525 enlisted in all, and in all divided into three combat teams of an infantry battalion each with a quota of the special units.

IV

The flight of Twining and McKean was on 17 July, but the information they brought caused no essential variation from the plan already drawn by that time. The day after this, while the two officers were still at Moresby congratulating themselves on being alive, Admiral Turner arrived at Wellington, looking grim. "Where's your operation plan?" were his first words as soon as the handshakes were over. When the Marines produced one the tension relaxed notably and his own G-3 officers sat down to draw the over-all plan on the basis of Vandegrift's detail for part of it, which is exactly the opposite of the way it technically should have been done. He also issued the welcome order that the attack would be delayed till 7 August, which gave a little more time for loading so that all the ships were buttoned up and steaming out of harbor by 22 July.

They reached Koro on the 28th and the men went into the rehearsal training whose value was instantly demonstrated when a number of the landing craft had engine casualties and could not leave the ships with the units assigned to them. The obvious arrangement to get around this was to pool all the landing craft instead of assigning each to a particular unit, and this arrangement was made. Meanwhile Fletcher's fleet had steamed in and command conferences began—the first time the leaders had met each other and with sailing day for the expedition less than ninety-six hours away.

There were four such commanders involved—Turner, Vandegrift, Fletcher as commanders of the three carriers and their retinue (Task Force 61), and Rear Admiral V.A.C. Crutchley whose screening force consisted of the heavy cruisers *Quincy, Vincennes, Astoria, Chicago,* with the Australian heavies *Australia* and *Canberra,* the Australian light cruiser *Hobart,* the American antiaircraft

13

cruiser *San Juan,* with destroyers quantum non sufficit. There were eleven big transports, six small ones that were warmed-over destroyers, and six big supply ships, these all under Turner's direct command.

As soon as the conference began it became clear that all the officers involved had utterly different concepts of the operation. The Marines down there at the ends of the earth knew of the war in general only that our forces had won a smashing victory at Midway. They had supposed this gave us full command of sky and ocean with all the time in the world to unload supply vessels when they reached Guadalcanal; with heavy warships cruising through the lagoon to furnish fire on call and carrier planes to dive-bomb in advance of the moving troops.

It was developed that this was by no means the case. Crutchley and his Australian ships were on loan from the MacArthur command and would have to return at an early date. Fletcher (who had been in action or close to it and consequently under heavy strain for months now and who looked pretty tired) held the view that his whole operation was a hit-and-run raid, setting the Marines on the beach and then getting away. It could be nothing else; we by no means had command by sea or air. From Rabaul and the upper Solomons the Japs could bring in land-based planes far more numerous than they could fly from the decks of their fleet carriers. In the background they had at least five carriers of their own and a whole division of fast battleships while Fletcher possessed but one. The disparity in the cruiser and destroyer forces was similar. Not we but they had command of the sea if they chose to exercise it.

The news appalled the Marine commander and his staff, who pointed out that in the twenty-four hours the fleet proposed to stay in the Guadalcanal area they might barely get the troops ashore, but certainly not their supplies. There would even be a shortage of hands for handling what supplies they did have. In that service it is usual for the replacement battalions to deal with such beachhead stevedoring labor and the 1st Marine Division had not yet received its replacement battalions. There was a long debate of the type one might expect from forthright men accustomed to command, and unhappily it was a debate without a moderator, for Admiral Ghormley, the only officer whose position enabled him to outrank all

14

present, had remained in Wellington, sending up a captain to represent him. The end was a compromise under which Admiral Fletcher agreed to keep his carrier force in the general area of the landing for three days, till D plus 4, Crutchley with his cruiser screening force to remain as long as necessary. The result satisfied nobody and none felt that the subject had been fully canvassed, but time had them in its tyrannous grip and they must sail at dawn.

Just before anchors were lifted some of the officers who had been clearing up fag ends of business in Wellington arrived by air. They brought with them copies of the local papers, which all through the staffs produced horrified exclamations of "Jesus Christ!" The page one headlines said "Americans to Attack Tulagi" and the story beneath carried a New York date line. For years after, no one in the 1st Marine Division would believe that there had not been a leak of a seriousness verging on treason; but it was not true, it was only coincidence verging on the improbable. Major George Fielding Eliot, the military commentator, had been moved to remark that after Midway our strategic prospect in the Pacific was much improved; the Japanese no longer possessed the offensive. Though Allied resources were probably not equal to long-range or large-scale attacks, they were probably good enough to undertake an offensive of limited envergure against some place within supporting distance from our bases. Say Rabaul, Tulagi, or Wake.

As far as he was concerned the names might have been drawn from a hat. They were there to indicate a wide range of possibility and Tulagi got in only because a Jap convoy had been smashed up there during the first phase of the Battle of Coral Sea. But there were representatives of the New Zealand press in New York, on the prowl for news with "local appeal" back home; and to them Tulagi was a familiar word. They cabled the story and, since cable tolls to New Zealand are high, they took out all Major Eliot's conditional and modifying words. "Americans to Attack Tulagi."

The flagship was the transport *McCawley*. Tregaskis the correspondent noted how a couple of the Marines on the weather deck had piles of half dollars and were trying to skip them across the water like stones in a pond. "We won't have no use for money where we're going," they said.

15

Chapter 2

Operation Pestilence

THERE WAS A TURN-TO AT 0200 FOR BREAKFAST, WHICH WAS large and accompanied by the type of conversation imagined to be humorous by men under strain. By 0400 it was growing faintly light; the fleet split into two groups right and leftward of the dark truncated cone of Savo Island where it seemed to float in the still water. Not a sound or movement came from the enemy as the ships shouldered their way in. "I can't believe it," remarked a lieutenant aboard the flagship. "I wonder if the Japs can be that dumb." He thought it might be a trick of some kind.

Of all nations the Japanese possess the widest and most successful fund of experience in beachhead operations, beginning with the Chinese War of the nineties and descending in unbroken sequence through the Russian conflict, the elaborate operation against Tsingtao in 1914 (they actually took the place three times, successfully making one type of landing and then drawing off to try it again in another fashion, using the unfortunate Germans as guinea pigs), and the long succession of operations on the China Coast during the twenties and thirties. In Malaya, the Philippines, all through the Indies, they had in this war demonstrated that they knew practically everything about the technique of converting a seaborne invasion into a successful land campaign. This had not escaped the attention of our Marine Corps planners. It was expected that an enemy who knew so much about the offensive across beaches would also understand the defense. The landing force had been warned to expect obstacles at the shore and interlocking belts of fire from machine guns carefully concreted into position along Tulagi, an island shaped like a banana, lying northwest and southeast.

Yet when Edson's Raiders charged from their boats onto Beach Blue, about two-thirds of the way up the banana with the steep slope of the island's central keel towering over their heads, there were only a handful of bullets peening past, only one man hit. The whole lagoon was still rolling with smoke and thunder, the single small Jap boat that had been found was blazing against the shore, an oil dump over on Guadalcanal was burning with smoky flame, and the wreckage of five float Zeros sinking at the seaplane ramp on Gavutu. (Only one of them had left the water and that was sent instantly tumbling back by a cruiser's guns.) Our own planes were weaving an intricate pattern overhead as they dive-bombed and strafed anything that looked like movement or a gun position. Edson's first wave was of two companies (B and D); they organized rapidly and began to climb the rough, wooded central mountain, keeping clear of the trail along the shore, which was commanded by lofty cliffs that would almost certainly hold dug-in Japs. Two more companies followed in fifteen minutes; all four strung out across the island and began working down through the rocks and trees in a southeasterly direction while Lieutenant Colonel Rosecrans's 2nd Battalion of the 5th Regiment came ashore.

About three-quarters of a mile from the landing point the central

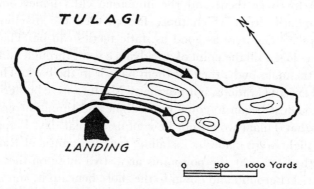

spine of the island runs out into ravines and small flats with limestone hills rising from them, steep and irregular. This region held whatever residences and business buildings the island had, and a "phase line" had been set just where the downslope begins in order to permit a halt for reorganization. No reorganization was necessary, but as the advancing troops reached the phase line it became apparent that the Japanese also had it on their maps. Sniper fire struck up sharply and was seconded by mortars. There were casualties, including the commander of Company B, and on the south flank of the island a little hill held a whole concentration of machine guns which had not been in the least damaged by the preliminary bombardment and which opened fire with the greatest energy. There was a good deal of battle savvy among Edson's Raiders. They spread out, took cover, and after about an hour of inching forward got the machine guns on the hill under by means of rifle and grenade. The Japanese kept up an intense fire and casualties began to accumulate, but their defense was strangely passive. They made no attempt to move, waiting for the Marines to come dig them out.

This took time—more and more of it as the Raiders on both flanks of the island worked down into the cricket ground area, which is dominated by a small hill on the west and a large one on the east. On the southern wing C Company was halted at this first hill; the fire became so heavy that the men could not move forward, nor from the configuration of the ground could they work around. On the northern side it was as bad. Among the accidented ground beyond the phase line our men encountered Japs tied into trees, under houses, behind rocks; sniping, sniping, sniping, with machine-gun fire to cover them and the limestone cliffs honeycombed by tunnel mouths from which more fire covered the machine guns. The Japs' tactics were as good as static tactics can be. The snipers would lie doggo till the point of an advance went through and maybe part of the main body, then let them have it in the back. There was no food except C rations, but not many Marines were bothering with that, though it began to come on twilight and simultaneously to be evident that Tulagi would not be conquered that day. Preparations for the night were made by installing two companies of Raiders on the north shore near the poisonous area, two more on the hill west of the cricket ground and down to the shore beneath it, and bringing up a company of Rosecrans's men to form a link between, pretty well back, since they tried three times unsuccessfully to clear a ravine north of the cricket ground.

Outposts were set and the men lay down where they were to get what sleep they could. They did not get much; as soon as the tropical night and rain closed in, the Japs pulled their trick out of the hat.

18

They sortied from their caves and pushed out in all directions like the fingers of a spread hand, using every trick in the book—firing to draw fire, which was returned by grenades in the hands of men who crept forward silently; screaming wildly, using knife and bayonet. On the southern flank they got between the two companies of Raiders and penned one back against the beach; at the center they lapped around both ends of the hill west of the cricket ground and made five separate, savage attacks on it. Twenty-six dead Japs were found within stone-throwing distance of our line there by morning. When sunlight drove the enemy back in their holes, the Raiders were tired men.

Yet they were not so tired or so beset as Major Williams' Parachute battalion on Gavutu. The landing there was not made till noon in order to be sure that the supporting ships and planes would

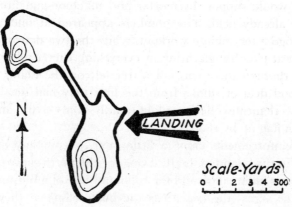

be clear of their tasks on the more essential islands. Gavutu rises sharply on all sides and is so surrounded by coral close to the surface that there is only one avenue of approach, toward the seaplane ramp and pier at the northeast corner. *San Juan* with the destroyers *Monssen* and *Buchanan* fired an intensive five-minute preparation; the dive bombers came over and gave the place ten minutes more, apparently doing very well, for they visibly knocked out a three-inch gun on a hilltop and at several points fires sprang up. But as the

19

boats charged in they found the seaplane ramp had been dug to tangled blocks of concrete by the preliminary shelling, no place to land. They had to angle rightward, toward the dock. The first boats got in all right and the men out of them, but then down came a storm of fire that instantly shot down one man in every ten. The remainder were pinned under the lee of the six-foot pier, being shot at from trenches across its base, from the hill on their left flank, and from Tanambogo Island to the north.

One boat did manage to get in a little leftward at the base of the slip and it fortunately contained some mortar men, who laid their fire with admirable accuracy on the trenches from which the most serious opposition was coming. By 1400 the Marines were able to get up on the pier, reach land and rush in, a handful at a time. They spread out up the steep slopes of Gavutu, whose surface was quickly won, though not without more casualties from the caves of Tanambogo. Major Williams had been hit; his successor asked for dive bombers on the other island and reinforcements to attack it, which move he would support by mortar and machine-gun fire from the place he already held. The bombers appeared at once and gave Tanambogo a ten-minute workout, while the two destroyers circled the place at close range, firing at everything they could see. When they got through there was not a tree left on the island and there was a good deal of smoke from the fires they had set. The parachutists were meanwhile spreading rapidly over Gavutu and had the American flag up by 1800.

The reinforcements came a little later, a company of the 2nd Marines in three landing craft, trying for the north shore of Tanambogo. It was falling dark and the brilliant blaze of a burning gasoline dump rose across the beach; as the boats came in they were silhouetted against it and received by so terrific a concentration of machine-gun fire that two were driven off again and the third only landed part of its people before being also forced to pull out. On Gavutu, meanwhile, there was a steady increase of sniping as the sun went down and in the night the experience of Tulagi was repeated, Japs popping out of their holes everywhere to snipe and throw grenades, with the additional trouble that a lot of them swam over from Tanambogo to the pier where the boats had landed and fired into the rear of our positions and the dressing station.

20

There was a good deal of confusion both there and on Tulagi during the night and somehow the casualty reports got mixed up so that when they reached General Vandegrift they said the Raiders had lost 22 per cent of their men and the parachutists between 50 and 60 per cent. Brigadier General W. H. Rupertus, deputy commander of the division, in general charge of the operations on these small islands, asked for reinforcements.

The reserve afloat was theoretically under the control of Admiral Turner, but the request gave General Vandegrift a good opportunity to reclaim them by setting them ashore. He accordingly assigned two additional battalion combat teams to Rupertus for dawn of the next morning, at which time the men of the Rosecrans command who had not reached the front on Tulagi the day before shifted toward the southern tip of the island. They and the Raiders worked along both shores, cleaning out caves one by one, and eventually got into positions from which they could put three-directional mortar fire into the main Jap concentration area. By midafternoon they had the place under control, though three separate sweeps across the hills the enemy had occupied each produced its quota of fresh Japs.

Even with the arrival of the two additional battalions Gavutu and Tanambogo were by no means done. The former was so honeycombed with caves and tunnels as to constitute a single big stone fort. Heroic and impossible deeds were necessary to get the enemy out of them—like that of Captain Harry Torgerson, who all day long kept running up to throw packages of dynamite with five-second fuses into these holes, while covered by rifle fire. The task was complicated still further by enemy fire from unconquered Tanambogo and it was not until late in the afternoon of that second day, 8 August, that a successful landing was made there under cover of still another naval bombardment. Two tanks accompanied the landing; one of them got ahead of the accompanying infantry, the Japs stalled it with an iron bar thrust into the treads and burned it out. But the other led a good advance, some of the parachutists joined by means of the causeway from Gavutu, and by 2100 of the second day organized resistance on Tanambogo was beaten down.

The harbor islands had cost 108 killed, 140 wounded. The Japanese dead were of the order of 1,500 (500 of them on Tulagi), of whom 600 were the conscript laborers whom the Marines instantly

21

named "termites," elsewhere miserable cattle but in the harbor of Tulagi fighting men of a valor and persistence not inferior to the best troops of the Empire. There were only three prisoners taken on Tulagi, only a few more on the other islands; the last man of a machine-gun crew, unable to operate his piece alone, invariably killed himself. Those who were taken said that about seventy more had escaped by swimming over to precipitous Florida Island, and as these were a source of potentially serious trouble, strong patrols were put onto Florida to hunt them down.

II

With its towering mountainous center Guadalcanal is a beautiful island from the sea and the day was so calm that all the cargo nets could be hung down the sides of the transports and used as ladders. The firing died away, the boats lined up and dashed for a white beach across which white waves broke and there was not a sound from the shore, on which bombardment had now ceased so that the men going in could hear the Tulagi battle, some 25 miles away across the water. There was no firing at the shore either; the two battalions of the 5th Regiment that were in the first wave formed rapidly there and pushed inland some 500 yards to where a little stream runs parallel to the beach to fall into the Ilu, forming a natural beachhead area. The boat pool functioned perfectly. The 1st Marine Regiment (Cates) followed the 5th ashore and as soon as it arrived Lieutenant Colonel Maxwell's battalion of the 5th crossed the Ilu by the sandbar at its mouth and began working along the shore. Cates's regiment slanted inland, taking a compass bearing on Grassy Knoll and cutting a path for transport through the lush jungle and the konai grass which is tall as a man. By noon the whole beach was a rubble from the passing of vehicles. Antiaircraft guns were ashore and being emplaced. Tregaskis the correspondent found one of the Australian guides leaning against a tree and consuming a coconut, who said, "I'm exhausted by the arduousness of landing against such heavy fire."

It would be a little after noon that the first Jap bombers came, 25 of them, very high up, which dropped only two or three eggs and then droned off to the southward, apparently looking for our carriers. They did not find them and three of the Japs were shot down. Ashore the advance went on—somewhat apathetically in Maxwell's direction, though he had the more open ground. He kept expecting to be counterattacked and threw out front and flank detachments in momentary anticipation of battle. Night found both forces up to the Tenaru[1] with the bridges for the 1st Regiment just getting into position and some of the minor units a bit scattered due to the inexperience of young officers in conducting operations through such country.

Night also found confusion in the beachhead. There had been a second air raid in the afternoon in which the destroyer *Mugford* was hit a knock, and this forced a delay in getting goods ashore, but by 2300 there was already so much material on the beach that it could neither be handled nor added to. The Pioneer battalion had labored itself into a state of exhaustion since dawn; the infantry reserve afloat, which might have furnished some of the muscle, had been drawn into the sudden whirlwind that blew up on Gavutu, and General Vandegrift dared not pull any of his combat troops out of the front line before making contact with those (estimated) 5,000 Japs. There was nothing to do but knock off unloading operations for the night. The casualty report for Guadalcanal that day was one man—cut his hand while trying to open a coconut.

In the morning the advance took up again. The jungle grew heavier in the sector of the 1st Marines and their progress was slow but they got hold of a couple of termite prisoners. By noon these had been screened through the interpreters, separately, and it became clear that an astonishing overestimate of the Japs on the island had been made. Their force did not exceed 600 fighting men; and these had fled to the westward, way beyond the Lunga, when our cruisers came in. General Vandegrift inquired about the latest reports from Maxwell's battalion. It was still making the same cautious advance

---

[1] It turned out that the river appearing on all the Marine maps and bearing the name of the Tenaru in all the early dispatches and war correspondents' stories was not the Tenaru at all. After the Army troops reached Guadalcanal they found this out and designated the river in all *their* correspondence and releases as the Ilu. But it was not that either; the correct name of the stream was Alligator Creek, and both Ilu and Tenaru are branches of the same stream. It seems preferable, in view of the fact that the Tenaru received so much publicity under that name, to keep the designation here.

through the coconut plantation, security detachments out wide. Colonel Hunt went to the front in person and during the afternoon pushed this formation more rapidly forward on a narrower front, so that by 1500 the leading elements were across the Lunga on a Jap-built bridge and moving toward the native village of Kukum and the lagoon that fronts it. Here a few bullets began to whistle among the trees. The battalion spread, went forward, shot a few Japs, and in thirty minutes had the rest driven out.

Colonel Cates's command had meanwhile worked out of its jungle into a region of open grass and had speeded its pace. Grassy Knoll, as one approached the place, became more and more a dominant terrain feature but a feature of such size that a corps four divisions strong would have been none too large to occupy it; clearly not this but the line of the Lunga was the place to hold. Almost as an after-thought the 1st Regiment took the airfield, where it found elaborate dependent installations, two radio stations, a pair of ice plants, an air compressor, a power plant, and camp buildings with yesterday's breakfast for the garrison still in the kettles. Among the abandoned weapons were some Springfield rifles '03 with markings showing they had come from Guam and even a few pathetic personal souvenirs belonging to Marines who had formed part of the Wake Island garrison. The fact was noted for future reference.

That day General Vandegrift had much of the unloading done on the beaches west of the Ilu, which speeded matters somewhat, but both this area and the original landing quickly became overloaded and there were still nowhere near enough men to dispose of the goods coming ashore while the amount of work done by those on the job began to fall off through mere human fatigue. At 1230 there was a truce to unloading when a formation of forty Jap dive and tor-pedo bombers came in low over Florida Island to stage a fierce raid. They seemed to have been after transports mainly, but ran into an AA screen of surprising force from the warships over toward Tulagi. The Japs tried to make their pull-out low among the transports, with the idea that our gunners would not fire at them. Their mission was not a success. Fighters from *Wasp* rode them in and took a heavy toll; they were wrong about the pull-out business, as the transports opened a hot concentration of automatic fire which brought twelve of the planes down and almost all the rest were picked off by the fighters.

24

But one in her death throes dived into the open hatch of the big transport *Elliott* and set a fire that could not be put out, so the ship had to be scuttled toward twilight with most of the supplies for a battalion of the 2nd Regiment. Another got a torpedo hit on the destroyer *Jarvis* and that was worse than it looked at first; the ship was able to steam out under her own power but was never heard from again; either broke up or a sub got her.

After the shooting was over and outposts set for the night a message came summoning General Vandegrift to a conference aboard the flag. He took off for it with a pardonable feeling of satisfaction. All objectives had been secured and the over-all casualties could be regarded as very light even though those on Gavutu had been heavy. The ship-to-shore work on which the Marines had been studying for so long had gone off with an admirable smoothness that completely justified both the method used and the Higgins landing boats the corps had forced a somewhat unwilling Navy to accept. Considering the amount of their training the performance of his men had been astonishingly competent.

True, there had been errors and surprises. The Japs were expected to be fanatics, but even so the fierceness of a resistance which genuinely went to the last man was somewhat unexpected. A few of his officers had not shown up too well under pressure. The arrangements for handling supplies after they reached the beach were fairly bad and it would evidently take a good deal of time to get everything ashore. The advance information, intelligence, was inadequate, especially with regard to Guadalcanal, where some of the combat troops might have been used in solving the supply difficulty if we had known how few the enemies were. The mistake about Grassy Knoll, which sent the 1st Regiment on its toilsome march, could have been avoided with good air photos. Still, the General had every reason to feel satisfied that his Marines were living up to the ancient tradition of being first when the chips were down.

III

A Japanese "appreciation" of American methods for the benefit of the officers who would have to fight us remarked some time later:

"The enemy is extremely sensitive to bombing, and just a few good hits are enough to rout several hundred of them."

The remark was evidently the result of exterior observation; but it could have been made by a nonexistent spy aboard the flagship *McCawley,* 12 miles east along the Guadalcanal coast that night before the command conference started. Admiral Crutchley came down after dark aboard *Australia,* leaving the rest of his cruisers on a sentry stretch north of Savo Island. He had won a V.C. "For Valor"; now looked tired and haggard and so did his supporting cast. They had not been able to claim more than two or three hours' sleep since the night of 6 August, what with stand-tos for fire in support of the fighting on Tulagi and Tanambogo. Admiral Turner looked tired and was a good deal worried by the loss and damage in the air attacks. Two destroyers out of action and a transport gone may not sound like a great deal to an outsider, but the losses were irreplaceable, there were no more ships behind these, not back in the States, not anywhere. At the present rate of attrition it would not be long before he was unable to conduct an operation of any kind. A wise commander does not wait till a situation which promises such disasters overtakes him, but applies his preventive when the indications become clear.

Admiral Fletcher was tired; anxious to get his carriers out of danger, which (he considered) they had escaped from the forty bombers only through sheer good fortune. A recon report told of a powerful Japanese task force approaching. It would enter Rekata Bay at Santa Isabel and presumably deliver a combined surface and air torpedo attack the following day. In fact it was not improbable that the surface attack would come before dawn, which might mean more losses. The transports were already in motion; the sense of the meeting was that all the ships must be withdrawn, not on D plus 4 as originally intended, nor on any more distant date because of trouble in handling supplies on the beach, but tomorrow, D plus 2.

General Vandegrift was thunderstruck. It was the argument that had taken place at Koro all over again, but now under worse conditions, since his men were already committed ashore; he could not withdraw if he wanted to. There was not even enough food for them to eat, to say nothing of ammunition and equipment items—hardly any shovels at all, for instance. The enemy ashore were off balance but quite capable of reorganizing and being reinforced.

There were probably some fairly bitter things said; but once more it was a case of each commander making the decisions for his own force since Ghormley, now in Nouméa, could not be reached. The end of it was the beginning; the ships would withdraw. The Marine commander left at a quarter before midnight, borrowing the mine-sweeper *Southard* to take him over to Tulagi for a conference with General Rupertus on what the supply situation was at his side of the lagoon. Crutchley returned to *Australia* and she turned her prow back to the north under pouring rain.

On Guadalcanal that night everybody was being drenched by the same rain, since the day's movement had carried them so late and far there was no opportunity for the shelter-halves, which were their only tents, to catch up from the beachhead. It would be after General Vandegrift got aboard his minesweeper that the sound of an airplane came from overhead. A parachute flare burst out in ghostly green and from the transports long red fingers of tracer reached up into the sky toward it, then gradually lowered their trajectory. Communications at the command post reported a message from *McCawley*: "Heavy enemy fire on Beach Red." Out in the lagoon another flare dropped; on its heels, far off to the north near Savo Island, arches of red and white fire sprang out of the dark. A ship was hit and began to burn like a torch; the multiple repeated thunder of a naval battle rolled across the sea and some Marines on guard at Lunga Point agreed that nothing but our big battleship *North Carolina* could rouse such turmoil.

"Enemy attacking Beach Red in force," said another message from *McCawley* to the CP ashore, but communications reported they could get no answer when they tried to talk back to the flag and ask them what made them think it was a counterlanding. Out in the lagoon near Savo the action intensified instead of dying down. There seemed to be a force to the north and one to the south, with the northern one clearly being worsted, for another ship and another were hit and began to burn while the flame of the first was suddenly quenched.

"Enemy landing on Beach Red right now," reported *McCawley* and the duty operations officer had to turn out a patrol to go down

27

there and see if it was true, while one battalion was alerted to make a counterattack in case the Japs really were landing. The flag still would answer no questions and it was near dawn before the firing in the north died down, the patrol came back with its negative report, and there was some opportunity to sleep.

It was still raining in the morning. Under the descending gray curtain two men near the shore saw the cruiser *Chicago* go by with part of her bow missing and a rumor began to spread that we had lost, not won the naval battle. About 0830 *Southard* pulled in with the General, and when the staff had a look at his face they knew things must be pretty bad. He called for all unit commanders and they had a conference around a fire under the rain, drinking half portions of coffee out of empty C-ration cans. He had undoubtedly hoped to get a reconsideration of the decision to withdraw the ships, especially since Tulagi had even less supplies than Guadal, barely enough food for eight days. There was no hope of any reconsideration now. In fact, there was very little left to withdraw besides the transports, for Crutchley's screening force had been nearly wiped out in the greatest disaster our Navy had seen, since there was no element of treachery, only a straight lost battle. *Quincy, Vincennes,* and *Astoria* were gone, shot through and torpedoed; the Australian *Canberra* was so bad she had to be scuttled; *Chicago* hard hit.

The transport force would leave immediately. The Marines were on their own, alone on a hostile shore whose surrounding waters were now in full command of the enemy.

It was probable, nay certain, that the Japs would try counter-landings. The first step would therefore be to set up at Lunga Point shore defenses as powerful as our means would allow. The supplies would have to be moved away from Beach Red at once (if the Japs had any sense they would try a counterlanding there or set fire to the mountain of stores), brought up to the Lunga Point area, dispersed, and put underground as far as possible. The Engineer battalion would turn to on the unfinished airstrip the enemy had left; air cover from a permanent installation was a necessity. The captured Japanese food would pass under control of the divisional quartermaster, who would issue on the basis of two meals a day until further supplies could be brought in. It would be dangerous to deplete these stores by using them faster. Meanwhile activity would be limited to vigorous patrols; there was too much work to do to permit of any large-scale movement.

IV

Afterward there was a violent controversy as to where the responsibility rested for the Savo Island defeat. The question is one which will probably never be settled in exact terms. It was primarily a fatigue defeat. Captain Riefkohl of *Vincennes*, senior officer present, wrote in his day book, "The enemy can reach this position at any time during the midwatch," and the midwatch being then approaching, turned into his bunk. It was characteristic of conditions at the moment. All the ships were on Condition 2, which sends half the crews below, and many of these crews never reached the guns they were supposed to serve. The guns that did shoot were fired in haste by weary men. They never hit a thing. Records showed later that *Astoria*, always before one of the prize gunnery ships of the fleet, had been firing at an estimated range of 6,000 yards, and at ships estimated moving at 16 knots speed. The actual range was 3,000, the actual Jap speed 26 knots; and only extreme fatigue could have led the *Astoria* men so to misinterpret their instruments.

But it was the decision of a tired commander to let them take their rest, in the expectation that the Japanese force would arrive on the schedule our intelligence had set for it, that is, at two o'clock in the morning. Nothing was added to the strength of the position by the fact that when Crutchley went down the coast for the conference aboard *McCawley*, the fleet was left without special orders for the apparently imminent enemy attack, and without a deputy commander. The tactical disposition also was about as bad as could be conceived—*Canberra* and *Chicago* south of Savo, the other three cruisers patrolling north of the island, each group out of touch with the other so they were certain to be attacked in detail, as was to be the case. *Chicago* exchanged shots with the destroyer *Patterson*, and possibly with our cruisers east of the island also.

But this is not the whole story. There were two destroyers (not enough, but remember two other destroyers had already been put out of action by air attack) patrolling the waters between Savo and Guadalcanal through which the Japanese ran rapidly to make their attack. One of them at least, *Blue*, had radar. She missed the Japs—

29

maybe due to an inexperienced operator who did not quite know how to pick them up under the loom of the island shore; maybe, again, because the operator was tired out.

There is also a responsibility at the high levels. It would seem that Admiral Fletcher received his recon report on the coming of the enemy force early enough to have flown off an air strike which, if it did not turn them back, would at least have left them in less than the first-class fighting condition in which they arrived at the scene; or he might have added some of his own ships to Crutchley's. But he too was a tired man, not with the local tiredness of seventy-two hours on duty, like the crews of the cruisers, but with the accumulated fatigue of many months of the most arduous command in the war. (In extenuation, it is worth noting that the reconnaissance was made by an Army plane, and the receiving authorities did not bother to transmit it for many hours. Since it was a report on moving ships capable of high speeds, most naval men would consider it nearly worthless when it did arrive.) Ghormley, who could have disposed of all forces, was not afloat but back at his headquarters in Nouméa.[1]

Never mind the responsibility. The salient fact now was that the 1st Marine Division had become engaged in a type of beachhead operation never foreseen in the books—alone, short on supplies, without air or sea support, subject to counterattack. It was not even properly distributed for meeting such an attack. Guadalcanal had 11,145 men all told, instead of something like 15,000, and the group of islands around Tulagi had 6,805 instead of fewer than 4,000 because so many had been drawn into the battle for Gavutu.

[1] To get the rest of the record straight on a matter that has caused endless speculation, some of which is likely to creep into the histories, the operation was planned approximately as it was carried out, as a high-speed raid. Rear Admiral Mikawa of the Imperial Navy was in charge; he had his flag in the heavy cruiser *Chokai*, and had with him the heavy cruisers *Aoba, Kako, Furutaka,* and *Kinugasa,* with the light cruisers *Tenryn* and *Yubari,* and either one or two (the records are not clear) destroyers. In the first action against the *Chicago-Canberra* group, he was thus able to oppose a broadside of 34 8-inch guns, 10 5.5-inch and 44 torpedo tubes to 17 8-inch guns and 4 torpedo tubes for the Allied ships, the torpedoes being particularly important in a high-speed close night action like this. In the second part of the action he had the same armament against 27 8-inch guns and no torpedoes on our side. He would have preferred to come through in two groups and get a crossfire, but these ships had never worked together before and he adopted a line-ahead formation to avoid accidents.

Chapter 3

Colonel Ichiki Arrives

L IEUTENANT GENERAL HARUYOSHI HYAKUTATE, A PROUD AND happy man, had received from the divine presence the mission of rounding off the dominion of Radiant Peace on its southern flank by the removal of the thorn that had stuck there since the beginning of the war—Port Moresby. His command was designated as the Seventeenth Army in the official documents, but he knew that according to custom it would now be referred to as "The Hyakutate Force" in conversation and the press. The detailed plans for a simultaneous advance across the Owen-Stanley mountains and a seaborne landing had already been drawn, the participating units were already in their rehearsal training. His staff had preceded him to Rabaul. He himself had already made his bows before the shrines of the august ancestors and was preparing to fly down from Tokyo when on 8 August the Imperial General Staff recalled him and handed him a file of dispatches.

They were from Rabaul, covering certain other dispatches received from Colonel Yano of the Kure 3rd Special Naval Landing Force, which had been established at Tulagi since May and from Captain Kodoma of the 11th Naval Billeting Unit, which had been working on an airfield at Guadalcanal since July. The Americans had attacked both places in great force the day before and as communications with both officers had since been lost it was probable that the men there had joined the illustrious departed souls.

Undoubtedly this unfortunate occurrence was the fault of the Imperial Navy (one can picture the staff and the General devoting some time to considering the shortcomings of the detested rival service), since as much as two weeks earlier Army Intelligence had predicted that there would be an attack on the place. The Navy had replied that there was nothing to worry about, the American advance would be intercepted by a powerful task force. It had not made the interception. Now the place must be retaken at once. It was essential to have the projected air base at the outer corner of the Empire, both as a means of protecting the line of advance toward Moresby and providing for that desirable further advance to New Caledonia and the New Hebrides that would sever the communications between America and her Australian ally. Lieutenant General Hyakutate would accordingly make the recovery of Guadalcanal his mission, and the task of capturing Port Moresby would be taken over by the Eighteenth Army, already in New Britain.

In view of its new purpose the composition of the Seventeenth would be somewhat different from that originally planned—a point which requires the explanation that in the Japanese service an army like Hyakutate's consists in the beginning of nothing more than a staff, which makes plans. The units that are to compose the formation are drawn from various places and assembled when the operation is about to begin. Estimates from air reconnaissance of the number of transports employed by the Americans, and from the few reports that had got through from the attacked positions, placed the number of Americans at 10,000. General Hyakutate was being given forces sufficient to crush such a group—to wit, two full divisions, one of them the famous Sendai 2nd Division, one of the very best in the Imperial Service; the other the 38th, which had a long record of experience in China; a heavily reinforced brigade (the Kawaguchi) almost a division in size; a shock regiment which had already fought surpassingly well in the Philippines and at Singapore, the Ichiki Detachment; the 8th Tank Regiment with an additional tank company and an Army Group artillery command consisting of no fewer than seven artillery regiments with six artillery battalions; a whole host of service units—say not much less than 50,000 men.

General Hyakutate was pleased with a generosity which indicated that exalted command's high sense of the importance of his mission; but not quite so pleased with the fact that the units of his army were pretty well scattered throughout the Co-Prosperity Sphere and that it would take some time to assemble them. The Ichiki was in Guam, whither it had gone when the landing on Midway, to which it had

32

been previously assigned, had proved impracticable. Most of the Sendai was in Java, the remainder at Davao in the Philippines. The Kawaguchis were in Borneo, the 38th Division in China, one of the antitank artillery battalions as far away as Manchuria, almost nothing directly at hand. This was very regrettable, as the Imperial Staff Manual on fighting Americans said quite clearly that "It can be seen that when they are pressed for time, the American dispositions and especially their organization of fire are not co-ordinated. Therefore we must not fail to move fast and attack quickly, giving them no time in which to prepare their positions." The staff themselves were quite insistent that matters be pressed home against the American landing force at once, before it had time to get set or to bring reinforcements in.

General Hyakutate flew down to Rabaul, where he met the good news that the Imperial Navy had partly redeemed its previous errors by conducting a very successful attack on the American ships off Guadalcanal. The enemy had already admitted the loss of two cruisers (one of them Australian) and damage to three more, which, considering how such matters are handled in the departments that make admissions, undoubtedly meant that one or more of the other cruisers were gone. Reports from a coast-watcher station on Florida Island, though partly garbled, seemed to make it clear that at least one of the American ships had sunk on the morning after the battle. This must be a very serious loss to their fleet; air reconnaissance had established the fact that their remaining ships had left the Guadalcanal area. The indication was that the Americans on Guadalcanal were in a state of considerable panic and disorganization. Did not the same Imperial manual lay it down? "The character of the Americans is simple and lacking in tenacity, in their tactics and battle leadership they also lack tenacity and if they meet with one setback, they have a tendency to abandon one plan for another. For this reason we must not fail to hammer at this weakness."

It was accordingly desirable to press the situation on Guadalcanal by every means and at once. Air attack was the obvious early resource, but unfortunately the squadrons based on Rabaul could operate against Guadalcanal only from the Bougainville fields, and these squadrons had already suffered serious losses in the first two days due to the great fire power of the American fighters. More planes were ordered in and a day and night bombing program was set up, as it was well known that not only do Americans suffer the most violent reactions to air attack, but also their lack of spiritual power makes them peculiarly subject to psychological discouragement when harassed. Forward operational airfields were begun on New Georgia and Kolombangara and an additional supply of laborers was sought to complete them with dispatch. For the present the field in the Shortland Islands was used as a fighter base, the bombers coming in from Rabaul or the expanding installations at Buka. Rear Admiral Mikawa called on 11 August to say that the Imperial Navy would be unable to keep surface ships on patrol in the area. The Americans were making great use of submarines and had torpedoed one of his best cruisers, *Kako,* a veteran of the victory off Savo, while she was entering Kavieng; she was the first cruiser lost by the Navy in the south, and he did not care to risk more losses among his slender stock of heavy ships. However, the 7th Submarine Division (*I-121, I-122, I-123, Ro-33, and Ro-34*) had been ordered down to the area to make vigorous and savage attacks on enemy shipping, and would co-operate in the campaign of harassment by shelling the American positions as well as maintaining an effective blockade. These were backed up by destroyers, which ran down during the night when American planes from carriers in the offing could not operate, and shelled the shore positions at dawn.

The Ichiki Detachment was the most readily available, arriving at Truk on 15 August. The day before, Intelligence had made a new report: "The enemy landing strength seems to be unexpectedly small. Not only are they not yet using the airfield but their activities are not vigorous. The enemy group has suffered losses." The report on which this was based seems to have come from Captain Kodoma on Guadalcanal, with whom communications of a sort had been re-established; he had beaten off an American attack with severe loss. One of the submarines reported that there was considerable movement of the American small boats in the lagoon and it was considered that the invaders were probably withdrawing to Tulagi to hold out in its more defensible terrain.

It seemed to General Hyakutate that in view of the disintegration and loss of spiritual power among the Americans the Ichiki Detachment might be sufficient to regain the Guadalcanal airfield by a

34

sudden and bold maneuver. Colonel Ichiki agreed. He worked out a plan on the excellent maps Intelligence had provided for landing at Kivu Point and near the mouth of the Ilu River, almost in the area where the Americans themselves had come ashore, with a quick crossing of that stream and a rapid march inland toward the airfield.

The Imperial Navy provided six of its best new destroyers (*Arashi, Hagikaze, Kagero, Tanikaze, Hamakaze, Urakaze*) to carry the advance echelon of 900 storm-troop infantry. A cruiser (*Jintsu*) and another destroyer were assigned as escort for two transports to carry the second echelon, largely mortar and artillery units, with a battalion of special landing force troops, the Yasuda, which the Navy somewhat unexpectedly contributed. All sailed from Truk on 16 August. As the transports were considerably slower than the six destroyers with the first echelon, they would not arrive till several days after, so Colonel Ichiki informed the troops of that group that they would unfortunately have little to do but the mopping-up operation. He was very energetic and ambitious, had fought Americans before, and had come thoroughly to believe in the words of the manual: "Our hand-to-hand fighting has decisive power and is greatly feared by the enemy." It seemed to him that mere numerical and material matters were insignificant in view of the spiritual superiority he would possess.

II

General Vandegrift was a soldier who had spent more time studying the subject in the field than from books, a complete denial in person of the statement in the Japanese manual (so carefully studied by General Hyakutate) that American tactics are precise but formal. The formal doctrine of modern war in such a position as the one he now occupied calls for a defense in depth around the central area of the airfield. But he had only five battalions of combat infantry; insufficient to man a defense in depth which would keep enemy advance beyond artillery range of the airstrip. There were more troops on Tulagi, but already on the night of the 11th a submarine had surfaced in the lagoon and plunked a few shells into the position. On the following morning another came up in broad daylight and chased a couple of Higgins boats into Tulagi Harbor under fire. This was followed by the attentions of nocturnal destroyers which would get

35

off a few salvos at daybreak before steaming away up the Slot, between the double chain of islands—which was to say that the Japanese had full control of the waters. An attempt to move troops across, at least until the Guadalcanal field was complete and could give air cover, would be an invitation to disaster.

On the other hand, country so broken and jungle-covered as that on which the beachhead abutted affords peculiarly good opportunities for infiltration attack, something in which the Japs were very adept. The point was convincingly demonstrated on the night when the enemy began to recover a little from his panic and appear as snipers, sometimes behind, sometimes in front, each sniper requiring an organized, time-consuming hunt by as much as a whole squad. One managed to establish himself somewhere in a tangle of trees (for instance) from which he crawled out each night and morning to fire one shot through Colonel Cates's tent. It was a matter of ten days before they got rid of him and even if nobody was hurt the tent was left looking like irregular brown lace.

In a spirit of the purest empiricism, therefore, the General threw all the rules overboard; decided to let his men deal with the snipers individually while his formal positions were established against the chief real danger—a counterlanding. The detail of the position established was that it ran from the highly defensible Tenaru westward to a point just beyond Kukum, where a high hill overlooked the beach and gave a strong point to anchor the left of the line. The beach defenses got a battery of naval 5-inch on each side of Lunga Point, a belt of machine-gun positions to sweep the shore, with 50-calibers, 37-mm., and mortars a little deeper in. The artillery was put into position south of the airfield, where it could fire in every direction. The emplacements themselves were covered on the south, landward side by a line of outposts manned by the Pioneer and Engineer battalions, the regular infantry battalions all being occupied toward the shore. Sandbags and wire were two of the items that did not get off the supply ships but all the positions could be fairly well bagged in by using the woven straw sacks in which the Jap occupation forces had carried their rice; the plantations were raided for whatever wire there was among them.

The General has left on the record his astonishment that the Japs used neither planes nor ships to burn out the stores on the landing

36

beach, though nearly forty bombers with full fighter escort came in on the 9th and nearly as many the next day. The enemy did not even bother the endless procession of trucks and amphitracs toiling along the single shore road to bring the supplies down to the point, where they were stored in piles of not over two-foot silhouette, a figure that had been worked out as providing maximum security from burst by observing what our own fire during the bombardment had done to the Jap supply dumps.

The first few days after the Battle of Savo Island were in fact a period of readjustment, personal and technical. The Marines, who thought of themselves as assault infantry, began as early as the 9th to become impatient about when the Army men would arrive and what beach they themselves would be called upon to assault next. Out on the perimeter of the position they showed a tendency to be trigger-happy, taking pot shots at stray cows and lizards and even coconuts swaying in the tops of trees, transformed by imagination into Jap snipers. The labor was hard, the food poor, the weather abominable, Japanese planes a constant annoyance—and they groused. Gradually the story of the naval defeat crept down through the ranks in the form of a rumor and was confirmed by the absence of American ships and planes. But these were hand-picked men, and particularly among the noncoms and the officers from major up there was a reserve of experience and savvy. Things quieted down; the shellings by night and bombings by day began to be accepted as routine and the 1st Marine Division was in the war.

Perhaps the key date for the completion of this process was that of the Goettge Patrol—the famous Goettge Patrol, particulars of which filtering back to the home-town newspapers through inadequate communications caused so much excitement that General Vandegrift was asked for a special report. The event fell out this way:

The leading weakness of the position was in the direction of Grassy Knoll, too large to bring inside the perimeter, yet dominating the whole left flank down to the mouth of the Lunga. Daily patrols were sent out to keep the mountain secure and they usually found something, more often than not a few of the miserable termite laborers, who would resist feebly before allowing themselves to be shot or would be brought in in the last stages of exhaustion. On 12

August a naval rating was among them, a sour, surly little man from whom the admission was at last extracted that a group of some consequence had assembled at a native village just beyond the Matanikau River. This checked with the report of another patrol which had been out in that direction and opened up with a heavy machine gun across the river, whereupon a large white flag was displayed on a pole within the village.

Goettge, as Intelligence officer, handled both sources of information. It seemed to him that the group at the Matanikau which was so anxious to hoist white flags wanted and could be persuaded to surrender and he proposed taking a patrol down the beach in boats after dark to bring them in.

The General did not like the idea but could not precisely put his finger on any flaw and Goettge, a persistent and very positive Teuton, talked him into granting permission—"Moreover, sir, it will be a humanitarian act to save the lives of those laborers besides what information we can get from the prisoners."

The patrol took off in the dark, 26 men and Goettge leading his Jap by means of a big rope around the latter's waist. As it reached shore at Matanikau there was a blaze of fire that killed the Colonel instantly and the patrol was attacked from all sides, only three men getting away by swimming. The "white flag," it developed later, had been the ordinary Japanese battalion battle flag which hung limp on the day seen and concealed the meat ball in the center.

That same day the airstrip reached a length of 2,600 feet; the last of the big banyan trees that stood in the way of the approaches came down. The day following the bad news about the Goettge Patrol, Martin Clemens came through the lines.

III

The Britisher said there were a good many scattered Japs back among the hills, starving, disorganized, weaponless, and lacking the power of coagulation. The Goettge Patrol had at least located the main fighting concentration around which these might gather at the Matanikau and it seemed likely that if this concentration could be broken up it would stay that way. With the matter of fortifications now as nearly under control as it could be, General Vandegrift decided to go for this group and assigned three companies of the 5th Regiment to the task. One was to move high up on Matanikau, cross and come down the west bank to the village of the same name, one to work across the sandbar at the river's mouth, and the third to move by night in landing boats down to Kokumbona to cut off the retreat of the Japs from Matanikau—a triple encirclement.

The upshot demonstrated what a difference there is between planning and performance in war—and also how a good plan which has not seemed to attain all the results desirable nevertheless accomplishes everything necessary. In the first place, the company that ascended the river found the going through jungle and cliffs so very tough that after making their crossing they had to bivouac for the night, which caused the operation to be postponed from 18 August, the planned day, to the 19th. In the second place, the company at the bar could by no means get across; the Japs had the whole place covered by machine-gun fire and pinned the attackers down. The landing-boat company were met by fire from the beach and just as they were going ashore at a slightly different spot a Jap destroyer showed up in the distance and began to shell them.

Yet the operation worked out anyway. The company from upstream found itself facing a ridge with prepared positions on it, but the Japs were mostly busy down in the direction of the bar and after our forces had taken a handful of casualties they got over the ridge and broke into the village. At the same time a mortarman with a good sense of direction knocked out the most serious of the machine guns that had been holding the bar. The Japs remaining in the village formed up shoulder to shoulder and came out in a spectacular yelling bayonet charge that cost them nearly all their lives. Those of Kokumbona ran away when their standard-bearer was shot down with his meat ball and our people had the whole position with 75 corpses at the cost of 11 casualties.

The result could not be called 100 per cent satisfactory. General Vandegrift planned another expedition westward to finish the job. It was unnecessary as it turned out—the essential step had been taken, enemy organization and stores had been destroyed, lack of food and the anopheles mosquito brought their casualty list up to the full tale of the original garrison. But our people did not suspect this for months or know it till years later and it was not for this reason that the mop-up patrol was never undertaken.

IV

Clemens's first act was to organize some of the natives in a service of information, which is not as silly as it might sound, since a good many of them were members of the Solomon Islands Police Force and knew a military position when they saw one. The earliest result was a report that way down to the east of our position the group of Japs had set up a radio station. It would be the equivalent of the Allied coast-watching system, capable of notifying them when and where our reinforcements and supplies were coming in. On the same 19th that saw the action at the Matanikau, therefore, Captain C. H. Brush with a company from the 1st Regiment started out to pick up this station. There were native guides and the patrol worked along the trails well inland.

Toward evening this patrol made contact with an enemy patrol on one of the jungle trails. Brush was astounded (at finding Japs in fighting shape out there) but not surprised. He deployed one platoon and sent the other to get behind the enemy. As the Japs came trotting blissfully along the trail without even security detachments out he let them have it from every gun in the company. They got a machine gun set up which cut down three of the Marines and wounded three more but it was knocked out by rifle and grenade, the Japs broke and were all shot but a couple who escaped into the bush. When the bodies were examined it was clear this patrol had been something special. There were thirty-five men, clean shaven and wearing new uniforms which bore the insignia not of the Naval Landing Force like all those hitherto, but of the Imperial Army. Four of them were officers; and they were carrying a lot of radio gear, far too much for a mere coast-watcher station. Brush searched the bodies for documents and found a good many which were immediately sent off to the command while he followed more slowly with his wounded.

The documents confirmed the obvious deduction from the appearance of the men. There was a special code for rapid ship-to-shore communication during action—also several diaries with entries

40

showing the force had left Truk since the American landing on Guadalcanal. This would be the advance scouting party of the counterattack, then, but how strong it was all told was unclear, and was it true that all had landed east of the perimeter as seemed likely? No data. General Vandegrift rejected the idea of using the single battalion he had in divisional reserve for a counteroffensive in spite of the attractive prospect of surprising their main body as Brush had surprised a part. Instead he pulled the right flank of his line slightly back from the upper reaches of the Tenaru, cut fields of fire for the weapons on this flank and threw out a screen of native scouts, with listening posts at the Ilu. That night there were Jap ships in the lagoon doing a good deal of firing. They caught two of the Higgins boats we had on antisubmarine patrol and sank them both. Toward morning there was a little rifle fire out toward the Ilu and some of the Marines in the river position complained of being eaten alive by ants. One of the enemy destroyers stayed till daylight. A B-17 arrived from New Caledonia, rather surprisingly hit her on the tail with a bomb and sent her out of there with a lovely fire burning.

The morning was the morning of 20 August, which started like other days, but that afternoon came the first good news. There was a roar of aircraft engines and it was not Jap bombers, but our own planes, Marine planes—a squadron of 19 F-4F fighters, Squadron 223, and a dozen Douglas dive bombers, Squadron 232, catapulted in from the escort carrier *Long Island,* far at sea. Now there would be something to say in answer to the daily attacks. "Morale has gone up twenty points this afternoon," one of the officers told Tregaskis.

About midnight that night flares went up from the listening post out eastward and presently their crews came tumbling in with word there was Jap activity all around them. Isolated scouts always tend to be nervous and not too much weight was given to the report, but the 2nd Battalion of the 1st Regiment was given a stand-to in its Tenaru position and the 1st Battalion alerted to move in in support.

The action was correct; Ichiki had arrived and the rustlings our men heard were their numerous scouting parties, which only by luck and the grace of the jungle night had missed picking up the listening forces. At the time the flares went up the Jap commander had already had a fairly good sketch of our position at the mouth of the stream and had determined how he would take it. Within another

41

hour he had his 70-mm. battalion guns, machine guns, and the grenade throwers our people called "knee-mortars," set up to smother with fire our position at the mouth of the river while his infantry should rush across the sandbar, here a hundred yards wide. At 0310 he gave the signal; all his pieces opened up with a crash that drowned the banzai as his men rushed, two hundred in the first wave.

The shock was terrific; in that first blaze of fire the Marines lost more men than they had so far on the island, the first rush of the Japs came right across the bar and into our outer positions, knocking out some of the guns and setting up some of their own. But quite a lot of the zing was taken out of the push by the single strand of barbed wire (which the Japs thought electrified) and still more by our machine guns, a couple of which really fired to the last man. This made the attack a group infiltration rather than a punch. A bright lieutenant named McClanahan managed to reorganize behind the broken front positions and with the help of some very accurate mortar fire drove the Japs back to their sandbar and re-established the line. The affair settled down to a fire fight of the most

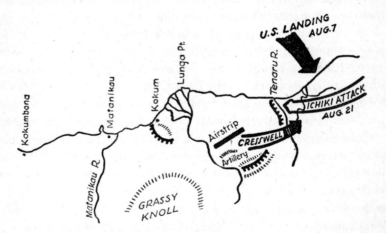

intense character in which our side did not have the worst of it, since the Marine artillery chimed in from the rear, combing over the whole grove in which the Japs must be lying.

By daybreak it was apparent to Lieutenant Colonel E. A. Pollock of the 2nd Battalion that the enemy force was not big enough to break his position. There was no action on his upstream flank, they were all concentrated down at the sandbar. It was therefore time to consider counterattack; Colonel Cates's 1st Battalion (Cresswell) was moved upstream to get across onto the enemy rear while the general dispatched five tanks to help out. The 1st Battalion executed its sweep without opposition till near the shore, where at the Block Four River it found the Jap rear guard in some native houses, a single platoon. Cresswell put a whole company onto this platoon; the platoon came out in a banzai charge and were all shot down.

It was now about 1000 and the rest of the battalion had reached the sea on one flank, the river on the other, and were closing in on the triangle of land that held the Japs. Progress was slow but steady, the Marines covering each other with fire as they made small rushes among the coconuts, while each individual Jap seemed determined to fight his own battle, and their occasional efforts to break from the closing net were disorganized.

As a matter of fact, Ichiki was not trying to break from the net except forward, still convinced that spiritual power was going to win the battle for him. He had filtered some of his men out along the reverse slope of the sandbar, where they inched slowly forward. About the time Cresswell's move really began to pinch his rear, he ordered a whole platoon to take the American position from the flank by swimming down the coast. American fighter planes unexpectedly appeared and broke up the sandbar attack by strafing; the platoon in the water was picked off by the rifle fire of Marines who very much enjoyed their target practice on the bobbing heads.

At about 1500 Ichiki's situation became worse yet; for Cresswell's men now had him thoroughly pinned in the contracting triangle, and across the sandbar appeared the ominous shapes of American tanks. The Ichiki Detachment was made up of picked men; they rushed the tanks and succeeded in disabling two with hand weapons, but the rest came right on, shooting in all directions, and now cruised back and forth through the grove, crushing the unfortunate remains of the Jap force into the ground where it lay pinned by increasing fire. The Colonel regretfully burned his colors and shot himself through the head. In his diary was found a neat schedule: "17 Aug. The landing. 20 Aug. The march by night and the battle. 21 Aug. Enjoyment of the fruits of victory."

By 1700 there was nothing left of the force but 900 dead, 15 prisoners, and some dozen men later reported as robbing native gardens among the hills to the south. The Marines had lost 34 killed and 75 wounded; but to balance this they had a loot of upward of fifty desirable entrenching spades.

Lieutenant General Hyakutate reported to Tokyo: "The attack of the Ichiki Detachment was not entirely successful."

V

The British carrier raid on Timor never did come off for reasons best known to HM Admiralty, but our raid on Makin did, though not till 27 August, while the troops on Guadal were moving into position for the fighting along the Matanikau. Lieutenant Colonel Evans F. Carlson was the commander, a skinny man with one of those faces that look like creased leather. His formation was the 2nd Raider Battalion—"Carlson's Raiders" henceforth and forever. Major James Roosevelt, the President's son, was his exec.

The trip down from Pearl was made aboard two old but gigantic submarines, *Argonaut* and *Nautilus,* on the theory that surprise could be had by coming up from underneath against the approximately 250 Japs supposed to be occupying this minor base.

Perhaps Major Eliot's too-accurate guess made the enemy think of Makin after the prediction about Tulagi had worked out so very closely. At all events the commandant on the island, which is a long finger of coral sand guarding the southeast flank of the lagoon, had a good prepared position ready to defend the vital areas of his radio station and supply dumps. There were snipers who had been slung in the trees for as much as three days and when the subs hove to off shore at dawn on 17 August all hands in the garrison were on the alert and even had their puttees carefully wrapped.

The strange part is that all this preparation failed to do the Japs any good; nor did they benefit from the fact that many of the motors on the rubber boats that carried our men ashore would not work, while the tidal swell proved so troublesome that all the boats had to make a confused rush at a single beach instead of two neat groups going in, each to a separate location.

Not a shot was fired as the Raiders went ashore and they were already forming under cover of the thick foliage in the first gray light when a rifle went off accidentally and gave the secret of their arrival away. Carlson at once rushed his Company A across the island to get on the main road down the lagoon side, while Company B got into the prepared Japanese position from the rear without a fight, so he evidently had his surprise after all.

Company A touched its flank to the lagoon and turned south; but after a half mile of advance with light now fully breaking, bullets began to whistle and then Japs tumbling off bicycles to be visible along the road ahead, with more of them in trucks behind. There was a powerful 55-caliber antitank rifle in the Raider equipment. It opened up on the trucks, they stopped and now there was a hot moving fire fight that lasted nearly all day, with the Jap snipers in trees extremely troublesome. The enemy were in pockets, usually centering around a machine gun. When the Raiders surrounded one the Japs would scream and shriek for a while to get their spiritual power worked up, and then all jump to their feet and run at the Marines, who shot them down and finished the job with knives.

Meanwhile there were difficulties with the radios, which worked only well enough to notify the two submarines that the Japs had a couple of ships in the lagoon, but not well enough to enable the Marines ashore to spot gunfire for our ships. *Nautilus* and *Argonaut* fired anyway, raking the whole lagoon, and they sank both ships; the natives said one of them had sixty soldiers aboard and they all drowned. Meanwhile also Jap planes had appeared a couple of times and in the afternoon they staged a regular performance, a formation of bombers coming over accompanied by one of the big Kawanishi flying boats. The bombers bombed and one of them landed in the lagoon along with the Kawanishi. As to the first, Colonel Carlson had just pulled in his flanks a little in the hope of drawing the Japs forward; the enemy bombers obligingly laid their eggs among their own people. As to the second, the antitank rifles were turned on the planes that landed; the Kawanishi burned up at once, the bomber got a couple of feet off the water and then crashed.

Now the Jap fire began to peter out and it grew dark. The Raiders were supposed to embark again and go on to Makin Meang, or Little Makin, some distance to the north. But when they tried to put the boats in the water serious trouble with the surf developed. The motors got wet, went out, and stayed out. The rollers came in so sharp and quick that paddling got the Marines nothing but the loss of their equipment and attempts to swim out cost the lives of five men. They kept trying and just after daybreak four of the boats did reach *Argonaut,* but there were still 120 Marines on the beach, now badly exhausted, many of them shivering since they had stripped for the paddling and swimming offshore, and with four stretcher cases among them. During the night a Jap patrol of eight men had shown up, three of them being killed by Private Hawkins before he himself was twice shot through the chest. There was evidently still resistance on the island and the coming of day brought Jap planes, so the subs had to go down.

It looked like disaster, but as Colonel Carlson remarked, "No matter how bad your situation is, there is a possibility that the enemy's may be worse." Making the best of a bad business, he sent one group toward the north end of the island in search of native outrigger canoes that would ride the surf and several patrols of others southward to search the more inhabited parts for weapons and food. The latter were interrupted by a flight of Jap planes which seemed to be in a fine state of confusion; they bombed the whole length of the island without hitting a single Marine and also laid some eggs on Makin Meang, results unknown. The food and weapon patrols had things unexpectedly easy, finding no Japs. They blew up the radio station, burned the storage tank with a lot of aviation gas, gathered some canned meat and crackers, and raided the house of the Jap commandant for his papers. Some of the natives said that practically all the Jap soldiers on the island had been killed; those who remained were termite laborers in hidey-holes somewhere and it was not worth digging them out even for the sake of getting prisoners, which had originally been one of the objects of the expedition.

That night Colonel Carlson got the remaining boats across to the lagoon side of the island and launched them in a group, all lashed to an outrigger canoe. He and his men were picked up at the lagoon entrance. They arrived in Pearl Harbor singing and piratical of appearance. Hawkins grew a magnificent red beard and allegedly cured himself of his chest wounds by getting up from the hospital bed and taking a walk. He was a Marine.

The Makin raid, the Battle of Tenaru, and the arrival of our planes marked a period not only in the struggle for Guadalcanal, but in the whole story of amphibious operations in the Pacific. Difficulties and deficiencies had appeared, notably at Makin, where the failure of the outboard gasoline motors nearly brought the expedition to disaster and the Marines did not know till they were forced to learn it that they had won a complete victory ashore.

In fact, looking back at those first few weeks of Guadalcanal, the really striking feature is how little anyone on the Japanese side realized that they were dealing with something bigger and tougher and a great deal smarter than they had yet encountered. The Marine doctrine really had functioned at Guadalcanal and Makin; the enemy had really been defeated at every contact. There were several reasons for this double failure of correct appreciation. The facts were overlaid by exterior circumstances.

General Vandegrift was an extremely tough-minded individual, but on short rations and isolated as he was, without even proper elementary tools, with a sea full of Japs around him and sniping on the perimeter all night, under constant air attack, with continual reports of additional enemy landings and the only apparent promise of assistance resting on the small driblets that could be brought in by the APDs,[1] it would be wonderful if he had considered his position good or his operation successful.

On the other side the Japanese had the universal record of their own success down through the Indies, Malaya, and the Philippines behind them. They had won a great victory at Savo Island—and all this confirmed what they had been learning not only from experience but also from indoctrination since childhood, ever since the early days of the Russian War. White men did not know how to fight. They relied too much on their mechanical instruments, on fire power; they were easily discouraged. It was true that the original garrison of the islands round Guadalcanal had disappeared and the Ichiki Detachment had now followed them into oblivion. But one must remember that there were no reports from these illustrious de-

---

[1] An APD is a small old destroyer converted to a transport by the removal of some of her boilers and armament.

parted souls to indicate why they had departed. To any normal command mind such a pair of isolated events must appear as exceptional, as up to this time they were. To a Japanese it would seem that there must have been some personal failure on the part of the Japanese commanders involved. The system was not wrong; it had produced spectacular results before and it would do so again.

Chapter 4

Flash from Radio Tokyo—
Airfield Taken!

THE YOUNGER OFFICERS OF THE IMPERIAL NAVY HAD FOR A
long time wished to increase the emphasis on carrier operations. Although most of the top brass was intensely conservative, Admiral Yamamoto leaned to their view and the success of the
carriers at Pearl Harbor provided the necessary impetus. A new
organizational setup was designed about that time under which the
3rd Fleet, previously consisting of cruisers only, should be erected
into a combination of scouting, screening, and supporting ships—
cruisers and carriers, with the flag in one of the latter. The loss of the
1st Fleet carriers at Midway made some such reorganization immediately imperative. Not much over one-tenth of the pilots who had
participated in that unfortunate incident were in a physical state
for service, but these were sent down to Kyushu to be the nucleus of
the new 3rd Fleet Air Wing. They were joined by young pilots just
out of the training schools, with whom they would work.

Admiral Takata, G-3 to the great Yamamoto, considered that the
losses at Midway were primarily due to over-concentration on attack
tactics at the expense of training in search. After the 3rd Fleet pilot
organization was set up on 15 July he prescribed two months of the
most rigorous training, particularly in search. Unfortunately the
American invasion of Guadalcanal upset this schedule. The Imperial
General Staff considered it necessary to send most of the 3rd Fleet
pilots to Rabaul at once and although the Navy complained bitterly
that the military were too concerned with their own fears and lacked
the true Bushido, the shift was made. It was mainly in the form of
reinforcing the 25th Air Flotilla, the Navy unit already operating
from the New Britain base.

In the meanwhile the new carrier *Hayataka* had come into service; *Shokaku* and *Zuikaku* had completed the repairs of the damage received at Coral Sea. The 1st Fleet could therefore mobilize four carriers (the other being *Ryujyo*) to escort General Hyakutate's troops to Guadalcanal. That officer was very insistent on the need for carrier cover, since it appeared that the Americans had installed planes on the island and the 25th Air Flotilla had difficulty in dealing with American planes operating so close to their own fields.

The General had not really expected Colonel Ichiki to do much more than administer to the Americans one of those "stout and crushing blows on the head" which would cause them to lose their initiative. Even as the valiant Colonel was burning his colors at the mouth of the Tenaru, Hyakutate was approving the orders prepared by Major General Kiyotake Kawaguchi, whose brigade would be sent in during August-September. These orders were carefully drawn to take advantage of the specifically American defects as stated in the Imperial Staff Manual—"The American soldiers are extremely weak when they lack the support of fire power. They easily raise their hands during battle and when wounded they give cries of pain. Their flanks and rear are extremely susceptible. Their training in reconnaissance and security is exceedingly inadequate."

In sum, the plan provided for a surprise attack on the flanks and rear of the American position from all directions at once, so that the enemy's fire power would be bewildered by the variety of impressions and unable to recover itself in the time necessary. The cover at Guadalcanal was good and given the American deficiencies in matters of scouting, there would be no particular difficulty in reaching the necessary positions without detection.

General Hyakutate ordered the Kawaguchi Brigade up to Truk, where the 1st Fleet had already assembled and whence the second echelon of the Ichiki Detachment had sailed several days before. The latter, known as the Kuma group since Colonel Ichiki's unfortunate demise, was worked into General Kawaguchi's plans, giving him a total of some 4,500 men and a certain amount of fire power. It would seem that at least one of the Japs who escaped the massacre on the Tenaru somehow got to a radio. At all events, the fresh group adopted "Remember the Ichiki suicide" as its watchword, and Kawaguchi's order stated that the purpose of the expedition was to "annihilate the enemy on the left bank sector of the Tenaru and thus give rest to the departed souls of the commander of the Ichiki Detachment and his men."

From the rest of the order emerges the detail that the brigade was to operate pretty much as a series of independent infantry battalions, four of them. Colonel Oka of the 124th Regiment, the biggest single unit of the brigade, would be landed with a reinforced battalion combat team from this regiment at the mouth of the Matanikau and would attack across that river. The remainder of the brigade would for secrecy's sake land even farther down the coast to the east than Ichiki had and work through the jungles across the ridges that step up to the central spine of the island. Said the order: "Passage through the jungles will be executed chiefly in the daytime; but be sure to make complete detour around grass fields by day. If passage through a grass field is unavoidable at night, try not to leave any footprints."

One battalion of the 124th would hit the inland, open flank of the American position along the Tenaru. The main "central" force was to strike across a dominating ridge south and a little east of the airfield directly upon it; this force consisted of the remaining battalion of the 124th with an attached battalion (the Aoba) and the infantry battalion of the Kuma group, whose guns would be added to the brigade artillery to provide preparation fires both on the front of this main attack and for the movement to flank the Tenaru position. Naval forces would enter the lagoon and conduct heavy diversional attacks on Lunga Point to convince the enemy that a counterlanding was taking place.

General Kawaguchi's order was far from clear and it made no provision whatever for either support or reserves, but the latter was not a defect from his point of view or from General Hyakutate's. It was a means of moving every Japanese warrior, filled with incomparable devotion to his Emperor, into personal contact with the enemy at the earliest possible moment. In war it is not the over-all number of men in an area that counts; it is the number actually in contact. Once contact was established the unquestionable superiority of the Japanese in hand-to-hand fighting would be decisive.

51

The 1st Fleet swept down from Truk with its transports well in the rear and a line of cruisers and destroyers in visual contact with each other fanned out ahead, while planes from the carriers flew searches still farther out to prevent such another surprise as that of Midway. Beyond them again ranged a few of the big Kawanishi flying boats that were Japan's most useful scouts. The intention was to sweep everything American from the eastern face of the Solomons while the transports entered the island chain past Sta. Isabel. Just before noon of the 24th, *Ryujyo,* the carrier nearest in, flew off a heavy strike to put the American field at Guadalcanal out of business, while the 25th Air Flotilla sent down more planes to co-operate. *Ryujyo* had hardly got her strike away when one of the Kawanishis reported a whole gigantic American squadron with two carriers out east of the Solomons and then stopped reporting, evidently shot down. The Admiral was annoyed—how had the Americans anticipated us? But he accepted battle and flew off his strike groups.

Actually the anticipation on our side was due partly to the persistent cracking of Jap code that had been going on since the beginning of the war and partly to an odd piece of luck. To the first can be referred the general information that the Imperial Staff had decided to take the Solomons campaign seriously and was committing heavy forces there. The groups built round *Wasp, Saratoga,* and *Enterprise* were accordingly held in the area south of the Solomons and another carrier group with *Hornet* at its center was dispatched from Pearl Harbor. The actual discovery of the enemy was a piece of luck—a long-range search plane from Espiritu Santo got well off its course 250 miles west and north of Guadal and sighted Kawaguchi's transports on the morning of the 23rd without itself being seen.

Hornet had not yet joined and *Wasp,* low on both fuel and provision, was on her way back to base. Admiral Fletcher came dashing north and got off a strike against the transports that had been seen in the afternoon, the 23rd. It missed them; they had changed course westward when a Jap sub in the area had reported American carrier-type planes going over. The point where the transports had been seen was so far westward that the strike missed the Jap fleet too.

The planes went into Henderson Field,[1] where the pilots spent an uncomfortable night getting what sleep they could in the seats of their machines while a Jap sub shelled the place. Fletcher had no doubt whatever that the enemy would keep on coming. The fact that he had lost track of them represented some trick which he could not exactly fathom as yet. Accordingly he worked steadily northward through the morning of the 24th, but made poor fleet speed because the wind was wrong and every time he took in or sent out planes he had to turn around and so lose mileage.

About the time the Kawanishi was getting off its final report his scouts found the Japs in two groups, spread all over the ocean. *Saratoga* and *Enterprise* flew off strikes and the Marines at Henderson Field were alerted, so their dive bombers came out also. The net result was the triple air battle known as that of the Eastern Solomons.

Over Guadalcanal the fighters of 223, a very hot squadron indeed, crucified the dual attack. They lost three planes but they shot down eleven Zero fighters, five of the Rabaul twin-engine bombers and five of *Ryujyo*'s bombing planes, and landed on the field hilarious and shouting. Captain Marion Carl, who had been at Midway, was one of them; he remarked that, although there seemed no difference in the flying of these Japs and those, "We got shot up a lot more there than we do here."

At sea the Jap striking force concentrated on *Enterprise* and she got hit—three times, with 169 casualties, and was out of action for a while. The Japs paid for that attack with 82 planes, mostly shot down by our fighters, though the battleship *North Carolina*, covering the carrier, knocked down ten or twelve and drove off several more which did not dare come through the curtain of fire she put up. It was the first suggestion our people had that the Jap pilots were no longer as good as those of Coral Sea and Midway.

Of our own strikes most of the *Enterprise* planes missed the Japs altogether under clouds. The Marines and *Saratoga* men all found targets, but not all the same targets. The Marine group got in on a heavy cruiser and punched her hard; the *Saratoga* men put a 1,000-pounder into a battleship and hit *Shokaku* twice. First prize, however, belonged to the *Saratoga* men who found *Ryujyo*. They hit her

[1] The Marines had named the field after the aviator who led the Marine attack at Midway.

with three big bombs and two torpedoes and left her burning brightly in the fading light. "She sank altogether too quickly," remarked one of the Japanese officers later. Moreover, their whole fleet got very few of its planes back. The big carriers had altered course so violently in getting away from our strikes that they could not be reached and *Ryujyo,* which was supposed to take in the planes for them, was gone.

The net result of the battle, then, was that on the evening of 24 August the 1st Fleet found itself not only unable to give air cover to Kawaguchi's transports but even without any for itself in the face of several highly functional carriers which would certainly come tearing north against them next morning. The Admiral ordered the whole fleet back to Truk. The transports were directed to the Shortland Islands under escort of Southeast Area Fleet units, where the Kawaguchi Brigade would be transferred to smaller craft to enter Guadalcanal in more normal fashion. There had reached the Shortlands some of the big power barges with dished-out bows for beach work, which had been found so useful in China and the Malayan campaign. They had the great advantage of being able to conceal themselves by day from American aerial observation among the deeply indented shores of the Solomons.

III

General Kawaguchi's troubles in getting his troops to Guadalcanal were not yet over. All during the battle the Kuma group had continued its plodding progress in slow transports toward the island. Under the peculiar Japanese system of war, what happens to another commander in the same area is not allowed to modify the obligation of any officer to carry out his orders to the letter. It would seem that the commodore conducting the Kuma group, under escort of the cruiser *Jintsu* and four destroyers, never received any orders to turn toward the Shortlands as the rest of the transports had. He must have known about the battle—all the radio channels in the Pacific were full of it—but he never thought of asking for a change in orders either; that would not be Bushido. Therefore he kept on; dawn of 25 August found him coming right along toward the strait between Florida and Sta. Isabel. The Marine planes from Guadal, out on the track of the retreating Jap fleet, stumbled on him there, instantly turned to on the little group, beat the bejesus out of one of the transports and got a heavy bomb on *Jintsu* forward.

Having his biggest ship badly damaged absolved the Jap commodore from continuing the direct line of his orders. He turned the transports towards the Shortlands, sent *Jintsu* back to Truk and dropped the destroyer *Mutsuki* behind to pick up survivors from the sinking troopship. While she was about it a flight of B-17s, alerted by the Marines, came over and found both ships stationary targets. They hit *Mutsuki* with a whole trainload of bombs and down she went. Her skipper, Commander Hatano, was picked up from a raft later, very much disgusted; his was the first ship sunk by the high-level bombers in the whole war. "I suppose even a B-17 has to hit something sometime," he said, "but why did it have to be me?"

On the island General Vandegrift had not misinterpreted the effort that failed amid all this thunder in the skies. It meant that the Japs were to make a renewed attempt on his position with heavier forces than before. Accordingly, on 21 August, the very first day when he had air cover for the job, he brought the remaining battalion of the 5th Regiment over from Tulagi and installed it as a reserve behind his position on the Matanikau. On the 27th, as soon as it was clear that fleet operations were at least temporarily over, he dispatched Lieutenant Colonel Maxwell along the coast with the 1st Battalion of the 5th to make a renewed landing at Kokumbona and clean out the remaining Japs on that flank by means of a backward sweep toward the Matanikau.

It would seem that not over a single destroyerload (150 men) of Colonel Oka's command of the Kawaguchis had arrived by this time, if that many; there may have been no reinforcements at all. Colonel Maxwell's men got ashore at 0700 without resistance and began going eastward at nearly noon. Fifteen hundred yards along the beach, the leading company came under machine-gun and mortar fire, halted and settled down to a fire fight. At 1500 Colonel Maxwell reported his position and that he was pinned down; wanted to know when the landing craft would come take him out of there.

The General exploded. Anyone could lay the position out on the map and see how the advance had moved forward only 300 yards an hour before meeting opposition. Moreover, the definition of "pinned down" had been established for Guadalcanal during the previous fight at the Matanikau.

"What do you mean, you were pinned down?" demanded General Vandegrift fiercely when Captain Hawkins, who had tried to get across the bar, made his report.

"Well, sir, I had three bullet hits on my helmet and they knocked the stock off my Thompson gun."

"You were pinned down."

There was evidently no such fire at Kokumbona; the almost total absence of casualties proved it. Maxwell was relieved of his command, Colonel Hunt of the regiment went down there to take over the operation. It was too late to do anything when he got there but he bivouacked for the night and at dawn conducted the flanking movement that should have been undertaken the day before along the ridges. Too late for that also now; the Japs had decamped, leaving twenty bodies, and the operation could be counted a failure.

IV

The moon was full during those last days of August and the nights brilliant. Major C. L. Fike, the air officer, made an effort to keep one or two planes up to see what the enemy were doing on the water. At midnight on the 30th one of these planes spotted two cruisers and a pair of destroyers down near Taivu Point, lying close in and stopped. Mangrum's dive bombers boiled out to attack them; no contact in the dark. Next night there were three destroyers there; and meanwhile the day patrol planes had discovered, near the southern tip of Sta. Isabel and under an admirable system of camouflage, a whole nest of big barges. The planes bombed; some of the boats burned but there was no fire nor any sign of Japs, nor was there any when another batch of boats was found and attacked near the same place on 3 September. The latter group had some big ones in it, 70-footers; it began to become clear that the Japs were moving down in this manner by night, hiding out during the day. Not very much could be done to interrupt them without real naval control of the lagoon.

It was, then, a question of getting them after they landed. Since a patrol had confirmed the intimation from the airmen that the main

56

enemy concentration was being built up east of the airfield that was the place to get them. The General had brought over Edson's Raiders from Tulagi. Now he attached what was left of the parachutists to them for a raid on this new nest of Japs, but there was a problem about transport. Taivu was some 20 miles down the coast from our lines, too far for Higgins boats if any surprise were to be attained, and besides Colonel Edson wanted the gunnery support that APDs could give. But persuading Admiral Turner to release APDs for a daylight job was not easy; Turner believed in not repeating past mistakes.

He had only six of these valuable ships in the South Pacific command. On 30 August one of them, *Colhoun,* had just been unloading some rations at Lunga when a flight of Jap bombers came over. There were only four fighters operational at the field that afternoon (there had been a heavy air battle in which eighteen Japs were shot down, but all except these four of our planes were so damaged that they could not take off), so the Japs had no opposition. Probably they did not know this; they ducked into some low-hanging clouds and began to drop bombs in the general direction of *Colhoun,* which got underway. One of the bombs hit her on the stern and blew it all apart; then another one got her and she sank in a few minutes. Actually it had been a lucky hit, a freak of the first order which would never again be repeated, but of course Turner could not know this at the time. What he did know was that *Colhoun* was gone, and leaving APDs in the lagoon during daylight was likely to get him nothing more than evidence of the increased efficiency of Jap bombers. Even at night . . .

There had been some suspicious-looking smokes going up from Savo Island and it seemed not impossible the Japs were occupying the place, at least with a coast-watcher station. Some of the officers persuaded General Vandegrift to send two companies of Raiders over for a "reconnaissance in force," a type of operation not much favored either by the General himself or by his operations department. (They considered a reconnaissance in force either too little or too much—the latter if information was desired, the former if the objective was to strike a blow.) The result bore out their dislike; the smokes came from the cookfires of apologetic natives who offered to

57

do their cooking at eleven in the morning to avoid future misunderstandings.

But after the Raiders had been brought home, two more of the APDs, *Gregory* and *Little,* were left in the lagoon on the night of 4 September. They took up patrol stations off Lunga Point. About 0100 they heard a crash of guns to the eastward, and pips developed from that direction on their radar screens. At almost the same moment the pilot of a night-prowling PBY had the brilliant thought that there must be a Jap submarine out there. He dropped a row of five flares, which admirably silhouetted the two little APDs for the Jap cruiser *Yubari* and a pair of heavy enemy destroyers which, having just landed some men near Taivu, came tearing past at 25 knots, searchlights on our unfortunate ships and every gun bearing. Both APDs were sunk in less than ten minutes and there were few survivors, since the Japs machine-gunned the men in the water.

This could be counted a failure in scouting (at Savo), or in liaison (the PBY man should have known), or just in the brain of the PBY man. The point that Admiral Turner saw was that two more APDs were gone, and when General Vandegrift wanted to use the rest for lagoon operations, the naval man was inclined to balk. There was an argument, which General Vandegrift won as for the use of the APDs, but with the specification that they were to be employed for a single day and under careful air cover, so that instead of an encirclement, the expedition was set up as a straight raid, with a landing beyond the easternmost point the Japs were known to occupy. It went in at dawn on 8 September, with the APDs firing on Tasimboko Village and the handful of Army P-40s giving close support, a job for which these planes had shown themselves peculiarly adapted. Colonel Edson's men reached the beach without opposition and worked westward along the shore till they came to a stream, the Kema, which spreads out into a marshy lagoon parallel to the beach. Here were Japs; they began shooting inaccurately from some field guns but a private in Company B put a stop to that by picking off the whole crew of the most annoying piece with his rifle.

Meanwhile another company had worked through the jungle to the south of Tasimboko Village. Just before noon the Raiders closed on the place in a rush from both directions, chased the remaining Japs into the jungle and killed those who delayed in getting away,

58

to the number of 25. The place turned out to be an artillery depot and supply dump—ammunition, food, medical supplies, and equipment for a whole brigade; flame throwers, land mines, antiaircraft guns, and a whole battery of artillery. Edson's men blew up and burned everything and got away with only two casualties, after one of the most brilliant little operations of the campaign and of the war.

It had an effect too. "It is maddening," wrote one of the Japs in his diary, "to be the recipients of these insulting attacks by American forces." Another: "Oh! All this is terrifying; I am surprised." General Kawaguchi set it down that our troops had occupied Tasimboko and angrily redrew his plan of attack to allow for the loss of the battery Edson's men had blown up. It had been intended that his three attacks should be simultaneous with the artillery covering all at once. Now the attack of the battalion behind the Tenaru was to be delayed till it could receive the support of all the guns, which by this time would have blasted a path through the American defenses south of the airfield. It does not seem to have occurred to the General that he had lost the secrecy which was so much of an element in his original plan, but if it had it would never have done to admit it since other elements of the Imperial Forces were already involved. Admiral Mikawa's cruisers with a pair of destroyers ran into the lagoon and shelled the American lines. The 25th Air Flotilla had now been built up by the planes originally intended for the 3rd Fleet and on both the 11th and the 12th it was possible to send down as many as 26 bombers with the elaborate cover of 30 Zeros. They reported they had done great damage to the American positions.

V

The stepping up of air operations, the nightly visits of Japanese ships, the fact that patrols to the east now almost invariably clashed with the enemy—all pointed in one direction: an imminent attack. Edson's raid had confirmed the reports of native scouts (not quite believed at the time) that there were three or four thousand of the enemy prowling around back there in the jungle.

General Vandegrift believed he could hold against that many but he was far from happy about his position as a whole. The aerial side was the worst; there was a continual drain of casualties from the

59

bombings and on 2 September a plane was hit on the field and blew up with a bad fire and some of the ammunition dumps exploding. Our fighters were getting a steady average of five to one but the Japs always seemed to have another five, and by the 11th the fighter strength of the field was practically zero.

The situation as to troops was not very good either. In the last couple of weeks there had been an outbreak of malaria that alarmed the medical officers—they had 48 hospitalized cases; and among the men untouched by the disease was a good deal of tropical diarrhea, traceable as much to fatigue as anything else. There were not men enough to hold the lines in any case. Thanks to the APDs and air cover, which allowed a thin trickle of supply ships to get in (seven during the first month), the men were eating again and ammunition stocks were adequate, but it had seldom been possible to get all the loads off ships before they had to pull out again, so equipment remained short. What was needed was a good big convoy with reinforcements and everything else implied in that word. General Vandegrift kept the communications channels hot asking for it—but most especially for planes, at once.

By the night of the 12th that convoy was already on the tide. Admiral Turner had made extraordinary efforts to assemble shipping (his major shortage) and had persuaded Ghormley that the 7th Marine Regiment could defend Samoa far more effectively up on the shores of Guadalcanal than where it stood. Now it was aboard and moving up, the carriers *Wasp* and *Hornet* seeing it in. Vandegrift's appeal of the 11th for planes caused a change; next morning the carriers left their intended course and stood up toward the southern shore of the island with twenty fresh Marine fighters aboard.

By that same date the General had made his arrangements to meet the coming storm. The eastern flank position along the Tenaru was strengthened and carried inward from the river's bank. Next to its termination there was a tall nameless ridge where the Raider battalion established itself and dug into what was rather a chain of foxholes than a formal position. At the right rear of this the Pioneers organized a position down to the Lunga; but beyond that stream Grassy Knoll still dominated the whole landscape and there were

60

not enough men to cover it. An attack there would have to be dealt with by a counterstroke from divisional reserve.

These arrangements were barely completed and Colonel Edson was just drawing a plan for reconnaissance in force when at nine on the night of 12 September a green flare exploded over the airfield and almost instantly shells began to crash into position from the sea. A Jap spotter plane (the Marines called him "Louis the Louse") buzzed overhead; a rocket went up from the jungle facing Edson's line, and with yells and a banging of mortars he was attacked. There were so many Japs they seemed to come from all directions at once. They got a lodgement at the center of Edson's line between two of his companies, and they filtered in men who cut all the communications wires, isolated one company at the western end of the ridge, and forced it back. There was hard fighting at close quarters till daybreak; when Edson tried to re-establish his position under the new light he found the Japs dug in in such strength that no progress could be made against them, so withdrew the entire position to some knolls near the northern rim of the ridge.

During the day Colonel Twining of the staff went up to look at the position. The reports from Edson were pretty encouraging, but it was always a good idea to have an eyewitness, especially with Edson, who was inclined to go too far in making light of his own difficulties. The staff man found the ridge held about as weakly as it possibly could be, a front of 1,800 yards in rugged jungle country with only 400 men in line, which meant that there were gaps everywhere, and no wire.

More alarming still was the condition of the Raiders. They had been sent there originally as to a rest area, having carried so much of the heavy fighting earlier. They had just fought desperately all night, with an unsuccessful counterattack during the day, and had undoubtedly given a good account of themselves against numbers obviously superior; but now they gave all the signs of men at the last limit of fatigue, lifting their feet high off the ground when they walked and mumbling their words. The Japs had nowhere withdrawn; it was evident they would attack again that night, the 13th. As soon as Twining could get out of earshot, he grabbed the nearest phone and told the General that the Raiders were done, they could stand no more, must be relieved.

Vandegrift ordered a battalion of the 5th Regiment from across the Lunga, but just as it was making the approach march, down came a savage dive-bomber raid, they had to take cover and could not cross the airfield. It was already falling twilight when they got through, and then too late to relieve the Raiders, so they did the best they could, which was move into a support position. At the front foxholes were dug and fields of fire cleared, not on the usual American system (for which time lacked) but by the Japanese method of opening a narrow tunnel in front of each piece.

As evening came on all the evidence spoke of a really stout effort for the night. The raid that halted the march of the 5th was only one of four; two of them heavy ones. The planes the two carriers had brought saved us; they got into the air raiders 15 miles from the field and made most of them jettison their bombs, shooting down eight machines at a cost of two.

VI

As a matter of fact that battle of the night of the 12th, which had taken so much out of the Raiders, was for General Kawaguchi no more than the move to his jump-off positions. There had been

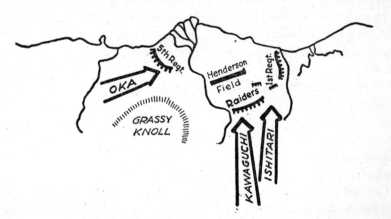

rather more casualties than desirable for such a preliminary operation but this might have been expected in crossing the zone where American fire power was dominant. The zone was now crossed; his three battalions were now in a position from which they could drive home the attack at close quarters that night. The General assembled his company commanders and made the assignments. While he was doing it there was a noisy air fight high above the American area and the men could hear the sound of exploding bombs, which cheered them greatly. The time for the main thrust was set very early, at 1830, so that the airfield would be clear of Americans by the time Admiral Mikawa's ships arrived at midnight. The battalion of the 124th (Ishitari) which was to take the Tenaru position would attack about that hour and General Kawaguchi expected to swing his own three battalions from the airfield against the rear of the same position. His situation as a whole was so favorable that he got off a radio message which led Tokyo (anticipating slightly) to announce that the airfield was Japanese.

VII

Under the jungle cover dark comes early and it could be counted already night when sniper fire on Edson's front began to step up and then on they came, screaming weirdly, shouting "Gas attack!" in English and throwing exploding smoke pots for distraction. The main thrust was straight against the center of the ridge under a strong barrage from mortars and artillery; but there was also a flanking movement through the jungle against the western end of the position (this would seem to have been the Kuma, Ichiki's avengers) with another smoke screen streaming through the trees to lend point to the "Gas attack."

The flank move fell on Company B, forced it back and completely surrounded one platoon, which took fire from three different directions and had to cut its way out. Through the gap thus created, through the interstices of the line, Japs infiltrated, cutting communication wires. Colonel Edson fell back on radio; and matters were not helped by the discovery that the Japs had our frequency. The men were tired out nervously and physically, the whole position began to shake, and the lines had become so closely interlocked that it was hard to bring artillery fire down on the enemy. By 2200 there were not over 300 Marines holding the position and Colonel Edson estimated he was being attacked by two full battalions. (He was wrong, as we know; it was three battalions). At 2230 came another

63

attack, chiefly at the western end of the ridge under a violent mortar barrage with calcium flares to illuminate our lines and shouting Japs running forward behind the lights. If there could be said to have been a crisis in that long-continued struggle, this was that crisis.

There is a small dominating knoll at the most northerly rim of the ridge. Colonel Edson pulled his lines back to this knoll, which was held by Company C, refused his right flank to cover against any effort to envelop him and called for artillery interdiction fire on the old positions and all the trails. Major Kenneth D. Bailey (who got a Medal of Honor for that night's work) strode from place to place through the fire, superintending everything, encouraging everyone. He carried the morale of the whole battalion. Down came the artillery with a crash, battery after battery of pack howitzers and 105s joining, and now it was seen whose men "give cries of pain when wounded" for the whole night was hideous with Japanese screams as the shells poured into them. They had been caught precisely in one of the most accurate barrages of the war. The attacks began to lose force and direction. When Mikawa's ships arrived a little after 2300 and began cruising around the lagoon, getting off a salvo now and then as they waited for Kawaguchi's flare to signal the fall of the airfield, there was no attack at all going on, the thing had settled down to a fire fight in the dark.

When the battle blazed up again a few minutes later it was to the eastward where Ishitari's battalion launched its attack on the Tenaru line. Unfortunately for that officer he lacked the support of guns; those of the Kumas were either otherwise occupied or had been put out of action in the American counterbarrage. Still more unfortunately he had to attack against wire across a grassfield which had been perfectly registered by Marine guns. Those guns could now be spared from Edson's support and they dropped a terrific shoot right into the middle of Ishitari's concentration. The attack stopped; Ishitari assembled his company leaders and made them a speech—this was a difficult operation and all must sacrifice their lives in the service of the Emperor. They attacked again; again that dreadful artillery fire fell on their heads, not an inch could be gained, and toward dawn—"Carrying our wounded we regretfully withdrew. The battalion commander, 50 officers, 180 men were killed, more than a hundred men so badly injured they had to be carried on litters." The battalion was in effect *zemetsu*—wiped out.

Meanwhile Colonel Edson, as he expected, was beginning to get some mortar fire from his left rear. The Japs had infiltrated there and were close to the division command post. But by 0230, though there was a tremendous amount of hardware still flying around, it was clear the position was going to be held. A good deal of the enemy fire was now sniper stuff and they evidently could not work up a concentration in the face of the Marine artillery. They did attempt more attacks, to be sure, but each increasingly feebler and rendered still more so by the habit of announcing the move with a red rocket, which instantly brought artillery down on the attackers.

By dawn it was nothing but snipers. American planes from the field began to comb the area and a few patrols to go out. They did not start soon enough to find the four Japs who popped up almost at the door of General Vandegrift's tent, yelled "Banzai!" one killing a sergeant with a sword thrust before they were shot down, but the battle for the ridge, Edson's Ridge, was over. It had cost the Raiders and attached Parachutists 143 casualties, 20 per cent of those engaged; but it cost General Kawaguchi nearly two thousand men, and after a jabbering conference with his officers, he decided to withdraw along the jungle trails and the routes of the mountains westward to the region of the Matanikau, where what was left of his force could be supported.

It was a hard, bad march. "I cannot help from crying," wrote one of his officers, "when I see the sight of these men marching without food for four or five days and carrying the wounded through the curving and sloping mountain trails. The wounds couldn't be given adequate medical treatment; there wasn't a one without maggots. Many died."

VIII

The fight at Edson's Ridge was the key action of the campaign but it was surrounded by a series of other events which tended to obscure that main issue. One of them was the attack by Colonel Oka of the 124th across the Matanikau. This gentleman seems to have been that rarity among Japanese officers, a cowardly braggart. Relations between him and Kawaguchi were bad; he received no support from the brigade artillery and it is possible that the delay in his own attack was deliberate. At all events, though his was the first of the forces to reach position, near Grassy Knoll, it was the last to attack—a sudden rush, made on the afternoon of the 14th after Kawaguchi had already determined on retreat. It was jungle but daylight; the Marine artillery pounded Oka into the ground and by night he was already pulling out. His casualties were few.

The other events were naval. There had been Jap submarines operating south of Guadal and one of them had slipped a torpedo into *Saratoga*'s ribs on 31 August, not sinking the big carrier, but sending her to dock. *Wasp* and *Hornet* had accordingly been ordered to conduct the cover of Turner's transports, bearing the 7th Regiment, from a region east of the Santa Cruz Island screen. They had failed to reach this position because of the need for carrying fighters to Guadal; but turned toward it and were sweeping eastward on the morning of the 15th when a recon report said Jap ships were out of Truk again and bearing down. This seemed more than likely in view of the enemy's operations on the island. *Wasp* and *Hornet* swung northward; and this brought them into the region south and a little east of Guadal.

As it happened this was exactly where the Japs wanted them. To their 7th Submarine Division the 8th had been added, making twelve submarines altogether. These were instructed to change their field of operations from the lagoon to the waters south of Guadalcanal as it appeared from the Battle of the Eastern Solomons that our carriers would come into this region. The movement from Truk was a feint intended to draw our forces on—a feint which would not have succeeded but for the fact that *Wasp* and *Hornet* had already run far from their intended course on the fighter transportation job.

Carriers and submarines approached each other then; and on the afternoon of the 15th the latter began to fire torpedoes. One of them hit *North Carolina;* she steamed out of the area at 27 knots but still had to go in for repairs. One of them hit the destroyer *O'Brien;* she reached port but after making emergency repairs and putting out to get more permanent ones, she simply dissolved and went down, her structure completely racked. One would have hit *Hornet* but for the amazing presence of mind of a young flier who saw the deadly thing approaching his carrier and dropped a depth charge on it. Three of the torpedoes hit *Wasp*; she burned and sank through a red twilight.

Under that same red twilight, far to the north in Tokyo, a crowd of 30,000 were pouring happily homeward through a litter of torn papers from a patriotic mass meeting at Hinomiya Stadium. They had heard spokesmen for the Imperial Army and Navy announce that Guadalcanal airfield had been captured and "the stranded 10,000 Marines, victims of Roosevelt's gesture, have been practically wiped out. Nothing is important but this."

On the last point the spokesmen were correct.

Chapter 5

The Attack of the Sendai: Preparation

T HE LOSS OF THE WASP HAD THE EFFECT THAT TURNER'S big convoy did not reach the island till 18 September, after jigging around for some time along the route while the submarine menace was cleared as well as it could be. The destroyers got two of them (it later appeared; they were not certain at the time) and the rest had to return to Rabaul for fuel and torpedoes, so the convoy went in. On the basis that the essential object of the campaign was Guadalcanal and the troops to hold Guadalcanal the Jap drive had been a failure, but it is perhaps just as well not to think too hard about that.

At all events there was the new regiment and in the period of relative lull that followed General Vandegrift and his staff reexamined the whole theory of the defense, for defense it still must be while Japanese control of the sea was unbroken and their willingness to put in forces unabated. Their movements and consequently their plan had been somewhat limited by the completion of a fighter strip beside the main field and by an increasing flow of planes, which by the end of the month gave our fliers 73 F-4Fs, 37 SBDs and a dozen TBFs, all organized under Brigadier General Roy S. Geiger, "a man who never knew what fear was like," with a heavy jaw, who had been one of the real pioneers of Marine aviation. These planes now began to swarm all over the central Solomons and their operations had quite evidently knocked all idea of using slow regular transports out of the enemy's head. Even the destroyers he did employ for ferrying in troops had to make fast runs so they would not be caught by daylight in the area where our planes were really effective—roughly about Kolombangara.

That meant he must make small-scale night landings followed by overland operations; and this in turn meant that the threat of a counterlanding along the Lunga shore was removed as a practical possibility. On the other hand, though there were now enough troops to set up some kind of a defense in depth along the flanks and back slopes where the next attack could be expected, the idea of a defense in depth was becoming dubious. The defense of Edson's Ridge had unavoidably possessed something of this character, and the Japs had infiltrated it so thoroughly in that rough country that the whole business was touch and go. The obvious solution was a really continuous defense line, all round the perimeter with a reserve inside to strike at anything that came through.

Now this is known in military textbooks as a "cordon"; and since Napoleon Bonaparte the generals of every nation have demonstrated how bad a system it is. The defect is that the enemy concentrates all his guns against a spot of the cordon, wipes out the defense there and rushes a big column of attack through to the center with a hurrah. But Japanese artillery practice had been distinctly bad up to this time; and considering the difficulty of moving cannon around in the jungle and the fact that their reconnaissance was poor it did not seem likely that their work with the guns would improve. Moreover, General Del Valle's Marine artillery had demonstrated at the battle of the ridge that it would have something very serious to say about the jungle trails. General Vandegrift boldly threw away the book and established a cordon defense.

In this arrangement the 5th Marines held the sector from the Kukum shore along the ridges to the winding Lunga; the 7th picked up there and carried the line past Edson's Ridge to the upper Tenaru where the 1st took over. All the special formations—Pioneers, Engineers, Amphitrac men, Raiders—were concentrated down by the shore around Lunga Point and formed the divisional reserve. The perimeter was wired in (there was wire since the big convoy arrived); foxholes were dug and splinterproof emplacements made for automatic weapons. This was a lot of work but there were now men to do it; the Seabees had arrived, dribbling in a couple of hundred at a time aboard the APDs.

69

There were 1,100 of them, the 6th Seabee Battalion, a "cub"[1] under Commander Joseph P. Blundon, the first unit of its kind to reach the wars. When they took over, the Marine Engineers, who had been thinking pretty well of themselves, were amazed to see how these men beyond military age made the Marston strip fly on the airfield. They turned over all their exiguous construction material to the Seabees and relaxed into straight military engineering; and the Seabees did everything. They drained the field, they built revetments; they put in concrete around the CP and built roads. The old Jap bridge across the Lunga had been in the habit of going out with every rain; the Seabees built a dandy new one, on piles made of coconut trees, with steel girders in it, that would carry a medium tank. They built a bake oven out of an old Jap safe and the Marines had fresh hot bread. They even found a Jap torpedo that had run up on the beach and took it apart. It was our Navy's first acquaintance, except on the receiving end, with that one piece of ordnance in which the enemy far surpassed us, and the big moments of the American submarine service date from the time when that torpedo went back to the States and our people learned to make them as good. There were also certain researches in the fermentability of various materials (dried jungle rations with sugar and yeast turned out very well), and the manufacture of portable stills—but these were unofficial.

II

The arrival of the 7th Regiment also made it possible to send out patrols of battalion strength to the west, in which direction considerable numbers of Japs seemed to be drifting through the jungle, probably the wreckage from the recent battle. One of these patrols got into serious trouble.

A battalion of the 7th under Lieutenant Colonel L. B. Puller began the movement on 23 September, sliding along the northern face of the ridge Mambula across the Matanikau to investigate the

[1] A cub is a unit peculiar to the Seabees. It contains all the units of construction and maintenance men necessary to some particular activity—in this case an airfield. It is composed of "acorns," which are smaller units each skilled and organized to undertake some phase of the activity. The 6th Battalion thus contained an acorn of specialists in road construction and repair, an acorn of drainage men, and one of experts in housing construction, plus various others.

country between it and Kokumbona. There was no effort to make speed—patrols like this occasionally came across Japanese caches of food or ammunition and it was a good idea to search the country for stragglers—so it was evening 24 September before the northwest flank of Mambula was reached. There were Japs, a lot of them, cooking dinner around fires. Puller had handled his security well, achieved surprise, and in a sharp little action drove the enemy from whatever positions they held. Night prevented him from pushing farther; he had 7 dead and 25 wounded and within his night lines more than this total of Japanese bodies, which gives some idea of the intensity of the fight.

During the night he was reinforced from the 5th Regiment (he had to send some of his men back with the wounded) and next morning he began to move again, reaching the upper Matanikau on the 26th early. He had been supposed to cross this stream but his original instructions also said that he was to return to the perimeter by evening of that date, so he did not cross but continued toward the coast down the east bank of the stream. Near the coastal track his advance parties began to get mortar fire from across the river. It seemed apparent that the force he had defeated the night before and the one now near Matanikau Village were not disorganized remnants of the Kawaguchis, but part of a new landing.

At about the same time he was joined by the Raider battalion, now under Lieutenant Colonel S. B. Griffith. (Edson had been moved up to command the 5th Regiment.) Puller and Griffith held a conference. They believed they could stage a repeat on General Vandegrift's encirclement of 19 August at Matanikau. Over the wires they succeeded in talking Lieutenant Colonel Twining (now divisional G-3) into the idea. Artillery and planes would furnish support next morning for a dawn attack. The Raiders were to move upstream, cross and come down on Matanikau from the rear, a battalion of the 5th to work across the sandbar at the mouth. Colonel Edson took general command.

Griffith with the Raiders started first as he had farthest to go, but half a mile upstream, still on the east bank, he encountered a force of Japs, apparently the reflux of the groups Puller had hit, coming back in a counterenvelopment. The Raiders deployed but instantly found themselves taking heavy mortar and machine-gun fire from

71

the front and both flanks. In that first blaze Griffith was badly
wounded and Major Bailey, his Medal of Honor exec, was killed.
When the company commanders tried to work out flankward they
got more fire, were pinned down with the casualties piling up. By
noon they were not moving an inch but in the confusion, under
heavy fire, a request about their position from Edson was answered
in a way that gave a clear impression they were over the stream,
though they gave no map co-ordinates because they had no map.

Edson, a driver, energetic and aggressive to the last degree, in-
terpreted the phrase to mean the Raiders were in position to make
their flank attack on Matanikau. The resistance Griffith's men
seemed to be meeting and the heavy fire still coming from across the
stream at his own position indicated that more pressure was needed.
He asked and got permission to send Puller's battalion of the 7th
down the shore by boat to renew the attack from the rear. It happened there was a destroyer (*Ballard*) in the lagoon that day; her
skipper delightedly offered to furnish support fire for the seaborne
landing. (Marines know almost by instinct what Army men seldom
realize—the power of ships' artillery, which makes even a destroyer
roughly equivalent to a battalion of medium guns.) The battalion
of the 5th was now to cross the sandbar.

It never did. Our guns could not reach the positions that covered
the bar and these positions stopped Edson's push. The Raiders still
were unable to move. Puller's battalion, under command of Major
Otho B. Rogers (the Colonel had remained with Edson) got ashore
all right, but when it reached a low bare ridge behind Point Cruz,
was pinned down by the same intensive fire that had stopped Griffith,
and Rogers himself was killed. He had confided his plans to no one,
so this battalion was without direction; and now, the Japs having
stopped the other moves, they turned to on it in style, working parties
through to cut it off from the beach and hitting it from all directions. The movement was seen from *Ballard*; it was clear the battalion would have to be pulled out at once and division headquarters
was notified. But fortune arranged it that just at this moment the
heaviest air raid that Guadalcanal had yet seen came pounding
down, 28 heavy bombers. A couple of them got through and one
laid an egg on headquarters, probably the most damaging single

bomb hit of the campaign, for it blew up the division switchboard and destroyed all communications.

Messengers had to carry orders for the Raiders to withdraw. The boats went out to pick up the lost battalion and *Ballard* moved inshore to shell the Japs along the beach while the Marines began to fight their way out. Up in the sky a squadron from *Enterprise,* which had landed on the field that day, leaped joyously into combat with the bombers. The planes did well; 35 Japs tumbled down that afternoon and the next when they tried their bombing stunt again. The destroyer did well. Caught between her fire and that of the Marines cutting their way through, the Japs along the beach gave way and Rogers's command escaped. But they had 43 casualties to pile on those suffered by the Raiders and the 5th and there was no question but the operation was a complete failure, another demonstration that successful war cannot be made on wrong information.

III

The failure had, however, the effect of drawing attention to the Matanikau area and General Vandegrift did a little hard thinking about the significance of the action and the fact that patrols in the Grassy Knoll region had to be made larger and larger and almost always had some action. It was clear that the Japs were getting heavier forces into the island for a new drive on the airfield and the very fact they were being deliberate about their move indicated that when the new attack came it would be well above those previous in both skill and intensity.

The General had been assured of more reinforcements in the form of Army troops and he knew that a naval reinforcement was also on the way, both PT boats, which could do something about the Japanese convoys at night, and heavy ships, to fight for control of the surface waters, but the over-all shipping situation in the Pacific was still extremely tight with all existing bottoms and new constructon being siphoned off for the operations in Africa. It was likely to be deep in October before the Army troops could reach the island and at least the same time before the Navy could cut off the flow of enemy units—if indeed they could. Well before that the Japanese effort could be expected.

Why were they so interested in the Matanikau? Our planes had seen enough of the stuff getting ashore to know that there was heavy equipment in it—tanks and big guns. Scouting and improved maps had rendered the geography of Guadal's north coast a known factor and it was apparent that there was only one route by which such heavy equipment could be moved from the western end of the island east toward the airfield—the route that crossed the sandbar at the Matanikau mouth. If they got across there nothing could stop them till the hill overlooking Kukum and the perimeter of the defense was reached. From a point outside that perimeter to the precious airfield was approximately 5,000 yards, which is good accuracy range for light artillery.

This is what they were up to, then; they were going to gain a position from which they could keep the airfield under fire and forbid it to our planes, then goodbye Guadalcanal. Even though he lacked men to bring the Matanikau crossing into the perimeter it would be necessary for the General to establish a battle position there. The southern flank was now well fortified and wired in and men no longer needed for labor details. A forward movement was accordingly ordered for 7 October. This was the plan:

Edson with the 5th Marines to reach and hold the right bank of the Matanikau. A special group had been made up of part of the 2nd Marine Regiment with a scout-sniper detachment of picked men under Lieutenant Colonel W. J. Whaling, who had been a not very effective exec of the 5th, but who had proved a hell of a good bushwhacking fighting man. This group to follow the 5th in, then circle Matanikau Village from the upper reaches of the river, crossing by a little bridge, the Nippon Bridge. Two battalions of the 7th (Colonel Amor Sims) to follow Whaling, extend his left flank and also attack toward the sea. If all went well, the 5th would pass through the other formations when they reached Matanikau Village, attack straight ahead, take Kokumbona and leave a small permanent garrison there to control the heads of the trails that lead into the back ridges. The Matanikau crossing to be held in force. Artillery and air co-operation were worked out with care.

IV

Lieutenant General Hyakutate was bitterly disappointed over the failure of General Kawaguchi's attack. He did not express it that way of course, remarking in his report that, although the attack had been successful, further efforts would be needed to mop up the American remnants remaining on Guadalcanal. The fact that there were remnants was primarily the fault of the Imperial Navy, which had given him inadequate air support and had been so slow in moving troops in that they arrived in insufficient force. He complained to Tokyo; and since the naval authorities, true to the principles laid down to them by the sacred Meiji, refused to mingle in politics even in defense of their own ideas, they received orders to second the Army more thoroughly. The Southeast Area Fleet was augmented by four battleships and a number of lighter units; three of the light cruisers were assigned to bring troops of the Sendai Division from Java to Rabaul and additional supplies of the naval aircraft were directed to the latter point to make good the losses suffered. The field at Buka had been worked on extensively and could now be used by any type of plane.

The 1st and 2nd Fleets were brought down to Truk to make another sweep toward Guadal and cover a major reinforcing move, this time to be made in transports. Meanwhile the Sendai were forwarded by means of destroyers operating at night, as fast as they arrived at Rabaul. The system was thoroughly satisfactory except for the continual annoyance of American planes, which attacked the men just after they landed. Complaints that the antiaircraft guns were ineffective were forwarded to headquarters with requests that more such guns accompany future units.

On 4 October Lieutenant General Masai Maruyama of the Sendai reached the island with his headquarters, assumed command, and went forward to make a personal inspection of the line. The initial regiment (4th Infantry) had now arrived with a number of artillery formations. The 16th and 29th were at Rabaul with the heavy guns, tanks, and a Naval Landing Force brigade, giving the General some 20,000 men all told, to whom could be added some 1,900 still remaining of the Kawaguchis, mostly Colonel Oka's command.

General Maruyama did not find conditions too satisfactory, either morally or tactically. The remaining Kawaguchis were nearly all infected with malaria and those who came through the jungles from south of the airfield were frightfully emaciated and very weak, but all had been forced to stay in their lines sick or not, because of the shortage of troops. To be sure, Colonel Oka's men with a good deal of help from the first comers of the Sendai had beaten off an American attack on 27 September, but these weak and hungry men had lost much of the true Bushido and told disgusting tales of horror to the newcomers. The Americans on this island (they said) were not the ordinary Army troops but Marines, a special force recruited from jails and insane asylums for their blood lust. Instead of according honorable death to the prisoners they cut off their arms, then staked them on the airfield and ran over them with steam rollers. A letter written home by one of his men was shown to the General:

"The news I hear worries me. It seems as if we have suffered considerable damage and casualties. They might be exaggerated, but it is pitiful. Far away from our home country a fearful battle is raging. What these soldiers say is something of the supernatural and cannot be believed as human stories."

On the tactical side it was perfectly clear to the General that Colonel Oka had been culpably careless in not keeping his lines close up to the American perimeter and insuring the passage at the mouth of the Matanikau for the guns and tanks with which to knock out the airfield. The Colonel complained that his men were worn with illness, and he had so much influence in high quarters at home that relieving him would only make trouble, so General Maruyama did the next best thing—pulled Oka's men out of the Matanikau position entirely and sent forward Colonel Nakaguna's fresh 4th Regiment. One battalion of the regiment was to cross by the sandbar, occupy the east bank of the mouth of the river and dig in; another to gain and hold the Nippon Bridge crossing farther inland, while the third battalion remained in reserve. This was to be done at once, as soon as the troops could be pressed forward, and they should all be in position by the night of 6 October. To brace morale a general order was issued:

"From now on, the occupying of Guadalcanal Island is under the observation of the whole world. Do not expect to return, not even one man, if the occupation is not successful. Everyone must remember the honor of the Emperor, fear no enemy, yield to no material matters, show the strong points as of steel or of rocks, and advance

76

valiantly and ferociously. Hit the enemy opponents so hard they will not be able to get up again."

The move was indeed begun but some American planes interrupted it, the regiment had to take cover and night found it still short of the objective. Colonel Nakaguna had his men dig in on the west bank as a precaution against night attacks. Two or three companies under cover of falling dark did manage to get across the sandbar and prepared to move farther out next morning.

V

At 0700 Edson's regiment started along the "government trail" that skirts the coast. It was a little after ten and still some 300 yards short of the Matanikau when the leading battalion began to get machine-gun fire, spread and developed the position. It might be held by a Japanese group of above a company strength. Another battalion worked leftward and by noon had reached the river higher up, while some half-tracks were brought up to fire into the enemy position and the advance resumed in the manner of advances against fire—slowly and with continual shooting. The Japs seemed quite willing to shoot back and night came down while the 5th was still well short of the river mouth.

Whaling's men and the 7th had encountered a small amount of sniper fire and some patrol activity. They halted for the night east of the stream and just short of Nippon Bridge. During the night Edson's men brought up some amphitracs which wallowed around like water buffaloes in the midstream region to give the enemy the impression a crossing was intended there. A company of Raiders was sent up from division reserve to reinforce the attack on the small Jap bridgehead. Whaling and the 7th were still to proceed as planned. Unfortunately toward dawn it began to rain with a violence seldom seen even among the Solomons. All the trails foundered and, though Whaling did indeed get across the Nippon Bridge, the continuing drench reduced his pace to an inch an hour.

Neither, under that downpour, could the Japs on the east bank all be eliminated, so they were penned against the stream and the Raider company on the extreme right reached the edge of the sandbar, where wire was hastily strung. It was decided to postpone the enveloping attack to the next day and everyone had begun to cuddle down for the night when about 1800 of the Japs on the east bank gave a unanimous whoop and broke for the sandbar, throwing smoke bombs in all directions.

There was a brief savage flash of hand-to-hand fighting in which a squad of Raiders was practically wiped out but the Japs who got away left 67 of their number behind. That night General Vandegrift got a message from SOPAC headquarters that air and submarine reconnaissance as well as code intercepts indicated a Jap movement of major proportions was imminent. His need, then, was to build up a general reserve. He changed plans, ordered the Whaling-Sims force to make its attack as before on Matanikau Village, but that would now be the end of their operation. When they reached the shore they would withdraw, the 5th Regiment covering, and two battalions would be left in the new forward battle position, horseshoe shaped, from Nippon Bridge to the river mouth.

The 9th broke clear; Whaling and Sims went forward and by 1000 had reached the shore on both sides of Point Cruz. A big ridge comes down to break just west of this spot. Lieutenant Colonel Puller, who had the battalion farthest west, discovered the wooded ravine under this ridge to be swarming with Japs, apparently concentrating for a counterattack. He brought up every mortar in the battalion to give the place a heavy pasting, at the same time calling for artillery fire and air bombing, and this so much discouraged the enemy that they gave up the idea of counterattack. Our forces pulled out without trouble, though not without casualties, 65 killed and 125 wounded for the whole movement. This could be compared with 253 Japanese bodies found plus whatever wounded they had—not a large score for a two-regiment operation. General Vandegrift was disposed to be dissatisfied; he might have been less so had he been able to see General Maruyama's orders or the dolorous report that gentleman was forced to make on having lost the Matanikau position—or the report of Colonel Nakaguna that one of his battalions had been nearly wiped out with 600 dead.

VI

The shellings to which the American airfield had been subjected from the sea had evidently failed of their object since the planes continued to operate. In view of Army pressure to carry this matter further as well as to get troops into Guadalcanal more quickly, Captain Ohmae, the staff planner at Rabaul who had set up the Savo Island victory, planned a combined operation. A big seaplane tender and two destroyers would run into Guadalcanal by a route south of the Russells on the night of 11 October, the tender carrying tanks and heavy guns, the destroyers troops. The 6th Cruiser Division meanwhile would run straight down the Slot and subject the airfield to prolonged and deliberate shelling which would destroy the planes in their revetments, accompanied by a single fast transport. The following morning would make it clear whether this result had been achieved. If not, the cruisers (*Aoba, Furutaka, Kinugasa*) would return the following night and finish the job; and on the night following that the remaining troops of the Sendai Division would set out in transports, which could be used since by that time there would be no American planes to bother them except a few B-17s that nobody minded. Rear Admiral Goto was in command of the ships.

No one knows whether this plan would have worked or not because it crossed a counterplan from the American side. Halsey, the raider of the Marshalls, had arrived at Nouméa to relieve Ghormley, who might be a good planner but certainly was not the kind of leader needed for the desperate dogfight into which Guadalcanal had evolved. The new chief brought naval reinforcements—not many, only a handful of cruisers, and there were still not enough destroyers —but what was far more important, he brought his own dashing, chance-taking leadership and all along the line of the naval service men began to pick up their heads and to think they might yet win this war.

It is necessary to remember that as of October 10, 1942, there seemed a very good chance that we would lose it. Coral Sea and Midway, yes; our naval air fought those and it covered itself with glory. The submarines were doing well. But the rest of the Navy, in fact the Navy as a whole, had not looked good. *Oklahoma* and *Arizona* had left the fleet forever at Pearl Harbor; *Lexington, Yorktown,* and now *Wasp* were gone, *Saratoga* and *North Carolina* were in for repairs. In the Java Sea we had lost a heavy cruiser and a whole division of destroyers; at Savo three cruisers more, and our destroyer loss now stood at fifteen ships. What had the Japs paid for this? The carriers of Midway, another one at Coral Sea, two cruisers downed by submarines and a few destroyers—not a Jap ship was sunk by the surface Navy. They were ahead.

Halsey's first act was to give them a chance to get still further ahead. On the very night that Admiral Goto came down to blow out the airfield four long gray cruisers slid through the twilight past Lunga Point and went to take up sentry-go between Savo Island and Cape Esperance, where the others had gone down. *San Francisco, Salt Lake City,* heavies; *Helena, Boise,* lights; with destroyers *Farenholt, Benham, Laffey, Duncan, McCalla* under Rear Admiral Norman Scott.[1] They steamed in line to and fro past the cape and *Salt Lake* catapulted a plane with flares but something went wrong and the plane blew up in a blaze of light just after 2300. Among our ships, officers cursed and stamped the deck thinking this meant the Japs had surely seen them.

They had; but Goto thought it was a flare from his own transport group south of the Russells, fired for reasons unknown, and pressed straight on in a column with two destroyers flanking ahead and two more at the tail. They showed as radar pips just as our ships completed a turn. Admiral Scott realized he was in a dream position of already crossing the enemy's T and ordered "Commence firing." Out blazed the guns in level sheets of lightning; back on Guadal the Marines roused from sleep wondered with an apprehension born from memories of Savo what was happening as thunder rolled across the black water and the whole sky was lit with the glare of a burning ship.

The flares and fighting died. Colonel Thomas ran with the dispatch into Vandegrift's tent where the General waited anxiously beside a single blue bulb; and the news was good, the bill for Savo had been met. We had lost the destroyer *Duncan* and two of *Boise's* turrets were burned out; but *Furutaka* was gone, broken in two and sunk by ten rapid salvos from *Salt Lake; Aoba* was staggering homeward, horribly mauled by over forty hits, and, with half her crew dead, would not see action again for many a month more; two of

[1] To compare with Savo Island, the Japs could now bring to bear 18 8-inch against 19 in our fleet, which would not have been a bad match, but we had the 30 6-inch guns of the light cruisers which upset the balance.

the big Jap destroyers (*Natsugumo* and *Fubuki*) were at the bottom of the lagoon and so was their fast transport.

Next morning all the planes from Henderson Field boiled out, the fighters covering *McCalla* while she rescued the *Duncan* survivors, dive bombers after the retreating Japs. The planes caught them near the northern end of Sta. Isabel trying to get *Aoba* in, and it cost them another big destroyer, *Murakumo,* to save her. While this was going on a little squadron of four PTs nosed into the lagoon and cast lines ashore. "I remember," said their commander, "one haggard, red- eyed youngster of a Marine with a Jap knife stuck in his belt, who said, 'Just teach the bastards to stay home in bed nights where they belong. Just do that and we'll remember you in our prayers.' "

The basis of Captain Ohmae's plan had changed but with that "tenacity" so much valued among his nation and so difficult for an Occidental to understand, he proceeded as though it had not. Indeed, there was something left of it; the seaplane tender had landed her heavy guns while the naval battle was going on and on the 13th they registered on the airfield from long range, cutting up the main strip so much that the fighter strip had to be used instead. That same night seven transports started down from Rabaul as planned; a division of the Southeast Area Fleet with two battleships in it saw them in, running through the lagoon and treating the airfield to the intensive shelling the 6th Cruiser Division had been supposed to give. It was extremely effective; of thirty-nine dive bombers in revetments when the sun went down only four were fit to fly the following morning.

But the essential feature of the plan had been to get rid of *all* the Guadalcanal planes through a two-night bombardment and they had not all been eliminated. Helped by the fighters they turned out on the 14th and there was a savage air fight all along the Slot in which one of the Jap transports was sunk and another hit so badly she had to turn back. The rest pushed on; they set their human loads ashore on the night of the 14th but before the supplies could reach the beach the dive bombers pounced on them again next morning and burned out three more, while still another was sunk by the Petes.

Sum up: General Maruyama had his division ashore, present and nearly complete for action, lacking only the men lost at the Matani-

81

kau. The airfield had not been put out of business; and it was the General's hard luck that the lost transports had carried most of the heavy artillery ammunition, nearly all the medical stores for his men, and a good deal of their food. The soldiers felt it on a diet of rice relieved only by taro and odd items like island lizards, and they wrote their worries in their diaries:

"The lack of sympathy by the headquarters is too extreme. Do they know we are left on the island? Where is the mighty power of the Imperial Navy?"

There were a good many sick, beriberi and malaria, but none could be spared for hospitalization. They had to march with the rest till they actually fell down.

Chapter 6

The Attack of the Sendai: Realization

THERE HAD BEEN A BIG CONFERENCE AT TRUK, FOR WHICH several members of the Imperial Staff came down. Under the nagging of the Army officers the Imperial Navy agreed to throw the full power of its carrier forces into a combined operation for Guadalcanal. The over-all plan was that the forces ashore should capture, or at least shell out of operation, the American airfield. The Navy would come down at the same time, sweep all American ships from the area, furnish some of the air support for the operation, and land carrier planes on the field as soon as it fell into Japanese hands. Six of the eight medium bomber groups available in the whole Empire were staged into Rabaul, both the 24th and 26th Air Flotillas being added, a good many of the planes pushing forward to base on Buka Field.

The fleets involved were the 2nd and 3rd, made up as Hyakutate's army had been, of units drawn from other commands. The Southeast Area Fleet furnished its four battleships—*Kongo, Haruna, Hiyei, Kirishima*—of which the first two fell under Admiral Kondo's 2nd Fleet command; he also had the new carriers *Hitaka* and *Hayataka,* with no less than six heavy cruisers[1] and the usual complement of destroyers. Admiral Nagumo, who had led the Pearl Harbor attack, was in charge of the 3rd Fleet, with three carriers— *Shokaku, Zuikaku, Zuiho*—and four heavy cruisers[2] plus light units. It would operate independently, and together the forces should give Japan crushing superiority, since the best of the carrier pilots were drawn, even from instruction groups, for this major effort.

[1] *Atago, Takao, Chokai, Maya, Myoko, Haguro.*
[2] *Suzuya, Kumano, Tone, Chikuma.*

83

Ashore General Maruyama's observation posts on Grassy Knoll were a good deal harried by American patrols but there were plenty of posts and his intelligence officer, Lieutenant Colonel Matsumoto, had been particularly diligent in getting information. Unfortunately they had had only one prisoner, wounded, who had been beheaded when it became clear he could contribute no information, but the submarines and air contributed something. There was even an American operation map found on a dead Marine. It was reproduced and distributed to all units along with a special study of Marine tactics which went a good deal beyond the Imperial manual. Matsumoto considered there was very little he did not know about the American positions and strength, and when General Hyakutate came down about the middle of October to lead the big push in person, that exalted personage agreed.

Hyakutate's plan was for a double penetration which would take advantage of the fact that the Americans had fallen into the error of setting up a defense in depth all round their position and omitting to have reserves. He would concentrate against points on this defense line and gain heavy local superiority. The 4th Regiment and Oka's command were to seize the crossing of the Matanikau. They would have the support of all the heavy artillery, most of the light, and a company of eleven medium tanks, for which a passage to the sandbar was cut through the jungle with only a narrow screen of trees at the outlet so their attack could be launched as a surprise. Oka's own force would seize the crossing of the Nippon Bridge while the 4th, led by the tanks, went right through the sandbar position.

As soon as this forward American outpost was captured tanks and artillery would file across the bar, knock out the airfield, and lay down a heavy fire along that part of the American lines which faced south along both sides of the Lunga, just west of the ridge where General Kawaguchi had experienced an unfortunate incident. The bulk of the Sendai (16th and 29th Regiments) with other formations bringing it up to a little better than the strength of a full division (part of the 230th Regiment, which really belonged to the 38th Division, some dismounted cavalry, and a battery of mountain guns) would attack this point from the south, reaching its take-off position by marches through the difficult but not impossible ridges of the Lunga mountains. The attack on the Matanikau was for 21 October,

84

a day ahead of the main effort along the Lunga. The task of the latter was undoubtedly made easier by the Americans using up whatever reserves they had in supporting the position at the shore. Maruyama in person was to lead the jungle attack.

Matsumoto had underestimated the American forces by a good deal, but he could hardly know that. What he might have known, however, was that the captured American map on which his whole plan was based had once upon a time been a captured Japanese map, showing their own positions before the Marines landed, which had been reproduced for our people as a matter of instruction with American lettering. Probably the only persons who could have made the identification for Matsumoto were among the departed souls.

There was also difficulty about getting into position for the main attack. Maruyama had planned the route on a map and had sent ahead an Engineer regiment with a stout working detail from the infantry to cut trails through the jungle. The engineer in charge, Captain Oda, reached the southern slope of Grassy Knoll readily enough, but here he ran into a maze of cliffs and incoherent ravines that brought his progress down to a couple of miles a day and carried him much farther to the south, up the stream, than had been originally intended.

It would have been a violation of the most elementary rules of military politeness to report to the exalted presence that he had failed to complete his task on schedule and he made no such report; which brought it about that Maruyama began his march on 17 October with his men carrying five days' rations as planned. By the evening of the 20th the head of column had touched the river, but they were still some distance from the American lines and all the men were dead tired from the terrible labor of carrying equipment along the trails and up cliffs where the guns had to be dragged by ropes. Maruyama had been forced to put them on one-third rations and it was clear the attack could not be made on schedule. The General passed the word by radio asking that the fleet delay its big sweep till the 26th. He also had all ranking officers informed that when the American General sent his offer to surrender it should be accepted at once, with only the condition that General Vandegrift must come to the sandbar of the Matanikau to arrange the details, alone except for an interpreter.

85

There was a crisis in aviation gasoline, so serious that ground crews were draining the tanks of planes wrecked on the field. Turner was doing his best to get more in, sorely hampered by lack of transporting vessels. He had received but one additional transport since the opening of the campaign, which fell a long way short of compensation for the loss of *Elliott* and the three APDs. Another APD, *McFarland,* pulled in on 16 October with a lot of gas in drums, but while it was being unloaded and some of the wounded being placed aboard for evacuation, down came a Jap air raid which sank one of the unloading barges and hit *McFarland* so badly that she seemed likely to sink too. The Seabees saved her; but now she was out of the picture and it was necessary to bring in gas by transport planes, which could carry only about six drums apiece, and by sending up more in a big seagoing barge under escort of the destroyer *Meredith*.

The barge was due in on the 16th, the same day *McFarland* got hit, but it did not show up. Two days later a handful of exhausted survivors arrived at the island with the news that Jap planes had found the little convoy on the 15th, sunk the destroyer and beat up the tug so badly that it could no longer tow. The barge was brought in eventually but this was clearly not a method that could be used again, and afterward it was necessary for quite a while to bring in gas on the decks of combat destroyers, a procedure that did not recommend itself to their skippers.

The airstrip also was given no little trouble by the attentions of a 6-inch gun emplaced somewhere near Kokumbona, which dropped in a few shells every day, cutting up the strip and forcing the abandonment of the Jap "pagoda" that had been used as a control tower, sometimes knocking out a plane. There was nothing that could be done about the animal, whom the Marines named "Pistol Pete"; time after time the bombers failed to find its position, which was so deep in it could not be reached by the 105s that were the heaviest guns on our side.

On the other hand, the air war itself was going well. A couple of Jap bombing raids were staged on the 17th and 18th for no apparent reason. (We know now, of course, that it was to cover the beginning of General Maruyama's movement along the trails, but no one on our side had any idea of this at the time.) Twenty fresh fighters which had arrived at the field the day before got into the enemy formations and cut them all to pieces, with the loss of 13 Zeros and 22 bombers, for which we paid with only three planes.

General Vandegrift also had reason to feel a little better satisfied with the development of the situation ashore after the Edson-Sims-Whaling action at the Matanikau. Whaling's scout-sniper detachment was an unqualified success, the picked men in it being returned to their normal units after a time and replaced by others. They not only improved the general quality of patrol work by a hundred per cent; the returned scout-snipers lifted the morale of the whole force with their tales of adventure in "the boondocks" on short rations and long marches. Men began to volunteer for the duty and the G-1 worry that the Marines would sink into the lassitude which everywhere enveloped garrison troops was disappearing.

One of these patrols captured a map with Jap lettering which showed, or seemed to show (it was hard to tell through the the abbreviated style of the language), that a three-division attack was imminent, one division each moving against the perimeter from east, west, and south. The patrols failed to confirm; there were so few Japs out to the east that the natives had come out of the hills back to their gardens, and to the south among the mountain slopes nothing had been found but a few drifting knots of half-starved vagabonds. There might be three divisions to the west, of course; the nightly runs of the Tokyo Express and pressure along the Matanikau made it seem that heavy forces were massing there. But the avenues of approach on that side were narrow and such an advance could be contained. Moreover, as the Jap bombing raids and intelligence from SOPAC indicated the big enemy push was near, it became possible for the General to compress his whole division toward the westward flank. The first Army troops had come.

They were the 164th Infantry, an "orphan" regiment squeezed out of the 41st Division when that formation had been changed from the old National Guard square to a triangle—under Colonel B. E. Moore—largely Scandinavian farmers from the Dakotas, big burly men, a little slow on the uptake. The regiment, being an orphan, had not undergone the intensive weeding process to which National Guard formations that remained in the divisions had been

87

subjected; a lot of the officers were of the old type, that is, over-age for their rank, lacking field experience, willing to do their duty but not realizing that wars are won by people who do more. They came in on 13 October—"the night of the bombardment," it used to be called as though there never was another—and had been assigned to a bivouac area on the Tenaru flank, where some of the shells fell among them with resultant casualties. This struck them as unfair and the effect on those Swedes was the phenomenon described as a "slow burn" which reached its maximum state of fury about two weeks after they got ashore.

III

This was perhaps just as well for our side. An annoyed Swede is a very good fighting man indeed and this lot reached their peak irritation just as the occasion arrived for some hard fighting. Maruyama's big push started on 21 October.

It began, as planned, with Oka's attack. His artillery fired a preparation shoot, his tanks steamed out for the Matanikau sandbar and the infantry went forward, only to turn back almost immediately when a crushing American artillery concentration came down to knock out the lead tank. The 4th Regiment could not even reach the bar, much less cross it. The whole thing was over so quickly that American Intelligence thought the whole thing had been intended as a patrol in force; Oka's own command never even got to the Nippon Bridge for their flank swing.

General Hyakutate went up to the front to find the men there growling they were caught at the river like rats in a bag and that it was impossible to make any movement in secret because of the constant presence of American planes. There was also difficulty about the heavy guns, already in trouble for lack of ammunition. The Americans had somehow acquired some long-range artillery of their own and their counterbattery work was so effective that two of the Japanese pieces were knocked out by direct hits, while the positions of the rest had to be changed several times.

General Hyakutate was himself so exalted an alp in the Japanese military hierarchy that he did not have to worry too much about Oka's influence at home. He sternly ordered that the attack should be renewed on the 23rd (it was, in a way, fortunate that Maruyama's movement had been delayed, for now the two drives would be better co-ordinated), conceding only that the entire force of the Army artillery should spend its slender store of ammunition without stint in beating down the American position. Oka himself was to lead the flanking movement along Grassy Knoll, and the General insisted that he get across the stream above Nippon Bridge at once, that night, and whether his men were able to march or not, in spite of his protests about their physical condition. One of the company commanders wrote in his diary: "I myself would be inclined to leave behind many of those who are not really fit. Can it be that I am not sufficiently ruthless? It is a matter regarding which self-examination is necessary."

The hour was set for 1800. That day there had been a heavy air raid by planes Hyakutate called down from Rabaul for a softening-up process and General Geiger's fliers met them with a new tactic of concentrating on the Jap fighters. It was a good trick; 20 of the 25 Zeros came down and the bombers jettisoned when they saw their protectors fall, so that although the beach was dug up not a bomb came near the airfield. As evening fell, the Marines began to take their ease; a red flare went up in the enemy lines and down came a terrific bombardment—mortars, heavy and light artillery, even machine guns from positions secretly hollowed out no more than 40 yards from our front lines.

Amid the shellbursts, with the reply from Del Valle's guns whistling over their heads, the Marines could make out the dark forms of tanks milling about at the end of the sandbar; they called for tank destroyers. A moment later the Jap machines rushed—down the secret track—with the 4th Regiment behind them giving that "bubbling shriek like a turkey gobbler's cry" which was the banzai. The direction of the tank attack was unexpected; the first one crashed through our barbed wire, crushed a pillbox and raced along the beach, followed by the rest. Private Joseph B. R. Champagne earned himself a Navy Cross by leaping from his foxhole to thrust a grenade in the lead tank's treads.

It was Captain Maeda's tank, the leader of the battalion; his machine swiveled around as he strove to regain control, got it, lurched half a yard and in that instant of stasis came into the sights of the first tank destroyer, just arrived. There was a violent explo-

89

sion; with a stream of flame leaping from its interior Maeda's tank was blown 20 yards into the sea. Behind him, before they could maneuver, before they could swing their guns to reply, tank after tank was hit by those half-tracks that had dropped from the clouds. In twenty minutes they were a line of flaming wrecks and the tank destroyers were pounding the remnants of the 4th Regiment, now fleeing under an artillery fire far more intense than its own support.

By midnight there was not even sniper shooting from the Jap positions and the patrols Colonel McKelvey sent out found several hundred dead, all the tanks of the battalion accounted for (three had been smashed by artillery), and hardly any Japs on the immediate west bank. Even so he did not know the extent of his victory. The 4th Regiment had been wiped out, *zemetsu,* and would not return, not even one man, to the district of the Sendai. As for Colonel Oka, he worked along the slope of Grassy Knoll all right, but never attacked at all. His report said: "The regiment endeavored to accomplish the objective of diverting the enemy, but they seemed to be planning a firm defense of this region."

IV

When on the 14th it was clear that the 105s could not reach the Jap heavy guns General Vandegrift put through an urgent request for a battery of 155s. He had been somewhat surprised that day of the 23rd to receive not one battery but two, one Army, one Marine. They more than did their part in the short hard fight at the Matanikau and now for the first time both headquarters and the men beneath began to have that most wonderful of all feelings in war, that in will and resource they had unlimited support, where up to now they had been marooned on a friendless shore. But the main attack was yet to come, heralded during the day of the 24th by reports from the scout-snipers that smokes were rising among the ridges to the south.

Patrols went out but found nothing. Nevertheless, the Japs were there all right, and at 2130 that night they attacked the positions east of the Lunga and south of Edson's Ridge under a pouring rain. Now it happened that this 7th Marine sector was held by a single battalion at the time, one of the others having been sent down to relieve the troops on the Matanikau battle position on the previous day and having been left there in the expectation the Jap attack might be renewed. The sector was 2,500 yards long and part of it ran through the densest kind of jungle. The Japs had a lot of mortars with them and charged again and again after concentrating their fire now here, now there along the line, working small groups

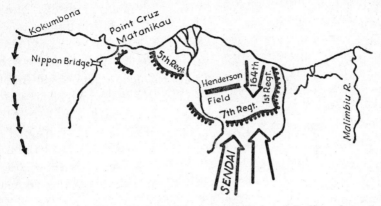

through the wire. By midnight Lieutenant Colonel Puller of the battalion had all his reserves in and the attack showed no signs of lessening. He asked for reinforcements and the General sent him the reserve battalion of the 164th.

The dogfaces did not know the country or the kind of country and they were new to battle. As they moved up along the muddy trails another Jap drive, the most powerful yet, broke a hundred yards into the position at one point while attacks continued along the line. It was necessary to insert the 164th in small parties, wherever most needed—just the circumstances under which whatever defects they had in leadership counted for least and their own fighting ability for most. They held; dawn found only the one real penetration. Marines and soldiers together put crossfire on it, worked in from both flanks and with the artillery laying interdiction fire along the trails to the Jap rear, re-established the whole position. The wire was full of enemy dead; one of the live Japs wrote as the last entry he would ever write in his diary that the Americans were inhuman demons.

During the day there were rearrangements on both sides. The men of the 164th were picked out of the little pockets they had occupied in the line and added part of it to the wing of their regimental position along the Tenaru, while Puller's battalion shortened its holdings. On the Japanese side the attack had been made by the 29th Regiment. Its colonel was now missing; one battalion had been practically annihilated along the wire and the second was in nearly as bad shape after being caught along the trails moving up by an American artillery concentration. However, General Kawaguchi believed some of his men had effected a firm lodgment in the American position. In accordance with the "expanding torrent" strategy which is fundamental in the Japanese war system, the thing to do was to exploit this break. The 29th was evidently too much weakened to push through without help. The 16th Regiment was now up; instead of employing it west of the Lunga, he therefore switched it along the jungle trails to pass through the 29th and renew the attack. What was left of the Kawaguchi Brigade and the 230th Regiment were to make a move on the right flank of this main attack, pushing into the American position toward the Tenaru. The attack for midnight. As all the troops were now farther forward, the synchronization would be distinctly better and one could hope to make several penetrations at once.

One's hopes were disappointed. On the American side there was now no lack of information as to the lines along which the attack would come, and as soon as it started, with long columns of Japanese moving up the narrow jungle trails, chanting "US Marine, you going die tonight," the artillery came down on them with everything it had. The supports were cut from under the attack before it was launched; the men in the forefront of the drive found themselves pushing against positions thoroughly wired in and steady as a rock. They could gain nothing, and neither could Colonel Oka on his front, where General Hyakutate had at last nagged him into making an attack that was something more than a show. There was another, weaker attempt by Kawaguchi on the night of the 26th, which only piled up casualties. It was featured by the extraordinary success of a mortar concentration from the Army troops, who caught a whole heavy weapons company moving up and wiped it out.

By the night of the 27th the southern front had settled down to isolated snipers' fire; by the night of the 28th all was quiet and the Sendai, like the formations before them, were broken men streaming off into the jungle. They had lost nearly three thousand among the ridges, more than another thousand at the Matanikau. In fact their whole attack, their whole system of attack, had been about as little calculated to succeed against General Vandegrift's cordon defense as it could well be. It was admirably suited to breaking through a defense in depth, isolating and wearing down the little knots of which such a defense is made up. But with its broad front of attack, its narrow avenues of approach on which the defending artillery had perfectly registered, Hyakutate's system was designed to accumulate the maximum possible damage from the fire of our artillery and from the weapons of our strong and solid line, every gun of which got into action.

Some sense of this seems ultimately to have reached Furumiya, the Colonel of the 29th, who had been left behind the American lines in a hide-out, with the regimental colors. They were among the most honored colors in the whole Japanese Army and he could not even set fire to them without detection, so he tore them in small pieces and wrote a note which he hoped somehow would reach General Maruyama:

"I do not know what excuse to give. I apologize for what I have done." Then a couple of diary entries:

"I am sorry I have lost many troops uselessly and for this result which has come unexpectedly. We must not overlook fire power. When there is fire power the troops become active and full of spirit, but when fire power ceases they become inactive. Spirit exists eternally.

"I feel sleepy because of exhaustion for several days.

"I am going to return my borrowed life today with short interest."

V

The planes at Rabaul and Buka were Imperial Navy units, since the Army had not deigned to send any of its own aircraft down to deal with the Guadalcanal plague spot. Admiral Nagumo, who was to be in general command of the great fleet sweep to the south, expressed himself as having little confidence in the Army's promise to put the Guadalcanal field out of operation by the time he moved, and desired the Rabaul bombers to make certain of the matter. As it fell out the report from the fighting front was that the rains had been exceptionally heavy on the nights of 22 and 23 October and observation posts on Grassy Knoll reported that the American planes seemed to have difficulty in getting off the ground. It rained again, torrentially, on the night of the 24th. A recon plane under Zero escort went down for a look. It cruised back and forth across the American field for quite half an hour without any fighters taking off in pursuit. Though this plane was unfortunately shot down by antiaircraft fire when it got too low, Rabaul was satisfied that American planes were grounded for the day and put out a major air effort, all day long.

On the island they knew that day as "dugout Sunday"; Condition Red lasted till dark. But the Jap planners were wrong about American planes not taking off. A lot of fighters did get away, including the famous Captain Joe Foss, who began his great record by shooting down four Zeros that afternoon. Thirteen more of them were shot down by other hands, and five bombers, but the Japanese command was fairly well satisfied over having smashed up or blown up the whole long line of planes waiting to take the air.

Admiral Nagumo received the cheering news aboard the flagship *Shokaku* toward evening. The other news of the day was not quite so encouraging. His carrier *Hitaka* had developed defects in her main condensers and had to be left behind; on the morning of the 25th a long-range American recon plane flashed past his formation into clouds before it could be intercepted; an American carrier had been sighted out to the east; and the submarines said there was another one, accompanied by a battleship, moving north from the New Hebrides. It looked as though they were aware of his approach. During the afternoon of the 25th, therefore, Nagumo turned his formations north again and ran in that direction till 1600 before once more taking up his course toward the south. Fortunately on this northern leg he picked up a storm front moving down.

What had happened was that Admiral Kinkaid had come tearing north from the New Hebrides, well east of the Santa Cruz Island screen. *Enterprise,* healed of her wounds at the eastern Solomons, was the center of one group—she was the carrier "to the east," seen on her way down from Pearl Harbor. With her was the new battleship *South Dakota,* the first one armed with a full set of 40- and

20-mm. guns, the heavy cruiser *Portland,* the antiaircraft cruiser *San Juan,* and eight destroyers. The other group had the veteran *Hornet* but there was no battleship to spare for her support, so she had to get along with the heavy cruisers *Northampton* and *Pensacola,* the antiaircraft cruisers *San Diego* and *Juneau,* and six destroyers.

The Japs were out; everyone knew it, and on the afternoon of the 25th *Enterprise* flew off a search strike but failed to find them. A little later came a PBY report that they had turned back north. Apparently they did not want to fight, but the fragmentary information about fighting on the island was not so good, so this might be a Jap trick. Kinkaid held on northwestward through the night.

Before dawn a night-flying PBY reported the enemy coming south again, shooting steadily toward the gap between Guadalcanal and Santa Cruz, under a weather front. At daybreak *Enterprise* flew off a 16-plane search and very little afterward a Jap recon plane was seen, which meant that our ships had been found while Kinkaid lacked certainty of the enemy's whereabouts and the strike groups were still on his decks. This looked bad; but about fifteen minutes later again a message came through from another long-range search plane which at four in the morning had located *Zuiho,* with her position, course, and speed as of that hour. The message had been vexatiously delayed for more than two hours in getting through from Espiritu. Kinkaid got his strike groups out at once. That from *Enterprise* was far less numerous than it should have been, partly because sixteen of the planes were out on the search, partly because the leader of the search on the evening before had allowed enthusiasm to carry him beyond the point judgment allowed and had lost eleven planes in water landings and deck crashes when he returned with insufficient fuel.

Some of the *Enterprise* search men found *Zuiho* about 0830, and after a hard fight with Zeros got in the first licks of the battle. There were only two planes with the light bombs searchers carried, but both of them hit her right through the deck and the Jap carrier staggered northward badly hurt and with smoke coming out. The rest was not so good, for thanks to the communication delay and some good Jap scouting, the enemy had launched all the planes of their four carriers and delivered the first really solid blows.

95

It was by the united air groups of *Shokaku* and *Zuiho,* the best pilots remaining to Japan. Twenty-seven planes broke through the combat patrols, through the crash of fire that downed twenty of them, and got two torpedoes into *Hornet,* besides six bombs and a dying plane that crashed her stack and demolished her signal bridge. The big carrier stopped; fires broke out below and she took a heavy list. *Northampton* took her in tow; three of the destroyers came alongside to fight fires and by noon it looked as though they were going to save her, though the towing speed was only 3 knots. But at 1600 the Japs came back in another co-ordinated dive-bomb and torpedo attack, hitting *Hornet* with two more fish, which gave her such a list that it was clear further efforts would be useless. What was left of her was scuttled.

Our own attacks were nowhere near as successful, the *Enterprise* group meeting with more misfortune on its way to the Japs when it ran into one of their strike groups in the skies and was suddenly attacked by Zeros from out of the sun, losing eight planes. *Hornet*'s strike groups had gone out in succession rather than together because of the distance (to save fuel) and their attack was a long stream rather than a co-ordinated punch. They did get in on *Shokaku* and landed six big bombs which tore her flight deck all apart, set fires in the hangar and left her with such leaks that the Japs thought she was going to capsize. *Hornet*'s second group missed the carriers altogether but turned to on the heavy cruiser *Chikuma* and hit her with three big bombs, killing everyone on the bridge and making such a mess of her after portion that Lieutenant Commander Widhelm, lying in his rubber boat where he had been shot down, compared everything aft of her funnel to taffy ready for the pull.

But it was round the fabulous *Enterprise* that the Battle of Santa Cruz was decided. It started badly for her; at 1100, with Jap planes already on her radar screen like a swarm of fireflies, the destroyer *Porter* stopped to pick up a torpedo pilot in the water and was torpedoed by a Jap sub; she sank in half an hour. Four minutes later the Japs came in, as in the *Hornet* attack too numerous for the combat patrol to handle, and from then on for an hour and a half over a hundred of the best pilots in the Japanese service kept after her continuously. But after this time there was a battleship for cover; *South Dakota* charged through the milling ships, shooting so rapidly that again and again our people thought her afire, and out of 33 planes that came within her range shot down 32. *Enterprise* took three hits but none so serious that they prevented her from recovering her own planes and *Hornet*'s too. *South Dakota* got a bomb hit as well, but on her turret top with no damage but a wound for Captain Gatch.

The big battleship followed the rest of the fleet south through the twilight, everybody aboard feeling cheerful and proud of themselves, and no wonder, this was the first time an air attack had been decisively beaten off. They were the only people in the American fleet who did feel that way; *Hornet* was gone, our carrier strength was down to a single vessel and that one in need of repair. We had lost 74 planes and 33 of their personnel, a Pyrrhic victory if not a defeat. "It was of dubious value to our cause," said the staff estimate, and editorials in the home papers began to inquire whether Guadal could be held.

But this was out of sight and mind of the Jap commanders. Admiral Nagumo, taking his damaged carriers back to Truk, whence they would have to go to Japan and lie in repair docks for many months, was in a state of fury and despair. This had been the big effort, using the last reserves of well-trained and fully experienced pilots in the Imperial Navy: 175 had left the decks that morning to wipe out the American fleet; not 60 had returned, and of these some had gone into the water and lost their planes. Japan was now in fact without a carrier service and it would be two years before she could have one again. Nagumo minced no words in telling the military people that it was the Army's fault that failing to capture the airfield on schedule. While the recriminations were going on, a message came in that lent point to what he said. The light cruiser *Yura*, following the fleet home after conducting a scout in the direction of the retreating Americans, had been caught by Marine dive bombers north of Sta. Isabel and sunk in less than ten minutes.

Chapter 7

The Battleships Go through:
End of Guadalcanal

FROM MINAMOTO YOSHITSUNE TO THE FORTY-SEVEN RONINS nearly all the Japanese worthies are in some form fighting men. The exception is the philosopher Ono-no-tofu, always represented as standing under a willow tree under the streaming rains of November and watching a frog which has made six futile efforts to get up a slippery bank and at the seventh succeeded. It was considered both by General Hyakutate and by Captain Ohmae, when the latter reached Guadalcanal aboard a destroyer on 31 October, that this was a highly favorable omen, especially in view of the fact that the next jump that the Japanese tried would be made almost exactly on the days sacred to the sage, at the end of the second week of the month, or "the days of the willow," as they poetically phrased it. It might even be worth some sacrifice in other directions to move it to precisely that date; sacrifice and timing would attract to their enterprise the blessing of the holy Amaterasu.

It was true that air support from carriers could no longer be counted upon and the 25th Air Flotilla had become so battered that it was now necessary to send it back to Japan. But the Imperial Navy had consented to make good this loss by moving in the 22nd from the Marianas and the 21st from the Marshalls, both of them formations which contained a number of experienced pilots. Besides, all these difficulties would clearly disappear the moment the Guadalcanal field was taken; the Americans were as badly off for carrier strength as we ourselves. There had been unpleasant incidents up to now but the fact must not be lost sight of that it was the enemy's main air base which was under siege, not Buka or Rabaul. A single victory would be decisive.

Approaching the matter in this rational and reasonable spirit, the naval man and the military now carried their consideration down into the domain of practical and specific measures. One of the reasons why Generals Kawaguchi and Maruyama had achieved something less than the annihilating success expected of them by the Imperial will was that they had spent too long in getting their troops ashore and assembling them for action. The Americans had thus been able to bring in reinforcements quite as rapidly as they. In fact the latest estimates showed there must be as many as 15,000 Americans on the island. Against these General Hyakutate could now assemble only about the same number and the difficulties of reaching positions where the invincible power of the Japanese soldier in close combat could be brought to bear were very serious. Moreover, many of these men were not in good physical condition. They were short of food and there were complaints even from officers of the small number and relative inefficiency of the antiaircraft guns. There was some help from the eighty big landing barges now assembled among the Shortlands, but the Americans kept bombing and damaging these and many were required to forward supplies for the much-needed new airfield at Munda.

The obvious operation was to bring in a really large convoy with a crushing number of troops aboard and all equipment necessary for a major campaign. There was such a force now available among the Shortlands, General Kagesa's 38th Division, called the Hiroshima, brought forward at last. During the period of the Sendai's operation there had been a change in staff planning at Tokyo and General Hyakutate had been informed that this division was to be detached from his command to the 18th Army for the capture of Moresby, from which the Americans and Australians were now making disquieting advances across the mountains of New Guinea. Now, in view of Admiral Nagumo's unfortunate experience, the Navy men were disposed to consider the American advance in the Solomons as more important than that in New Guinea. The 38th was returned to Hyakutate's army. Naval headquarters softened the edge of its criticisms and recalcitrances in other matters by agreeing to detail twelve large transports for this convoy operation, most of them 7,000-tonners that had been on the Australian run before the war, though two were bigger. In return they detached the battleships *Kongo* and *Haruna* from the Southeast Area Fleet.

The plan was for this fleet (Vice-Admiral Abe) to use his two remaining battleships (*Hiyei* and *Kirishima*) with fifteen destroyers to run in and bombard Guadalcanal field on the three successive nights of Ono-no-tofu, 12, 13 and 14 November. This would not only put all the few American airplanes out of action but would keep them out through damage to the airfield and would pick up any replacements in planes as fast as they were brought in. A further group of twelve destroyers under Rear Admiral Tanaka, designated the Guadalcanal Reinforcement Force, would cover the transports against attacks from the motor-torpedo boats which the Americans had so annoyingly brought into this area. (One of the Americans blew up a second-class destroyer in the lagoon on the night of 6 November and two or three of the big barges had been sunk by them.)

Admiral Mikawa's force was now designated as the Outer South Seas Supporting Unit and was greatly strengthened, now having three of the big heavy cruisers (*Chokai, Suzuya, Maya*) besides his original *Kinugasa*, two light cruisers (*Isuzu, Tenryu*), and six destroyers of the largest size. This force would hang north of Sta. Isabel, beyond American plane range, till Admiral Kondo's bombardiers had quitted the Slot; then run in to give the convoy their powerful antiaircraft support against whatever few American planes remained operative and also be prepared to beat off any attempt by American surface forces to repeat their action of 11 October. Long-range recon planes and the 7th Submarine Division, now on duty between the New Hebrides and Guadalcanal, had furnished a pretty accurate count on American ships in the area. The enemy did not have above three heavy cruisers and a light, so Mikawa would enjoy a comforting fire superiority besides what he would gain from superior Japanese torpedo attacks. Naturally the newly arrived 21st and 22nd Air Flotillas would make vigorous attacks on American airfields and ships in the vicinity.

It was originally intended to land the 38th east of the airfield and all but a single company of the 228th Infantry Regiment (this company had already been sent ashore at Buna for the Moresby job) was moved in in destroyers to prepare a beachhead during the night

100

of 3 November. But the more General Hyakutate considered the matter the less he liked the idea of making the double attack on the American position that this would imply. "Co-ordinated attacks always fail to co-ordinate." He exercised a commander's privilege of changing his mind, ordered the big convoy to land along the shore at Tassafaronga and Doma Cove and radioed the regiment already ashore on the east to come around by means of the trails the Kawaguchi Brigade had cut.

II

The physical shape in which General Vandegrift found his men after getting rid of the Sendais was not encouraging. They were tired out and 15 per cent of them were hospitalized malaria cases, a figure which caused the gravest concern among the medics, as yet unaware that the Japs just beyond the lines were nearly all suffering from the disease and formed the source of infection which would be eliminated only with the end of the campaign. He had been forced to send out the parachutists (on September 18), now down to 200 men and with all their officers above lieutenants killed or wounded; and the 1st Raiders (on 13 October) who were in nearly as bad shape. Even if he had received the 164th, and the total of Americans on the island had reached 27,727 as the month turned into November, a large part of this imposing force was composed of airfield personnel, Seabees, and similar formations which could take defensive duties only in an emergency. There was a definite lack of combat infantry for offensive purposes.

Nevertheless, an offensive across the Matanikau seemed indicated after talks with Colonels Thomas and Twining, for morale in our own troops—it was important to let them know that they still had the old Marine kick; for moral effect on the enemy—"We want to give them a sense of futility, especially that concentration up at Buka," said Colonel Thomas; for the purely tactical effect of driving Pistol Pete and his playmates out of Kokumbona to a point where they could not drop shells on the airfield. The 5th Regiment was the only formation rested enough to undertake the drive and it was so far down in strength that it could hardly do it alone. General Vandegrift accordingly got the troops by bringing over from Tulagi the two remaining battalions of the 2nd Regiment and

101

adding to it for the attack the Whaling group and a battalion of the 7th. It was quite a complex little operation, since the presence of considerable enemy forces was counted upon and the country was even more intricate than that usually found on the northern shore of Guadal. Nine batteries of artillery were assigned to give the region beyond the Matanikau a heavy combing, with special attention to a narrow draw and stream bed 1,500 yards east of Point Cruz. The bombers, including B-17s (the airfield had now so improved that a squadron of the big planes was based there), were also to give the place a heavy pasting and the mediums were to remain on call for close support. Captain Ryan's Desron (*Fletcher, Radford, O'Bannon*) was also to furnish call fire.

The Engineers would build bridges on the night before the attack across the Matanikau just below Nippon Bridge. Over these the 5th would pass, attacking westward, then curving toward the shore. The 2nd, with the Whaling detachment leading, would take the Nippon Bridge, covering the left of the 5th and sweeping around it to hit the shore near Point Cruz. Behind the 2nd the battalion of the 7th would similarly do a wide right wheel and also turn toward the shore.

D day was 1 November; at 0630 the artillery barrage began and two hours later the troops went forward. The Japanese front here was under Colonel Oka (General Hyakutate had to use him because he was getting a little short of high officers, Maruyama having committed suicide in the hospital and Kawaguchi being missing back in the boondocks); as Oka displayed his usual courage and competence, the whole American operation ran like a grandfather's clock. This does not mean there was no hard fighting or casualties— Major W. K. Enright's battalion of the 5th Regiment, which had the rightmost position in the attack, encountered a big pocket on a ridge at the base of Point Cruz. Three attacks were beaten off under considerable fire from 1-pounders and antitank pieces.

The plan was flexible enough to allow for that. Next morning another battalion of the regiment pushed past the Jap pocket while Whaling's snipers formed a link between it and the battalion that had been stopped the day before. The Japs were gradually pushed into a narrowing net. There was a rocky ravine at this point which had machine guns set up in the sides, just like Tulagi; each one had to be knocked out by handwork. The men of the 1st Marine Division had by this time become pretty competent about such business. They finished the job on the next day, 3 November, with a flourish by making a really successful bayonet charge, the only one in the history of the island. They found a 75, a dozen 37-mm., and 187 corpses besides a number of others who were bumped off as they tried to swim out. One of the dead was a colonel—not Oka, who was preserved to be a help to the Americans in other ways.

The formations from the 2nd and 7th Regiments had pushed forward to their objective lines meanwhile and ran into another pocket of resistance 3,500 yards from the Matanikau. Some of the 164th were sent up to relieve the front and preparations were under way for an attack on Kokumbona and the Pistol Pete position when the operation had to be called off.

The reason for this was that Japanese 228th Regiment, which had begun to come ashore from its destroyers on the night of 2 November with attached formations, such as artillery and transport. A code intercept told SOPAC headquarters, who told General Vandegrift that a new landing would be attempted in that direction. On 1 November he sent Lieutenant Colonel Hanneken's battalion of the 7th out toward Koli Point on patrol. The boats were being used to support the Matanikau movement, so the battalion had to be trucked down to the Ilu and march forward from there. It was an exceeding hard march, marked by a grotesque tragedy when a big coconut tree fell over, killing two men and wounding four more, not for any reason except that it got tired of standing there. On the night of 3 November Lieutenant Colonel Hanneken with the battalion was at the mouth of the Metapona; he found no Japs but did find he could cross the stream only by wading waist-deep to the sandbar at the mouth. That night he bivouacked on the eastern bank; it rained and under the rain in the dark Jap ships could be made out standing in, more of them and landing many more men than had been expected, near the village Tetere, just east of them. Hanneken tried to notify headquarters but his only radio had gone out during the hard march and it stayed out.

At dawn the Japs attacked and the battalion learned for the first time that the enemy had artillery. It was time for our men to get out, especially as they ran short on mortar ammunition. They successfully negotiated the Metapona, but could not hold the left bank as the Japs came around from the jungle side in an encirclement and they had to pull back still farther on the Malimbiu. Late on the afternoon of the 4th word of Hanneken's plight reached division by runner; air support was sent at once and another battalion of the 7th by boat to Koli Point. The 164th was pulled out of the Tenaru position, and instead of going to the operation beyond the Matanikau, was moved east by inland routes to get at the Jap rear. General Rupertus took over-all command; and Colonel Carlson with his 2nd Raider Battalion was brought westward by inland trails from Aola. The beach track would have been more convenient, but they were Raiders, and didn't want to get involved in any formal war.

This battalion had landed that day, the 4th. On the chart Aola looks like a nice little harbor and Admiral Turner had put the battalion in with the idea of building another airstrip beside it, but there had been the usual trouble about maps, and when Carlson landed he found the site of the proposed strip was occupied by a ridge and swamp.

The two battalions of the 7th of course brought matters to a stand at the Malimbiu and with naval support put the Japs on the defensive. Jungle delayed the march of the 164th so that it was 7 November before they began to take the enemy from the rear and even then they could not completely close the net. The Jap 228th retreated to the Metapona and holed up on the east bank of that stream. On 8 November they were closed in there and with no less than five battalions of artillery supporting, Marines and soldiers began to clean out the pocket, an operation which required two days. It produced 450 dead Japs at a cost of 40 of our men.

Once again some of the fish got off the hook. Colonel Suemura of the regiment with something more than a battalion of his men slipped southward up the Metapona and began to work to the east along the jungle trails cut by the Kawaguchis long ago. Unfortunately for the remnants of the 228th, Carlson's Raiders, coming from Aola, got on their tracks before the movement had barely started and never let them go. The Raiders were fresh, full of ginger, had an inspiring leader and by this time a solid background of training and experience in jungle work. The 228th, whose previous service had been at Macao, Hong Kong, and in garrison at Amboina, had none of these things.

Carlson used an entirely unorthodox system of tactics invented by himself. Normally in such a retreat movement a fairly strong rear guard is left out and when the pursuit, following the track of the retiring formation, runs into this rear guard, there is a fight which is in effect a frontal attack on a prepared position. The Raiders gave Colonel Suemura every opportunity to think that this was what he was dealing with. A patrol would contact his rear guard, fire a few shots and apparently settle down to wait for reinforcements to come up. Actually Carlson would be moving on a parallel route well off to the flank of the Jap main body; when his strike came it was always on the rear of the prepared position, knocking it out and picking off a few more men. Again and again the trick was repeated in the following weeks. The 228th never did fathom it; the Raiders clung to their heels all through the back country, across the Tenaru, across the Lunga, up into the hills where the Matanikau has its sources, a long march on which Carlson never even reported to headquarters except to ask for food. He reached the perimeter down the Matanikau on 4 December; and by that time the 228th was all gone.

III

The Japanese plan for moving the 38th Division in crossed one by Admiral Turner for the reinforcement of the island. Down at Nouméa a new Army division had been organized, the only one without a number, the Americal. It was under Major General A. A. Patch, whose infantry regiments were the 164th, already on the island, and the 182nd; eventually they were to relieve the Marines. Four transports, three supply ships left on 8 November with the divisional artillery, part of the 182nd, and a few special units, all they could carry on this trip.

Turner knew the Japs would be reinforcing heavily and knew most exactly the date, 13 November. He expected violent land-based air attack as a preliminary and also expected the Jap fleet would take part with battleships and two carriers, *Hitaka* and *Hayataka*. (He could not know, of course, that the Jap carriers were so short of both planes and pilots that their presence in the upper Solomons

105

represented only a bluff.) His plan was to get the transports unloaded by the 13th, using Rear Admiral Callaghan's force (*San Francisco, Portland, Helena, Atlanta, Juneau,* with eight destroyers) to beat off the air attack with the planes from Henderson Field, and then bring *Enterprise* up from the south to smash at the Jap transports and surface force.

This was the background. Action in the foreground began at 0930 on the 11th, when the supply ships were unloading, with an attack from 9 dive-bombers covered by 15 Zeros. They went for the transports and hit *Zeilin,* one of the APDs, badly enough so she had to go back to base. The antiaircraft fire was good but nothing special; all the bombers were shot down and 5 of the Zeros, mostly by fighters from Henderson, who themselves lost the unusual number of 6 planes, being a new formation with inexperienced pilots. Two hours later another bomber group came in, 25 this time, not pressing home so closely. They lost 8 and we won this bout. As twilight drew in, our cruisers got underway and moved out into Indispensable Strait.

Next day, 12 November, more transports arrived and so did more Japs, 25 torpedo planes at 1405 with 8 Zeros for escort, low over Florida in a long line like water out of a high-pressure hose. There was adequate warning from a coast-watcher up the line; the transports got underway with the cruisers around them in a semicircle and the destroyers came back from putting out of business one of the Pistol Pete guns which had decided to become annoying. All the fighters went up, to the number of 29. As the torpedo formation darted in along the water where fighters could not get at them, the ships opened up one of the fiercest AA barrages ever seen; most of the planes that survived it dropped their torpedoes haphazard and were caught by the fighters in the pull-out. The action lasted fourteen minutes; when it was over one lone Jap plane was staggering northward with smoke coming out of his engine, all the rest shot down. *Buchanan* had been hit by our own fire and one Jap exploded into *San Francisco*'s after battle station, where 30 men were killed.

While this was going on, the long-range searchers reported the Japs bearing down from the Shortlands and in position to arrive by midnight with two battleships, a cruiser, and a destroyer. *Enter-*

prise had been busy with her repairs, was still far south, and so could not reach position to do business before the next day. In the lagoon, in the area there were only the cruisers and the supply ships still being unloaded. In a counsel of almost desperation Callaghan was ordered to fight a delaying action, hold them off, prevent the bombardment of the airfield, and disengage so that our carrier and the field planes could get a whack at that big enemy convoy on the following day.

With twilight the Admiral put the supply ships out to the east. It was after midnight when he came nosing back along the shore all in line with destroyers *Cushing, Laffey, Sterrett,* and *O'Bannon* leading; then the cruisers *Atlanta, San Francisco, Portland, Helena, Juneau;* finally the other four destroyers *Aaron Ward, Barton, Monssen, Fletcher.* Admiral Turner had told the Marines ashore there was going to be fight that night; their headquarters got chairs out under the palm trees to watch and the defense battalions set up their instruments.

Near Lunga Point at 0124 *Helena,* the only ship with SG radar, picked up the signals of enemy ships in three groups: Admiral Kondo's fleet, two battleships, a light cruiser, and fourteen heavy destroyers, bigger than ours;[1] expecting to bombard and loaded with ammunition for that purpose, but with three times or more than three times the American fire power and at least three times the American torpedo power.

Callaghan's little fleet was heading straight into the southernmost of the three enemy groups, the one near Guadal shore. He turned rightward in succession to get across their bows, then left again to close. There was confusion in his line as he plunged toward the charging Japs, shouting "Commence firing; give 'em hell, boys!" at 0145 and all the guns blazed out across the lagoon. Ships plunged in every direction, friend and enemy inextricably mingling amid searchlight glare, gunflash, and the waterspouts of exploding torpedoes. "All we

[1] For the record, these ships were *Hiyei* and *Kirishima,* battleships; *Nagara,* light cruiser; and the destroyers *Amatsukaze, Tokitsukaze, Terutsuki, Akatsuki, Inadzuma, Ikadsuchi*—these were very big destroyers with eight guns, really small cruisers—*Asagumo, Murasame, Samidare, Yudachi, Harusama, Shigure, Shiratsuya, Yugure.*

could see was one hell of a dogfight," said one of the Marines ashore; and out on the water they could discover little more.

At the head of our line *Cushing* got off three fish and was badly hit aft, coasting on momentum through the Jap formation, listing and beginning to go down. Behind her *Atlanta* and *Juneau* hit a pair of big Jap destroyers again and again before both ships were torpedoed, *Atlanta* drifting down toward Guadal without lights or power, *Juneau* trying to get away with her keel broken, still shooting slowly in local control. *Cushing's* skipper from the bridge wings looked south and saw outlined against the intermittent light the fantastic form of a Japanese battleship with the destroyer *Laffey* shooting at her bridge. *Laffey* was hit and began to burn. "Get on that God-damn pagoda!" shouted someone over TBS and *San Francisco* was doing so, dueling with *Hiyei* at a range so short that armor was meaningless and the big Jap could not depress her guns far enough to get at our cruiser's waterline. She hit the cruiser's upper works, a whole salvo of 14-inch that went through the bridge and killed every man on it including Uncle Dan Callaghan, one of the best-loved officers of the Navy. The turrets went into local; it was probably at that moment that one of them fired on a ship which they thought Jap but which was actually *Atlanta,* killing the other admiral, Norman Scott.[1]

In the wild tumult *Portland* had taken a torpedo aft that ruined her steering gear and *Barton* blew up. *Monssen* began to burn from end to end, hit by a whole series of salvos. But the Japs were paying: *Sterrett* got two fish into *Hiyei* and either she or *Fletcher,* perhaps both together, launched a series of torpedoes that blew up *Yudachi.* Nearly every Jap ship was hit and now they turned in disorderly retreat, firing wildly, sometimes at each other, as they ran.

Helena, the only undamaged ship on our side, was trying to assemble the squadron as the morning came, and all the boats of Guadal put out to pick up survivors while planes droned overhead. *San Francisco* was in the hands of a lieutenant commander; *Atlanta* was lying near the shore with her foremast over the side and it could

---

[1] Unfortunately there seems no doubt about this. *Atlanta's* later injuries were discovered to be caused by 8-inch shell when they inspected her in the morning, and the Japs had no ship in action using this caliber. Besides, these shells employed green dye, *San Francisco's* color.

not be cut away. They had to take her people out and let her go. *Portland* and *Aaron Ward,* the former without steering, the latter without power, were still in the lagoon. On the horizon over beyond Savo there was a crippled Jap destroyer, *Akatsuki,* which *Portland* sank with six salvos. But what most excited all the Marines at Guadal and the sailors picked out of the sea was the news that still farther beyond Savo lay a Japanese battleship which seemed to be having trouble with its rudder.

It was *Hiyei,* the flagship, which had taken more than such a vessel could stand from the much smaller Americans, over eighty-five hits. The flotillas with her had been cut to pieces; besides the two sunk, *Amatsukaze, Tokitsukaze,* and *Inaduzma* of the cruiser-destroyers and five of the normal type[1] were so battered that they could not be used again in that campaign, but the battleship was the main issue, an absolutely irreplaceable unit which represented exactly one-twelfth of Japan's major battle power. Back at Truk, Admiral Yamamoto leaped up so vigorously that he overset his chair when he heard of her plight. "The ship must be brought back home at all costs!" cried he, and instantly removed from command Vice-Admiral Abe, who had taken her in there and got her hurt. Fighter planes were ordered down from Buka to cover her in relays and the Outer South Seas Supporting Unit to detach some of its destroyers to protect her from surface attack.

It was not enough. The fighters had to come a long distance, which meant they could stay only briefly above the damaged giant, while it was only a half step for Geiger's pilots from Henderson Field. They loaded with torpedoes and had full cover (eight of the Jap fighters who tried to interfere were shot down) and about 0800 put four more fish into *Hiyei,* while Major Sailer knocked out one of her AA positions with a bomb. The big ship staggered on. There was a brief moment of excitement on Guadal when she seemed to be coming back toward the island, but it was only the eccentric circle that was now all she could steer and the merry-go-round carried her back in the other direction. At 1430 the fliers staged another attack, co-ordinated bombs and torpedoes. Two of the latter were duds but three were not, and the dive bombers got three of their 1,000-pounders into her. She took a list, her AA fire went out, and there was

[1] *Asagumo, Harusame, Shigure, Shiratsuyu, Yugure.*

smoke in the region of her fore turrets but the damned thing would not go down.

"We've got to sink her," said one of the eager airmen, "or the admirals will stop building carriers and start building battleships all over again." It would be about this time when it occurred to someone that the torpedoes had been running with the shallow setting normally used against the light-draft Japanese craft of the region, and must be exploding against the armor belt of the big ship, depressed by the water she had taken aboard. Another torpedo attack with deep settings went out in the twilight and there were two more hits. *Hiyei*'s stern was glowing cherry-red and one of the Jap destroyers was alongside, taking people off. Next morning there was only an oil slick two miles long, shining iridescent on the swell.

IV

We lost a ship too that day, with nearly all hands, the poor old *Juneau,* torpedoed by a sub on the way out because our destroyers were so smashed up their sound gear was no good. Ashore the day was quiet and everybody wondered whether the Japs were not cured of their intentions. It seemed like it; the search planes reported a group of transports out beyond New Georgia, retreating slowly toward the Shortlands.

Actually the Japs were not cured at all, had only made a quick change in plans after battle damage cut down the bombardment force so badly they could no longer do a proper job on the Guadalcanal field. Admiral Mikawa's Outer South Seas Supporting Unit, the one with the heavy cruisers, was assigned to take over the job and get rid of those Henderson Field planes that night, Friday the 13th, so the transports were held out to the north till he had done it.

The transports would now arrive on the night of the 14th, being covered during their daylight approach by Mikawa's retirement. While they were unloading, a reconstituted bombardment force, now under Vice-Admiral Kondo, would protect them and give Henderson Field the necessary second night shelling. Mikawa would have no surface opposition (he was told); the American surface forces had been eliminated.

110

This proved approximately correct. Mikawa came in at 0220 and began a deliberate bombardment. Of all the shellings the Marines on the island had to bear they considered this the hardest; they cowered in foxholes and some shed actual tears, tired out. But they did not have to bear it long, for the Petes slipped out of Tulagi, six little boats, and fired a spread of torpedoes into Mikawa's ships.

One of them hit and a very important hit was that, for it left Mikawa with a crippled cruiser.[1] He ceased fire at once and started back, running south of New Georgia, to get his cripple beyond airstrike range before dawn should bring the planes down on him. The best speed he could make was insufficient; the dawn search from Guadal found him within range and a strike went out immediately. Unfortunately for the Japanese commander the Rabaul fighter planes had been so badly used up over *Hiyei* the day before, and were so much occupied covering the transports, that there was no support for the cruiser squadron. The American fliers rode down a slide of flak to administer a heavy bomb hit to his flagship *Chokai* and smashed two torpedoes into *Kinugasa*. The Admiral knew that Yamamoto felt pretty strongly about losing more ships; he had intercepted the radio dispatch removing Abe from his command the day before. Accordingly, although *Kinugasa* was burning and in bad shape, he slowed up still more in an effort to see her home, convinced that the Marine planes could not come back at him again for a matter of hours.

He was perfectly right about that but another factor had now entered the situation—*Enterprise,* tearing up from the south. She was looking for the Jap transports but there was no information about them via radio, so a dawn search was flown out, which found Mikawa and his gang under some fleecy clouds near Rendova Island, just as the Marine strike group soared away. The searchers attacked and both secured hits. *Enterprise* had no other targets at hand for the moment; the full dive-bomber group of a major carrier fell on Mikawa a little after 1100 and gave him a terrible going over. *Kinugasa* was hit by three big bombs and down she went, burning and exploding; *Chokai* was hit again; *Maya* had a turret knocked off,

[1] Which one we do not know; the damage was overlaid by what happened later.

and *Isuzu,* the light cruiser, was so badly beaten up that there was long doubt whether she could be got home.

Of course this had the effect that Mikawa was forced to clear the area in a hurry unless he wished to lose still more ships, and he did clear it, considering himself extremely lucky that the American fliers did not return. They were after other game by this time—the transport fleet which Mikawa was supposed to be protecting and which now had only Rear Admiral Tanaka's twelve destroyers plus whatever fighters Rabaul could send. The leaders of another nation might have halted the march of those ships after Mikawa's trouble showed that the bombardment had so little damaged Henderson that American bombers were still able to come out in force. Not the Japanese; they considered that the Mikawa misfortune would divert our attention from the main object, so right on down they came with nearly all the 38th Division aboard, the 229th Infantry Regiment, the 3rd mixed, the 38th Engineers, artillery corps troops, and all the rest.

At 0949, just after the Mikawa strike had left her deck, an *Enterprise* search plane found them, in the Slot between New Georgia and Sta. Isabel. The searchers reported to both ship and Guadal. All the planes on the island, Marines and Navy Air Group 10, poured out as fast as they could be organized and then again as fast as they could reload. The first strike went in a little after noon; the cover shot down half a dozen Zeros, the bombers hit two of the transports (they were briefed as the primary targets), and the torpedo planes two more.

From that time on it was one of the most horrible nightmares the war had seen. Ship after ship was hit as the *Enterprise* fliers joined in. The transports began to burn and the men in the skies could see through torn decks the inner structure of the ships outlined in metal glowing bright red as though touched by paint. Ship after ship went down; for a mile around the water was covered by the tiny dots of heads. At the field there were grim jokes about buzzards; up in the Slot the Jap destroyers deserted the doomed convoy and the heads one by one disappeared beneath a sea that was genuinely tinged with blood.

Twilight fell; a Marine pilot out to look for another who had been shot down could see far below him only five flickering points of light that were as many of the transports, burning but still moving toward

Guadalcanal. As he watched one of these hissed out in the dark; the others pressed on.

V

Between being badly shot up in the attack on Mikawa's force and having mechanical trouble, there were only two of the Petes fit for service that night. The report was the Japs were coming down with heavy forces to bombard and the two went out to stop them, their crews feeling a little lower than worms, for what could they do against a fleet? To their knowledge they were the only surface force left to the U. S. Navy in the Solomons, the only force that could fight at night. They were off Cape Esperance at midnight, waiting for the Japs to come with the battleship,[1] and it was well that they were there for their TBS registered the most dramatic order of the war:

"This is Ching Chong Lee. Get out of the way; I'm coming through."

The battleships had arrived.

After the losses in Callaghan's action, Halsey had made the difficult decision to put those giants in there among the narrow channels and Japanese torpedoes after dark. They were all he had to put in; if they were lost or even seriously hurt, the Japanese could bombard with impunity, and in spite of the favorable position of the fighting ashore, anyone could figure out the consequences of that. The field would be out of business and all the hard fighting the Marines had done would count for nothing. He had put in Ching Chong Lee then, with *Washington, South Dakota,* and the destroyers *Gwin, Preston, Benham,* and *Walke.* They circled Savo once; at 16 minutes after midnight, south of the island heading round again, there was a wild babble of Japanese on the radiophone circuits and pips on the radar screens.

"Commence firing," said Ching Chong Lee evenly. Back on Guadal the Marines started into wakefulness at the jar of the heaviest guns afloat. There was no such melee as in the other battle. Admiral

[1] Actually the Japs had more than a battleship; Kondo's reconstituted bombardment force contained, besides *Kirishima,* the heavy cruisers *Atago* and *Takao; Sendai* and *Nagara,* light cruisers; big destroyers *Ikadsuchi* and *Terutsuki,* and other destroyers *Shirayuki, Hatsukaze, Asagumo, Samidare, Uranami, Shikinami, Ayanami.*

Kondo had come down with his light cruisers and destroyers well in the lead and they let loose shoals of torpedoes that dealt hardly with our destroyers, sinking *Preston, Benham,* and *Walke* all three. But *Washington* skipped among the missiles like a toe dancer and poured three rapid salvos into *Kirishima,* every shell hitting, smoke, steam, and a long tongue of flame pouring out. Behind her *South Dakota* was caught in the searchlights and being hit all over by 8- and 6-inch shell. She had many dead in the upper works but returned every blow with one twice as heavy. The lights died and the Japanese voices died from the radio; Ching Chong Lee was steaming back toward base and the Japanese Southeast Area Fleet had ceased to exist as an effective unit.

For *Kirishima,* like *Hiyei,* was gone; *Atago* and *Takao* had taken 16-inch shell aboard and would not fight again for long; Mikawa's squadron was out of action. There were only the light cruisers and some of the destroyers left. Nor was the report that presently came through from General Hyakutate any more encouraging. The men aboard the four remaining transports had performed miracles in keeping those ships running so that all pushed up on the beach that night, after the naval battle. On two of them the fires were even got under. But that was no good either, for on the next morning the Marine fliers from Henderson and an American destroyer, *Meade,* came along and finished them all. As for the men, the men of the 38th Division, who were to take Guadalcanal in a big sweeping operation—of them all not 6,000 reached the shore so much desired; and those 6,000-minus, naked, many of them burned or wounded, with no equipment or food beyond ten days' supply of rice, fit cases for hospitalization but not for war.

"After Guadalcanal I knew we could not win the war," said Captain Ohmae, long later. "I did not think we would lose, but I knew we could not win."

Chapter 8

Guadalcanal: L'Envoi

T HERE ARE A FEW ODDS AND ENDS TO TIDY UP AND MAKE THE picture complete. After the big battle the Japs went back to using destroyers only in the Slot, sometimes as many as twenty in a single expedition. There was a very bad show with these on the night of 30 November, known as the Battle of Tassafaronga, when Halsey tried to break up this system by sending in a cruiser squadron. The Japs had nine of their destroyers in that night, close to shore where it was hard to pick them up on radar. Carleton Wright, the American admiral, apparently did not believe the report of his leading destroyers that they had found the enemy, or else he wanted to get in closer where he could use the guns of the light and four heavy cruisers that made up his force. He held fire so long that the Japs were able to work up speed, make a torpedo run and escape, all but one destroyer, sunk by gunfire. Four of our ships were hit: *Northampton* went down, *Minneapolis* and *New Orleans* lost their bows, and *Pensacola* was badly hurt, all in exchange for that one destroyer.

This did not affect the strategic balance of the campaign. The Jap ships had come not to bring reinforcements but to take out what men they could, most technical personnel and higher officers, including Colonel Oka, who left a note for his men telling them it was the duty of the Japanese soldier to shift for himself and keep up his spirits, no matter how discouraging the circumstances. The Tassafaronga expedition was nearly the last; on the night of 12 December a reinforced group of Petes got into another destroyer formation, sank the big *Terutsuki* and beat up another of the heavy destroyers so badly that all were taken off the run.

On 9 December the command of the area was turned over to Major General Alexander Patch of the Army's XXIV Corps with Vandegrift's 1st Marine Division being relieved as fast as the operation could be carried out.

The 2d and 8th Marines were now occupying positions west of the Matanikau. On 4 January the advance echelon of the 2d Marine Division under Brigadier General Alphonse DeCarre and the 6th Marines under Colonel Gilder T. Jackson landed.

For the first time the 2d Marine Division was fighting as a unit. Both the 2d and 8th Regiments were worn down badly; the 2d had been present since the beginning, the 8th had arrived early in November, and elements of the 10th Marines (Artillery) had been in action equally long. Both regiments were riddled with malaria and fatigue and the 8th was beginning to show the effects of its sojourn in Samoa—filariasis, known to most of the Marines by its Polynesian name, *mumu*.

The Marines jumped off from a line running inland from a point just west of the base of Point Cruz, for the final drive up the coast. The Army moved along the left, inland flank. The campaign had become a grim and relentless business of hunting out small, determined groups of the enemy who fought hopelessly until killed.

The 2d Marines and the 1st battalion of the 8th left Guadalcanal on the 31st of January. The remainder of the 8th followed on 9 February and by the 19th the 2d Division had cleared Guadalcanal with the exception of a battalion of engineers. Marine air base, base defense, and service troops would be present on the island for many months to come, but for the Marine infantry the operation was over.

Malaria, beriberi, enteritis, starvation, and lack of the most essential equipment got all the Japs in the end.

All told they had put 42,000 men ashore and something less than 10,000 got away. The rest were dead, as was over half of the 38th Division in that butchery under the planes on 14 November. The American dead for the whole campaign were 1,979; the wounded approximately 6,000, a difference in the figures that is perfectly amazing when one considers the slenderness of General Vandegrift's resources during most of the campaign. The disproportion was so great that nobody on our side would believe it until we began to get into the Japanese records, and the consistent underestimate of the enemy's casualties ashore is even more striking than the consistent overestimate of his casualties on the sea.

Of course, one obvious reason for the high enemy losses is that the Jap medical service broke down completely, while ours was very good. Of their huge casualties, well over 10,000, probably nearly 20,000, were medical—disease and wounded who died for lack of medicaments and care. But this itself looks back to another failure on their side. Why did the Japanese medical service break down? Partly at least because medical supplies did not get to the island; they were bombed out and burned out on the way in, chiefly by the planes which flew from the island itself. Partly also the medical failure was only a portion of the bad staff planning which distinguished, or failed to distinguish, the whole Japanese operation for the recovery of Guadalcanal.

The staff work on our side was by no means perfect and plans frequently did not succeed. This is what one expects in war, where every contact is the result of the impact between two mutually exclusive plans. But if there is any one thing that stands out in the whole campaign it is how well our cause was served by the twenty-year background of training, planning, and experience possessed by the Marines. General Vandegrift and some of his staff were (as we have seen) pretty much worried in the beginning by what they considered the lack of training among their men and there was a good deal of beefing afterward to the effect that more physical hardening was needed. But they were looking at it from a very high standpoint, the standpoint of the U. S. Marine Corps, professional soldiers who had long ago worked out the answers to most of the problems involved. Japanese commanders, to note only one small but significant detail, complained they could not get their men to use the latrines; but sanitation is one of the first things a U. S. Marine thinks of when going ashore, especially in the tropics.

At another point there is a marked difference between the two forces involved. One is struck by the fact that the Japanese leaders, naval and military, were always waiting for somebody else to do something—the Navy for the Army to take the airfield, Kawaguchi for Oka, Oka for the Navy to shell out the American planes. It was the tradition, almost the doctrine of the Marines that, being given a job, they should go ahead and do it without yelling copper to anybody. The thing was carried too far sometimes, as in the Puller-Edson attack at the Matanikau, where the forces were simply inadequate for the job those two very energetic Marines tried to carry through. But the system has its bright side also; the dog-tired Raiders did not ask for help in the Battle of Edson's Ridge (except from the artillery, to which help they were normally entitled) and against all expectation, including that of General Vandegrift's staff, found they could hold the place.

In actual contacts, of course, much of the Japanese failure can be traced to the mystical belief that a man with Bushido and a knife is better than a man with a tommy gun and a bellyful of beans. This piece of irrationalism is fundamental; without it, or something like it, the Japanese would never have gone to war against a nation so superior in every material resource. But whether criticism really lies on this score can be questioned. Most acts of war, most of war itself, are not very rational, and the history of human conflict is full of instances where apparent material odds were overcome—within the purview of this book, at Edson's Ridge for example, and in Callaghan's desperate naval action. The true failure lies rather in that tenacity, that particular type of tenacity, of which the Japanese were so very proud—their persistence in error, their unwillingness to alter a plan once it had been set in operation. After Admiral Abe and then Mikawa had failed on successive nights to put the Guadalcanal planes out of business, one would naturally expect planners of even elementary intelligence to realize that the transports carrying the 38th Division were walking into the dragon's jaws.

In all the operations of the Marines on the island there is only one case of a similar inflexibility on our side, the move at the Matanikau when Edson, Puller, and Griffith got into trouble. Even here there was the excuse that the Americans involved were acting on faulty intelligence. At first sight it would seem that for many of the Japanese failures a similar excuse could be made; that this is the only explanation of why they put in first the Ichiki Detachment, then the Kawaguchi Brigade, and finally the Sendais against forces that were always so much superior to them. But on examination the general plea of faulty intelligence on the Japanese side does not stand up very well. Their intelligence was often faulty, but not in any

118

fundamental way. The original Japanese G-2 estimate of the number of Marines on Guadalcanal was far more accurate than the intelligence on which General Vandegrift had to work when he made the landing. All through the operation the Japanese were exceedingly well served on the sea by both their submarines and their air scouts, and if their air reconnaissance ashore was distinctly faulty, their patrols and listening posts in the Grassy Knoll region covered everything so completely that General Vandegrift could hardly cut his fingernails without having it reported across the line. After the war it was revealed that the Japanese had been extremely acute about intercepting and making use of American radio messages.

The Japanese command simply chose to disregard the intelligence it received. It went right on making elaborate plans, like that for the attack of the Sendai, as though the whole thing were a sand-table problem, in which the enemy's action need not be taken into account, with no room for the unit commander to exercise his discretion. After the plan was once made it was never on any account altered, either from above or below. The last feature is sufficiently puzzling; and at least one high American officer who has studied the problem considers that some of the difficulty here may lie in the fundamental character of the Japanese language, a poor instrument for either ratiocination or the rapid communication of ideas.

But there is not only the question of why the Japanese lost; there is also that of why the Marines won. The difference is pronounced when one sets procedures of the Marines against the specific reasons for Japanese failure. Marine training, Marine doctrine, or, to add it up, Marine experience gained through the years of peace, said very clearly that war could be made only by giving subordinates a task in fairly general terms and then letting them alone. If the officer assigned proved unequal to his task he was relieved before he could mess anything else up—and in this connection it is interesting to note that officers who flopped on one job not infrequently panned out very well on another, different kind of task, or even under another leader, with whom they could establish a more effective rapport. The system that succeeded on Guadalcanal was in fact one of treating each campaign and each part of a campaign as a separate operation, to be solved by the men on the job with native intelligence and in the light of the peculiar special conditions surrounding the

119

case. All war is, of course, made up of special conditions, but in practice this flexibility and confidence in subordinates is one of the most difficult of all things to attain and can be attained only when men have worked together for a long time on similar tasks and understand much of what is to be done without specific and detailed orders.

Chapter 9

Peripheral Operations

WHEN NEXT THE MARINES SAW ACTION IT WAS IN A different world. Guadal's a major base now, Camp Crocodile, with a lot of top brass running around, most especially Richmond Kelly Turner, who is there to plan a new operation, while planes go out all day long. Some of them are the new Corsairs, F-4Us of VMF 124,[1] first of all the squadrons to use this new plane which could really match a Zero for acrobatics. The Navy fliers had complained that not all the bugs were out of it yet and at least one air officer refused to have it aboard his carrier, but for the land-based status of VMF 124 it was just the dish. Captain Kenneth A. Walsh proved it by winning a Medal of Honor for himself for tackling a Jap formation of fifty planes singlehanded and shooting down four of them before being forced to a dead-stick landing; and later he ran up a record of twenty-one enemies before he got his leave.

There is a seaplane base at Halavo on Florida Island now; a new officers' club rising on the hill above Tulagi Harbor. Heavy Jap naval units are no more seen; they only run destroyers and some of the old light cruisers along the Slot at night. We have command of the seas south and north; if there is still only one American carrier (*Saratoga*) in the area she is supported by a British vessel of the same class, while to the south no fewer than three of the new battleships are on the prowl in case the Japanese want to make something of our forward movement. The close support is in the hands of two divisions of light cruisers and as many of destroyers, with all the men upon their bridges whose names are to stand most for dash

[1] Marine Fighter Squadron.

121

and daring in the war—Pug Ainsworth, Tip Merrill, 31-Knot Burke, Mick Carney, Fritz Moosbrugger, Cooke, and Francis X. McInerney. The new landing craft are here, to be used for the first time in the war and a fresh Army division, the 43rd, under Major General John H. Hester. Vice-Admiral Aubrey Fitch is air officer; out of the Guadal fields (there are four now) he can put on the morning of the operation 213 fighters, 170 light and 50 heavy bombers—what a change from the day when Henderson Field had only four planes fit to fly!

The operation—capture of Munda at the northern end of New Georgia Island. The Japs had an operative airfield there, having cleverly concealed its construction by cutting the tops of palm trees and slinging them on a screen under which they worked. The site was well chosen. A mad network of coral reefs made it immune to approach from the water, and approach from the land side involved a long march through pestilential jungle where the ground was always at least half liquid. They had another airstrip over at Vila-Stanmore on Kolombangara Island, northwesterly across Kula Gulf, and had worked out an ingenious system of logistics to keep both places supplied in spite of the fact that American planes dominated the area by day and American cruisers went hunting at night. Big ships brought goods from Rabaul to Buka off Bougainville. Here destroyers which could run fast or barges that could lie in concealment took over and made the run down through Blackett Strait to Vila, where they unloaded. More barges carried supplies across the gulf to Bairoko, and a jungle trail led from the shore there to the back door of Munda.

The process was not unattended by accident. On a night in January Pug Ainsworth's cruisers slipped into Kula Gulf without being spotted, caught everyone in bed and got rid of 2,000 Japs in a quick, crashing bombardment whose effect was made the worse because the first shells killed all the medics and laid the hospital flat. On a night in March, Merrill's cruisers caught the destroyers *Murasame* and *Minegumo* just after they had unloaded at Vila and sank both without taking a hit in return; and on 8 May there was the worst disaster of all. The Japs knew we were putting mines in various places because occasionally one drifted up on the beach, but Tokyo had so few minesweepers to spare that it would send none to the

Solomons, where these very tender vessels would come under American air attack during the day, the only time they could work effectively. Japan did not think, however, that our minelayers would venture so far in as Blackett Strait. Error: on the morning of 8 May as a division of big new destroyers was just making out after a supply run, one of them, *Kuroshio,* ran on a mine and began to sink at once. The others stood by to take her crew out; at this precise moment a squadron of Marine dive bombers came piling out of a rain squall on them. The destroyer *Kagero* was badly hit and as she attempted to evade ran on another mine. *Oyashio* was blown all apart by the bombers, and the fourth destroyer, *Michishio,* was so badly battered that she had to be beached twice on the way home.

The losses in planes also continued to be extremely serious. Nevertheless, Captain Miyazaki, senior air staff officer of Rabaul, was beginning to be convinced that the American advance could be held. He now had three air flotillas—24th, 25th, just returned from Japan, and 26th—and by a policy of using them only for major operations and in great strength, was managing to keep their numbers up while (he believed) inflicting serious damage on the Americans, in both ships and personnel. He had 250 operational planes from the Navy, the largest number since the beginning of the war; and the Imperial Army had been somewhat reluctantly persuaded to send down 50 of its own.

The Americans occasionally brought in cruisers to shell his fields at night and there was a certain amount of loss among planes caught in the revetments, but in no case were the airstrips dug up beyond what a few hours would repair. He felt that the losses were worth it for the deterrent effect his planes exercised on the Americans, who had twice begun massing ships near Guadalcanal as though for a move and had then thought better of it after being attacked by air. They were stopped; and even if they were not, even should they bring in forces powerful enough to capture Munda, the place could be spared. New fields had already grown up at Kahili and Balalle on Bougainville; there was a seaplane base at Rekata Bay and another at Soleken Harbor. It had taken the Americans six months to get Guadalcanal; let them spend as much time and effort on each of these other successive outposts of empire and they would grow

123

tired of all the business; Nippon would get a good negotiated peace.
A problem in military mathematics.

II

Admiral Turner's problem was the reverse; that is, the problem
of getting Munda quickly and cheaply. He did not know, of course,
that the Japanese carriers would be out of business for another year,
but he did know that after their losses in the November battles the
Japs had pulled all naval forces that really meant anything out of
the South Pacific Area and, with the new battleships floating around
to the southward, he did not particularly care if they came back.
That is, our command of the sea was limited only by occasional Jap
aerial operations. The Guadal fields would give him command of
the air when and where he wanted it; not absolute cover against
every kind of raid, but good enough. The question was purely one
of operations ashore.

In addition to the 43rd Division, there was the 37th in the background and the 25th if he needed it. He planned to use the whole of
the 43rd plus a battalion of Marine Raiders and the 9th Marine
Defense Battalion (an artillery organization) against the estimated
8,000 Japs in the Munda area. This time there were good maps and
the place had been persistently photographed; it was possible to say
with some accuracy where to put the finger. Our numerical superiority would not be absolutely crushing but in such operations a nose
count is deceptive; our air with artillery superiority on sea and shore
should be decisive.

The Marine Defense men, under Lieutenant Colonel W. J.
Scheyer, were to land on the north shore of Rendova Island about
11,000 yards from Munda and its airstrip. They had two batteries
of 155 Long Toms, borrowed from the Army, for which guns the
distance was child's play. They could give the advancing troops
good support besides wrecking any installations the Japs had in the
area. The boats carrying the 43rd would work through the passages
in a small screen of islands south of the curving New Georgia coast
and land there for a 6-mile overland push against the Japanese positions, driving the enemy into the open area around the airfield
where our shells and bombs could get at them.

124

It seemed to Admiral Turner that it would be pretty important to keep the Japs from feeding more men into the position as they had on Guadalcanal, since this factor had so conspired with our naval difficulties to prolong the campaign. The Raiders were accordingly to be taken around into Kula Gulf and put ashore at Rice Anchorage, where there was a practicable beach (most of the shore is mangrove swamp), for a push down to where they could cut the overland trail from the Bairoko barge terminal. From this point they

would come down on the flank of the Munda position. The Raider battalion was the 1st, back to the wars after a rest in New Zealand and a period of refresher training in New Caledonia to work in the new men. To it was attached a battalion each from the 145th and 148th Army Regiments of the 37th Division. The whole force was placed under command of Colonel Harry B. Liversedge, "Harry the Horse," a giant of a man who had been a shot-putter in the Olympics and, like nearly all those Raider commanders, had been hand-picked for his job by the heads back in Washington. The date for the Rendova strike was June 30, 1943.

The Rendova-New Georgia operation clicked off very neatly in its beginning stages. Daybreak was the time set; everything got ashore on the island with insignificant opposition from a handful of machine guns manned by the eighty Japs who were there, most of whom were killed by the guns of our destroyers. A Jap scout plane saw the whole business, but Miyazaki's attack aircraft were being kept back at Rabaul because of American bombings at the forward fields, and besides he had to delay sending them in, since the new pilots were not far enough advanced in their training to make night take-offs. It was 1500 before a raid could be mounted against the American beachhead. When it came it was severe enough, 130 planes, mostly torpedo carriers, one of which got a fish into the old McCawley that was ultimately the end of her. The Japs paid for it by losing no less than 101 planes in the fighting in the skies, 58 of them to Marine pilots.

There were a few hitches of course, which caused notes for future operations to be made by Scheyer's 9th Defense Battalion. The men operating the landing craft and boats became trigger-happy and peppered the trees ahead of the landing in a manner which annoyed their friends far more than the enemy. The gunners in the big landing craft shot at our planes until the 9th Defense put some observers aboard who could tell a Betty from a Corsair. There was also some of the same trouble with unloading as on Guadalcanal—the Seabees assigned to the job were too few in number, became fatigued, and had to quit while a lot of aviation gas in drums was still below high-water mark. Fortunately the Japanese aviation was so hard hit that it could take no advantage of the beach congestion.

Radar equipment gave trouble for another thing; that of the Marines had been given a low landing priority in the expectation that some of the less efficient Navy 602 radars going ashore would serve until the Marines' own big instruments were set up. One Marine instrument did get ashore, but someone had filled the generator tank with oil instead of gasoline, and it was out of action. It rained heavily on 2 July and the 602 radars failed. The Marine instruments were not yet operative and the result was that a raid of a hundred planes got in without warning that day. They missed the batteries which were their targets, but they caught everybody in the open and caused a number of casualties in the nearby hospital and command areas.

After this the 9th, later reinforced by some of the 11th Battalion, settled down to a steady pounding of the Munda positions and the rest of its history for the operation is a record of rounds fired.

III

Actually, there had been an overestimate of the number of Japs on New Georgia and underestimate of their positions. The core of the troop command there was the Kure 6th Special Naval Landing Force, opposite numbers of our Marines, the men who had established the base, with part of the 13th Infantry Regiment, which had taken some fairly heavy losses getting in, and a couple of indepandant machine-cannon companies. Along with them were a few men of the 229th Regiment from the unhappy Hiroshima Division, who had reached shore after their transports were sunk during the previous November. They arrived at Munda in their shirttails, but there had been time to rest them up a little and to re-equip them, at least to the extent of small arms and grenades: 6,000 all told, under command of Colonel Toyoharu Muda, and by the time our men landed, all suffering a good deal from exhaustion, which is one of the reasons why the defense was almost purely passive.

The exhaustion had been achieved as a result of producing positions in which a passive defense might be valid, and these positions were something new in American experience. The Japs went down five feet or more into the coral sandstone that lay under the greasy topsoil and lined these pits with coconut logs, nearly impervious to gunfire; this log barricade being carried a couple of feet above the ground with narrow firing slits. The roof was more coconut logs; on it lumps of coral were piled, earth over the whole, with jungle plants and coconut shoots in the earth. Within a couple of months over-

127

growth made such a pillbox into nothing but a kind of mammary on the jungle floor, almost undetectable, invulnerable to anything but a direct hit from a heavy gun (for which it was too small a target, considering where the 9th Defense had been placed) or from the heaviest kind of bomb (which could not find the pillboxes under the rain forest). Tanks might have been the answer, but there was not a medium tank west of San Francisco at this date, the guns of the lights were no good against the coral blocks, and their armor was too weak to stand up against the Japanese machine cannon at close ranges.

By 4 July the advance had already begun to show signs of stalling among these obstacles, and Liversedge's flank operation assumed an importance it had not previously possessed. Ainsworth took his cruisers, *Honolulu, St. Louis,* and *Helena,* in that night with the destroyers *Nicholas, O'Bannon, Strong,* and *Chevalier* to put the shore batteries out of business while seven APDs, covered by as many destroyers, moved in on Rice Anchorage. It rained and the night was pitchy-dark; the cruisers swung on a southerly course, pounding away at the Vila-Stanmore guns, then came round the curve to run northward out of the gulf. At this moment TBS carried an anxious "Hurry—come quick" and the radar screen on *Honolulu*'s flag bridge showed only one destroyer out ahead. The missing ship was *Strong,* hit squarely amidships by a torpedo from one of those nasty Jap two-man submarines and now breaking up rapidly. *Chevalier* stood in to pick up her crew; as she did so a Jap plane overhead dropped flares and a battery of four 4.9s at Enogai Inlet, undetected by previous air photos, began to shell the rescue operation. They may have killed a few men; and *Chevalier* not only collided with the wreckage of the sinking *Strong,* but was further damaged when the latter's depth charges went off.

Nor was this an end of the misadventures of the night. While the racket, flares, and shelling were going on down in the base of the gulf, some 8,000 yards away at Rice Anchorage the Higgins boats towing rubber rafts with Liversedge's men had come across a narrow but shallow bar and touched bottom. It was necessary to lighten load and as men who are going into action do not dispense with their weapons or ammunition, it was the food that went over. About the

128

time they got free and began to draw in, the Enogai battery decided it had made all it could of the *Strong* affair and shelled the landing area, adding to the confusion caused by the bar and a last-minute change in landing priorities made by the task group commander when he discovered there were not enough boats for all the men he brought.

The sum of all this was not a little disorganization down at Rice, and it was added to by the fact that in this area no satisfactory contact had been made with the natives, so the trails down to Bairoko were pretty much unknown. The march began at dawn but intense rain came down during the day and by 1600 the Liversedge force had covered only the distance to the Gizagiza River, eight miles, through rain forest with mud that was truly ankle deep and still further encouraged the men to lighten their loads. No Japs yet; but the command had to ask for food-drops from the planes, and then this food had to be carried up from Rice Anchorage, which reduced the number of fighters who could be put in line and left all something less than well supplied.

The next river is the Tamakau, only three-quarters of a mile from the Gizagiza as the crow flies; as Lieutenant Colonel Griffith of the Raiders remarked, receiving the reply from one of his men: "That may be, Colonel, but we ain't crows." Proof of the point was immediately forthcoming. The three-quarters of a mile was all mangrove swamp and it took three hours to reach the Tamakau, where there was only a single log to cross the stream and a good many men fell in. Nobody drowned but the command did not get across till 1600, when it was time to bivouac again, if bivouac it could be called in a swamp one to three feet deep in mud and water.

In the morning, 7 July, the advance went on. Now it was time to consider tactical operations. The nearest local Japs were supposed to be down at Enogai and against them Liversedge took his Raiders, sending the battalion of the 148th toward Bairoko to set up a trail block and so isolate the point he was attacking. (The 145th's battalion was guarding the original beachhead.) There was a trail junction on high ground at a place called Triri; that afternoon there was a little fight with a strong Jap patrol, the enemy being driven off and some maps captured showing what his positions were, or had been. Colonel Liversedge brought up two companies of the

145th to hold Triri, making it the point for the next food-drop, and himself leading his Raiders forward for the attack on Enogai.

It took two days to reach the place, including one false start in which the command encountered an impassable swamp, but on the 10th Enogai was carried with a rush. That afternoon the 145th brought food and water up to the Raiders, who had been without either for thirty hours. Up to now the operation could be considered as a somewhat qualified success. We had 125 casualties and the Jap dead counted 350; an additional point d'appui on Kula Gulf had been seized. But much time had been spent and this was only the apéritif before the main dish at Bairoko, since it was clear the Enogai was a shore post only, not even having a trail connection with Munda. The enemy patrols were active and it seemed likely he would not give up Bairoko without the application of more force than Liversedge could put in. He stationed his men of the 148th at Triri, moved his headquarters to Enogai, and called for reinforcements.

They came in early in the morning of the 18th, the 4th Raider Battalion of Lieutenant Colonel Michael D. Currin. Preparations were made for an attack in two columns, the rightward and heavier one consisting of the two Raider Battalions leaning their flank on the shore as they pushed toward Bairoko, while the leftward column, which was the 148th's battalion, moved out along the Triri trail. The 19th was spent in patrolling and feeling out the enemy's positions, with the attack set for the 20th. Toward afternoon of the first day it became evident that the Japs were much stronger and better situated than had been previously supposed and Colonel Liversedge decided to ask for air support for his attack in the morning.

The request produced one of those unhappy incidents that are the result of trying to apply formal principles in a type of war which is essentially a series of improvisations. The messenger had to go some distance to reach a radio. When he did reach one it was 1700, and Airsols (now under Major General N. S. Twining of the Army) had established an ironclad rule that such requests must be in by 1600 in order to insure proper assignment and briefing. The request was refused; Liversedge attacked without air support.

On the northern flank the first contact came at 1015. Almost immediately the 1st Raider Battalion found itself up against a system

130

of the same sort of emplacements as were stalling the Army over on the other side of New Georgia. There was little gain; Liversedge put his 4th Battalion in as an extension leftward of the 1st and pushed on again. By 1430 he had taken two lines of emplacements in fighting of the most intense character, but at this point the Japs opened up mortar barrage far heavier than our own, and at the same time began firing from a well-concealed 4.7.

The casualties piled up so fast that at some time during the next hour or so that shadow line was crossed where more men were occupied in caring for the wounded than there were on the firing line. At the same time word came from the Army men that they were up against equally formidable obstacles and were now being counterattacked. Harry the Horse reluctantly gave orders for a general retreat and a few days later the force was withdrawn, its operation a failure, with 243 casualties in that last fight, and the Japs' nowhere near that many.

IV

Well, why did it fail? The point that leaps to the mind at once is that we have here another case of defective intelligence, this time so defective that not even the addition of another battalion and the fact that the 1st Raiders were highly skilled jungle fighters could save the operation. The loss of food at the Rice Anchorage bar and the failure to locate the 4.9 battery at Enogai early enough for the cruisers to take care of it were the first failures in intelligence. There was a lack of knowledge about the jungle trails, which made the movement so slow the Japs had plenty of time to get set. From the activity of their patrols it seems likely they had a good count on the Marines and had pretty well taped out their lines of approach before the attack began at all. There was a somewhat forgivable lack of knowledge about those coral and coconut pillboxes.

But there seems also to have been a lack of intelligence in the other sense of the word and higher up the line than anyone at Rice Anchorage. What was the operation in essence? An attempt to take a fortified position defended by artillery with unsupported infantry. The books all say such a stunt can be done only by means of surprise, and someone in the upper echelons should have known that you are not going to get surprise in a rain forest, where the characteristic move-

131

ment is that of the three-toed sloth. The only answer to the kind of position Liversedge encountered is powerful air and artillery support, as the Army men proved on the other side of New Georgia. Artillery support at Bairoko could be given neither from the sea nor from the land. If it be answered that those higher echelons did not know Bairoko trail was fortified, well, they should have expected that it would be. The reason the attack was made was to cut off a Japanese lifeline, and if it were important enough to deserve an attack of this weight it was certainly likely the Japs would be dug in.

Finally it was a dispersion operation, contributing very little to the main campaign. After all, if the Japs did determine to reinforce Munda from Vila they would have to make a trip something over seven sea miles every time they did it. The ships or barges that made that trip would have to lie somewhere within view of our planes during the day and be under the menace of attacks by our destroyers in Kula Gulf during the night as was proved when the enemy gave up the whole reinforcing idea after the two naval battles in the gulf. The Raiders could have been far better employed on the main approach to the airfield, which went so badly that General Hester was relieved and most of the 37th and 25th Divisions were brought in under a corps organization before the approximately 6,000 Japs were eliminated by 5 August.

Nevertheless, though there was fumbling and grumbling all through the operation, one fact must not be forgotten—that the bank pays off on the winner. It took six months to take Guadalcanal; it took one month to take Munda, sweeping our airplanes all the way up to northern Bougainville and permitting our destroyers to run the Slot o' nights and win victory after victory. American sea power was beginning to tell in the war; and the savvy so hard bought by General Vandegrift's men was spreading like a liquid through all levels of the services.

V

There was one more operation before the Marines entered upon their wider sphere as the dominating influence in the Central Pacific war—the Choiseul diversion, as different from the Rice Anchorage affair as day is from night. It began when Lieutenant Colonel V. H. Krulak, in command of the 2nd Parachute Battalion, then encamped on Vella Lavella, was called down to Camp Crocodile to see General Vandegrift, now in command of the corps. The date was October 20, 1943; the situation was that the Americans had eaten up the Solomons from the tail as a pig eats a snake, till only the head was left— Choiseul and the big island of Bougainville with its air bases and as many as three divisions of troops. We were going in on Bougainville (the General said) on the night of 31 October-1 November and if our forces could make it stick, that would be pretty much the end of Rabaul, the great and menacing base from which the Japs had for two years fed all the fighting in the South Pacific. It would be so close in range from the Bougainville airfield we expected to establish that we could maintain fighter and light bomber patrols over it, inhibiting use.

The Japs would hold hard; might even bring their long-absent fleet out for major operations to retain this vital base. If we could have them, surprise and deception were much needed. For this purpose Colonel Krulak could take his battalion ashore on Choiseul a few days before the main offensive and make a great noise, shooting out patrols in all directions and contacting as many Japs as possible to give the impression that he was the active vanguard of a great force. His battalion would be reinforced up to 700 men by extra machine-gun formations. With any luck he ought to persuade them to send reinforcements over from Bougainville, at notice of which he would be instantly withdrawn.

Choiseul is the most rugged and wooded of the Solomons; it lives in a perpetual twilight under the shadow of banyan trees larger than anywhere else in the world, and the Japs there were supposed to be along the coast, living in huts, in poor shape and badly armed, since most of them were refugees from the islands lower down. (They used to take them over to Choiseul by barge from Kolombangara and Vella Lavella when our destroyers permitted, march along the trails to the northern end of Choiseul and then make another barge trip to the Shortlands.) There was believed to be a concentration of the enemy at the northern end of the island and a base of some sort on the offshore island named Guppy there; another concentration at Sangigai halfway along and a third at Kakasa near the southern tip, where submarines had been observed, either bringing in supplies or taking them out.

The details were up to Krulak; and the maps, even those compiled by careful photographic reconnaissance, were bad because of the overwhelming vegetation. He decided to land at a place called Voza, some eight miles north by the coast trail from the Sangigai concentration, and he did so on the night of 27-28 October. There were four Higgins boats for rapid shore-line operations, which were concealed under the overhang of trees at an offshore island with a platoon to guard them. A coast-watcher came out of the bush with some natives; the latter had cut a trail a mile or so uphill into the jungle to where a stream runs round three sides of a sheer cliff, a very defensible place. There Krulak set up camp, spending most of the morning getting in supplies and preparing a dummy beachhead down at the water's edge for the convenience of the Jap bombers that were pretty sure to come around.

Toward noon the battalion left camp and began pushing along the coast trail toward Sangigai, finding Jap lean-tos all along the edge of the jungle but no enemy. The native scouts reported through the coast-watchers that the nearest Japs were at the settlement whither they were bound and at the Warrior River in the north.

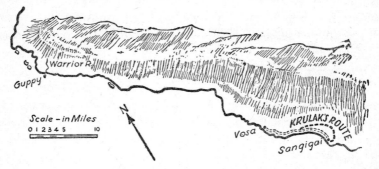

Our men camped along the trail that night. Next morning Colonel Krulak personally took a patrol out to reconnoiter, using native guides and keeping well inland across the spurs of the central mountain. The Japs were in Sangigai all right, somewhere between 100 and 200 of them. When Krulak rejoined his main force at 1500 a plan to attack the place was made, a double envelopment on a small scale. One company would work right down the coast road, going slow. Krulak would lead another company up the back alleys and along precipitous slopes to come on Sangigai from behind.

Krulak figured that the Japs would get into their foxholes at the settlement when the coast-marching company attacked, before his own detachment arrived. The move to positions began at 0900 the following morning, 30 October; five hours later Krulak and his company were closing in on Sangigai from the southeast, down the spur, not a little concerned at having thus far heard no burst of fire to signal the arrival of the other attack. Fifteen minutes later it came, the heavy whump of mortars as the coastal company shelled the town. As the Colonel's own command worked forward through the green gloom, it was surprised to run head on into the Japs, who had evacuated their town and unexpectedly tried to make back into the hills. There was a brief, sharp fight in which Krulak's men, too numerous for their opponents, worked round both flanks and shot them down or sent them tumbling back into the arms of the other company. The enemy conducted their retreat in the usual form, putting snipers into the trees, and the Colonel himself was wounded by one. Seventy-two Jap bodies were found when the two companies met in Sangigai; maybe 30 Japs got away down the coastal trail southward, whom Krulak made no effort to pursue, as his objective was publicity rather than concealment. The rather surprising thing was that the bodies turned out to be not those of refugees but strong, well-fed men with the insignia of the Yokosuka 7th Special Naval Landing Force.

The town turned out to be a minor base, as predicted, with a lot of food, medical stores, a big landing barge at the shore, and several radios which were smashed or burned. One piece of booty was a collection of Japanese charts; that evening when the command was back in its mountain hide-out language officers discovered that they had won first prize. The charts contained the complete layout of Jap minefields among the northern Solomons with the schedule of the enemy's barge movements. Krulak got off both pieces of information to Halsey's command by radio at once and they greatly simplified the whole Bougainville operation.

That same night after dark Major Bigger took 200 men north to the Warrior River to stir up the Japs in that direction. They landed just south of the mouth of the stream, worked across it and through a swamp; and next morning began to plaster Guppy island with mortar shells, starting some fires. There was quite a violent reaction;

the Japs boiled out in barges in considerable numbers and landed behind the little force at the mouth of the Warrior.

Now Bigger was in trouble, for the heaviest weapon he had was a 60-mm. mortar. There was nevertheless an answer; Colonel Krulak, advised by radio, requested and got some PT boats over from Vella Lavella. The Warrior River force fought its way through to the shore under cover of their guns. A good many more Japs were killed here; but now it was 1 November and off to the northwest toward Empress Augusta Bay the Jap air snoopers could see for themselves the big transports going in and be sure that Krulak's move was a lightweight feint.

They turned on him with everything on Choiseul, including some troops brought over from the Shortlands, and closed in from all directions. All along the trails there were practically hourly encounters with Jap patrols and Colonel Krulak estimated that nearly 1,000 of the enemy were coming from the north, another 800 from the south. The Marines mined and booby-trapped the trails and got out that night with casualties of 9 killed, 16 wounded, having knocked off over 150 of the enemy, stolen his mine charts, and persuaded him to shift his troops off balance before the big attack— about as much as could be asked of a single battalion. The scale of the operation was small so that some of the command and logistics problems that beset larger movements were missing, but it is noteworthy how the maximum was extracted from the accurately expended force employed without allowing victory to carry the command to overextension.

Chapter 10

Tarawa: The Tough Nut

O N SEPTEMBER 4, 1943, THERE WAS A CONFERENCE AT PEARL HARBOR. Present: Admiral King, Admiral Nimitz and his staff, Admiral Spruance and his, Major General Holland M. Smith of the Marines and part of his. The offensive in the Solomons had been pushed to the outskirts of Rabaul, MacArthur's in New Guinea was already in the phase of swinging westward toward the Philippines and he had adequate force for that enterprise. Attu and Kiska had been recovered, but weather, distance from our bases and nearness to the Japanese, left no future to an offensive along that line. The spine of the German submarine war had been broken, the naval forces in Europe were adequate to their present task.

On the other hand, the fleet that had once been down to a single carrier now counted six of the largest size plus five of the new light carriers and eight escort carriers. There were six of the new fast battleships and as many of the older free for Pacific operations. We had a surplus of unemployed force and the Joint Chiefs of Staff had decided to use in in an offensive straight across the clouds of Central Pacific islands against the heart of Japan. The Marines would spearhead the attack.

Thus Admiral Nimitz, explaining why they were met. He went on to announce that Spruance would have general command, with designation as head of a new organization, 5th Fleet. There would be two simultaneous attacks in this new move, one under Richmond Kelly Turner against Nauru, one under Rear Admiral Harry Hill against Tarawa in the Gilberts, with a small offshoot of the latter to take Apamama, also in the Gilberts. General Smith—who bore the picturesque byname of "Howling Mad" for no other reason except that it fitted his initials—General Smith was to be in over-all command of operations ashore, his organization being called the V Amphibious Corps. This corps contained two divisions, one of them the Army 27th Division of the New York National Guard under the Army General Smith, Ralph C., the other the 2nd Marine Division. The infantry regiments of this latter outfit were the 2nd, 6th, and 8th; we have met two of them in the Solomons where they saw a good deal of fighting. Both now ranked as veteran, formidable organizations, now thoroughly rested. The division commander was still another Major General Smith, Julian C., a rather strange personality for a Marine officer, at least outwardly—self-effacing, with a soft voice and a dreamy eye; but his brain ticked right along and there was nothing wrong with his fighting heart. He was patient and stubborn. They gave him Edson of Guadalcanal as a chief of staff.

It is to be noted that this was America's first offensive across oceanic areas against positions really held in force, with the possibility involved that the Japanese fleet would come out for a fight while it was on. The naval commander who has to do battle with a convoy under his wing, even if the troops had already been landed, is like a boxer trying to operate with an iron ball chained to his foot. Everyone at the conference knew it. There was also the virtual certainty implicit in the Japanese strategic arrangements, that they would stage vast quantities of planes through the Marianas and Carolines to their numerous fields in the Marshalls, and from those points let our shipping have it hard. Even among the Solomons, where the supply runs were short and transports could clear the unloading areas at dark, putting to sea under strong shore-based air power, we had suffered considerable losses under such attacks. In the Gilberts none of the favorable factors would be present. Moreover, the operations ashore promised to be tough in the extreme. The Japs had long been in possession of these islands and, if Munda was any criterion, would have fortified them extensively and intensively. The atolls were flat, never more than ten feet above water; there would be no accidents of ground or jungle cover to enable our men to get close to these fortifications along routes defiladed against fire. Nor would there be friendly artillery, except afloat—or, to sum up, this was the first truly amphibious operation.

138

The Marines, of course, had a background of doctrine for such operations which they had accumulated through the years. General Holland Smith and his staff possessed a considerable amount of training experience, having been in charge of preconditioning the troops for that attack on Kiska which was never made because the Japs got out. For the rest it was all new; but novel as the problem was in practice, the V Amphib Corps staff began gravely to doubt the plan as soon as they sat down in front of the intelligence reports

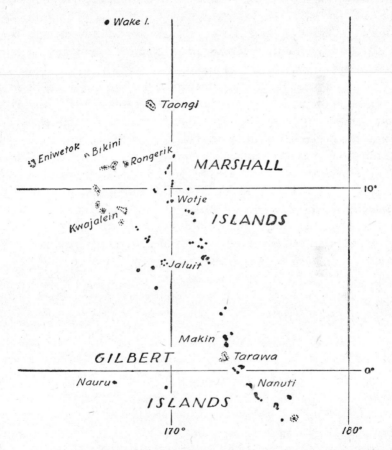

and photos on Nauru. The place is not an atoll but a monolith of limestone with cliffs nearly 100 feet high behind narrow beaches; surrounded at a considerable distance by a coral reef which has few penetrations. The cliffs were honeycombed with caves which now housed gun positions; they would almost certainly have every entrance through the reefs calibrated to the inch and it would take a direct hit on a pinpoint target to put one of those guns out of business, a thing very difficult to obtain from the distance at which the reef would hold our ships.

The corps staff took the matter up with Admiral Spruance and Spruance took it up with Nimitz. "What would you substitute for Nauru as a point of attack?" asked the latter, and Spruance unhesitatingly said, "Makin," pointing out that if that place were taken in addition to Tarawa we would have two mutually supporting airfields and Nauru would lose significance, because it could be kept ineffective by shuttle-bombing from planes running between the new Gilbert fields and the Solomons.

Makin it was, then, and assigned to it Admiral Turner's force afloat and the 27th Division. This force organized at Pearl Harbor, the 27th having been on garrison duty in the outer islands of Hawaii since the beginning of the war. The fleet in immediate support was formed round the old battleships *Pennsylvania, Idaho, New Mexico,* and *Mississippi* with four heavy cruisers and Rear Admiral Mullinix's division of three escort carriers. Cruising free to hit the Japanese fields in the southern Marshalls, and to intercept the expected air attacks from that region, would be two groups of carriers under Admirals Radford and Pownall, one of a big carrier and two lights (*Enterprise, Belleau Wood, Monterey*), the other of a big carrier and a single light (*Yorktown, Cowpens*). There were supposed not to be many more than 600 Japs on Butaritari, the main island, where Carlson's Raiders had gone ashore the previous year.

II

Tarawa loomed as a much tougher enterprise; it would be handled by the 2nd Marine Division, coming up from New Zealand. For immediate support of this job there would be the old battleships *Tennessee, Colorado,* and *Maryland,* heavy cruisers *Portland* and *Indianapolis,* light cruisers *Birmingham, Mobile, Santa Fe,* twenty-one destroyers and five escort carriers under Admiral Ragsdale. Cruising off to furnish air interception and support ashore as needed would be Rear Admiral Montgomery's group of two big carriers

140

and of a light (*Essex, Bunker Hill, Independence*). Moving everywhere needed in support of the carriers, ready to tackle the Japanese fleet if it poked its nose out of Truk, Willis Augustus Lee and the six fast battleships with a retinue of light cruisers and destroyers. Holland Smith and the corps command to be aboard *Pennsylvania* in the northern group; Spruance in *Indianapolis*.

The key island of Tarawa is Betio at the southwestern angle of the delta-shaped atoll. The island itself is a very elongated triangle, its point toward the east and the other islands that form the delta's base. The whole center of Betio is occupied by a big airfield. A long pier jutted north into the lagoon from opposite the center of this field. The air photos of the place had been carefully taken and were extremely good (compare Guadalcanal). Lieutenant Colonel T. J. Colley, of divisional G-2, estimated that the place was held by some 2,742 men, undoubtedly belonging to one of the special naval landing forces. They were provided with so many guns that the whole tiny island, about 4,000 yards long and 800 wide at its widest point, bristled with them like the back of a fretful porcupine. G-2's preliminary estimate of the situation indicated heavy coast defense guns with 8 4.7s, 11 80-mm., 14 40-mm., 4 25-mm., 69 heavy machine guns, 45 pillbox-emplaced machine guns, with 37 emplacements that could be used by the Japanese mobile artillery, of quantity unknown.

The question of taking one of the adjacent, less heavily fortified islands first and using it as an emplacement from which to beat down these defenses by artillery fire came up at the conference.[1] Navy said no. It would take a day at least to capture the subsidiary island and get the guns in; another two would be required for the bombardment plus whatever time would be needed for capturing Betio itself. All during this time the transports must lie off the island, loaded with Marines. With a chart and a pair of dividers it could be calculated that this would allow plenty of time for the Japs to stage their air reserve through Nauru and the Marshalls for those air attacks which were almost bound to prove costly, not to mention

[1] The two best short-range histories of the Pacific war both say that Army men advocated such course, but it is not true and needs correction before the idea gets embalmed into permanence. There were no Army men present at the planning for Betio; strictly a Marine Corps operation.

141

submarines. The man aboard a transport is the world's most help-less soldier. Not only this; there was more than a fair possibility that by the third or fourth day, when the island-to-island advance became possible, our carriers and gunnery ships alike would be called away to do battle, which would mean an attack without gunnery support from the sea.

No: the time factor demanded that Betio be attacked directly and in the first rush. The obvious method of such an attack was a landing on a broad front along the south beach, coming up out of the sea, but air photos showed the Japs had thought of that. Their heaviest concentration of guns and pillboxes was along this shore and they had fringed the reef off the coast with underwater obstacles of the most difficult type, heavy concrete pyramids with horns and probably mines, wired together. There was constant bad surf on this beach with the whole sweep of the Pacific behind it; only five days of the month offered landing conditions even if there were no obstacles. The narrow west beach held some of the same obstacles, offered little room for maneuver, and above the water's edge was studded with tank traps.

This brought matters down to the north, the lagoon side, where the underwater obstacles were limited to a little wire that could be easily by-passed. There was a reef off this beach, part of it sometimes exposed at low tides, but information from former British residents was that at the central part of reef and island it could be crossed by amphitracs (here to be used in combat for the first time) and the smaller, Higgins type of landing craft at all stages of tide. There were not enough amphitracs. The division burned the air with radio messages asking for more; eventually it got them, but only as the convoy was already arriving off Tarawa.

The decision was to attack on the north side, then, with three battalions going in abreast on the first wave, two to the west of the pier, one to the east, where the angle of the airstrip would give this last battalion a good field of fire to cover the advance of the other two as they cut right across the island at its middle. One of these battalions would be furnished by the 8th Regiment, two by the 2nd; the other three battalions comprising the two regiments would follow as a second wave. The 6th Regiment to be held aboard ship as corps reserve for employment as occasion dictated, either at Tarawa

142

or at Makin. With the six battalions on the beach the Marines would have a two-to-one superiority over the estimated number of Japs—a dangerously low figure, the book prescribing at least three to one for attacks on fortified positions, but there was no way to get more in.

There was to be a strong preliminary bombardment, beginning with long-range B-24s up from Funafuti, the rest from carrier planes, 1,500 tons of bombs all together, with the naval vessels putting in 2,000 tons of shells. The staff planners wanted a feint against the south beach to disperse the Japs at the moment of attack, but Navy vetoed this idea. It meant setting up destroyer protection against subs for an additional transport area; and the shortage of destroyers was such that this in turn meant taking away about half the destroyers supposed to furnish close-in fire support for the landing.

This was the plan signed Colonel Merritt A. Edson, Chief of Staff; approved, Julian C. Smith, Major General, USMC. As an annex there was provided that the V Amphib Corps reconnaissance company would be set on Apamama by a big submarine as soon as Tarawa was secured, enough troops joining this company later to clean house on the island, where not much resistance was expected.

III

In August, 1943, Rear Admiral Keichi Shibasaki took over the command of Tarawa, with general supervision of the Gilbert Islands group. The muster rolls he received for the headquarters island showed a command consisting of the Sasebo 7th Special Naval Landing Force, 1,497 men; the 3rd Special Base Force, 1,122 men of the same background and training, who had originally belonged to a special naval landing force but had now changed designation; a pioneer and construction unit, 2,217 strong; 400 men of an air base unit—5,236 all told. Of course the labor troops were not fighting men, but most of them had done at least some military service and two-thirds of them were assigned to battle positions, as either emergency riflemen or ammunition handlers, the remainder being listed as stretcher-bearers in the event of an attack on Betio Island.

The naval situation was so insecure that it had become quite probable the island would be attacked. In fact, this question had been one of the main items on the agenda during the strategic planning conference at Truk in May, when Vice-Admiral Kusaka, the new commander of the Southeast Area, met with Vice-Admiral Kondo (now heading the 2nd Fleet) and the unit commanders of the various island groups. The general plan laid down at that time was to hold the 2nd Fleet with all the main battle units at Truk, "ready for any eventuality"—by which was meant that it would either rush to the northern Solomons, in case of a heavy American attack there, or to the support of Nauru, Ocean Island, or Tarawa.

The situation with regard to aircraft was bad, due to the heavy losses in the Solomons and the defective training of new pilots arriving there. A group of twenty Army planes, for instance, had recently left Truk in flight for Rabaul and only two of them arrived. The conference decided that as fast as new planes and pilots became available they should go to Rabaul in northern New Britain. The Marshall-Gilbert area would have to get along with the units of the 22nd Air Flotilla now stationed there—some forty bombers of the 97 type and thirty fighters.

In the event of an attack on islands of the Marshall-Gilbert group there would be a counterattack in four phases: an air strike by long-range planes from the Bismarcks, which would land among the Marshalls; a continuing attack by short-range planes staged through from Truk and even Rabaul (if they could be spared); an attack by a powerful squadron of submarines; and finally, while the Americans were still astride their beaches, a major blow by the 2nd Fleet. The whole plan was designated as the "Waylaying Attack," or "Yogaki."

In the meanwhile the outer islands of the network, Nauru, Ocean, Tarawa, Mille, Maloelap, would be reinforced with troops and construction units, and everything dug in to hold an American assault at the waterline for long enough to allow Admiral Kondo's counter-stroke to develop. Admiral Shibasaki expressed himself as pleased with the progress of construction on Betio when he took over the command in August. Ashore nearly the entire island had been ringed by a barricade of coconut logs at the edge of the beaches, the logs well wired and stapled together. Tank traps were set up both east and west of the airfield and everything but the airfield itself covered with rifle pits and pillboxes well dug in, built of coconut logs with coral sand piled on their roofs, many of them concreted in addition.

144

The bulk of these were tied into the beachhead barricade, at it was planned to make the main defense at the waterline, and they were arranged to give flanking fire along the lines of wire with which the beaches were covered. There were 62 such positions for 13-mm. machine guns[1] alone; of pillboxes housing lighter machine guns there were 44. The Sasebo Force had arrived with fourteen light tanks mounting 37-mm. guns; Admiral Shibasaki had these dug into the ground and their turrets camouflaged with palm fronds. His nine 37-mm. antitank guns were similarly emplaced, but behind concrete.

Of heavier artillery there were fourteen 70-mm. guns, most of them the normal mobile battalion artillery. These also were emplaced, the island being too small for anything but static defense. There were ten 75-mm. howitzers; four 5-inch dual-purpose; six 80-mm.; four coast defense 5.5s and four fine 8-inch coast defense pieces in turrets, brought from the British defenses at Singapore, where they were no longer needed since that place had received its new name of "City of Radiant Peace." The last two sets (5.5s and 8-inch), being heavy enough to duel with warships, were mounted at the ends of the island, a pair at each end, served from bombproof ammunition rooms.

If the Americans came they would in all probability approach from the south shore. Along the fringe of reef here there had already been begun a defense system of horned concrete tetrahedrons, wired together and with mines scattered among them. Closer in to the beach were fences of clamped coconut logs that would stop an amphibious tank. Admiral Shibasaki planned to carry these obstacles right around the entire barrier reef protecting the island, but by 19 September he had achieved only a partial series at the western end of the island, enough to canalize any boat approach into fields of fire for the 70- and 80-mm. guns mounted there. After that date work on the reef barrier went much more slowly. The night and the following day were marked by a violent attack from American carrier-type[2] planes which burned up some of the buildings and

[1] The 13-mm. corresponds to our 50-caliber.
[2] It was a special task force of the new heavy carrier *Lexington* with the new light carriers *Princeton* and *Belleau Wood,* covered by three new cruisers, *Birmingham, Santa Fe, Mobile*; marking the acceptance of all these units onto the first team.

destroyed one of the observation towers, not only making reconstruction work necessary, but interfering both with pouring concrete for the obstacles and with the use of boats to carry new tetrahedrons out to position. There was also some shortage of cement; the Americans interrupted shipping.

This carrier attack also upset things at the planning level by making it clear that the Americans had some of their new carriers in service. The situation with regard to Japanese carrier aviation had deteriorated badly since the Truk conference as a result of the summer fighting in the central Solomons.

A great many planes had been lost and it was necessary to send to Rabaul even the air groups that had just been recognized for the carriers *Hitaka, Hayataka* and *Ryuho,* with the result that these ships were inoperative and no air support could be given to Tarawa except from land bases. The place being on the outer rim of defense, it was thus impossible to protect it against American carrier thrusts. Under such conditions there was no security for planes at Betio and Admiral Shibasaki had his aviation ground crews taken out at once, as capable mechanics were so urgent a shortage, and there was no sense in getting any of them killed under circumstances where their special skill could not be employed.

In November there came a further and still greater setback to the plans for Waylaying Attack. The Americans had unexpectedly landed a force at Empress Augusta Bay in Bougainville during the night of 31 October-1 November. When Admiral Omori took the Rabaul cruisers down for an attack on the transports at this place he was intercepted by a powerful American force. There was a battle; Omori reported that he had instantaneously destroyed four American cruisers, but he brought back his own force in bad shape, minus the light cruiser *Sendai* and the destroyer *Hatsukaze,* two more destroyers in sinking condition, and the heavy cruisers *Myoko* and *Haguro* suffering from gunnery damage so serious that both had to go to dock.[1] He estimated that the Americans had four heavy cruisers remaining in the area.

[1] Actually no U.S. ships were lost in the battle and only two destroyers even damaged.

146

Now the enemy could by no means be permitted to make good their hold on Empress Augusta Bay; they would put fighters in there and end the utility of Rabaul as a base. It had in fact already been necessary to remove the 26th Air Flotilla from Buin as a result of their occupation of Vella Lavella. Admiral Kondo accordingly sent down the 4th, 6th, and 8th Cruiser Divisions from Truk to make a major naval effort against the American beachhead by night, to be followed next morning by a heavy air raid. The ships reached Rabaul late on 5 November, expecting to refuel the next day and go in that night; but next morning, as they were peacefully minding their own business in harbor, a perfect torrent of American dive bombers came pouring through the overcast that just touched the tops of the mountains.[1] It was a complete surprise, since Rabaul was at that time served by only a single radar station, out on Cape St. George, and the planes had not come from that direction. The bombers nearly wrecked the whole force; *Atago* had bad leakages, *Takao*'s fore turrets were burned out, *Maya* got a bomb in the engine rooms which started a fire that burned all day and night, *Mogami* was badly hit aft, *Tone* lost her bridge and fire controls, *Agano*'s decks were cleared and all her antiaircraft guns smashed, the destroyer *Naganami* sunk, the cruisers *Chikuma* and *Kumano* were holed.

This was a dreadful affair, for it took out the cruiser screen of the 2nd Fleet and without cruisers the naval portion of the Yogaki Attack became impossible. Within the week it was followed by another disaster. Admiral Kusaka had no intention of giving up the Empress Augusta Bay area without carrying things through to the last effort. By tapping Truk for even the flying instructors he managed to assemble enough aviation for a major effort, to take place on the 12th. On the 11th he was hit as surprisingly as before by a still larger force of American carrier planes.[2] A good many planes were smashed on the ground at Rabaul; those from the satellite fields managed to take the air and out north of the Solomons found a group of three

[1] They came from the carriers *Saratoga* and *Princeton*, with which Admiral Sherman had hurried up from the south on hearing of the Jap cruisers in Rabaul.

[2] It was *Saratoga* and *Princeton* again; this time helped by Montgomery's three carriers, *Essex, Bunker Hill*, and *Independence*, which had run in all across the Solomons Sea from the north.

147

American carriers. Unfortunately they also found an extremely alert combat patrol which shot down over sixty of them in a furious air battle and as the survivors were trying to reach home a lot of Marine land-based fighters jumped them and brought the total losses up to eighty-seven.

This made it impossible to execute the aerial phase of the Way-laying Attack as planned. If the Americans were to hit the islands of the outer perimeter before the cruisers were repaired or air strength restored, the garrisons would have to depend upon fortifications and the unconquerable Bushido of the Japanese soldier. It does not appear that Admiral Shibasaki was notified of the changes in plan except for one rather vague message advising him that air forces in the Marshalls would soon be reinforced directly from Japan. The Admiral knew something was up, though; he sent through a requisition for 690 kilotons of cement and for enough more labor troops to let him construct immediately 23 additional artillery emplacements, 7 for tanks and 24 for heavy machine guns, with the weapons to fill them.

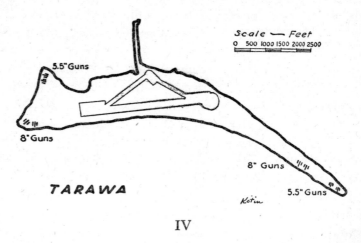

TARAWA

IV

"Are you afraid?" one of the correspondents aboard the flag of the transport group asked. "Hell, no, mister," was the reply, "I'm a Marine."

Colonel Edson was not afraid either, but he failed to share the optimistic estimates of the aviators and naval gunfire men that the huge tonnage of explosives put into Betio would enable men to walk ashore standing up—if, indeed, there were any island left for them to walk ashore on. "We do not intend to destroy the island," Admiral Hill had said. "Gentlemen, we will obliterate it."

Edson was more temperate. "We cannot count on heavy naval and air bombardment to kill even a large proportion of the Japs on Tarawa; and neither can we count on taking it in a few hours," he put it while briefing the correspondents. They were surprised; up to this point things had gone with a smoothness to which most of them were not accustomed in this war of improvisations. The loading at Wellington had clicked; several ships at a time, each done in less than twelve hours and all by 29 October. The rehearsals at Efate from 7 to 12 November had clicked far better than those for Guadalcanal and all the ships had been smoothly refueled. At D minus 2 the rendezvous with Turner's force was smoothly made at sea; on D minus 1 it turned westward and away from Makin and a big flight of B-24s went over to lay the eggs of the preliminary bombardment. There was no Japanese interference or even sighting; the carrier planes joined the B-24s and reported that nearly all the aboveground structures of Tarawa were down, they had been able to strafe at low levels and were met by only weak antiaircraft fire.

The destroyers of the escort made contact on a sub that night and the ocean heaved with the shock of their depth charges. (It was *I-25* and she never returned to Japan.) Toward midnight, as the parade of ships swung around the atoll from the south, the Japs ashore woke up and turned all their searchlights, swinging them in every direction, but not far enough out to catch the convoy, so that it was only a show.

At 0220 the transports hove to in the area northwest of the island, which loomed black down the path of the big moon. There was a little maneuvering and shuffling, since the charts were out and some currents interfered with dispositions. By 0320 Marines were getting into their boats and amphitracs with a good breakfast in their bellies. H hour was 0830, still some time away, but that meant the moment when the boats would hit the beach. First sign from the shore was just before 0500, when someone there fired a red flare; then at 0507 there was a series of flashes under the light rising across Tarawa and splashes began to go up near the ships. Just two minutes later the

149

men on the transports heard a great dull boom off to the southwest and our battleships had gone into action.

One of the earliest salvos hit something ashore and a sheet of flame soared 500 feet into the breaking day while the Marines stood on the decks and cheered. (After it was all over they found that one of *Maryland's* 16-inch armor piercers had exploded inside the "bombproof" magazine for a pair of 8-inch.) The bombardment went on like the slow beat of an enormous drum till 0542, when the shore guns had fallen silent and an order was given to cease fire in preparation for the carrier air strike that was to follow instantly. The planes were late for a reason which no one, not even the commanding admirals, was ever able to ascertain; nor did word of the lateness get through either because aboard the flagship *Maryland* the shock of her own heavy artillery had damaged some of the communications equipment and the rest was overloaded. (Everyone in the Tarawa operation seemed possessed of an irresistible desire to express himself on the air.) There was also to be a bombardment by Army planes, B-24s, from Funafuti, but they never came. It seems the unit was not too experienced, and the first plane, the squadron leader, crashed in the water at the take-off. So did number 6, and the remainder of the pilots, eighteen of them, refused to take off with such loads, as they had a perfect right to do. The four in the air had no leadership and were not even sure the island they reached was Tarawa. It was not.

Instead the Japs ashore began shooting again, this time dropping shells right into the transport area, with straddles on two of these very tender vessels and the certainty they would soon get hits. The size of the splashes was the first certain knowledge given our people that the Japs had 8-inch and 5.5s in there. The transports scuttled northward with the boats already in the water following as best they could; *Maryland* led the line in again and took up the matter of these shore guns. She did a good job of it; one of the 8-inch was found later with its whole barrel blown off by a direct hit and at least two of the 5.5s seemed to have been put out of business at this time, but the remaining Jap artillery kept dropping shells among the transports and they had to move still farther seaward. The carrier planes grew later and later; Admiral Hill signaled that H hour was postponed to 0900.

150

At 0620 the planes came at last. The schedule called for twelve torpedo bombers to hit each of the three main battery positions with a 2,000-pounder each, the scout bombers to use 1,000-pounders on the dual-purpose batteries, the remaining torpedo bombers to drop sticks of 100-pounders and the fighters to strafe. The whole island heaved in a tumult of smoke and dust; it was found afterward that the last of the 8-inch guns had taken a direct hit from a 1,000-pounder dropped by one of *Chenango's* fliers. Yet amid that tumult which so impressed less experienced observers a few men were growling. Marine officers who thought they knew the explosion of a 2,000-pound blockbuster when they saw one and who had not seen any. They were there, but not as many as expected; the Army planes that were to bring more 2,000-pounders never showed up at all, and the total weight of bombardment amounted to less than half of the scheduled 1,150 tons.

Never mind that now; the little boats had begun their long walk across the water while ahead the minesweeper *Pursuit* was pushing into the lagoon to lay a smokescreen, and outside the battleships and cruisers paced up and down, firing steadily now on area targets, the whole island being so covered with the smoke and dust of explosions that nothing specific could be seen. Nevertheless, there was recurrent fire against *Pursuit;* the destroyer *Ringgold* moved in to cover her and was herself hit three times, right amidships, one of the hits putting an engine out of action. There was another hitch here; the day had come in bright and clear, but with a strong unseasonable wind sweeping in from southeast across island and lagoon. The skipper of the minesweeper found that when he laid his smoke pots the wind would blow it right back in the faces of the advancing Marines and asked permission (granted) to call the smoke-screen project off.

The men in the boats did not worry too much about that; there was plenty of smoke on the island from shell bursts. But as they reached a point 3,000-4,000 yards from the beach there began to be airbursts over the landing craft from Japs 75s, then the water was stirred by long-range machine-gun fire and some from 37s. There were no casualties yet, the bursts were too high and too small, the fire of the smaller guns wide. A scout-sniper platoon under Lieutenant William Deane Hawkins pushed right through it to make the first contact, on the long pier. The scout-snipers worked expeditiously in toward the shore, cleaning out a couple of storehouses with flame throwers, while a gasoline dump at the end of the pier burned furiously, throwing off a long rolling tail of smoke.

V

Now came trouble. As they reached the reef the Marines found that the southeast wind had blown the water off it beyond all expectation; only the amphitracs carrying the first wave could get through, the Higgins boats behind grounded. The men in the latter had to jump out into water up to their necks and wade inland for nearly a mile, loaded with heavy combat equipment. Precisely at this junction (for it was now 0900, H hour as set) the fire of the fleet lifted from the beaches except that of the destroyers *Ringgold* and *Dashiell* in the lagoon having a private fight with some guns east of the pier. As we have seen, most of the heavy coast-defense pieces had been disposed of by shellfire or bombing; but the 37s, 13-mm., and heavy machine guns of the beach barricade, well covered in, were immune to anything but a direct hit on the aperture from an armor-piercing shell and there had been very few such hits. The cease fire at 0900 gave the men in those defenses just enough respite to recover from the shock of the bombardment, and now they all opened up at the Marines wading for the beach and the amphitracs that had crossed the bar.

Amphitracs were hit in the water and every man in them killed by mortar and 37 shells. Amphitrac drivers in the new machines that had come out at the last moment were killed by small-arms fire when it proved that these had no protection for the driver. Waders were killed right and left, something like 20 per cent of the terrible casualties at Tarawa taking place in those few minutes. As the men of the first wave hit the beach at 0917 they found themselves on a ten-yard strip of sand raked by fire and with a high coconut sea wall behind it. The moment they tried to climb the wall more machine guns fired into them; a good half of the men who tried to work inland were cut down, and in the area just west of the pier, where Lieutenant Colonel Amey's battalion of the 2nd Regiment had landed, it proved utterly impossible to run the vehicles through or over the wall as planned. Six of the battalion amphitracs were hit in the water. Amey

152

himself was killed and Major Rice, his replacement, was pinned down in a shellhole, out of communication.

Major Henry P. "Jim" Crowe's 2nd Battalion of the 8th Regiment got to land east of the pier with light casualties, chiefly because the destroyers were working over that area, and two of his amphitracs slipped through the barricade to reach the northward projection of the airfield. Then they were stopped by a big blockhouse on their left which opened fire on them with 37s, and heavy machine-gun fire ahead. There was another blockhouse to right of Amey's battalion which squeezed it down toward Crowe's position. The same structure with a number of others had driven the 3rd Battalion, 2nd Regiment, well westward and out of touch with the others to the tip of the island, where the big Jap batteries had been.

This was Major J. F. Schoettel's battalion. At 1500 he was still in a landing boat offshore, isolated from his men as they were isolated from the other landing teams, and Major Ryan had to take over command till a positive order from General Smith sent Schoettel in to "land at any cost." This battalion managed to get one message through—"Issue in doubt"—but it was about the only message they did get through except by means of amphitracs taking out the wounded. The TBY radios had been drowned during the wading process and failed utterly. There were no others. Neither the warships shelling other parts of the island nor the carrier planes cruising overhead could get any word from the beach, any identification of our line, or give the support they were so anxious to render.

By 1000, except in Major Crowe's area, the beachhead was nowhere more than 20 yards deep and that 20 yards still held concealed snipers who shot men in the back. Colonel D. M. Shoup of the regiment had come ashore and now called for reinforcements, the 1st Battalion, 2nd Marines in the same area as the 2nd Battalion and the 3rd Battalion, 8th Regiment, in Major Crowe's area. Some light tanks began to get in. But the 3rd Battalion, 8th Regiment, was caught on the reef in Higgins boats and heavily shelled so that it was completely disorganized by time it reached the shore by wading in on both sides of the pier. There was no artillery, the Jap guns were too heavy for the light tanks. All the units on the beach had lost a lot of officers and became much intermingled so that the whole thing turned into a soldiers' battle. At the main landing there was still no

153

word from the Schoettel-Ryan battalion down at the peak of the island. The condition at the beaches was bad, ammunition and everything else needed, unloading slow. The fire from the anti-boat guns did not cease.

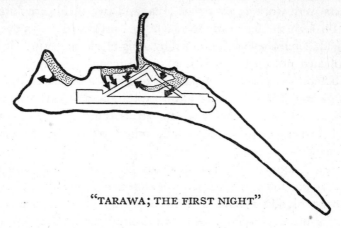

"TARAWA; THE FIRST NIGHT"

A report went out to General Julian Smith: "We need help; situation bad." Early in the afternoon that officer asked for the use of the corps reserve, the 6th Regiment, still aboard transports. As things were going so well up at Makin that it evidently would not be needed there, he got it. It would be just after this that Major Ryan at last got a radio working and reported from his isolated station. He had six tanks in action and had made a nice gain, a full 150 yards down the western beach, though there were still some fortifications north of the airfield that kept him from reaching eastward and hooking up with the main movement.

That was the situation by the night of the first day,—the 3rd Battalion, 2nd Regiment, solidly established at the island's tip; two battalions of the 2nd and two of the 8th maybe 75 yards along a floating, uncertain line at the pier. These last four battalions had had something like 35 per cent losses and these losses had fallen where they could least be afforded, on key men, like company commanders and platoon sergeants. The units were disorganized, the men were tired, and the commanders awaited a Japanese counterattack with something like apprehension.

That counterattack might have been very serious under such conditions, but it never came. The Marines did not know it at the time but they had derived an unexpected benefit from the preliminary shelling. It had completely knocked out the Japanese communications system, not a line of wire working, not a portable radio working on the island. There were many hundreds of the enemy still alive, well hidden in the bombproofs and full of fight; but they were isolated little groups who could not get in touch with one another even by runner because of the constant presence of our fighter planes, strafing everything that moved in the Jap-held parts of the island. A few of them stuck their heads out of holes, but the Marine division was well trained and battle experienced; there was no wild firing to give away positions, and the Japs ducked back.

During that night of D day, 20 November, in fact, a crisis was met and passed—a double crisis on sea and shore. Instead of a counterattack there arrived in the area around the pier the guns of "Pres" Rixey's battalion of the 10th Regiment. They were pushed right up to the front, where the single bulldozer on the beach built embankments around them. (When they opened fire next morning the first shot was at 75-yard range.) The men got some rest and had a chance to find that more of them were alive than dead; they knew reinforcements were coming.

The crisis on the sea was in Admiral Spruance's cabin on *Indianapolis,* rocking to the long Pacific swell. After dark had fallen officers began to come aboard for conference. The operation was a failure (they said); it was likely, nay certain, that under the present leadership there ashore Betio would not be taken for days, and all the airplanes in Japan would be down on the fleet through the Marshalls. Let us do this, let us do that, let us relieve one officer and put in another, row, row, row. Spruance heard them, his granite face impassive. When they had finished, he said:

"Gentlemen, there are a number of Marine officers on that beach in whom I have the utmost confidence. The operation will proceed as I planned."

VI

Through somebody's failure to pass along an order, the remaining battalion of the regiments ashore (1st Battalion, 8th) had remained in the boats most of the night, grouped around the minesweeper *Pursuit,* which was the control vessel. As soon as this was discovered

155

they were ordered in but did not get away before 0530, at which time it was already breaking light. There was the usual trouble with the reef (the southeast wind held steady) and as the men began to wade and swim ashore they took a good many casualties from machine guns mounted in the wreck of an old freighter near the pier, to which the Japs had swum out during the night. Air support was called for and a file of fighter-bombers came over to drop all round the wreckage, only two of them hitting her, but that seemed to be enough. When the battalion reached the beach it was faced westward at the limit of the 2nd Regiment's position. The 2nd and 3rd Battalions, 8th Regiment similarly formed a line facing eastward, while what was left under Colonel Shoup received orders to work toward the south shore of the island, across the airstrip.

He made slow progress at first and there were some pessimistic messages to Division Command, where Julian Smith was trying to work out the best method of employing the 6th Regiment. The 1st Battalion, he decided, should be put in at the western end of the island down toward its southern tip, where the outer main Jap battery position had been. There was a tangled maze of fortifications just beyond the end of the airfield there and the 3rd Battalion, 2nd, did not seem strong enough to deal with them. The 3rd Battalion, 6th, was ordered to Bairiki, the island just east of Betio; toward dawn air observers had reported some of the Japs getting across the narrow water gap between the two and it was desirable to stop them. This battalion took some artillery with it for long-range directed fire against the eastern end of Betio. Meanwhile there were those discouraging reports from ashore. General Smith quietly ordered the organization of his headquarters and communications men as a final reinforcing battalion of the division and prepared to take them to the beach under his own leadership to fight through.

He did not have to carry matters so far. After a holdup at the airstrip, which the men quite understandably hesitated to cross since there was no cover and it was swept by a good deal of fire, the 2nd Regiment began to filter through by twos and threes. Sometime after noon its advance elements reached the south shore and were taking Jap beach defenses from the rear, working them over methodically with TNT demolition charges and flame throwers. The valiant Lieutenant Hawkins was mortally wounded in that operation after fight-

ing in a manner which led to a posthumous Medal of Honor and
designation of the airstrip as Hawkins Field.

At the western end of the island the Schoettel-Ryan battalion also
made good progress by infiltrating, and a little after 1700 the 1st
Battalion, 6th, under Lieutenant M. K. Jones was released for landing. They mostly went in in rubber boats, since mines had been detected off and at the shore. The wire of the beach obstacles was too
much for the rubber boats and when they tried a gap in it they found
the Japs had this gap exactly registered from a pillbox which was still
an active volcano, so they had to work up to the northwest tip of the
island and pass through the men already there. Even so one of the
only two Higgins boats they used blew up on a mine and everyone
in it was killed.

Their objective was a big blockhouse at the western end of the
field, one of those which had given trouble to the 2nd Regiment.
They did not get it that night but their methodical cleanup program
so much reduced the anti-boat fire that on the evening of D plus 1
jeeps and self-propelled guns were coming in over the pier. The Japs

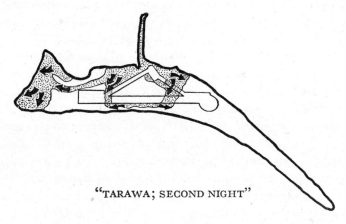

"TARAWA; SECOND NIGHT"

got one of the 5.5s at the eastern end of the island back into action
that night and began to fire shells slowly; the destroyers had to put it
back out of action again.

Next morning, 22 November, General Smith came ashore. On his
arrival he found things in pretty good shape. Jones's battalion had
cleaned out the big blockhouse and the pockets surrounding it except
for mopping up; the 1st Battalion, 8th, was making steady progress

157

westward toward a junction with the 3rd Battalion, 2nd, and the two destroyers in the lagoon were now giving steady effective support. The remainder of the 8th Regiment was working eastward to just beyond the end of the airstrip where there was a long tank trap, on its way laying siege to the big blockhouse that had given trouble all through the two days. The Colonel said he could take it (he did) but that his men were so beat up they would have to be relieved that night. It would be about the time this interview was going on that Tokyo reported all communication with Tarawa had ceased.

General Smith brought the 3rd Battalion, 6th, in over the now secure western beach and planned a general concentration toward the eastward, with the 6th Regiment carrying the ball. His intention was to exchange the fought-out 8th Regiment with the 2nd Battalion, 6th, over from Bairiki, making the shift that night. In this was another of those misfires in which Tarawa abounded. There were no boats available to move the men. When the landing teams had been boated originally the skippers of the transports had insisted upon a general unloading into the boats—all sorts of items, food, ammunition, trucks, gas and oil, into each craft as it came along. There had been no opportunity to unload most of these supplies and there they still were, jamming the boats floating around in the lagoon.

As it turned out the 2nd Battalion, 6th, was not really needed on Tarawa. That night, the night of D plus 2, the remaining Japs had been crowded closely enough into the eastern tongue of the island so they could get in touch with each other and they put on a counter-attack—not a very good one in a technical sense, since it bore some resemblance to a banzai charge. The island was so flat that our people could see the Japs assembling under the moon. Fire was called for from the supporting artillery, from the guns on Bairiki, and from a destroyer. All three of the Jap attacks, which were made at four-hour intervals through the night, were really broken up before they got underway, though they came on boldly enough and there was some hand-to-hand work in the battle positions. 475 dead Japs were counted there in the morning; and by 1330 of the next day the island was declared secure, all resistance over. This was not quite true, as there were isolated snipers there for days, but for practical purposes it stood up. Tarawa had cost us 985 Marines killed, 2,183 wounded; something like 100 Navy killed and twice as many wounded. All the

158

Japs except 17 wounded prisoners were dead; we also captured 129 of the labor troops, who were Koreans and willing to surrender.

VII

Makin had fallen to the 27th Division with comparative ease; there were only 848 Japs on the island. Apamama was almost a joke. The reconnaissance company of the V Amphib Corps landed as planned from the submarine *Nautilus* but as it progressed met fires, so the men took position and asked *Nautilus,* which had big guns, for support. A passing destroyer joined in and the two of them made such good practice that when the advance was taken up again our people discovered that all the Japs not killed by shellfire had committed suicide.

From what has been already said it will be clear that the expected naval and aerial counterattacks did not develop. Spruance kept his fast carriers moving around rapidly, hitting Nauru with them on 19 November, while Radford and Pownall's groups went in on Mille, Kwajalein, and Jaluit three days running, the 18th, 19th, and 20th. The Jap planes on Nauru tried to strike back, a torpedo attack at dusk, and lost eight of their number. Of course the 22nd Air Flotilla did what it could in the way of bomb and torpedo attacks, chiefly at night and along the lines of those which had given fairly good results during the fighting in the Solomons. On 21 November they got in on Montgomery's group just taking planes aboard west of Tarawa and managed to hit *Independence* in the stern with a torpedo—not very serious damage but enough to take her out of the campaign. This operation also cost eight planes. Planes were sent down from the Empire as our people had expected—the 24th Air Flotilla, down to forty bombers and thirty fighters. As usual with these emergency arrangements, the group had neither completed its re-equipment nor properly trained in its new men after the hard experiences in the Solomons. They did not reach the Marshalls till 25 November and by that time it was too late. Most of the Marines who had fought so hard for Tarawa were already re-embarked, the transports were out of the area, and the airstrips both there and at Makin were in operation, with patrols of land-based fighters and B-25s working out of the fields. Under these conditions neither the 24th Air Flotilla nor the remnants of the 22nd could undertake any real operations. They settled down to a routine of daily scouting and nuisance raids at night by one or two planes.

The submarine divisions had a little better luck. Like the reinforcement air flotillas they were too late in reaching the area, not making it till 23 November, when the show ashore was practically over. But toward dawn of the next day one of them, the big new *I-35,* managed to make an approach on the escort carrier *Liscombe Bay* and got a torpedo into her. Magazines and gas storage aboard the jeep carrier exploded, she became a mass of flames in a matter of minutes and 712 men lost their lives, including Admiral Mullinix. *I-35* paid for it with her own life, however. Working south toward Tarawa from the area of her success, she was spotted by a plane which summoned the destroyer *Murray* to the scene. *I-35* dodged and held out until late in the afternoon when two other destroyers, *Meade* and *Frazier,* caught up with her and she disappeared forever from contact and surface.

None of the other submarines accomplished anything and one of them, *I-19,* got herself sunk by the destroyer *Radford* three days later, when she tried to get nosy about what was going on near Makin Island. Admiral Kondo did bring four of his battleships with a couple of divisions of destroyers forward to Eniwetok but he failed to reach the place before 3 December. He had no carriers at all, was very short on cruisers, and, when he found his air cover would consist only of the battered 22nd Flotilla and the ragged 24th, considered it too dangerous to push on toward the Gilberts. He would get nothing there anyway but a naval battle, since the radios were proclaiming that both Tarawa and Makin had fallen.

The whole Yogaki plan was thus a complete washout in a strategic sense, and it deserved to be, for essentially it was a plan that demanded much more time than the slam-bang attack of the Marines allowed. Ten days would not have been too much for the execution of Kondo's scheme, even had his cruisers and air arm been intact; a week was absolutely essential. It is possible that if the original landing had been made on Bairiki a week would have been taken, but under the circumstances there was no chance whatever for a counterstroke.

On the other hand, it was not entirely a case of whistling in the dark when Imperial Headquarters issued a bulletin on Tarawa which, after referring to the defenders as "the flowers of the Pacific," remarked that "there were simply not enough men; but we have learned valuable lessons about the defense of islands." There had been radio reports from Admiral Shibasaki until the afternoon of the 22nd. They seem to have been clear and very accurate as to the details of the Marine tactics, fire, and air support methods. The Japanese had also been assiduous in picking our radio messages out of the air and had learned a lot from them.

On the operation as a whole our side probably learned more; certainly more that was of immediate value. The Japanese were much better dug in than expected and their positions were much less vulnerable to both bombs and gunfire, but the key point here was quite clearly not so much the strength of the positions or the fact that the original estimate erred as to both the number and caliber of the defending guns. The crucial question was the lack of co-ordination between our infantry attack and its preliminary and supporting fires; the fact that less than half the promised tonnage of bombs had been put into the island (the Navy exceeded its promised shell tonnage by a little) and that even delivery of this reduced amount of bombs was badly co-ordinated. There would have to be a good deal of tightening up in this respect for the future and the matter was immediately a subject of intensive study. At the same time it was obvious that these coconut and coral prepared positions could be taken only by infantrymen crawling on their bellies. There was no easy way.

There were other lessons as well, one of the most common being the value of good communications. D day at Tarawa would not have been half so bad but for the failure of those miserable TBY radios, a Navy model of the walkie-talkie which was too complex in any case and then not waterproofed. When good communications were available on the night of the 22nd the destroyers in the lagoon laid their fire only 50 yards ahead of the lines with the utmost success.

Finally, there had been a good deal of trouble about boating, attended by often frantic efforts on the part of control officers to discover which of the loaded Higgins craft out in the lagoon held a case of mortar ammunition or blood plasma that happened to be urgently needed at the moment. After Tarawa the amphibs detailed a certain number of landing craft as floating supply dumps to be

161

held offshore, with the contents of each clearly indicated so things could be found when needed.

Tarawa produced another effect also, an effect on the country at large. There had been battles and heavy casualties in this war before, but they trailed out over long periods of time and space. Here on an insignificant lump of coral over 3,000 men, nearly a quarter of a division, had been hit in the space of seventy-two hours. The reaction was one of shock and horror; and for many it was the first realization of what war against a nation of fanatics really meant.

Chapter 11

The Marshalls: Offensive in High Gear

WHEN ASKED ABOUT THE PROJECTED WAR WITH THE United States, the great Yamamoto had remarked that the Imperial Navy was confident that it could maintain itself victorious for two years, "But after that I don't know." The question, he continued, was one of industrial potentials. The U. S. was quite capable of building a very formidable fleet in two years' time, and peace should either be conquered by that date or the Japanese position rendered secure against attack so that the development of the Southern Resources Area could be carried forward to the point where Japan's own industrial potential matched the Americans'.

Yamamoto was gone, shot down over the Shortlands, before his two-year period reached its term, but the Navy General Staff he left behind felt that nothing had happened in the interim to invalidate his preliminary estimate of the situation. They had always been a little restive under the "Manchuria Gang," as they called the men who seized power with Hideki Tojo at their head; and in October, 1943, they considered the time was ripe to bring pressure through the Jushin for the removal of the Premier.

The Jushin was one of those Japanese corporate bodies whose position it is so very difficult for an Occidental to understand—probably because it cannot be precisely defined. The word means senior statesmen; they were mainly ex-premiers, nominally retired and without official position except as a few of them held memberships in the Privy Council. Nearly all were close to the Emperor and their indirect influence was immense, especially on matters of broad policy. They had a tradition of always acting slowly, and only on the most elaborate and convincing evidence, which gave the greatest weight to anything they said. In preparation for an approach to this august body the Navy General Staff appointed a member of its ministerial section, Rear Admiral Soichi Takagi, to prepare quietly a careful over-all study of the war, with special reference to naval, aerial, and merchant ship losses, how they affected the development of the Southern Resources Area and the transport of supplies to metropolitan Japan.

In any polity where so much is done as a result of gossip it is impossible to keep an enterprise of this kind secret, and Admiral Takagi had hardly begun his study before Tojo became aware of what was going on. His answer was only semipolitical (in Japan military operations were politics and vice versa); he ordered the organization of a series of amphibious brigades under control of the Army for the reinforcement of the outer islands of empire. This would bring these islands, where the American attacks were falling, under Army rather than Navy command. It would also reduce the Navy's Special Landing Forces and Special Base Forces to the role of subsidiary units; would require any reports from the battle areas to reach the Jushin and the Emperor through the Army; and would enable the Army to have more voice in controlling the movements of naval vessels and aircraft, since the security of Army troops would be involved.

The first of these brigades was naturally organized in the Manchurian Army, the source of Tojo's power. It had a foundation of infantry but an unusual number of mortar, machine-cannon, and artillery units. It was unready at the time Makin and Tarawa fell but after that double event it was at once sent out to the Marshall Islands, the activity with which the Americans were attacking these places from the air making it likely that their capture was the next thing on Pearl Harbor's agenda. The situation with regard to the aerial defense of the Marshalls was no better than it had been at the time of the Tarawa attack. Planes were lacking even for the reinforcement of the 24th Air Flotilla. But the reports from Tarawa were so eloquent about the value of fortifications that the 1st Amphibious Brigade was given a large allotment of concrete, steel, and other building materials, scarce though these were in the home islands.

To Rear Admiral Monzo Akiyama, commanding the Marshalls region, it seemed obvious that the Americans would make their first attacks on Mille and Maloelap, the outermost atolls of the chain, in order to obtain tactical surprise. It was to these that the earliest arrivals of the 1st Amphibious Brigade were sent, together with the bulk of the construction materials and contingents of laborers. The movement was severely interfered with by American planes up from Tarawa and Makin, which attacked everything on the water. It became dangerous to send large supply ships farther forward than Eniwetok. Their cargoes were either warehoused there or trans-shipped at once into small vessels of 100 tons and less, which stood a good chance of evading American aerial observation and would not represent heavy unit loss even if discovered. Several of the larger submarines were requisitioned for the transport of small-bulk, high-priority cargoes. At the atolls underwater obstructions and beach defenses on the lagoon side received first priority. The fact that the Tarawa attack had come from this side was very astonishing and since the Americans had gained their objective by such a procedure, they would evidently try it again.

II

As early as July of '43, while the fighting was still going on on New Georgia, Admiral King's staff had sent through a general directive naming the Marshalls as the next point of attack following the Gilberts operation. This directive contemplated a break-through in the line of the eastern Marshalls, Maloelap, Jaluit, Wotje. But when it reached CINPAC doubts arose. In a military sense this would be frontal attack, the most expensive and difficult form, the only advantage to be gained from it being surprise. Admiral Nimitz's staff did not think the surprise would be particularly surprising if the operation followed that of Tarawa. They came up with the idea of attacking the enemy across his line of communications, at the rear atoll of Kwajalein.

This involved serious difficulties and Admiral Spruance, who was in command of the whole operation, was the first to point them out. The march up would have to be made into a perfect maze of Japanese air bases and the amphibious forces off the beach must lie under aerial attack from all points of the compass—from Wake in the north, from Eniwetok in the northwest, the Carolines to the southwest, Nauru almost directly south, and the outer screen of the

165

Marshalls to the east. At this date the Japs in the central Solomons were still staging strong counterattacks by air and no one at Pearl Harbor had any conception that their squadrons were in the shape that had led the Imperial Naval Staff to approach the Jushin. Spruance's objection seemed well founded and was passed on to Forrest Sherman, the flying admiral who had the old *Wasp* and had just come in as Nimitz's war plans officer.

He believed the Jap air bases could be neutralized. There would be two additional heavy carriers available by the end of January, when the Marshalls attack was to take place, *Intrepid* and the new *Lexington;* four more escort carriers; and four of the new light carriers, *Cabot, Monterey, Belleau Wood,* and *Langley.* Not counting the help of the Army's 7th Air Force, land based, these should be enough to put such concentrations on Eniwetok, Nauru, and the eastern Carolines that the enemy would find it difficult to stage in any really formidable attack groups. By moving the fleet up the western flank of the Gilberts there would be land air cover from Funafuti and from the new bases to be seized at Tarawa and Makin.

The plan was set up on that basis although Spruance was still disposed to disagree a trifle. General H. M. Smith's V Amphib was the corps organization in charge. Kwajalein is one of the largest atolls in the whole Pacific, and preliminary intelligence reports indicated that two of its islands, Kwajalein itself at the southern end and the double island of Roi-Namur on the north, were strongly held. Two divisions of troops were earmarked for the task of taking the atoll—the Army's 7th Division (Major General Charles H. Corlett) for Kwajalein, the now-veteran outfit which had taken Attu in the Aleutians; and for Roi-Namur a brand-new Marine division, the 4th, under Major General Harry Schmidt, in training at Camp Pendleton, California. This outfit's normal training was almost insensibly carried over into rehearsals for the Kwajalein attack. The division had the usual three regiments of infantry (23rd, 24th, and 25th) and one of artillery (14th). An extra regiment of Marines, the 22nd, not attached to any division, was to be held aboard transports in corps reserve and so was an extra regiment of Army infantry, the 106th of the 27th Division. The total force for the expedition was thus two regiments larger than that for Tarawa-Makin.

In other respects also the lessons of Tarawa were taken to heart and worked into the plan as the day for Kwajalein approached. Submarine and air scouting had given a good picture of the atoll as the headquarters and central distributing point for the whole Marshalls group and it had been noted that after Tarawa there were considerable troop movements into the region. Intelligence estimated that there were not less than 7,100 fighting men there, a figure that might be run up to 12,000 by last-minute arrivals. They would have far

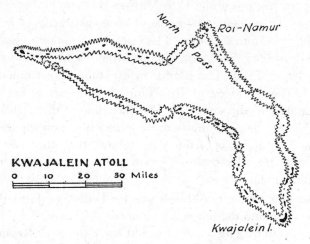

KWAJALEIN ATOLL
0   10   20   30 Miles

less gunnery support than Tarawa, since the most careful scansion of the Roi-Namur photos failed to reveal more than one coast defense gun (probably a 5.5), two twin-mount AA pieces, ten 37s, and nineteen heavy machine guns, with seven blockhouses and thirty smaller pillboxes. But with so many Japs present who could hide in a hole in the wall, it was decided to take no chances in the way of preliminary bombardment.

It was desirable to keep the carriers on the move and ready for the omnipresent possibility that the Jap fleet might come out or strong air squadrons be staged down through Eniwetok for a counterattack. Therefore the scheduled bombing was made far less than at Tarawa but the total of naval bombardment was nearly doubled, and it was arranged that this bombardment be delivered in a two-day period of deliberate, observed fire against specific targets. Destroyers in close support had worked so well down in the Gilberts that three of these craft were assigned to move into the lagoon with the transports, getting close enough so they could spit in the eye of the enemy ashore and furnish both preliminary and call fire.

By time the final plans were drawn Tarawa was over and done, where the enemy had not come down in the air strength expected; and since in any case the success of the operation depended upon putting his supporting fields out of business, an operation lasting several days could be contemplated. There were dots of land flanking Roi-Namur on either hand. It was decided to take these in a preliminary operation, install the 14th Marines on them and give the landing teams the immediate support of their own artillery in addition to all they got from the ships. There was no question of lack of time on this operation; land-based planes would hold off interruption if the carriers did not. The islands in question were Ennuebing and Mellu to the southwest of Roi-Namur; Ennugarret, Ennumennet, and Ennubirr to the southeast. One battalion of the 25th Regiment would handle the preliminary overrunning phase on the former pair with two battalions of artillery to follow, the other two infantry battalions to take the southeast group with again two artillery battalions coming in later.

This attack on the out-islands was for D day, 31 January, during all which day and the following night the ships were continuously to shell Roi-Namur. This method would leave the 25th Regiment in a convenient position to act as reserve for the other two, which were to go in next morning when it had become fully light, the 23rd Regiment with two battalions abreast on Roi, the 24th in a similar formation on Namur. The two islands are connected by a causeway and are widely different in character, Roi almost completely occupied by a big airfield with its strips in a figure 4, so that all defenses were at the beaches or underground. Namur had a heavily wooded section, which might conceal traps, occupying its northeastern portion and a great many aboveground structures of one sort and another, supposed to be chiefly barracks and supporting installations for the airfield on the sister island.

This time there were good tide tables, checked by submarine reconnaissance, but all the same there would be none of those Higgins boats so useful on the sand beaches of the South Pacific, so much a hindrance among coral reefs. There were nineteen or twenty big LSTs in the task force; on their decks and in their holds they carried

110 amphitracs of a new organization, the 10th Amphitrac Battalion, with forty-four armored amphitracs from another organization attached. They were to move into an area close off the northwest of Ennuebing, where there was a pass into the lagoon. There they would 'set the amphitracs into the water, with the armored vehicles carrying the artillery. All the night of the first day, while the outer islands were being conquered, the LSTs would hold position. As Higgins boats brought men from the transports farther out they would shift to amphitracs at the LSTs and pass into the lagoon for the main assault. Spruance had had tests conducted after Tarawa and was satisfied that an amphitrac was the only thing that could work across the coral. A few of the new DUKWs, "Ducks," were available but they were sent down to Kwajalein for the Army to try out, the Marines being doubtful about how their rubber treads would go with coral. Finally the TBY radios were discarded wherever replacements could be had, and Army-type walkie-talkies were taken ashore for handling close-in communications.

As before, Admiral Turner had the attack force working with the Army troops, down at Kwajalein Island. He led the old battleships *New Mexico, Idaho, Mississippi,* and *Pennsylvania,* with the heavy cruisers *Minneapolis, New Orleans,* and *San Francisco,* twelve destroyers, and the immediate support of the escort carriers *Natoma Bay, Coral Sea,* and *Corregidor.* The new battleships *Indiana, Washington,* and *Massachusetts* would work with him if not called away by the Jap fleet, as would "Black Jack" Reeve's carrier division of *Yorktown, Enterprise,* and *Belleau Wood.* At Roi-Namur, 50 miles to the north, the general operation was under Rear Admiral J. B. Oldendorf. The ships were *Tennessee, Colorado,* and *Maryland,* the Marines' old friends, the heavy cruisers *Louisville* and *Indianapolis,* the light cruisers *Santa Fe, Mobile,* and *Biloxi,* and eleven destroyers. The immediate support in planes came from Ragsdale's division (escort carriers *Suwanee, Sangamon, Chenango*). The detachment from the main fleet would be the fast battleships *North Carolina, Alabama, South Dakota,* and Montgomery's carrier group of *Essex, Intrepid, Cabot.* The firing areas were arranged so that while some units were giving flat trajectory fire others would be far enough out to let their shells fall plunging in on the anticipated roofed pillboxes. The two new battleships *Iowa* and *New Jersey* with other carriers

169

Bunker Hill, Cowpens, Monterey, Saratoga, Princeton, Langley and an array of heavy cruisers would roam at large under Willis Lee and Marc Mitscher to give support wherever needed or strike first at an interrupting surface enemy. All told it was nearly the greatest fleet ever assembled, with far more fire power than both enemies together had possessed at the battle of Jutland.

III

By time this plan was perfected it was well down into December and events had brought variations into the arrangements on both sides. The difficulty Admiral Akiyama experienced in getting his supplies and reinforcements forward to the outer atolls has been mentioned; it was mainly the reflection of an incident on 4 December when, with Tarawa secure, Spruance sent the fast carriers up for a flash raid into the Marshalls. They were intended to strike the airfields primarily, and did chew them up to some extent, with ten or more planes smashed on the ground. But as it happened the fliers arrived over Kwajalein simultaneously with a big convoy, the cruisers *Nagara* and *Isuzu,* with half a dozen transports and freighters of large size as Jap freighters go. The planes jumped this juicy target, sinking all the commercial craft and hitting both cruisers, *Isuzu* so badly that she was unable to steer for days and lay in the lagoon a sitting duck if our people had only known where to find her. She was eventually patched up enough to get back to Truk but not till after the turn of the year.

Of course Akiyama whistled up all the planes in the Marshalls and during the dusk they made a concerted rush against the American carriers with the torpedo. One of them got a fish into the new *Lexington,* right in the stern, almost the same way *Independence* had been hit two weeks before; few casualties and no serious damage, but she was out of the campaign. They paid sixty-three aircraft for it.

Akiyama got off a report which led Tokyo to produce a bulletin saying that the current Roosevelt-Churchill conference had been called "to cover up a disastrous naval and air defeat in the Pacific. The enemy is hiding an acute dilemma in his heart" and had lost four carriers. The real effect on Japanese planning was that Akiyama became very nervous about the situation at Mille and forwarded to it at once all the troops that had come in the 4 December convoy.

170

This brought it about that he had only 2,900 men left on Roi-Namur and 5,600 on Kwajalein as of New Year's Day, 1944, when the air attacks from the Gilberts became so intense that he could bring no more in. The Roi-Namur men belonged to the 6th Base Force (Naval) and the 61st Naval Guard Force, with the ground crews of the naval air group normally stationed there, including a very high-striped vice-admiral, Yamada of the 22nd Flotilla. The freighters had not been unloaded when they were hit and part of their cargo was concrete mixers, so that work on the new fortifications did not proceed as rapidly as planned. Even his division of six submarines Akiyama could not use. They were requisitioned by the Army to carry supplies to the outer atolls, the military leaders complaining bitterly that the Navy's supply arrangement was so defective it had been necessary to make the soldiers out there grow gardens, just as though they were common laborers.

The other change in the situation was precipitated by Spruance, who sent Admiral Lee down to Nauru with the six fast battleships between operations. The place had been airbombed repeatedly but it didn't seem to do much good. The Japanese always repaired the damaged runways in a few hours and they could fly planes out from the Carolines without difficulty. A pair of carriers, *Bunker Hill* and *Monterey*, accompanied Lee to provide air cover; it was good enough to give him complete surprise so that on the morning of 8 December the Japs woke up to a breakfast of 16-inch HC ammunition. The battleships steamed slowly back and forth for a couple of hours. When they got through, the shop installations of Nauru were so thoroughly wrecked and so many of the personnel killed that, although an occasional scout continued to come from Nauru, the island was never again a factor in the war.

This indirectly produced two last-minute changes in the American plan. One was for Admiral Oldendorf to take *Louisville,* with the three light cruisers of the Roi-Namur group and six destroyers, up to Wotje on 30 January, D minus 1, to see what could be done about the big airfield there. The ships pounded it hard, but *Anderson,* a real hard-luck destroyer, got in close enough to be hit by a 5.5, which burst right in CIC,[1] killing her skipper and five others and wounding

[1] Combat Intelligence Center, the brains of a modern warship, to which all information is relayed in battle.

171

eight. The other alteration was a definitive plan for the seizure of Majuro atoll at the center of the Maloelap-Jaluit-Wotje triangle as a fueling station and anchorage alternative to Kwajalein for future operations. The desirability had been recognized during the early planning in July, as Majuro has one of the best anchorages in the Pacific, while Kwajalein is full of coral heads. But there had been some question about keeping Jap air away from two bases at once. With Nauru out of the running Majuro became possible and the reconnaissance company of the V Amphib was sent down aboard the APD *Paine* to settle the conflicting reports on whether the atoll was in Japanese occupation or not. If so, it could not be by many of the enemy; a battalion of the 106th Regiment was assigned for occupation, the cruiser *Portland* for gunnery support, and a pair of escort carriers to furnish air.

With these alterations in the lines the curtain was run up on the main show. Up to now all American operations had been peripheral, to secure points of lodgement on the outer glacis of Empire. Now the assault on the main ravelin had begun.

IV

The rendezvous was near Hawaii on 26 January. The fleet cruised wide to the south of the Marshalls, refueled, and came up west of the Gilberts. The fast carrier group split apart; Reeve's *Yorktown* group to Taroa, Ginder's (*Saratoga*) to Wotje, Montgomery's (*Essex*) to Roi, and F. C. Sherman's (*Bunker Hill*) to Kwajalein. Off Roi-Namur at dawn of D day the transports and LSTs moved to their assigned areas and Marines lined the rails to watch the low-lying pencil lines of islands in the distance, looking like bald heads that still held a few vestiges of coconut-palm hair. The double island was smoking and battleships were striding up and down to the north, hammering away after a fashion that caused the comment: "Taking their time about it, aren't they?" They were; and for the most part firing by observation.

The APD *Schley* had pushed into the lagoon the night before and landed an underwater demolition team which established that neither Ennuebing and Mellu, nor Roi-Namur itself, had any trace of offshore obstacles. The Ennuebing-Mellu landing would be from

172

the sea side. There was trouble at the start; there had been no opportunity to practice such an unloading and it took a lot longer time to transfer men from the Higgins boats to amphitracs than had been anticipated by guesswork. The swell was heavy, the amphitracs were rolled and drifted, they took long minutes to get into formation, and it was 1000, an hour behind schedule, when the men of the 1st Battalion, 25th, hit the beach of Ennuebing. On Mellu the attack was still later, there had been such heavy surf on the northern flank of the island that it was impossible to land there as planned, and the boats had to circle south. But the destroyers provided good fire cover and there were not many Japs on either island in any case. Hardly a man was hit when at 1035 Ennuebing and a little later Mellu were reported secure while the artillerymen began to sweat over mounting their pieces.

The second wave, for Ennumennet and Ennubirr, was to leave at 1130, but now came more grief. The first group of amphitracs had been very slow getting rid of its troops at the beach; not all of them had returned to the LSTs and some of those that did return had trouble finding their parent ships since there was no means of identification. To cap all, the destroyer *Phelps,* which was supposed to be control ship for the amphitracs, marking their line of departure, was suddenly called by fleet command to run down southward through Mellu Pass and cover a group of minesweepers going into the lagoon. She transferred functions as she went past by megaphone to a subchaser carrying Brigadier General J. L. Underhill, in charge of landing operations. Few of the amphitracs heard this, practically all their radios had gone out of business early (like the miserable TBY, they were not waterproof) and the subchaser had no good radio anyway.* Many of them accordingly pursued the destroyer toward what they thought was the new location. The total of these mischances was that the attack on the two islands east did not reach its beaches till 1515. But once more the delay was canceled by good preparation fire and light resistance, and both small islands were overrun by 1628.

* Throughout the war, Navy designed or specified radios were consistently bad. They always strove for communication on too many channels, instead of good communication on a few.

Meanwhile an order had come through from Rear Admiral R. L. Connolly, "Close-in Connolly," commander of amphibs for Roi-Namur, that Ennugarret would be attacked at 1600 as it was important to take it that night and post the Marine artillery into close supporting position. It could not be done on that basis; not all the men were even landed on the first two islands from amphitracs when the order came through, already after 1600. When they had landed, the amphitracs insisted on pulling out at once for a rendezvous with the LSTs on the east side of the lagoon under orders from their own battalion commanders.

General Underhill had almost no communications since the radio sets of his subchaser had now begun to go out of order, but he managed to keep five of the amphitracs under his own command, and, through a night running pencils of fire in all directions, overloaded them with Marines for the short haul to Ennugarret, which was secure by 2000. Out in the lagoon the LSTs had failed to show identifying lights and some of the amphitracs were in vain hunting for their mothers. Occasionally one would run out of gas or develop motor trouble and then it usually sank; an amphitrac needs to keep going to stay afloat. Alongside other LSTs weary amphitrac men, who had already been laboring since dawn, were trying to get their vehicles oiled or otherwise serviced—not with much luck, for the LST skippers stood on Navy dignity and refused to allow the Marine amphitrac men so much as a cup of coffee. It was one of the curious command problems that arise in amphibious war, fundamentally stemming back to the question of whether an amphitrac is a seagoing or landgoing vehicle.

V

Destroyers had fired on Roi-Namur through most of the night, more to keep the Japs on edge than for direct effect. At daybreak Close-in Connolly brought his battleships and cruisers to 2,000 yards (*Louisville* was even hit by a ricochet) and took up the battering again, while the LSTs of the attack wave lined up in the lagoon and prepared to discharge their cargoes. Officers with glasses could make out that many of the pillboxes sited to fire from flank along a beach barricade resembling that of Tarawa had been knocked out by direct hits. Dive bombers came in; some of them had 2,000-pounders and

174

some had depth charges, with which they effectively leveled most of the remaining forestation on Namur; fighters came over and dropped bellytanks of gasoline which made not bad incendiary bombs.

H hour had been set for 1000, but there was a stiff breeze, the water on the lagoon was rough, and there was the same trouble as on the previous day in getting the amphitracs assembled at the line of departure. Everyone became cross and jumpy as H hour was set back to 1100, then to 1200, and finally to 1215; but this time communications worked perfectly, naval gunfire and planes were on call and delivered when wanted.

At 1215, then, they hit the beach. A few pillboxes remained in action and opened up; a few Marines were hit as they launched out

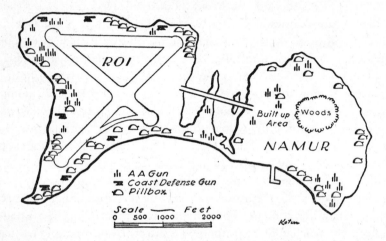

on the beach of Roi, but surprisingly few. They began working rapidly across the devastation of the airfield island. There were live Japs in there, all right, most of them in the drainage ditches of the field or in hide-outs of a new type—"spider holes," which were merely depressions in the ground covered with palm fronds. The enemy practiced the usual Jap trick of letting the first group go by and firing into the second. From the drainage ditches they could be extracted only with bangalore torpedoes, and the green men of the 23rd Regiment became trigger-happy, firing at anything and everything till they were quieted down. But the resistance as a whole was insignificant. Most of the enemy were dead, those caught alive had idiot expressions and fell asleep immediately when placed in boats,

175

their nervous organization completely destroyed by the red rain that had fallen on them for days. By 1315 the 23rd had reached its reorganization line, with some difficulty holding back the attached tanks that wished to push farther without orders. By 1530 the regiment was jumping off for the conquest of the remainder of the island and by dark this was complete except for mop-ups of the few Japs still scuttling around the drainage ditches, and for the problem of disposing of the enemy dead, a very serious one, since many had been killed in the early bombardment and had ripened considerably under the tropic sun.

Namur was a more serious proposition, as might be expected from the nature of the cover. The 2nd Battalion, 24th, went in on the right, the 3rd on the left. Both were bothered a good deal by the shortage of amphitracs and after they reached the beach both were bothered still more by the fact that the amphitrac men insisted on firing over their heads at nothing. Resistance at the beach was minor, but just above the waterline a big antitank ditch kept the amphitracs from penetrating as planned and the men had to push along on foot. They encountered spider holes as on Roi, and these were hard to locate because the whole ground was littered with torn trees from the bombardment. There were also pillboxes and blockhouses still in action and any number of Japs concealed in the ruins of their buildings, keeping up an active fire. The action was of the usual type against such defenses, the attackers crawling in with satchel charges while others covered them. The advance was proceeding in a satisfactory manner when at 1245 there was an explosion that seemed to shake the whole Pacific Ocean.

Three thousand feet up an observation plane from *Colorado,* which had been planting 16-inch shell ahead of the advance, was shoved flatly sidewise in the air. The aviator saw a mushroom of smoke and flame shoot past him into the skies, spotted with debris, and with a shock realized that part of the debris consisted of an entire palm tree, root and head. Ashore at least 20 Marines of the 2nd Battalion were killed, another eighty wounded, and all the rest more or less stunned. Later it was discovered that the main magazine of the island, loaded with torpedo warheads, had gone up in that gigantic blast. Why? There are various stories—one to the effect that some Marines had crawled on the roof of the structure, dug a hole through it and tossed in a grenade under the impression they were dealing with another blockhouse; but the men of *Colorado* insist that it was an armor-piercing shell from their ship that did the business.

It does not matter; what does matter is that although more Japs than Marines were killed in the big bang, Battalion 2 was set back on its heels by the jar, followed at short intervals by two more that would have been gigantic but for the one that preceded them. Colonel F. A. Hart of the regiment decided to commit his reserve battalion. These men hit the beach late in the afternoon, when the 3rd Battalion had already reached its phase line, but there was a delay in getting tanks ashore and not till 1730 could the advance be taken up again. When it was resumed a maze of ruined buildings and pillboxes was encountered with many live Japs. Night came down to find the regiment still a quarter mile from the north peak of the island. The order was given to dig in.

Twice during the night the Japs tried small counterattacks and on 2 February the Marines found they had to go back to many of the pillboxes already conquered, which the obstinate enemy had reoccupied. But by afternoon of that day the island was won, the 1st Battalion losing its lieutenant colonel, A. J. Dyess, in the process. The only other accidents were that the unfortunate *Anderson* ran on a coral head and twisted her screws while twenty-three of the amphitracs sank.

The cost had been 190 killed, 547 wounded, total 737; of the enemy 3,742 were killed, 99 idiot Jap prisoners taken, and 165 Korean laborers. Admiral Akiyama was killed down at Kwajalein, where the 7th Division encountered more of the enemy and took more time. Despite the difficulty over the amphitracs, which showed plainly the need for better training and control of these extremely useful vehicles (down at Kwajalein Island the Army had placed its amphitracs in charge of a regular tank battalion and had no trouble), it had been the easiest and least costly conquest of the Pacific war. The reasons were clear enough—the strategic surprise which brought the attack down upon that one atoll of the whole Marshall group least prepared to receive it; the crushing, accurate naval bombardment that reduced the defense to a few isolated knots of men. "Maybe we had too many men and too many ships for the job," said Richmond Kelly Turner when it was over, "but I prefer to do things that way. It saved us a lot of lives."

The system of dealing with island defenses had been discovered, our people told themselves in a mood of legitimate self-congratulation; and Pearl Harbor sent through a suggestion that since Roi-Namur had been taken so much more rapidly and at so much less cost than anticipated, it might be a good idea to attack Eniwetok in a week or less. Majuro had been in the meanwhile captured in an incidental manner without a man being hurt; construction of the airfield there began on 3 February.

VI

Aboard the carrier *Saratoga* they got out a skit during the middle days of February. It was a glimpse into the future, date uncertain. The carrier and her companions of Admiral Ginder's group (*Princeton, Langley*) had been working on Eniwetok for these many years, according to the document; seniority had brought all the enlisted up to chiefs and warrant officers and all the fliers up to rear admirals with long beards. As Rear Admiral Gish lands he reports to the Vice-Admiral in charge of air intelligence that the Japanese are still in occupation of the atoll; there is an outhouse standing.

Aboard the ships of that group they felt out of things. After Kwajalein it was clear to everyone, including the Japanese, that Eniwetok would be the next point of attack. It had a good airfield on Engebi Island at the north flank of the circular coral formation; and of all the atolls it was the only one through which planes could be fed from either the Empire or the Carolines into those Japanese positions among the eastern Marshalls, now converted into agricultural projects by American ships with their bases at Kwajalein and Majuro. If Eniwetok were taken, if our land-based air were established there, the Imperial atolls would be permanently innocuous, the forces in them permanently immobilized. The American fleet would be set free for any operation its commanders chose to undertake.

It was also evident that for some reason at which our high command could only guess (they were very far from imagining the Japanese situation in carrier pilots to be as bad as it actually was), the enemy either would not or could not commit major forces to the

178

defense of Central Pacific islands at this particular time. The capture of Eniwetok was thus merely a question of applying readily available forces to produce an important result—if it were done soon, before the strategic situation or the Japanese mind had altered. This was why Admiral Nimitz had indicated to Admiral Spruance that he would like to have the place attacked right away.

Admiral Spruance examined the refueling situation and the reports on Kwajalein and replied, no, he didn't think it could be done that way. It was only on 2 February that the decision had been taken to go to Eniwetok. The V Amphib Corps reserve that had not been used at Kwajalein (106th Army Regiment and 22nd Marines) would carry the ball and Rear Admiral Harry Hill would have the over-all command. It was 4 February when the conference was held aboard the command ship *Rocky Mount*, with Admiral Turner,

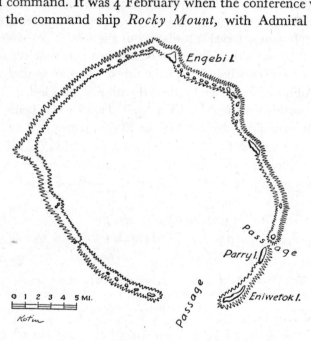

Admiral Hill, and General Holland Smith present to lay down the general lines of the plan. That plan now required to be broken down into details by the staffs involved and something had to be done to obtain better function from the amphitracs, all of which would take time. In the meanwhile, however, here was the fleet, Task Force 58, six fast battleships (*Washington* and *Indiana* had been in a bad

179

collision and were not available), twelve fast carriers, fully refueled at Majuro and with Marc Mitscher champing for action. Admiral Ginder's detachment would not reduce this force by much and the old battleships and cruisers of Harry Hill, destined for the Eniwetok attack, would not reduce it at all. Spruance proposed to attack Truk.

In the light of subsequent events it is hard to realize how terrifying an enterprise an assault on that mysterious and formidable place of arms seemed at the time. The skipper of *Essex*'s Air Group 9 has said that when he heard where they were bound "my first impulse was to jump overboard"; and he was a man who had seen a lot of war at its worst. The place was stronger than Pearl Harbor, a huge atoll enclosing a variety of islands supplied with airdromes aboveground and and underground, armed to the teeth with antiaircraft and coast defense guns, any number of supporting planes, the major Japanese naval installation of the world. No white man had been there since the days when it belonged to Germany; and out from it for two years had flowed the tide of the war against us.[1]

To it Admiral Kondo had returned with his 2nd Fleet units after the futile sortie into the Marshalls while Tarawa was being taken. When a pair of B-24s led by Marine Major James R. Christensen flew over it at 24,000 to take pictures on 4 February, the ships were still in there, two carriers among them, secure in their defenses. The operation was an attack on a major fortress with a naval battle to be carried on simultaneously.

Or was it? Our submarines had been around the secret terror since the beginning of the war. *Skate* sank a torpedo into the battleship *Yamato* there in December and *Guardfish* knocked off the

[1] Actually, Truk was a good deal of a falseface, like most bugbears. The place had never been a true major base, only an anchorage where there was no refueling dock, and most of the shop installations were for servicing submarines. Up to the beginning of the war it was not even very much fortified, and Vice-Admiral Hara, who then commanded the place, has told how he used to get "the South Sea blues" when he heard American radios describing it as impregnable. During 1943 quite a lot of artillery, chiefly antiaircraft, was moved in, and the place had never been so strong as it was on the day of Admiral Spruance's strike. He ruined it; the aboveground installations were almost completely destroyed, so were most of the ammunition dumps and the fuel storage; and since it is composed of a number of islands, the place was badly pinched from that time forth by the destruction of all the barges and sampans in the harbor, which there was no means of replacing.

destroyer *Umikaze* as she was trailing a convoy in there on 1 February. But Major Christensen's bold 2,000-mile flight was the first time an American plane had appeared over the place, and the Japanese naval command, in a considerable state of nerves over the idea that this might mean increased submarine attacks and possibly a land-based air assault, ordered Kondo out westward to base on Palau and the Tawi Tawi passage in the Philippines. It does not seem to have occurred to Vice-Admiral Hitoshi Koyabashi, in command of Truk, that the removal of these major fleet units increased instead of decreased the danger of an American attack. When, on the morning of 15 February, his recon planes reported no signs of American approach, Koyabashi grounded his snoopers (he was very short on fuel), had his attack planes defueled and relieved of their weights of bombs and torpedoes, and sent the pilots to barracks on islands separate from the airfields. The only other news he might have received was from the submarine *I-43*, out scouting to the north; but as she surfaced, possibly to make a report, she was torpedoed by USS *Aspro*. The result was that at 0714 on the morning of 17 February, dotted with fleecy white clouds, he got the word that hundreds of American planes were approaching the great base.[1]

The fighter commands were alerted at once and a good many of them got into the air though not all; on one island the alarm did not sound till the attackers were overhead. Mitscher had sent his own fighters in for the first sweep. There was a violent dogfight in the skies as the two groups of planes bumped into each other, the Japs diving down through our formations at full power to hide in the clouds below if they missed. "They fought as though they were in a daze," said one of the American pilots, and this was substantially true, for the enemy had had no time to form in those tight squadrons under a leader, on which they so much depended. Japanese planes dropped all over the place—127 of them according to the estimates of our Intelligence, though subsequent information from the Jap

[1] They came from Reeve's carrier group of *Enterprise, Yorktown,* and *Belleau Wood;* Montgomery's of *Essex, Intrepid,* and *Cabot,* and Sherman's of *Bunker Hill, Cowpens,* and *Monterey.* The supporting vessels were battleships *North Carolina, South Dakota, Massachusetts, Alabama, Iowa, New Jersey;* heavy cruisers *New Orleans, Minneapolis, San Francisco, Wichita, Baltimore;* light cruisers *Santa Fe, Mobile, Biloxi, Oakland, San Diego;* and numerous destroyers.

records made it much smaller—only about 35. American dive bombers following in jumped on the airfields and shipping in the lagoon. Pickings were rich, since Koyabashi had not been able to bring the pilots and planes of his strike groups together and there was a big group for Rabaul awaiting ferry pilots at the fields; nor had most of the ships time to work up steam. No fewer than 235 planes were destroyed on the ground or water, 21 of them multi-engine jobs. (Our estimate was much less here. We did not know that the Rabaul group caught fire from one another and all burned.) Some 13 transports and supply ships were seen to sink and admitted; 17 more actually went down, including a 20,000-tonner. So did the destroyers *Fumitsuki* and *Tachikaze* and the cruiser *Naka*. The destroyer *Oite* was so badly hit she could not move. The cruiser *Katori* and the destroyer *Maikaze* did make out of the lagoon and were escaping to the north in a somewhat battered condition when they ran into *Iowa* and *New Jersey*, the two most powerful battle-ships in the world, and were sunk in a couple of minutes.

Spruance led his forces right around the atoll to attack again from another direction next morning. Now was the chance for the Japanese system of defense by quick assembly of aircraft from adjacent areas to justify itself and Admiral Koyabashi summoned units in from all over the Carolines. They began to arrive on the night of the 17th and all night long drove at the carrier force in energetic but badly co-ordinated attacks. One of them got a torpedo hit on *Intrepid*, which left her temporarily without steering but unhurt in speed or ability to handle planes; but the Japs paid for that with the loss of over half their squadrons. Next morning Mitscher's planes hit Truk again, finished off *Oite* and some of the cargo ships that had only been damaged the day before, wrecked everything above-ground and then soared back to the fleet. They had accounted for a grand total of 296 Jap planes besides all the shipping; and they were not through yet, for Spruance sent *Intrepid* back to Pearl with *Cabot* and a battleship for company, and went rushing north through the Central Pacific to Saipan, the enemy's big base in the Marianas. He was approaching it on the 22nd when spotted by a scout plane. The carriers put up their combat patrols and fought through the night against the usual torpedo attacks, next morning going in. They shot down 29 planes and got some 80-odd on the ground, but not many ships there, since most of them had time to get away.

VII

Note Spruance's strategy, which operated both in the psychological domain, effectively to exorcise the ancient demoniac ghost of Truk, and also on the chessboard of the ocean, to impose a moving screen of force between Eniwetok, which was attacked on 17 February, and any attempt to interrupt the operation by sea or air.

Aside from Engebi on the north, where the airfield was, the main islands of the group are two, Eniwetok itself and Parry, on the southern edge of the circle, each flanked by a passage deep and wide enough to admit heavy ships. Reconnaissance had failed to show any important forces on the latter two islands.

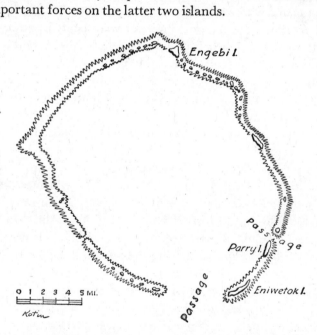

These features determined the hastily drawn plan of attack. The fleet would steam right into the lagoon and a seaplane base would be set up there, the planes working from tenders. Engebi would be attacked first, by Colonel Walker's 22nd Marines with artillery on the flanking islands as at Roi-Namur, two battalions going in abreast, the third in reserve. The 106th Infantry was short one battalion, which had gone to Majuro. One of the remaining battalions ought to be enough for Eniwetok Island, with the second in reserve, and when that was cleaned up the 106th would move to Parry. Fire support was to be from *Colorado, Tennessee,* and *Pennsylvania,* with heavy cruisers *Louisville, Portland, Indianapolis,* and seven destroyers; air support from Ginder's group of carriers and Admiral Ragsdale's escort carriers, *Sangamon, Suwanee,* and *Chenango.*

The first part of this scheme went exactly as written. The ships steamed into the lagoon and tore Engebi all up with their discharges while a Jap lieutenant ashore wrote in his diary that "What must come, has come. I am amazed at the severity of the bombardment; my stomach is upset," and distributed sake to his platoon. All day the guns pounded; as dark fell *Schley* put out her rubber-boated demolition teams who worked in and buoyed channels for the landing craft. At dawn the men of the 22nd were boated and at 0842 were on the southwest beach of Engebi a little ahead of schedule. (The control arrangements had vastly improved and in addition the assault teams had the support of a number of LCI gunboats, used for the first time against Kwajalein Island, where they had proved vastly effective.)

Machine-gun and rifle fire along the beach was sporadic and generally inaccurate. The two battalions worked in rapidly for about 100 yards, set up effective liaison—and discovered something entirely new in the line of Japanese defenses. The Marines called it a "spiderweb"; it was made up of a number of empty gasoline drums laid end to end to form a pipe, and well dug in. A number of such tunnels would radiate from a central spider pit or pillbox. As soon as the latter came under fire the men in it were off through their pipes to turn up 50, 75, 100 yards away, full of fight and still under concealment, diving down again as soon as they had fired once. The whole operation turned into a feverish pursuit of moles by cats with our forces rapidly dominating the surface of the island, yet being sniped at from all directions. At 0955 the 3rd Battalion of the regiment was put ashore. It had to go for every pillbox and hole on the way to the front, if front it could be called, just as though it were the first group on the island.

One of our men wrote later: "That night was unbelievably

184

terrible. There were many of them left and they all had one fanatical notion, and that was to take one of us with them. We dug in with orders to kill anything that moved. I kept watch in a foxhole with my sergeant and we both stayed awake all night with a knife in one hand and a grenade in the other. They crept in among us, and every

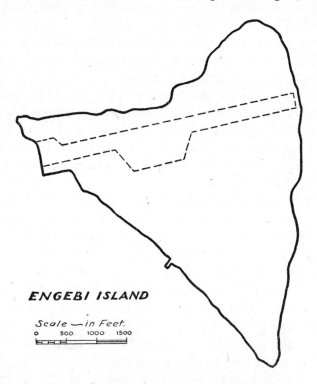

ENGEBI ISLAND

Scale — in Feet.

bush and rock took on sinister proportions. They got some of us, but in the morning they lay all about, some with their riddled bodies actually inside our foxholes. Never have I been so glad to see the sun."

That sun looked down on the last resistance of Engebi; but a hitch in the original plans was caused by the discovery in the raddled headquarters post of the island of documents indicating that the jungle and thick brush of Eniwetok and Parry islands held a good many more men than had been thought in the beginning, including Major General Nishida of the 1st Amphibious Brigade. There was a quick conference and General T. E. Watson, in charge of the land

185

forces of the operation, stepped up his force for Eniwetok Island to put in both battalions of the 106th Infantry with the 3rd Battalion, 22nd Marines, in reserve. The 27th Division men landed midway along the island at 0915 of that day, 19 February, meeting little resistance at the water, but considerable as they worked inland, and it was difficult to get the troops moving. They lacked both the training and the drive of the Marines and were encountering a series of well-prepared positions from which the Nips retreated in good order, one after another. At 1330 the Marine battalion was put in, penetration across the island was achieved, and the troops began to sweep it out northward and southward. It was still not cleared by night and the Japs infiltrated vigorously into the loose, indeterminate lines, producing another night fight like that on Engebi. Next day both grenades and satchel charges ran short; more had to be flown in from Kwajalein, but resistance was finally put down by the morning of the 21st.

That left Parry. It had been intended to use the 106th there, but the General was not too confident of the performance of those infantrymen and switched his plans to make it the 22nd Marines, with the reconnaissance and scout companies and part of the 10th Defense Battalion as a reserve afloat. The landing was on the morning of 22 February, while Spruance was hitting Saipan. It was a savage fight. The place had some natural caves which had been developed into a spiderweb system, many Japs had survived the naval bombardment delivered by *Tennessee* and *Pennsylvania* from no more than 1,500 yards, and some of them managed to put an enfilading fire along one of the beaches that forced its evacuation half an hour after landing. One battalion landed out of position and, calling for fire from a destroyer, got it under the smoke on what should have been lines to its right, but what was actually the beachhead; a bad business. But by evening most of the island was overrun; and the rest of it next day, after the ships had kept the place bright all night with star shell, to make things difficult for the Japs who popped out of their holes in the usual night attacks.

So Eniwetok was ours at a cost of 299 killed, 766 wounded, mainly on Eniwetok Island and Parry. Of the Japs, 3,400 fell and we got 66 prisoners.

That was the conquest of the Marshalls, the first true amphibious operation—not in a sense of fighting across beachheads to a self-sustaining operation ashore, for that had been done at Guadalcanal and several times in MacArthur's campaign along the coast of New Guinea, already a serial story by the time Kwajalein began. The Marshalls operation was amphibious in both a wider and a deeper sense: the sense of combining strategy at sea and ashore. It involved the conception that, although the opposing parties in a war may control fortresses, base areas, whose geographical interlocking it is almost impossible to resolve, victory will rest on the banners of that party which holds the open areas among the fortified positions. This is to say that the side with the best communications will win; or to put it another way, that amphibious operations and sea power are inextricably linked. As soon as a new base becomes self-sustaining the fleet is free to attack other points, transport its own special type of troops (Marines) to a spot where they can conquer a new, a more forwardly base. The effective conquest of the Marshalls by the capture of only two atolls was the perfect answer to earlier complaints about island-hopping strategy; it swallowed a quarter of the Pacific at a gulp.

Air enters the picture, of course. One of the best reasons for the conquest of bases in the island network was to provide airstrips on land from which planes could take off at any hour of day or night to oppose enemy interjections. Admiral Yamamoto had seen this very clearly. His trouble was—or the trouble of the lesser men who attempted to carry out his doctrine—that they saw the mission of land-based air too clearly. They thought it the most important factor and almost the only factor. They never imagined that the strategic mobility of a fleet could be so great or that of an air force so restricted. The dreadful surprise at Truk, where an entire air flotilla had been concentrated in spite of the need of planes elsewhere, and the complete failure of the counterattack there, show how far they erred.

No Japanese seems to have realized what the American Marine leaders realized from the beginning—that in amphibious operations, island warfare, time is more essential even than lives. Parenthetically,

187

the time factor is the most difficult of all in war to grasp and when you have a commander who really understands what a clock is good for his name is Napoleon.

If the time factor had been right, if the Marines had not upset the Japanese time schedule, there was nothing really wrong with their system of defense. Admiral Kondo, for instance, could have attacked the 5th Fleet by surface, subsurface, and air in the Gilberts while that fleet was still burdened with its transports and tied to a narrow area, unable to engage in an all-out action. The Japanese devoted all their planning and skill to methods of gaining time from Guadalcanal down, in fact, yet they never succeeded in gaining enough to make an effective counterattack.

Why? Not an underestimation of American industrial power, for Yamamoto, if no other, had accurately estimated that from the beginning. It could hardly be a failure to use the best tactical methods either, for they continually came up with something new in this field, even though the results tended to resemble those of the fox competing with the cat in Aesop's fable. Rather it was the Japanese failure to grasp the large picture; to understand that operations at the shore and among islands and those on the sea form parts of a single complex. No Japanese ever got hold of the idea that it did not in the least matter how many islands they held as long as the American fleet held the seas—certainly not till after the Marshalls had fallen.

At all events the American fleet now clearly did hold the high seas, Truk was almost as useless as Wotje (unless they could induce us to assault it), and the Japanese defense line was forced back to the Marianas, Yap and Palau, the inner bastions. The realization of this, the obvious fact that, in a manner no Japanese could understand, the Japanese military system had failed, shook to its foundations that dictatorial government which had ruled the country for more than a generation.

Admiral Takagi had just completed his task of gathering data. He pointed out that essential raw materials were not coming forward from the Southern Resources Area, and in view of the growing shortage of merchant ships—the Americans appeared to have discovered some new and deadly type of torpedo—it seemed unlikely that they ever would. It had already been necessary to cancel most of the building program on heavy ships to provide new escort vessels for convoys. This was reflecting back into the general naval situation, for the Americans were at sea with powerful new battleships and carriers that weighted the balance heavily in their favor. Moreover, advices from the Army in China and the publicity of the Americans themselves, indicated that bases were being set up there for long-range air attacks on metropolitan Japan. The Admiral considered it was time to seek a compromise peace, even at the cost of withdrawing from China and Korea.

Naturally this report was not made in writing; things are not done that way in Japan. Instead Takagi called on old Admiral Yonai, a former premier and one of the most respected members of the Jushin. After the ceremony of the teacups the junior officer set forth his case. Yonai confessed that other members of his informal but powerful organization had been agitated by fears that all was not well in the war; and when his visitor had left, himself called on several of the other Jushin. One of them was another retired admiral, Keisuka Okada; he had just received information to the same general purport from his son-in-law, Hisatsune Sakonizu, who was a member of the Cabinet Planning Board. The two old men quietly sent word to Tojo that it would be best if he withdrew, and as they had of course consulted others of the Jushin before doing so, Tojo could get no other advice anywhere.

But Hideki Tojo was by no means willing to give up his position as the most powerful subject of the Emperor since the days of the Ashikaga Ministers of the Left, back in the thirteenth century. He retorted by a counteroffensive, directed in both the military and the political fields against the Navy men whom he rightly placed at the core of the intrigue to remove him. He asked the resignation of Admiral Osami Nagano, who had stepped into Yamamoto's place after the latter's death. The attack on Truk was the ostensible cause, but in order that face should not be lost, nor the appearance of solidarity against the Empire's opponents, Field Marshal General Sugiyama, Nagano's opposite number in the Army office, was also eliminated, both men being elevated to the Jushin. Tojo himself took over the Army staff; the Navy went to Admiral Shigetaro Shimada, one of the few men in his service who had all along been a supporter of the "Manchuria Gang."

189

On the strictly military side an offensive into Southeastern China was ordered for the seizure of the potential American air bases, a program which presented no great difficulties. Admiral Shimada demanded and received assurances that the pilots now in training would not be at once sent to the front in New Guinea, but be reserved enough for the new carriers in order to bring the fleet up to something like equality with the American. Additional steel was allocated to speed up the construction of six more carriers—the six that had been begun as battle cruisers. The Army heads remained adamant about the use of submarines to supply the isolated forward bases, but Tojo conceded that this was not a proper naval function and set up a new Army bureau to build submarines that would be under Army command. Admiral Shimada was glad to detail naval officers to give the necessary technical help.

Chapter 12

Bougainville: Beachhead in Jungle

ON JULY 11, 1943, ADMIRAL HALSEY CALLED A CONFERENCE and set up an organizational plan. The campaign for Munda, if not proceeding brilliantly, was at least making sufficient progress to guarantee its ultimate success. The next long step would be to capture a naval base and airfield at Bougainville, both to eliminate that island as a center of Jap aerial bases and to furnish fields from which we could put light bombers under fighter cover over Rabaul, which would effectively neutralize that enemy center. For this job Rear Admiral Theodore S. Wilkinson was named commander of a new unit, the 3rd Amphibious Force, Task Force 31, with general leadership of the forces afloat and on the beach. Under him was Vandegrift, now a lieutenant general, as head of the I Amphibious Corps.

This corps was a South Pacific command, originally composed wholly of Marines—the 2nd and 3rd Divisions, with the Raiders, parachutists, and several defense battalions in its organizational setup. It paralleled the Army XIV Corps, under Major General Harmon, the aviator, which contained the 37th Division and the Americals, ready for early action, and the 25th, which had fought hard on New Georgia, and was entitled to some rest and recruitment. The Army command had had charge of the last operation, calling for whatever help necessary from the Marines. The next operation was to be Marine, with help coming from the Army. (It is not to be thought that interservice questions were confined to Japan, but the difference is that we solved them in good humor and on a basis of reasonable co-operation.) Before the Bougainville attack could be planned, however, the 2nd Marine Division was taken away from its Corps for Tarawa. The result was that after a good many paper-work changes which caused staff men many sleepless nights and severe cases of mental indigestion, the 37th Army Division became a part of the new corps for this operation.

The beachhead force of the corps was still the brand-new Marine division, the 3rd, commanded by Major General A. H. Turnage, just organized and in training among the mountains of New Zealand. The three Marine infantry regiments were the 3rd, 9th, and 21st, the last two of them new but with sizable cadres of experienced men. It had an artillery regiment, the 12th; a regiment of engineers, the 19th; an attached Seabee command; and for the purposes of the operation there was added to it another new organization, the 2nd Provisional Raider Regiment (Colonel Alan Shapley) which had been formed by boiling together Carlson's old 2nd Raider Battalion and a new 3rd Raider Battalion—the Raiders being not now so much needed in their specialty, since the days when we had to think in terms of raids were pretty much at an end.

Bougainville is the largest of the Solomons, inland a ferocious jumble of rocky jungle in which nothing but an insect can live. Flatlands along the coast allow the construction of numerous airfields, an opportunity of which the Japanese had not failed to avail themselves. They had a good field at Kieta on the northeast coast; a pair on opposite sides of Buka Passage in the north, where Bougainville faces the smaller Buka Island across a strait so narrow as hardly to be a passage at all. At the southern end of the big island a complex of shoals and smaller spots of land makes access from the sea as difficult as at Munda; here the enemy had a whole series of airfields with fortifications and coast artillery.

The first plan of the new amphibious force called for a direct attack on this complex, to secure a naval base and airfield, but as soon as recon reports and intelligence began to come in, it was clear that General Vandegrift's corps would not be big enough for the job. These recon reports were unusually complete; our submarines worked all around Bougainville, photographing the beaches by periscope and landing parties of two or three, who slipped into the interior to make contact with coast-watchers. The latter had the natives (who on this island are mostly Methodists and Seventh-Day Adventists) well in hand and there was a good count on the enemy

192

forces. The Shortlands in the south held some 6,000 Japs; around the airfields across the bay there were 3,000 more, with another 17,000 in the immediate area. There were 5,000 at Kieta, say 4,000 in the Buka area—about 35,000 altogether.

On 5 August, therefore, the plan was redrawn. Now it was to take the Shortlands only and put the airfields inshore out of business by long-range gunfire. The accumulation of evidence showed this as not much better than the original idea. The beaches at the Shortlands are not wide enough to set any sizable force ashore in the important first rush, and suppose we did put the enemy's fields out of action by cannonade, how would that help us get an airstrip of our own? There was, moreover, the big strategic picture. Down through that summer it was becoming increasingly clear that the Japs suffered from no shortage of manpower but a very serious one in shipping; and that their air force, if not actually wearing out, was sustaining losses that could not be borne forever.

Why not (argued the staff) attack them at points where these weaknesses could be made to count? That is, by seizing an area of our own on Bougainville and setting up an airfield there behind a perimeter defense, along the lines toward which the Guadalcanal operation had unconsciously developed. The Bougainville terrain was far worse than that on the island earlier taken, the only practical trails for large bodies of troops are close along the coasts. The enemy could not move men by these routes nearly as fast as we could reinforce by sea, and whatever troops he did move would be subject to air attack and naval shelling all the way, with the result that he would have the same difficulties about transporting heavy weapons as on Guadalcanal; more serious ones still in keeping his troops well supplied and healthy.

At about the time this idea was under discussion, some of the SOPAC staff returned from a visit to MacArthur's headquarters, with the report that he too took a dim view of an attempt on the Shortlands. Lae, Salamaua, and Finschaffen in New Guinea had lately fallen into his hands and Rabaul was already under air attack from this direction. He was projecting an advance by leaps westward along the coast, and would like Admiral Halsey to investigate the possibility of by-passing the Japanese concentrations on Bougainville by seizing some spot on the western coast of that island. As

Bougainville fell into the area of MacArthur's over-all command, it could be considered that his desires were entitled to weight. The new idea was a more landgoing version of the same strategic plan that lay behind the campaign for the Gilberts and Marshalls—seize a base in the center of enemy holdings and by means of mobile forces pin them all down in passive defense.

The place actually selected was on the north shore of wide Empress Augusta Bay, where the fishhook-shaped Cape Torokina juts out toward two islands, Puruata and a tiny dot of land named Torokina. It is a nasty neighborhood, lacking a good anchorage and with no shelter for ships from the winds that often blow onshore

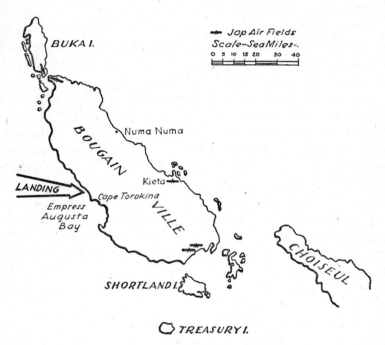

with great force; the beach only a few yards wide before jungle shoots up like a wall. But the land behind was flat for some distance to the hills and an area some eight miles long is nicely boxed in by two deep winding sluggish streams, the Luruma and Torokina. Puruata Island was held by the enemy, but not in any great strength, and the forces ashore behind it were estimated at 1,00 men—mostly at Mosigetta, a station where the main coastal trail cuts inland briefly. This lack of probable resistance was another reason for selecting the Empress Augusta Bay region. Most of the big ships that could give crushing fire support against a defended shore were needed to cover the oceanic move to Tarawa-Makin, and the Navy could spare for the Bougainville show only three squadrons of destroyers (23) and a division of light cruisers (4).

The detailed plan called for a landing on a front running from Torokina Cape northwest for something better than two miles, along twelve designated beaches. The three battalions of the 9th Regiment would go in abreast on the left, beyond a small river called the

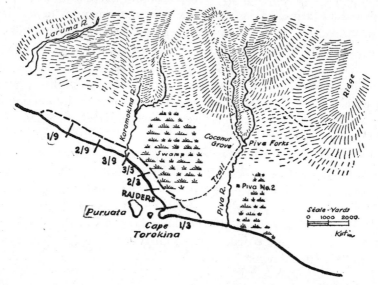

Koromokina. East of the stream two battalions of the 3rd Regiment would land with a battalion of the Raiders just north of the cape. The remaining battalion of the 3rd would land on the cape itself; the other battalion of Raiders would take Puruata.

This would give a broad, quite shallow beachhead, thus getting all the men the twelve transports could carry ashore in a few hours. General Turnage was most desirous to push patrols inland early to find airfield sites, and wanted to be able to shift his forces from one beach to another in case lines of resistance developed which were not visible to the camera. Each transport had one battalion and its equipment; they would have to make a second trip or more for the

2 1st Regiment and the 37th Division. As they would have to go back immediately for these troops, cargo loadings for the original expedition were cut to 500 tons per ship, the very minimum needs in food and ammunition for ten days. It was estimated that this amount could be unloaded in the five or six hours that would elapse before dark of D day put an end to the business. Jap planes would come at night.

The 3rd Marine Division had been subjected to a rigorous conditioning process under the rain of New Zealand. Before it embarked there were careful conferences, first of regimental and battalion commanders, then company officers, finally of the noncoms and individual Marines. Everything was laid out on maps to the last detail and every man was taken over and over the process till he knew, not only what his unit and he himself were supposed to do in the landing, but toward what objective every other man in the beachhead force would be working. The rehearsals at Efate went off well. Probably no command new to combat went into action in the Pacific with its lessons more exquisitely learned. The date was set for 1 November.

An annex which had always been part of the over-all scheme called for the seizure of the Treasury Islands off the southeast coast of Bougainville as a motor-torpedoboat station and staging airfield, a day before the Bougainville landing. This project was entrusted to a New Zealand brigade, and need not concern us further except to remark that it was carried out smoothly and with light casualties on the designated day.

II

The Bougainville commands were under the general direction of our old friend Lieutenant General Hyakutate, then at Rabaul.[1] He

[1] We know less about the Japanese in this campaign than in almost any other. A large number of them were the wreckage of the big command on Kolombangara, which the Japanese had evacuated, or attempted to evacuate, after the American seizure of Vella Lavella. They had lost heavily when our destroyers attacked their transport in the Slot during the process and on arrival at Bougainville many of them were brigaded into new, temporary organizations. Most of these secondary groupings were destroyed in the disaster of March, 1944, and their records and diaries went with them into the jungle mud.

was a somewhat subdued man since the Guadalcanal campaign; forced to think in terms of the defensive, a form of war he did not like and for which he considered the Japanese Army ill-prepared. Nevertheless, there is nothing to indicate that he had any particular apprehension about Bougainville. The troops in the Shortlands area were grouped around the Kure 7th Special Naval Landing Force, an organization which had come out full strength and had been very little depleted by casualties. There was nearly a full division of Army troops with them, made up of fragmentary organizations that had originally been in the lower islands, and a new, full division, the 6th Infantry, assigned to Hyakutate's army when the Guadalcanal campaign went sour and sent forward to Bougainville in December of 1942, when it appeared that the Americans might strike farther north along the Solomon chain.

This division, like the other troops, had its headquarters around the Shortlands air bases, as it was considered that an American attack must be delivered in that area, though there was a full regiment to protect Kieta and something over a regiment in the region of Cape Torokina on the southwest coast, where it was just possible that the Americans might put men ashore for an overland flanking effort in connection with their main drive at Shortland. The formation at Torokina was Colonel Kawano's 23rd Infantry Regiment, supported in its position by the bulk of the 6th Artillery, the divisional force. The regiment had been in that station for nearly a year now, had become thoroughly familiar with the ground, and had dug itself in with the semisubmerged, grown-over coconut log bunkers and pillboxes that had proved so successful on New Georgia.

The nature of the position was this: at a point southwest of the Torokina River the main coastal trail cuts inland to avoid a vast tropical swamp which picks up a few hundred yards inside the foreshore and runs to the foothills of the central mountain, over a mile. This swamp is always deep in water with mud beneath it and huge trees growing up out of it, bound together with thorny vines, a natural abatis. The swamp is split by the small Piva River, along whose western bank is a narrow strip of dry ground. A trail, the only one crossing the central ridge of the island, comes across from Numa Numa and Kieta, past the source of the Piva to meet the coastal trail at Piva Forks. Regimental headquarters was there with a system of defense around it. From Piva Forks the double trail runs almost due south with swamp on its right, river and swamp on its left, to Cape Torokina, there becoming the coastal trail once more. The cape itself was provided with a bunker system well thought out and with good interlocking fields of fire—Colonel Kawano had been besieged by the Chinese during the Hankow operation and knew the importance of this. The island off the cape, called Motupena by the Japanese, was similarly provided with defenses from which the shore could be swept where it curves away northwestward. Beyond this point up to the Luruma, the coast fell out of the area of Colonel Kawano's command, but he noted the surf was always bad there and did not think he should worry about it.

III

There were some changes in Marine commands during the period of preparation. General Vandegrift was going home to be commandant of the whole Marine Corps, and after the preliminary planning was done, turned over the I Amphib to Major General Charles D. Barrett; but three weeks later Barrett suddenly died and on 8 October Vandegrift had to take command again, with Major General Geiger, the aviator, as his deputy and heir apparent to the command of the Amphibs. This did not disturb any of the other arrangements, such as those for air bombing which was begun in force on 15 October, with B-24s attacking Kahili and Buka Fields daily and fighter sweeps from Vella Lavella to keep any Jap planes on the ground, which was pretty successfully done.

On 30 October General Vandegrift boarded the transport *George Clymer* and the campaign was on. Next morning "Tip" Merrill with his four cruisers, *Cleveland, Columbia, Montpelier, Denver,* and Arleigh Burke's "Little Beavers" of the famous Desron 23, pushed out of Purvis Bay and ran fast up the southern flank of the Solomons to give the Buka airfields a heavy shelling, still further to keep Jap planes on the ground. There were still some snoopers about. They saw the transport fleet coming before dawn of 1 November and alerted all Japanese commands, which stood to their battle stations while General Kanda of the 6th Division got off a message saying that an American attack on the Shortlands was commencing. He still thought so at daybreak; the streamlined shapes of Merrill's cruisers caught the first light as they ran in on Shortland Island and began to shell.

Colonel Kawano at Cape Torokina could see with equal clarity twelve transports push into Empress Augusta Bay and dish out amphitracs, while destroyers ran past to shell his positions and dive bombers came down from above. At 0710 the race to the beach began; the landing craft immediately came under a heavy crossfire from Puruata Island and the cape, the latter supported by a 75 so well hidden that neither ships' guns nor bombs could do anything about it. This fire hit the 1st Battalion, 3rd, and the 2nd Raider Battalion hardest; blew up the command boat of the former, smashed five others, and so disorganized the landing waves that no group reached the beach in precisely the place or order assigned to it. The fire was not heavy enough to halt the Marines (though it killed Lieutenant Colonel Joseph P. McCaffery of the 2nd Raiders almost as soon as he set foot ashore), but it drove men out of position in little groups so that even squad leaders could not gain control of their commands. But now the careful briefing told; the men recognized the ground they were on, knew what was to be done there, and followed any leader they could find toward their objectives.

Sergeant Robert Owens of the 3rd personally disposed of the 75 by worming into the firing port of the bunker and driving the crew out the back, getting himself killed and a Congressional Medal for it. The other bunkers were one by one reduced in a rifle-knife-grenade fight, the crossfire became disorganized and by noon most of Cape Torokina was in our hands. The 2nd Raider Battalion pushed patrols out along the solid ground by the trail to Piva, finding ever more defenses and making it evident that any Jap reinforcements would come from that direction. The 3rd Raiders spent all day in a hard fight to subdue Puruata.

Meanwhile the 9th Regiment on the left had encountered special difficulties. The surf was high on all three of its beaches and immediately behind the surf line was a 12-foot bank. Boats and tank lighters began to broach and be swamped as soon as they approached the beach, eighty-six of them altogether, including almost the entire equipment of the three transports working the area. Before a third

199

of the trips from the ships were made these beaches had to be abandoned and the men of the 9th with all their supplies put ashore by means of other ships' boats on the beaches already occupied by the 2nd and 3rd Battalions, 3rd Regiment, to march along the beach to the positions intended for them. These two battalions of the 3rd worked rapidly across the beaches and sent their patrols out toward the assigned phase line for the first night, some 200 yards inshore.

They encountered the swamp. The men were never less than knee-deep in mud and water and sometimes right up to their necks. Thorny vines tore at them, there were occasional Jap bullets, and the vegetation was so thick that it was almost impossible to maintain communications even straight back to the beach, while as for obtaining liaison with formations to the left and right, it was flatly impossible.

While this struggle was going on, General Turnage brought the 1st Battalion, 9th, down to Cape Torokina to cover the flank of the 1st Battalion, 3rd, now pushing along the more solid ground toward the Piva. The force buttoned up for the night, landing successful, though it had been all handwork with the value of the fire support negligible.

There was still some apprehension that night. During the afternoon a big Jap air raid came down, the transports had to cease unloading and move out to sea, while many of the supplies did not get ashore. The original allotment had been so slender that this looked bad. To complicate matters still further there had been so much confusion due to the three useless beaches, the swamp and jungle behind had proved so unexpectedly tough, that it was very hard to move or even to sort the supplies that had come ashore. Under the tropical twilight artillerymen, engineers, signalmen, and even medical detachments toiled at the job, cursing fervently. After dark it clouded up and came on to rain; some of the men in outposts had to sleep sitting up in water to their waists and a general blackout was imposed, under which at least one roving Jap tumbled into a foxhole on top of a Raider, who stabbed him as he squealed in excellent English "I'm too young to die." Under that same night there were lightning flashes and a rumble of thunder from seaward; a phone at the CP rang and the officer who answered it repeated:

"Condition Black—You may expect shelling from enemy ships followed by counterinvasion."

It was not thunder; the reconstituted Southeast Area Fleet had come down from Rabaul to break up the landing—heavy cruisers *Myoko* and *Haguro,* light cruisers *Sendai* and *Agano,* with eight destroyers—and out on the midnight water were locked in battle with Tip Merrill's Hollywood Squadron, their inferiors in guns, speed, armor. But when dawn of 2 November broke it was the Japanese condition that was black; *Sendai* and two of their destroyers were on the bottom and 31-Knot Burke was chasing the rest back toward Rabaul, in such shape that they would stay in dock for a long while. Only one of our destroyers was badly hurt; and that morning of 2 November, when the air forces from Rabaul came down with a group of 67 planes to sink the American "cripples" (instead of going for the piled supplies on the beachhead, where they might really have achieved some damage), Merrill's squadron shot down 17 of them and sent the rest back empty-handed.

IV

Documents found on the bodies at Cape Torokina showed pretty clearly what the Jap order of battle was and that a counterattack might be expected from Piva Forks if at all. General Turnage accordingly brought the 2nd Battalion, 9th, down to join the 1st at the cape, pulled the 1st Battalion, 3rd, back into reserve (it had taken most of the comparatively light casualties—39 killed, 39 missing, 104 wounded that first day); and brought the other Raider battalion over from Puruata Island to form a solid front with its strength on the right. That day and the next and the next were spent in edging through the swamps, the worst country the Marines had ever seen or ever would, while Seabees and bulldozers toiled at the immense task of building roads. For the time being amphitracs were the only vehicles that could move; most of the supply was by hand.

General Turnage intended to bring the remaining battalion of the 9th also down to his right flank, but lateral communications being what they were, the move had not yet been made when the second echelon arrived on 6 November—3,548 men composing the 1st Battalion, 21st Marines (Lieutenant Colonel E. W. Fry), and the advance elements of the 37th Infantry Division. Perhaps it was just as well the shift had not been made; while the transports carrying these troops were lying offshore General Hyakutate tried his counterattack.

One of the most remarkable things about this officer was his persistence in the single plan of action he had worked out for destroying American beachheads. At the same time the 6th Division was added to his army he acquired another from the forces in China, the 17th Division, which had been in the Hankow campaign and was rated as veteran. A good many of the troops of this unit had already been forwarded to southern New Britain to meet the MacArthur menace across the Bismarck Sea, but there was something better than a regiment of infantry with a couple of machine-cannon companies at Rabaul. These he intended to land at Atsinima Bay and the mouth of the Luruma, just beyond the American west flank. They were to hack trails into the interior of the island and come down from there on our perimeter, infiltrating and acting as guerrillas, while Colonel Kawano would be reinforced up the trail from the Shortland area by part of the 45th Regiment and deliver a heavy attack from Piva. Hyakutate estimated the American force ashore as 7,000 (actually it was nearly 18,000 by this date) and, though the number of his own troops was less, still thought the balance would be made up in spiritual power.

It was the Guadalcanal plan used by Kawaguchi and Maruyama with variation in two details only. Admiral Kondo was persuaded to send down the heavy cruiser force of the 2nd Fleet, which should be ample to wipe out the remains of the American cruiser squadron in the area, and at the same time to subject the beachhead to a powerful preliminary shelling that would make Kawano's task easy. Unfortunately there was a shortage of destroyers since the battle of the 1st and they could not be used to carry in the 17th Division troops. These men would have to travel by barge and landing boat. As there was also a shortage of barges, the troops would move in three separate echelons, the first on the night of 6 November.

Now, as we have seen (page 147), the cruiser force got itself caught in Rabaul by the air groups from *Saratoga* and *Princeton* and was so used up it was eliminated from the combination. But even if Hyakutate had not followed the normal Japanese method of going ahead with the plan when one of the legs that supported it had been cut off at the hip, it was now too late to recall the first echelon from the 17th Division, some 1,200 of whom were toddling along in their barges toward Atsinima Bay.

They reached it during the night of the 6th. A couple of barge-loads became confused in the dark on an unfamiliar shore and land-ing east of the point where the Koromokina River spreads into a lagoon at the water's edge—that is, behind a strong outpost of the 9th Marines. Firing broke out there at dawn, the outpost began to retreat east, but found the Japs too numerous, and they had to be taken out by sea, though not before they had eliminated some thirty-five of the enemy. The Japs who landed in the right place pushed across the Luruma, made contact with the advance group, and dug in along a line facing the west flank of the 3rd Battalion, 9th, about 150 yards distant.

Whether they were waiting for the remaining echelons of their group before attempting the move upcountry was uncertain; they may have been too closely held in combat by the Marines, for Gen-eral Turnage had plenty of force at his disposal and promptly at-tacked. A pair of PT boats ran along the shore and shot up the barges with whatever supplies had reached the beach. The 1st Battalion, 3rd, was brought back to assist the 3rd Battalion, 9th and the 1st Battalion, 21st, pushed up into reserve in the same boats in which it had just been landing at the cape. On the afternoon of the 7th both the fresh battalions attacked with an artillery and mortar barrage to help. The attack went all right but they could find no tenable line so withdrew to their original positions during the night. The next day the 1st Battalion, 21st, passed through the lines to attack again after a new and even heavier artillery concentration. This time they went right through the positions the Japs had hastily constructed and the rest was mop up. The few Japs who escaped the fighting all died off in the interior from disease and the activity of the Fiji Island scouts who prowled the area. Our loss—16 killed, 30 wounded. Jap rifle marksmanship, never very good, was noted as outstandingly bad in this affair.

V

On the other flank the Raiders had penetrated some 2,000 yards by this time and had set up a road block on the trail from Piva across the mountains (the Numa Numa trail) about 500 yards west of the point where the two trails joined. Colonel Kawano had not received his reinforcements from the 45th Regiment, but he seems to have been an impatient man, and began an infiltration attack on the road block during the night of 5 November. The only thing it achieved was to bring all the Raiders to the front while on their side the Japs dug in with their flanks on the swamps.

There Colonel Shapley's men attacked them on the 8th and again on the 9th under artillery cover. It was slow going, along a narrow and muddy causeway that tanks could not negotiate, but the fire power was on our side and the enemy continually raked by planes to which he could make no reply. On the 10th two battalions of the 9th Regiment passed through the Raiders, took up the drive and carried it through Piva Village, wiping out its defenders. We lost 17 killed, 32 wounded; buried some 200 Japs.

Corps headquarters was now in and most of the 37th Division. The latter was given the old left flank of the position with the mission of pushing beyond the swamps to the upper Koromokina, where some flat ground offered a site for bomber strips while the fighter strip was laid out on the cape itself. The Marines took over the perimeter along the Piva, the 9th Regiment close to the shore, Raider Regiment farthest inland, 3rd and 21st Regiments between. There was another Piva Village in this area, Piva No. II, with an extensive coconut grove just north of it. The enemy's main positions seemed to be on the far side of the stream, from where he continually threw in an annoying mortar and rifle fire. The coconut grove and all the country north along the Numa Numa trail were terra incognita, except that a reconnaissance company of artillery had been fired on from this region. On 13 November the 2nd Battalion, 21st, was pushed out in this direction to develop the small Jap outpost expected to be found there.

The battalion encountered difficulties. Under hurry-up orders from division, Lieutenant Colonel E. R. Smoak sent one company well in advance; it ran into a Japanese position in strength, was pretty badly shot up, and reduced to the defensive. The remainder of the battalion had to be put in as fast as it came up to the rescue, that is, piecemeal, and then a second disengaging move made, after which the battalion dug in for the night. In the morning a squadron of planes combed the whole area with 100-pound bombs, and the artillery laid down a beautifully accurate concentration, thanks to the intelligent action of a corporal who had counted his paces as he walked back wounded. Under this fire the battalion again went forth, but encountered more trouble when two of the accompanying tanks got lost in the dense vegetation and fired on our own troops, producing a momentary confusion that was less serious than it might have been because the intensity of our fire kept the Japs pinned down. By evening both the grove and Piva Village No. II were taken and there was only a little mopping up still to do. Loss: 9 killed, 42 wounded; Jap dead counted, 19—but there were plenty more, all right, never found under the jungle. It had been the main Jap position in the area, the junction of the two trails.

It was a position which Colonel Kawano was nearly ready to abandon in any case. He had thrown a road block across the Numa Numa trail and had a reinforced company holding it, with the bulk of his forces, now including some of the 45th Regiment, well back on a series of north-south ridges east of the east fork of the Piva.

All this area fell within the designed limits of the perimeter since from the high ground the proposed airstrips could be both observed and fired upon by light guns. On 11 November the moves began to take it away from the Japs, with the 3rd Battalion, 3rd, moving north, parallel to the Numa Numa trail on one hand and the advance elements of the 37th Division on the other. They had to work forward slowly, their supply problem being acute thus deep in the roadless jungle, but on the 15th their left made contact with the 37th Division men, behind whom the Seabees had now built a road up from the beachhead circling the swamp. On 17 November the battalion located Colonel Kawano's road block; at the same time the 1st Battalion, 21st, found a Jap outpost between the two branches of the Piva.

Two days later the 3rd Battalion, 3rd, went forward with light tanks; by-passed the road block, hit it from its flank, and drove its defenders out. They counterattacked the battalion from flank and rear the following morning, but Lieutenant Colonel R. M. King, commanding, had expected exactly that and shot their hearts out, pursuing eastward right across both forks of the Piva. Here he found a prepared position, a long line of foxholes rather hastily dug, but now without troops enough to man them effectively. The battalion attacked at once, carried the position, and found it had taken a covering position for the main Jap defense line east of the Piva.

Meanwhile the 2nd Battalion, 3rd, had passed through the troops along the east-west trail, reduced the outposts between the river forks and crossed to the east bank, getting mortar and machine-gun fire from a series of pillboxes. A platoon under Lieutenant Cibik, working slightly leftward, began to climb, under fire and beating it down. They presently found themselves atop a 400-foot ridge from which the entire Empress Augusta Bay region was visible. There was not much opportunity to enjoy the view; the Japs immediately attacked in force and Cibik's command was gradually built up by small reinforcements till over 200 men were involved in some pretty desperate fighting before the Japs gave it up and our command began to construct a regimental line involving the ridge.

It was now the evening of the 21st. The 2nd Battalion, 3rd, had its ridge ("Cibik Ridge," it was later called) but was unable to get any farther into the Jap lines and that night was relieved by the 1st Battalion of the same regiment. As the 2nd was moving to the rear the enemy heavily counterattacked the salient that had been thrust into their lines; the 2nd Battalion had to stay on the job and gladly accepted the assistance of a heavy patrol from the 21st, which was next in line. The positions held; and all the next two days were spent by observers spying from Cibik Ridge, registering Jap installations for shoots by the artillery, preparatory to the break-through attack. Colonel George B. McHenry of the regiment noted with pleasure that the Jap positions had been mainly set up facing south to resist an attack toward the hills. He proposed to sweep right down the main trail, taking each in flank.

The attack jumped off on the morning of 24 November, the 2nd and 3rd Battalions abreast, after an artillery concentration of no less than seven battalions, which was considered the heaviest barrage Marines ever had to help them. They needed that much; most of the prepared positions were found occupied only by the dead, but the Jap artillery was both accurate and in strength. It inflicted the heaviest casualties of the campaign on the 3rd Regiment men and when they had penetrated 500 yards they were counterattacked on both flanks by the Jap reserves. There was a hand-to-hand fight that lasted till nearly twilight and died down only because of lack of material. Colonel Kawano was dead by that time and his regiment had joined the list of *zemetsu*. It was the last heavy fighting while the Marines were on that line.

VI

They went looking for action on their own, however, and found more than they wanted. Scouts and coastwatchers brought reports that the Japs had some men at Koiari Beach, where Empress Augusta Bay turns wide to the southward, 10 miles down. On 29 November, Major Richard Fagan's 1st Parachute Battalion, reinforced by a company of Raiders, was thrown on the beach there to see what could be done about it. Apparently the Japs were expecting friends; an officer waded out and began a conversation. "There is no record of his subsequent proceedings," says the report, dryly. But that was the end of the easy going; the parachutists and Raiders had no sooner installed themselves in a little perimeter of 350 by 180 yards ashore when they began to get heavy rifle, machine-gun, and mortar fire from every direction, followed by Jap attempts to break into their lines. By noon it was evident there would be no raiding that day; by early afternoon Major Fagan was requesting evacuation.

The Jap fire continued to increase in intensity and the parachutists, who were old hands and knew what they were talking about, estimated that there were between 1,000 and 1,200 of the enemy besieging them. The fire became so heavy that the boats could not work in. Things began to look bad; ammunition was nearly gone and so small a perimeter would be very difficult to hold in the dark. But now some planes came over and the destroyer *Fullam* worked along the shore. The latter proved an excellent gunnery ship, a battery of 155s in the Torokina beachhead opened up from long range, nicely directed by an artillery observer with the Raiders, and they got out through the twilight with 22 men killed, 99 wounded. Maybe the Jap casualties were heavier but the operation was no success—defective preliminary intelligence again.

That was the campaign as far as the Marines were concerned. They began to be pulled out on 21 December as the Americal Division moved in and a week later the exchange process was complete, the whole area being turned over to the Army XIV Corps. It had been a highly successful affair, with 390 killed, 1,097 wounded of Marine forces (the 37th casualties were negligible) against the wiping out of the Japanese 23rd Regiment and the 1,200 men they tried to land in our rear. But the count on casualties does not tell the story; the essential airfield had been taken, the three Jap bases on Bougainville knocked out, and Rabaul converted into a ghost base by the pinch between Empress Augusta Bay and the positions MacArthur had seized.

Looking upon it as a whole one cannot but be impressed by the manner in which the difficulties encountered in the earlier jungle-island campaigns had been overcome, the errors made in those campaigns eliminated. Bougainville was the Guadalcanal attack as it should have been delivered. Of course, at Guadalcanal the means were lacking to make the attack this way. There was no strong force of cruisers and destroyers patrolling the beach every night to keep the enemy from landing reinforcements. (The enemy did try once during the campaign, with five destroyers, while the Marines were fighting for Cibik Ridge, but Arleigh Burke's Little Beavers caught them off St. George's Channel and sank three of the Jap ships without losing a man.) At Guadalcanal we had no command of the air. The 3rd Marine Division counted that it was bombed ninety times during the operation and was inclined to feel abused about it, but on General Vandegrift's island they used to have that many Jap air raids in a week. But above all the success of the expedition was due to the fact that the strategic use of the amphibious forces had been better learned. The enemy's strength ashore was underestimated at Empress Augusta Bay, the position was not at all what either scouting or air reconnaissance had promised it to be (that swamp!), but these errors made not the slightest difference. Neither did the fact that there was trouble about getting supplies across the beachhead—the one problem not yet solved.

The place was expeditiously and cheaply taken and it was ultimately held by the same means of perimeter defense as that at Guadalcanal. The method is certainly not suited to the general conditions of land warfare and is probably valid only for the special case of amphibious work in thick country.

The Japanese helped us prove that it is valid for such cases. They managed to assemble their forces around the Bougainville perimeter at the end of February and in early March, 1944—for an attack down the ridges on the land side of the position, as one might expect from Hyakutate, who directed the operation from Rabaul. The fighting lasted three days; once the Japs got as much as 75 yards into our lines; but the over-all result was the same as at Guadal. They went trailing back into the jungle, losing men at every step from malaria and enteric, since it had been impossible to move supplies up with their troops, the medical stores were all gone and no more reaching them across seas now thoroughly in our control. At the end of that year there were not 12,000 left of the whole Jap force on Bougainville and those who were left were devoting their attention to sweet potatoes. "The seasons do not change," said the commandant of Truk, caught in a similar situation at the same time. "I try to look like a proud vice-admiral, but it is hard with a potato hook in my hands. It rains every day, the flowers bloom every day, the enemy bombs us every day, so why remember?" In Japanese it forms a poem.

Chapter 13

The Marianas: Plans and Preliminaries

IN DESULTORY CONVERSATIONS AND OCCASIONALLY DURING THOSE staff conferences held every morning in the dun-colored building overlooking Pearl Harbor from Makalapa Drive, Admiral Nimitz had not infrequently expressed his desire to see the Star-Spangled Banner floating over Truk, which still held its place in American imaginations as the mighty fortress of Japan in the south and the symbol of the enemy's power by sea. There was even some talk that the CINCPOA[1] might fly his own flag afloat for such an operation, which would surely bring the long-invisible Japanese fleet forth for that showdown battle every American seaman desired. The suggestion came less from the Admiral himself than from those juniors who are quick to expand every hint into a statement, but it illustrates the state of mind: and it was a state of mind shared by the Joint Chiefs of Staff in Washington, as Nimitz was informed at one of the periodic meetings between himself and Admiral King when the two came together on the Pacific coast, the one flying across the continent, the other across an ocean.

The original long-range plan was for an assault on Truk in September, 1944, when so many new fleet units would be ready and so many troops available. But now two things had changed: the Japanese air force had shown itself both weak and timorous during the great sweep of Task Force 58 from Truk to the Marianas, and our own losses on Bougainville had been so unexpectedly light that no fewer than three divisions of Marines with nearly a fourth would be ready for action by June. These were the 2nd, 3rd, and 4th Divisions with the 1st Provisional Brigade, containing the Raider regi-

---

[1] At this period Admiral Nimitz's title had been ·changed from Commander in Chief Pacific to Commander in Chief Pacific Ocean Area.

ment, the parachutists, the 22nd Regiment and attached troops; add the Army 27th and 77th Divisions, and there would be a force two corps strong.

The position at sea was not less favorable; three of our carriers were temporarily out of action but one of these (*Lexington*) would soon be repaired and there were three new ones. The escort carriers had shown themselves capable of providing the necessary close support for beachhead work. It was thus possible to contemplate detaching the whole of the fast carrier force for a fleet action without seriously decreasing the help given from sea to the Marines ashore.

The invasion of Truk was accordingly advanced from September to June and the planners began to work on it. But before March had run its course opposition to the idea began to develop, it would seem chiefly from the group centering round Admiral Spruance. Truk, these officers insisted, now had no more importance than Wotje or Jaluit; neither our submarine scouts around the place nor the B-24s now bombing reported major Japanese ships there. It was time (they said) to apply on an oceanic scale the doctrine of seizing an advanced base in the midst of the enemy's holdings; time to go not to Truk but to Saipan and Guam in the Marianas—break through the Japanese defense line running down those islands from metropolitan Japan by way of the Bonins, Iwo Jima, and the Marianas to Yap and Palau.

It was a bold concept, but not too bold for Nimitz who, at a staff conference in earliest April, asked proponents of each view—Saipan or Truk—to sum up their cases. When they had finished the Admiral asked one question: "Which will damage the enemy most?" and the matter was decided.

Nevertheless, there were lions in the path. From Eniwetok, whose fine anchorage would make it the forward staging base, it is over 1,000 miles to Saipan; from Pearl Harbor to Eniwetok it is 2,375, totaling an oceanic distance. It was clearly impossible to consider reinforcement convoys moving in several echelons across such spaces, as they had done at Bougainville; the expeditions, with all resources for a major land campaign, must go in a single piece. The project was not dissimilar to invading the shores of Europe direct from New York. The enemy could stage in his own land-based planes from the Empire; we would have none. Yap, Ponape, Woleai, and Truk were

211

within bombing range of the areas where supply ships must lie till unloaded. Above all, there was the intimate prospect that the Japanese Navy would come out for a final reckoning while the invaders were astride the beaches. Every prewar military and civilian examination of a Japanese-American conflict[1] had reached the conclusion that the great battle of the navies would come when our forces attempted to repossess Guam and there were in existence maps with a cross 100 miles or more southwest of that island where the clash would most likely take place.

These were the problems. Admiral Spruance had over-all command, as head of 5th Fleet; he could see further into the complications of such a situation than any other leader and would keep his eyes more steadily on the overruling consideration of establishing our forces ashore. For the fast fleet, Marc Mitscher, his flag in a carrier; for the battleships, Willis Augustus Lee. Under Spruance also, Richmond Kelly Turner led the amphibious forces; clearly the best man in that business, though explosive and temperamental; but he had worked much with Spruance in the past, the two understood each other and got along together. Holland Smith, now lieutenant general, was given command of all expeditionary forces, tantamount to an army in strength; but as there was no other landing force Corps Headquarters with skill and experience for so wide a project, he held a dual command as head of the V Amphib Corps, with a second staff for that purpose.

This corps would attack Saipan on 15 June with the 2nd and 4th Marine Divisions, the Army 27th Division being in reserve afloat. As soon as the success of that operation was assured, which should not be too long, as intelligence estimates showed only some 5,000-6,000 Japanese on the island, the III Amphib Corps, under Major General Geiger, would be called up from Guadalcanal and launched against Guam. It was anticipated that at most two regimental combat teams of the 27th would be called into the Saipan fighting, probably in the last stages. This organization could thus serve as a reserve for the Guam attack also. As soon as Saipan was clear the V Corps would take Tinian. These were the only important Marianas. Rota had an airfield but it would be insignificant with the larger installations of Guam-Saipan-Tinian in our hands. The Japs would hardly have

[1] Cf. Hector Bywater, *Great Pacific War.*

time to complete the strip on which they had been rather unimpressively toiling on Pagan Island, and the remainder of the Marianas were hot rocks inhabited chiefly by melancholy seabirds. The 77th Division was to remain in distant reserve at Hawaii.

Rehearsals at Maui went off with a pleasing smoothness. The cap-

tain of each transport visited the unit he was to carry and had a long talk with his officers, so that the loading went smoothly also, delayed only a single day by the Pearl Harbor explosion, when an LST blew up on 2 May while loading ammunition and communicated the fire to six others, all being lost plus 200 men. On 8 June the armada rendezvoused at Eniwetok, much cheered by the radio flash of Eisenhower's men at last in France, and the occasion was celebrated with

213

beer and gin in the newly opened officers' club. If the fleet that went to the Marshalls had been one of the largest that ever sailed, there was no question about this: the exclusive superlative could be applied without modification. The ships were 775 in number and could not be seen by a single eye, even from a plane; there were 100,000 marching men and a quarter million sailors.[1]

[1] For the record and because it was important later, Mitscher's fast force had the carrier group of Admiral Clark—*Hornet, Yorktown, Belleau Wood, Bataan,* with the attached cruisers *Boston, Baltimore, Canberra, Oakland, San Juan* and destroyers *Izard, Charrette, Conner, Bell, Burns, Boyd, Bradford, Brown, Cowell, Maury, Craven, Gridley, Helm, McCall;* the carrier group of Montgomery—*Bunker Hill, Wasp, Cabot, Monterey,* with the battleships *Iowa, New Jersey,* cruisers *Santa Fe, Mobile, Biloxi,* destroyers *Owen Miller, The Sullivans, Stephen Potter, Tingey, Hickox, Hunt, Lewis Hancock, Marshall, Selfridge, Mugford, Ralph Talbot, Patterson, Bagley;* of Reeve—*Enterprise, Lexington, San Jacinto, Princeton,* with the battleships *North Carolina, Washington, Indiana, South Dakota, Alabama* and destroyers *C. K. Bronson, Cotten, Dortch, Gatling, Healy, Cogswell, Caperton, Ingersoll, Knapp, Dewey, Hull, Monaghan, Farragut, MacDonough, Dale, Aylwin;* of Harrill—carriers *Essex, Langley, Cowpens,* with the cruisers *Vincennes, Houston, Miami, San Diego, Reno* and destroyers *Lansdowne, Lardner, McCalla, Lang, Sterrett, Wilson, Case, Ellet, Charles Ausburne, Stanly, Dyson, Converse, Spence, Thatcher.* In the attack force for Saipan Admiral Turner led the battleships *Tennessee, California, Maryland, Colorado,* with the cruisers *Louisville, Indianapolis, Montpelier, Cleveland, Birmingham;* the escort carrier divisions of Admirals Bogan and Sallada comprising *Fanshaw Bay, Midway, White Plains, Kalinin Bay, Kitkun Bay, Gambier Bay,* and destroyers *Halsey Powell, Benham, Yarnall, Twining, Stockham, Remey, Wadleigh, Norman Scott, Mertz, Monssen, McDermut, McGowan, McNair, Melvin, Bailey, Coghlan, Porterfield, Callaghan, Cassin Young, Irvin, Longshaw, Morrison, Prichett, Phillip, Cony, Newcomb, Bennion, H. L. Edwards, Robinson, Ross, A. W. Grant, Bryant,* minesweepers *Palmer, Chandler, Howard, Zane.* Close-in Connolly had the Southern Attack Force for Guam; his ships were battleships *Idaho, New Mexico, Pennsylvania,* cruisers *Wichita, Minneapolis, New Orleans, San Francisco, Honolulu, St. Louis;* escort carrier groups under Admirals Ragsdale and Stump comprising *Sangamon, Suwanee, Chenango, Corregidor, Coral Sea,* and destroyers *Stevens, Harrison, John Rodgers, McKee, Murray, Ringgold, Schroeder, Sigsbee, Dashiell, Phelps, Shaw, Fullam, Guest, Bennett, Halford, Hudson, Anthony, Wadsworth, Terry, Braine, Colahan, Erben, Walker, Hale, Abbot, Stembel, Bullard, Kidd, Black, Chauncey, Haggard, Franks, Hailey, Johnston;* minesweepers *Swallow, Sheldrake, Skylark, Starling, Hamilton, Holmes, Hopkins, Perry, Long, Hogan, Stansbury.* Six more destroyers—*Pringle, Waller, Saufley, Conway, Eaton, Sigourney*—and six destroyer escorts—*Sederstrom, Fleming, Tisdale, Eisele, Barron, Acree*—covered the reserve afloat. And these were the fighting vessels alone; only such a catalogue of the ships can convey beyond figures an idea of how a like mass migration this attack on the Japanese inner defense line was.

214

Yet no one thought it would be easy. Three times since the preliminary estimate planes had flown over Saipan for photos and each photo showed almost feverish work on the new defense positions, each plane saw new ships in the harbor, and our submarines reported traffic heavy from the Empire to the Marianas. The final G-2 estimate jumped the number of troops on Saipan to 10,000-12,000.

On the command ship *Rocky Mount* General Holland Smith was not elated. "We are through with the flat atolls now. We learned how to pulverize atolls, but now we are up against mountains and caves where the Japs can dig in, and a week from today there will be a lot of dead Marines." As the correspondents left the room where they were being briefed, Richmond Kelly Turner indicated the General, as he remarked to correspondent Bob Sherrod, "He can estimate the enemy capabilities better than any man aboard."

II

Vice-Admiral Chuichi Nagumo, commander of the Central Pacific Fleet, had moved his headquarters to the Mariana Gunto. He was an extremely big pot, who had commanded the forces afloat in the Pearl Harbor attack and later at Midway and Santa Cruz—though not quite as big a pot as he thought he was, for after Yamamoto was shot down in the Solomons, it was revealed that that officer had named as his heir to his own high office not Nagumo but the unfortunate Yamaguchi, who had been killed aboard the *Hiryu* at Midway. The command ashore was not the normal assignment of such a magnifico, but the political pressures in Tokyo had been building up so seriously that a major naval officer was believed to be needed in the Inner South Seas Defense Area. Under the impulse of the Jushin, Shinusuka Kishi, of the Commerce and Agriculture Department, and Manoru Shigemitsu, the Foreign Minister, had threatened to resign. Tojo would evidently have to reconstruct his whole Cabinet, and the Navy people were hopeful that in the reshuffling that would inevitably attend such a process a revision of the unsatisfactory chain of command in the Central Pacific Area could be achieved.

This chain of command was itself the result of the haste with which Tojo had been forced to revise both his political and his military arrangements after the simultaneous attack on Truk and loss of the Marshalls. That double event foreshadowed an attack by the Americans somewhere in the Central Pacific and without even consulting the Navy the Premier set up a new 31st Army command with the aged, solemn and respectable Lieutenant General Saito at its head, for the defense of the island barrier. The General received his command on 25 February; made obeisance at the palace the next day and on the 27th was in Saipan. Three days later he went down to Palau by seaplane to wait on Admiral Koga, commander of the Combined Fleet, aboard his flagship *Yamato*. The two officers had dinner and then discussed strategy, after which Admiral Koga remarked that he had no orders from the Imperial Naval Staff in Tokyo relative to command in the Central Pacific, and Saito flew back to Guam, where there was a good deal to do. The transport *Sakito Maru* had been sunk by an American submarine with the 18th Infantry aboard and the survivors had just arrived in a deplorable state, without arms.

The General was busy with these men and with inspecting the shores of Saipan when on 10 March, to his intense surprise, he received an order from Koga unifying all commands in the area under the authority of the Central Pacific Fleet. The staff officer who brought it was very disagreeable, pointing out that the Navy controlled all supplies. General Saito considered the procedure indecent and the scheme of command set forth in the order as vague and irritating. There was a series of debates, acrid and hissing, which lasted for weeks, during which the troops sent down from the Empire for the defense of the Central Pacific Area underwent some remarkable shufflings, the case of the 8th Expeditionary Unit being typical.

This was one of Tojo's amphibious brigades under a new name. It embarked at Fusan in the Matsu No. 2 convoy on 1 March under orders for Truk by way of Saipan. En route the Imperial General Staff decided to strengthen the Saipan garrison instead and placed it under Saito's command, but before it could reach him, Admiral Koga's order was issued. The Tokyo staff suddenly realized that under the terms of the order the 8th Expeditionary Unit would now be under naval command, so they ordered it to Truk after all. In the meanwhile one of the American submarines, which were becoming very annoying, got into the convoy and sank one transport, also the escort flag, the cruiser *Tatsuta,* which had all the unit's records aboard.[1] A new set of records had to be prepared while the convoy lay over in Saipan Harbor, and as this was being done the Navy insisted that since the unit was afloat it was under naval command and could be sent wherever they pleased.

The result of all these and similar arguments was naturally a compromise which satisfied nobody. The general lines were that Army and Navy commanders should continue to control their own troops (Special Naval Landing and Base Forces in the case of the latter) under ordinary circumstances. "It is unnecessary that certain forces be organized under a unified command," said the document initialed by staff officers for the heads of both services. Naval and Army troops were not to trespass on the areas under the other's command. But as soon as the enemy commenced a landing operation on any island all the forces there would immediately fall under the authority of the senior officer present, whether he belonged to Army or Navy. The Navy should be responsible for developing each island's resources for defense, the necessary laborers being furnished by the Army. General Saito would be responsible for the land defenses of the Bonins and the Mariana Gunto, the Navy for the land defenses of the Carolines; but Navy base forces in the western Carolines should take orders from the Army General commanding in that area as regards operations ashore. (This is somewhat difficult for an Occidental mind to understand; the answer is that the Orientals did not understand it either. It was one of those arrangements common among Japanese who cannot agree, purposely over-intricate, so that the question of who is to give the effective orders in any case is thrown into the domain of individual personalities.)

A secondary result of these debates and command shufflings was that until the matter was settled to the dissatisfaction of both services no reinforcement convoys at all were dispatched to the Inner South Seas Area, that is, for nearly a month. When they resumed, American submarine activity had been greatly intensified and the attacks on these craft added to the confusion of commands. In April, for example, the submarines sank almost an entire convoy bringing part of the 52nd Division down past Saipan for the Carolines. Only

[1] This was the work of *Sandlance.*

300 men of the 150th Infantry Regiment from that division were rescued and there was a good deal of question about whose command they were now under.

Nevertheless, the Imperial Staff persisted in its reinforcement program. By early June it had succeeded in furnishing General Saito with 22,702 Army troops, the bulk of which belonged to the 43rd (Nagoya) Division and the 47th Independent Mixed Brigade, commanded by Colonel Oka.[1] These troops were all in good shape with the exception of one regiment of the 43rd which had been torpedoed in its transport, the soldiers losing all their weapons. There was a tank regiment with fifty medium and about twelve light tanks; a couple of vehicle companies, the survivors of the 150th Regiment, with similar weaponless survivors from the 9th Expeditionary Unit, two mortar battalions, an engineer regiment, and another tank regiment. Arms were lacking for some 7,000 of the people, who were the relics of the Tateyama convoy, which lost five big transports out of seven in a concerted and persistent submarine attack of 4-6 June, when over 2,000 soldiers drowned.[2] Admiral Nagumo had the 1st Yokosuka Special Naval Landing Force, a few Naval Guard troops, and the men and planes (120) of the 22nd Air Flotilla, totaling 6,960 men on morning report.

The submarine activity that cut the number of troops in the Mariana Gunto also interfered with the construction of defenses, to which General Saito addressed himself as soon as the command problem was straightened out. He considered Saipan the most vital of the islands and had sent only 4,700 to Tinian and 13,000 to Guam. A single battalion held Pagan. Inspections both on the ground and from the air led him to the conclusion that at Saipan there were only three areas with beaches suitable for the the American type of landing—on the extreme southern face (but that was covered by reefs), around the island's main town of Garapan about halfway along its western flank, and at the southwestern tip of the

---

[1] There is no absolute certainty that this was our old friend of Guadalcanal, who sneaked off after leaving the farewell note for his troops, but the name is not particularly common in Japanese and it is most unusual to find a colonel in command of a brigade unless he has a good deal of influence, so this is probably the same old Oka.

[2] This was the work of *Pintado* and *Shark*, second of the name, which attacked the convoy throughout five days.

island, embracing the sugar-mill town of Charan Kanoa, the most probable point of attack. Desirable as it would be to construct positions around the ravines and natural caves of Mt. Tapotchau at the center of the island, the General held (in accordance with normal Japanese doctrine) that island defense could most successfully be conducted at the beach. Since materials and labor were lacking for the construction of both beach and mountain projects, he used what he had to build up positions along the Charan Kanoa shore.

SAIPAN

0   1000 2000 3000 4000 YDS.

The intent was to line this full 4-mile strip with barriers and pill-boxes giving flanking fire from machine guns, 20- and 37-mm. anti-boat guns, as in the Tarawa defenses. Behind these and at the first ridge line mortars were to be in place and registered on the beaches; behind these again, on the rising slopes, the artillery. The tank regiment and the bulk of the infantry forces were to be held approximately at the line of the battery positions, ready to counterattack any survivors of the American force who remained on the beaches when darkness fell. Unhappily, several shiploads of steel and concrete for the beach defenses were lost through "the hazards of the ocean" (as the General put it) and replacements had only begun to come by May. Some work was done by that time, including the digging of field trenches; now everything was pushed forward more vigorously and guns began to be mounted. The General reported at this time that he considered the Mariana Gunto as "the final defensive position of the homeland" and that he would complete his "strong positions which will make fire point a backbone" by the middle of August. By November he expected to have fortified a series of cave and terrace positions in from the beach line and around the important Aslito airfield at the southern end of the island.

The precise state of affairs in June was that sixteen 105-mm. howitzers, thirty 75-mm. field pieces, and eight 155s were in position behind the Charan Kanoa and Oreai beaches—divisional and brigade artillery, immobile because the prime movers had been sunk on the sea, and with the emplacements around them incomplete. At Agingan there were a pair of British 6-inch from Singapore; on Nafutan Point four more, and another pair at Garapan covering the harbor, which is known as Tanapag. All around Magicienne Bay, which was a Navy command area, and which Admiral Nagumo expected the Americans to use as an anchorage, were batteries under his control. They aggregated four fine 200-mm. mortars, three 140s, and four 120s. Aslito Field had eight dual-purpose 120s and a pair of 75s. Both ammunition chambers and emplacements for all but the divisional and brigade guns were incomplete; nor had any positions been made ready for six more 200-mm. mortars and thirty-two 120s in Garapan Naval Depot.

A meeting of all officers was called by the Chief of Staff, who told them for themselves and for their soldiers that there had been too much of suicide in the other islands. They should by no means consider destroying themselves if the enemy made progress. One lieutenant wrote in his notebook that he was deeply moved by this speech. "We shall crush the enemy by living." Admiral Nagumo meanwhile had become very apprehensive about the slowness of the Army men in getting things done. On 14 June, in an effort to stir them, he showed Saito the report he was sending to Tokyo—"It is a certainty that the enemy will attack the Marianas this month or next."

III

The estimate was only accidentally accurate and was by no means shared either in Tokyo or aboard the flagship of the Combined Fleet. In both places there had been much speculation about the next point of American attack following the blow in the Marshalls, but in both speculation had gradually yielded to almost-certainty as American forces landed at Emirau in March, Hollandia in New Guinea during April, and Wakde in May, to the accompaniment of heavy carrier strikes all along the range of the Carolines. It seemed clear that the Americans had established themselves at Kwajalein and Eniwetok not so much for the sake of any advantages they would gain by holding these points as to eliminate them as Japanese observation and air-attack stations, clear them out of the direct path from Pearl Harbor down to the New Guinea shore, give the U. S. Fleet free movement in that direction. General MacArthur was using major forces of troops in his leapfrog offensive; he had had the support of main American fleet units; he was doing a great deal of talking about the return to the Philippines. It was perfectly comprehensible to the Japanese that this politically potent officer had been able to impose his strategic views on the American Navy. It was the sort of thing that happened in their own country.

Accordingly they envisioned the next move of our fleet and its attached Marine force as an attack on some point in the Caroline Shoto—Palau, Yap, or Woleai for choice. These points received the bulk of the reinforcements and construction material that sifted through the submarines. The Combined Fleet, in no very good shape when the New Guinea move began (*Yamato* was still recovering from her torpedo at that date and no pilots had been received by the

221

new carriers), was coming around nicely and as May lengthened pilots and planes were receiving actual training aboard their ships. Of these new carriers and new air groups there were now nine— *Shokaku* and *Zuikaku*, fully healed of their battle damage; the splendid new *Taiho*, largest carrier in the world; *Hitaka* and *Hayataka*, and the light carriers *Zuiho*, *Ryuho*, *Chitose* and *Chiyoda*, the last three new—nearly five hundred planes. This was no bad match for the American force. The battle line had suffered a misfortune during the previous summer when *Mutsu* got into a new-laid mine field while entering harbor and went down; but there were still nine fast battleships, including the great *Yamato* and *Musashi* with their 18-inch guns. It was close enough to the strength of the fast American force to make success a matter of tactics and technique.

When it became so probable that a combined MacArthur-Navy offensive against the Caroline Shoto was in prospect, all the fleet units were assembled at Tawi Tawi Anchorage, where the Philippines joined Borneo, to give Tayoda freedom of action in time and space. 60 per cent of the available combat planes in the Empire were flown into the Southern Area, a figure which is even larger than it looks, since most of the 40 per cent remaining had their pilots still in the advance student stage and were not fully organized as combat air groups. (One of the Bonin sector squadrons, for instance, had ten instructors and twenty students and was to be employed for combat in an emergency only.) As a final preventive a double line of twelve scouting submarines was fanned out in an arrowhead formation with Truk at its point—six covering a line north to Guam, six covering the sea south of the Carolines to Manus Island.

The operations of this last group had a remarkable result. On 21 May one of them, probably *Ro-117*, was sighted by an American long-range scouting plane which attacked her. The pilot bombed as she went down, thought he missed and so reported to Halsey's headquarters. Now it happened there was in this general area a division of destroyer escorts (*England*, *Raby*, and *George*) which had been looking for and had lately sunk a big supply submarine (*I-16*) trying to work into Bougainville. The Admiral ordered the three to go look up the sub seen by the airplane. They never found it; nobody ever did, she had left the scouting line damaged and on her way back to Japan for repairs was picked up by a PBY. But they did find, so far from the position given that it could not have been the submarine they were after, the first vessel of the Japanese scouting line, *Ro-106*. The destroyer escort *England* was one of the most efficient anti-submarine vessels that ever sailed; she sank *Ro-106* on 21 May, and still running toward the desired position, found *Ro-104* and disposed of her the next night. There was now evidence of pattern in the Japanese arrangements. The *England-Raby-George* unit worked right along the scouting line and on the five succeeding days accounted for *Ro-116, Ro-108,* and *Ro-105*. It was a clean sweep. On one day Koga's scouting submarines were furnishing completely negative reports, on the next day they were gone without making any reports; they had simply ceased to exist.

Submarine scouting is a dangerous profession, but nothing like this had ever happened before, anywhere. Out of a group of six one would expect at least some member to survive long enough to furnish some clue to the mysterious destruction that had overtaken the rest. The Tawi Tawi Admiral and the Imperial General Staff reacted as men with their preconceived ideas of American strategy might be expected to react, or even as men without preconceived ideas when encountering an event so wholly beyond precedent. They deduced the presence of an enormous American fleet with elaborate air patrols and a whole host of destroyers on its wings, so many that a submarine stood no chance.

It was the final article of conviction which made almost-certainty into certainty absolute. The Americans were sweeping down on Yap, Woleai, or Palau. The air patrols over all this region were doubled; the Combined Fleet was alerted to have steam for full power on three hours' notice; and Admiral Nagumo's estimate of the situation at Saipan was received with a sniff and filed away in mothballs.

IV

One of the oddest features of Operation Forager, as the attack on Saipan was called, is how correctly and yet incorrectly the Japanese commanders had divined the American plan. The Admiral was perfectly right as to the date, but he had set up his portions of the defenses around Magicienne Bay where Turner had no intention of attacking. The General would not believe a word his colleague

223

said about timing, but had selected for his main defense precisely the area where the Marines were going ashore, on both sides of Charan Kanoa, with the 2nd Marine Division beyond a jutting pier at the north end of the town, which formed a convenient divisional boundary landmark, and the 4th Division south from there to Agingan Point.

The plan was for the regimental combat teams of the 23rd and 25th Marines to land abreast in the latter area, those of the 6th and 8th Regiments to land abreast in the former, two battalions of each in the first wave. They would have the cover of a battleship and four destroyers in the south (*Tennessee, Bailey, Robinson, A. W. Grant, Norman Scott*), two cruisers at the center (*Birmingham, Indianapolis*), and a battleship and three destroyers at the north (*California, Halsey Powell, Coghlan, Monssen*), while off beyond the line of fire twenty-four LCI rocket gunboats formed line to throw in those missiles that had been so effective in Kwajalein.

This time there were plenty of those small craft like PCs and SCs to act as control ships for the transfer of troops from Higgins boats to the amphitracs which would carry the men across the reef line to the beach. There were eight battalions of these amphitracs, four manned by Marines, four by the Army; DUKWs would handle the artillery. The CVEs would furnish close air support; their fighters would be supplied with the new "Holy Moses" rockets, to be employed here for the first time, where numerous caves and ravines promised them a particular utility. The aviators had trained with them but regarded the new weapons with unconcealed distrust, and Army air observers with the expedition thought that this whole idea of close air support was, in the expression of their own field manual, "dangerous and unprofitable." A number of planes for the preliminary strike had white phosphorus bombs and belly tanks for burning off the cane fields in which the Japs might take cover.

The two remaining regiments (2nd and 24th) were to move up in their transports to the Garapan area with the battleship *Colorado* and a couple of destroyers covering, to make a bluff at a landing, allow themselves to be apparently beaten off; then move down to the actual beaches and go ashore before dark of D day. As soon as the beaches were sufficiently clear the 10th Regiment (Artillery) would follow the 2nd Division Infantry and the 14th Regiment the 4th

224

Division; and as soon as it was possible after this an Army formation of heavy guns, the XXIV Corps Artillery, would follow the Marine cannon in, taking over all counterbattery work at the earliest possible moment.

It was hoped to reach the first phase line in the center of the position by night of D day, a region not far from 3,000 yards inland, enclosing the crests and looking down reverse slopes of the high central hills at that part of the island. The 2nd Division would then hold on its left and swing its right toward the slopes of Mt. Tapotchau; the 4th would branch out from it in a direction generally rightward to the southeast to get the big airfield, Aslito. There was a small airstrip right along the beach north of Charan Kanoa, but with the fire it would take and the fighting across it, there was little likelihood it could be used by anything more than grasshopper artillery observation planes for some time after the landing.

All told in that first landing group there were 21,746 officers and men of the 2nd Division and its attached elements, 21,618 of the 4th Division, 2,582 of the XXIV Corps Artillery. The key idea of the operation was to get this massive force on the beach quickly, under crushing fire from air and sea to break up the defensive formations which were expected to make their main fight at the beaches.

This was the amphibious plan then, and it looked airtight; but the amphib plan was something less than half of what Admiral Spruance had to keep in mind. He must count on interruption from all the planes in the Empire and from the fleet invisible since the night of Santa Cruz, located by our submarines off Tawi Tawi, its air arm presumably again recruited to full strength. The plan worked out to protect the movement ashore against these counterstrokes, to throw confusion into the counsels of Japan, and obtain surprise for the action at the beachhead—this plan went up even beyond 5th Fleet's level to embrace all the American forces around the rim of an ocean that occupies a quarter of the world.

D day was 15 June; but the first air strike on Saipan would be on the 12th from the fast carriers running ahead of the transport fleet, heavy fighter sweeps to ground any Japanese planes in the Marianas. Simultaneously planes of the 7th Army Air Force in the Central Pacific and of the 5th Army Air Force in the Southwest Pacific were to attack in whatever force they could muster all the islands of the Carolines with Wake and Marcus. Far in the north more planes had come out of Adak for a blow against Kuriles and mysterious Paramushiru. Admiral Small's cruisers from Dutch Harbor would run in before dawn (using radar if there were fog as there was almost certain to be) and shell the same place.[1] Far to the west runways and bases for the B-29s had at last toilsomely been set up in Southern China. As Mitscher's carriers approached Saipan the big planes would take off and make a reality of what had been a nightmare to every Japanese since the war began by bombing the home islands.

Tinian and Saipan are within eyesight of each other; Spruance and Mitscher with the battleships and fast carriers were to run between this group and Guam, swinging north up the west flank of Saipan, and for a day the fast battleships would shell the place while the air attacks continued. This would be on the 14th; by that date the slower escort carriers would be so close in that their planes could take over part of the aerial bombardment duty. It was expected that the enemy on Saipan would by this time have notified the homeland of the impending attack and need for reinforcement and that reinforcements would be on the way. On the night of the 13th, then, Indian Jocko Clark with his own carrier group and that of Admiral Harrill would run fast to the north, flying their planes off against Iwo Jima. They should catch the reinforcement just coming in and shoot them up in a fighter sweep, following this with a dive-bomber attack against Iwo Jima's shops and runways. The Japs would repair the latter quickly; but they could hardly do it in less than twenty-four hours and those twenty-four hours would be the crucial period of the landing.

Having struck at Iwo Jima, Clark and Harrill would turn back and join the fleet west of Saipan, then all the fast carriers together run down to Guam and Rota to complete the destruction of the airfields and shops there, lying off to await the coming of Admiral Koga's fleet. There were six big seaplane tenders with the expedition, their squadrons of patrol planes still back at Eniwetok. By time Clark and Harrill had rejoined Mitscher and the Guam fields had been bombed, it was expected that the operation ashore would have

[1] These hard-working, unsung ships were the heavies *Chester* and *Pensacola;* light cruisers *Detroit* and *Concord,* with Desron 49.

proceeded so far that Admiral Turner could clear the anchorages off Saipan of some of his transports and support ships. One or more of the tenders would come in and fly out planes for a long-range search to the west to supplement the work of the submarines which were always out there but which could cover comparatively little of the ocean.

The plan was as intricate as a piece of buhl cabinetwork and as closely jointed. It did not, however, depend essentially upon this jointing but upon the fact that at every moment the immense reserve of force represented by Task Force 58, Mitcher's carriers and the battleships, would be free to meet whatever form of counterattack the enemy close—that there were now in fact two American fleets, one to hold the sea and one to support the Marines across the beaches. Japan had only one; it was probably stronger than the second American fleet, but getting at that fleet and the transports it covered without encountering Task Force 58 demanded something pretty special in the line of deceptive tactics.

Chapter 14

Saipan: The Shock at the Beaches

ADMIRAL NAGUMO ALSO HAD A SQUADRON OF SUBMARINE SCOUTS of the "small Ro" class, like those knocked off by *England* in her sweep to the south. Believing as he did that an attack on the Mariana Gunto was approaching, he fanned them out toward the Marshalls, which he correctly estimated as the staging area through which the American fleet would come. One of them, *Ro-111,* was the first casualty of the campaign, picked up on sound by the destroyer escort *Bangust* as the latter was conducting some rear echelon vessels between Kwajalein and Eniwetok, and sunk before she could get off any information. The rest seemed to have been in the wrong place; or, in other words, Nagumo's eyes under the sea did not function.

His eyes in the air did. A pair of Saipan-based snoopers penetrated the C.A.P. running ahead of Mitscher's force on the afternoon of 10 June. Both were shot down, but there seemed no doubt aboard the flagship that they had had time to get off messages announcing their discovery. Now, the distance to the Marianas was still considerable; but Mitscher quickly made the command decision to send his fighters in at once, a day early, feeling that he would gain more from the strategic surprise than he would lose by creating that gap in the plans. He stepped up his fleet speed and as soon as he was within reasonable range of Saipan launched out two hundred fighters on 11 June, a Sunday. The Japs came up to fight—there was nothing else they could do, in spite of the fact that the 22nd Air Flotilla was still mainly in its final training stage and not well organized. Of course they lost heavily, one hundred and twenty-four planes shot down that afternoon, twenty-six of them by *Hornet*'s very hot Fighting 2 squadron. We lost eleven planes.

There was still Japanese aviation left in the islands, a few of their planes coming out to drop flares around Task Force 58 that night. Their report convinced both Nagumo and General Saito that they were going to be heavily attacked, though as yet they seemed to have expected only a strong raid, like that on Truk in February. They ordered two convoys bringing fuel and construction materials to turn back, sent their troops to battle positions and buttoned up everything ashore. The attack came in next morning as expected, dive bombers and torpedo planes which reported back to our fleet that Saipan was sending up heavy and pretty accurate flak. Mitscher had taken the normal precaution of flying off distant searches. One of these, from the carrier *Essex,* found the nearest of Admiral Nagumo's convoys burning oil at a great rate as it tried to make back toward Iwo Jima. The searchers whistled up the dive bombers and the *Essex* group made a concerted attack on the convoy. Two of its escort vessels went down, so did seven of its cargo carriers and a big tanker; most of the remainder were hit.

Next morning, the 13th, the searchers went out to pick up the relics of this convoy. They found it had scattered, but the dive bombers jumped on two more cargo carriers and an escort, sinking them all. At the same time Nagumo's other convoy was found, way out at the limit of plane range. It was already afternoon when the sighting was made and no bombers were then available, but the fighters from *Yorktown* and *Hornet* went out, a 700-mile round trip, and abused the five ships of this convoy so badly that two of them never got back to Japan. The shore bombing also went so well that Mitscher got off a jubilant message: "Keep coming, Marines; they're going to run away."

That day also one of Nagumo's submarines, *Ro-36,* tried to interfere with our advancing escort carriers and the destroyer *Melvin* sank her.

But these convoys and contacts had now become a minor issue. That morning Willis Lee's fast battleships began shelling Saipan and a pair of electric messages were laid before Admiral Spruance. One was from the submarine *Harder,* on patrol off Tawi Tawi. The Japanese fleet there was coming out, steaming up north through

Sulu Sea. The other, from a coast-watcher on Helmahera, reported the northward movement of fleet units past that island. At the same time Radio Tokyo declared in clear:

"It has been announced here that the Japanese Navy in the near future will win a great naval victory in the Pacific. We are all waiting for the news."

The prospect for the great battle of the Pacific looked hopeful, but hope is poor material to weave into operational plans and Admiral Spruance in his cabin could prick the chart with a pair of dividers to see that even if the Japs were coming it would be days before they would arrive. Proceed as planned; that night Jocko Clark and Harrill stood fast to the north for the strike on Iwo and next morning, the 14th, both the escort carriers and Turner's old battleships closed in on Saipan to bombard. They drew return fire from Nagumo's batteries (Saito's were under orders not to reveal their positions); *California* and the destroyer *Braine* were both hit and had dead aboard. The counterresult was that most of the Jap naval guns were put out of action. Saito reported at close of day that the losses to his materiel and personnel were slight, morale was high, and though the shelling had been severe there were no transports in sight nor any signs of an immediate landing.

At twilight there was a slight flurry down toward Nafutan Point, where *California* had been working over the gun positions. After she moved out for the night the Japs suddenly opened up with their medium pieces against the light cruiser *Birmingham* and some destroyers which had gone in to put down harassing fire during the night, and as these vessels did not have battleship armor, they had to pull out under a smoke screen. *California* came back with *Colorado* to blast down the cliff where the guns were concealed, while over at the west side of the island the underwater demolition teams worked in, buoyed the reefs, sketched everything they could see and swept the shelf, where no mines were found.

II

The turn-to was at 0530; fifteen minutes later the covering ships opened fire and at 0700 the planes began to come in with bombs and rockets. Smoke and dust rose in tall pillars all along the beach

230

and back into the country and fliers reported the sugarcane fields burning merrily. Correspondent Sherrod thought the whole place looked like a furnace, and the ships offshore were wrapped in clouds of orange-yellow smoke; but he set down in his notebook that the Japs could hold out for a long time in a smoking ruin. Out beyond the reef line there was considerable swell but H hour was delayed only ten minutes from schedule, a contrast to previous landings.

The new time was 0840; at that hour the long line of boats touched the beaches while up at Garapan the waves made semblance of finding fire too heavy, broke up and circled back to their transports. *Colorado* took an artistically contrived list and began to draw out of range. As it happened this ingenious fake accomplished little but to provide some fun for the boys all along the line back to Tokyo. Admiral Nagumo reported that he had sunk an American battleship "probably the *New Jersey*," which must have caused some astonishment to the Imperial Naval Staff, which knew what kind of guns he had. But although General Saito held his 135th Regiment to the north in the Garapan area, it was only a little beyond the position it was supposed to take in reserve for opposition to a Charan Kanoa landing.

It was time to get *Colorado* and her attendant destroyers out of there anyway; an emergency had arisen. The fire from General Saito's divisional guns was beyond all expectation heavy, not out in the water as at Tarawa, but on the beach line, and supplemented by excellently calibrated mortar bursts which walked right along the narrow strip of sand, taking a heavy toll of both Marines and amphitracs. Nor could the latter work inshore to the phase line before unloading the troops as planned because of the sharply rising ground and heavy growth of trees. The aviation did not seem to be able to find the Jap guns or the cruisers in the center of our bombardment line to get them under, since most were firing from reverse slopes. At the right flank near Agingan Point, *Tennessee* had been hit hard by a shore battery over on Tinian which she had to put out of business, so that the 4th Division was deprived of a good deal of its covering fire. In addition a couple of tank-carrying LCMs capsized going in.

Admiral Turner quickly ordered the tanks to debark directly on the reef and work in under their own power. *California* dropped down to *Tennessee's* position and covered the landing of the 25th

231

Regiment while *Colorado* took *California's* place in support of the 2nd Division. As soon as the units on the beach could get a little observation, rocket-armed fighters went after the Jap artillery positions. The rockets were an outstanding success. "Never use anything

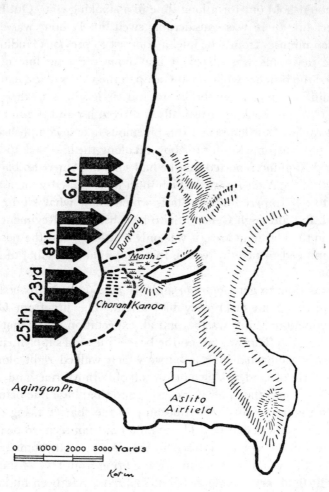

else as long as I live," said one pilot, landing on his carrier. "You just drive right in on them and they haven't a thing they can send back."

By noon the 2nd Division landing teams were about 400 yards inland, past the first zone of fire, the 8th Regiment had its shore parties working and supplies coming across the beaches. Fire was still heavy, the 6th Regiment on the extreme left flank was being counter-attacked and attempts to penetrate toward the terraced interior island were meeting resistance that made it evident the enemy positions were organized in great depth. But the burning of a big ammunition dump hindered Jap artillery observation, and an effort to mass for a counterattack around Lake Susupe behind Charan Kanoa had been blown up by the Navy. Everything looked all right there.

On the 4th Division front things were by no means so good; indeed one officer reported the position critical. The Japs had only small stuff on Agingan Point but they had so very much of it that the right flank unit, Battalion 1 of the 25th (Lieutenant Colonel H. U. Mustain), was driven to a landing 500 yards to the north of where it should have come ashore. There was a considerable rise behind the beach where the battalion did land and it was full of Japs; the cross-fire from there and the point pretty well cut this battalion to pieces, so that when the landing was an hour old it had penetrated only 12 yards and Colonel M. J. Batchelder was putting in his reserve battalion.

The arrival of tanks somewhat loosened up the situation but the regiment was nowhere near taking Agingan Point by 1700, when it became time to dig in for the night, and the beaches were badly congested. Leftward of this the 23rd Regiment also had trouble; it worked through the ruins of Charan Kanoa town readily enough against scattered sniper fire, but beyond the town was faced by a swamp surmounted by rising terraces and the troops took heavy casualties from mortar and artillery fire at no more than 700 yards range. A communications officer noted the number of requests for air attack against mortar positions, but they could not be met, the mortars were too well hidden. At noon Colonel L. R. Jones of the regiment reported that he needed close artillery support and that he had the beaches clear enough so the guns could get in. The 14th Regiment came ashore during the afternoon while the other boats brought the divisional reserve, the 24th Regiment. By twilight Colonel Jones had reached his phase line but the crests were still above him; he had no sure contact with the 2nd Division on his left, and did not think the position tenable against the night attack he was most certain to get. He pulled back some 800 yards. The divisional command post came ashore but was set up only 50 yards from the beach; except for the morale feature it could have been handled more efficiently from shipboard.

On the 2nd Division's front that night found not only the 2nd Regiment committed from divisional reserve, but also a special reserve, the 1st Battalion, 29th, that had to be landed to deal with a specially bothersome nest of Japs who were enfilading the beaches from Afetna Point. By night the 8th Regiment was still a good 1,500 yards short of the hill crests that were its phase line; both front-line regiments were being fired into heavily from artillery among those hills and on the slopes of a deep gulch known as Charan Kua, which leads northeast toward the flank of Tapotchau.

At twilight the destroyers worked in, using fires all night and firing on call. They were needed; the Japs made no fewer than four separate counterattacks all round the developing perimeter. One on the south, right flank; they hit the center of the 25th Regiment's position and drove it in some 400 yards before it could be halted. All night small parties tried to infiltrate the front of the 23rd, and the 2nd Division drew attacks in form. One came down the beach from Garapan, accompanied by some barges from which a counterlanding was attempted; the 6th Regiment had to fight from midnight to dawn, while our landing craft drove off the barges with their own guns; when morning came 700 Jap bodies were counted on the beach. The attack against the 8th Regiment was spotted as it formed in the Charan Kua gulch by some of the last aviators up for the day and ships' guns took most of the zing out of it. The persistent Japs then worked to their own right and attacked along the division boundary, just as day of 16 June was breaking.

They got through the floating left flank of the 23rd Regiment and some of their small parties worked right down to the beach, where the stevedoring parties had to drop their boxes and beat off the enemy with rifle and grenade. This appeared greatly to encourage the Japs, for the first planes in the morning found them once more massing in Charan Kua gulch. The cruisers and the battleships worked in to help Marine artillery ashore and a heavy strike from Mitscher's carriers break this up, while the 8th Regiment and the 1st Battalion, 29th, cleared the noisome Afetna Point area.

The 4th Division now had all its troops in line. The 25th retook the ground it had lost during the night, and with the help of a battalion from the 24th cleared Agingan Point. But when darkness of the second day fell no troops were beyond phase line for the first, and nobody was near Aslito Field. The casualties of the 2nd Division to this point were 2,310 including half the division's battalion commanders; those of the 4th were about the same, or a total of approximately 10 per cent in both units.

III

The Divine Presence himself sent down a message to encourage the defenders of Saipan that day, 16 June, a message which, on being read, was instantly burned lest the Imperial word be polluted by the touch of those American barbarians who smell so much like sheep. General Saito expressed his gratitude for "the boundless magnanimity of the Imperial favor which we hope to requite by becoming the bulwark of the Pacific with 10,000 deaths" and set about gathering his resources for an attack that would drive the invaders into the sea that night. It would be made, the General decided, down the gulch of Charan Kua toward the airstrip on the beach and Afetna Point; a form of attack that would permit cover by the still-valid artillery units along the sides of the gulch and afford some protection to the accompanying tanks as they massed.

The staff roused each other with words of courage while this plan was being made, but it was obvious to each individual that their main resource now lay in the boundless inspiration of the divine words and the hope that the Navy and its air force would come to their relief. As the staff reported to Tokyo, the positions protected by concrete had withstood American shells very well and dummy emplacements had been particularly successful in causing the enemy to waste his fire; but the shelling had been so violent that the minds of many were confused, and communications were not working at all well, since all the normal routes along the shore were in American hands. It had been impossible to move troops or even to send messengers by daylight. This brought it about that the men could not be assembled in the gulch till well after midnight, though it would have been desirable to begin the attack itself at that hour, allowing time for the break-through before dawn again allowed American naval gunfire to become accurate.

Even so the number of men brought together for the attack was far less than the General wished. The tank regiment had suffered some casualties, but it was in fairly good shape; but the 135th Regiment, brought down from Garapan, had to form the bulk of the infantry column. Some elements of the 136th were present but that regiment had lost heavily. It proved very difficult to establish communications with Colonel Oka, whose 47th Independent Mixed Brigade had been holding the front south of Charan Kanoa, and when he was reached he reported that the enemy fire on his front was so intense that he considered it inadvisable to attempt a lateral movement to Charan Kua. He would continue to hold his position with the greatest constancy.

Captain Shimamura, the naval observer at Army headquarters, had noted that "without command of the sea and air island defense cannot be maintained against naval shelling" and freely expressed the insulting opinion that only defensive maneuvers should be adopted until the Combined Fleet made its appearance. He knew it was coming, of course; had only recently left the conference at Palau, where Admiral Toyoda and his staff had canvassed the various American capabilities and accepted the Imperial Staff plan for the then unlikely case of an American attack in the Marianas instead of in the south. This plan recognized that an American landing in the Mariana Gunto would constitute the extreme emergency in which the still incompletely trained Bonin Sector air squadrons would be employed in combat, as well as those planes still farther back in the homeland.

When, on the 14th, General Saito's first message about the heavy shelling and air attacks on Saipan arrived, the aerial counterattack plan was placed in operation and Admiral Toyoda was advised to execute the naval portion of the movement, toward which he had already made the preliminary dispositions. Should the American attacks at Saipan be a feint, these movements would seriously deplete the Empire's dwindling fuel resources, but it would be important to catch the enemy on the beaches.

The naval plan called for Group One to run north through Sulu Sea, pass through the Philippines by the Strait of San Bernardino, then head eastward. The necessary refueling would be done at about 130°, Group One (which contained most of the new carriers) then running rapidly eastward to cover the advance of the 3rd Fleet up from its station among the former Dutch islands by a route east of Mindanao, west of Palau. At about 136° or 137° all planes would be flown off for an attack, landing in the Marianas fields after they had hit the American fleet, since the carrier pilots had not yet received training in night deck landings. The gunnery ships would be running in under this attack to protect the carriers from American surface action, and all ships would refuel that night while the planes were absent.

In the meanwhile the planes from the Empire and the Bonin Sector would also have attacked the Americans the same day, and under the combined assaults of over five hundred carrier planes and something like three hundred land-based, the enemy should be in pretty bad shape. All the planes were to refuel and rearm during the night at the Marianas fields and attack the Americans again at dawn the next morning, the carrier planes returning to their decks for another arming and assault on the second day of action. American aerial counterstrokes on the first day would be prevented by the fact that our carriers would be too distant from them, for the Japanese squadron would be making a long straight run to the land bases while the Americans would have to go out and back, thus having only half the range. On the second day counterattacks would be prevented by damage to the American vessels and the fact that after dawn of that day our carriers would have their own planes directly overhead.

It was an extremely ingenious plan to strike without drawing a counterattack, but unlike Spruance's plan it rested upon the dovetailing in time of two independent movements—upon the precise simultaneous arrival of the planes from the Empire and those from the fleet. Group One in fact steamed out of Tawi Tawi and Group Two from the Dutch islands on 12 June; but already another bit of sand had slipped between the closely meshed gears of the plan, and it was to prove as damaging as that introduced by the unexpected operations of the destroyer escort *England*. The marplot was the American submarine *Harder,* which had left Exmouth Gulf, Australia, on 27 May (while *England* was chasing her subs) and pushed up through the Java barrier on patrol to the northeast coast of Borneo. Near Tawi Tawi Anchorage she was attacked on 6 June by the destroyer *Minadzuki*. The submarine was surfaced at the time and the destroyer came right on her at high speed. There was no time to seek safety under the sea, so *Harder* fired three torpedoes right down the destroyer's throat and with a wonderful shot blew her all to bits.

Commander Sam Dealey of *Harder* was one of the most aggressive submarine skippers who ever lived. He had already sunk a destroyer that was looking for him on his last previous cruise and this new experience gave him the idea that destroyers were not such tough customers for a submarine, after all. He began inviting them to attack him and then hitting back, with intense success. On the 7th he sent *Hayanami* down; and on the 9th wound up with a grand slam by getting *Tanikaze* and *Urakaze* in a single barrage of torpedoes, then hung in the neighborhood to report. Now, it was as unheard of for a submarine to sink four destroyers as for a destroyer escort to sink five submarines. Admiral Toyoda's staff (Koga was lost in a plane accident at the end of March) once more drew one of those perfectly understandable deductions every military commander must draw from the combination of events and experience. The Americans had somehow found the 2nd Fleet and had concentrated against it an immense force of submarines; countermeasures were ineffective. The Admiral's orders from Tokyo about the Mariana Gunto battle plan were permissive and preparatory only, resulting from Nagumo's report of the fighter sweep over Saipan on the 11th; but he steamed up in Sulu Sea at high speed on the morning of the 12th to get away from the ill-omened Tawi Tawi Anchorage. He was a whole day and a half early; it was not till noon of the 14th that the land-based air part of the plan was set in operation.

IV

Far to the north of the Saipan beachhead Jocko Clark's carriers ran into heavy weather with low overcast, squalls of rain, and seas that set the big ships pitching wildly on the morning of D day. He ordered the planes out anyway (there was some bitter comment from air officers) in a double strike at Chichi Jima in the Bonins and at Iwo. The dive bombers did not make good practice, most of them having to hunt for a long time to find holes in the cloud cover, but at Iwo the fighters shot down 5 planes, claiming another 16 grounded, and at Chichi they got rid of 13 more, all airborne. The gale rose toward evening when a second strike was flown and during the night a plane crashed on the deck of *Belleau Wood,* burning so vividly that everyone thought the carrier was gone. But next morning she was flying planes again with the rest in moderating weather, just in time to catch the first reinforcement groups of the Bonin Sector command, on their way down to Saipan. They were neither well formed nor well led; Clark's fliers disposed of 47 more, dug up the runways, and turned to steam fast back to 5th Fleet.

Clark's radio report was one of the items on the agenda at Spruance's staff conference in the evening. The original plan had been to make the landing on Guam, W day, on D plus 3, but accumulating information now threw this idea into serious question. The number of Japs on Saipan had evidently been much underestimated, our troops were well behind the hoped-for schedule and would evidently become more so. All divisional reserves were already engaged and if the important Aslito airfield were to be taken in a hurry it would be necessary to commit the 27th Division at once, not as a mop-up force but in full combat. This would leave the Guam attack without any reserves; the nearest available being the 77th Division, now back at Hawaii, 3,000 miles away. The fighting ashore still needed the full support of the escort carriers, which meant that they could not be spared to cover a Guam landing. From Clark's report it seemed fairly clear that the Japs would indeed reinforce by air from the Empire, so that at least part of the fast carrier force would be needed close at hand. Above all, there were the indications that the Japanese fleet really meant to come out for battle for the first time since Santa Cruz. They were certainly no longer in Tawi Tawi; and the submarine *Flying Fish* reported some of them had passed through San Bernardino Strait on the night of the 15th. During the day of the 16th some ships in the Jap fleet broke radio silence so that a direction finder fix had been obtained on them. The point of origin was about 12° north, 127° east, on a line whose extrapolation would bring them right to Saipan. A great naval battle could hardly be conducted at the same time as a landing operation.

Cancel W day for Guam. What Admiral Spruance wanted now, he explained, was long-range air scouting and a good radar fix on the Jap fleet, since radio finders have an error of 100 miles at such

239

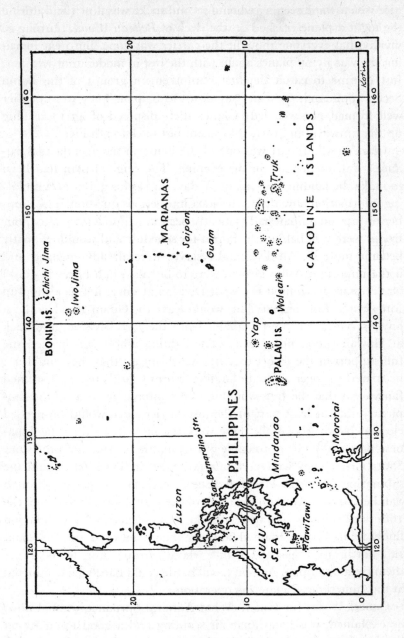

a range. To obtain that he would have to have anchorage and pera-
tion space for his seaplane tenders. In anticipation of the battle, in
order to make room for the tenders, would not Admiral Turner get
his transports and supply ships out of the anchorage near the beachhead, taking them into the clear east of the island, which would have
the additional advantage of making them less a responsibility during
the coming battle? No, said Turner, he could do nothing of the kind;
the obstinate Japanese fire on the beaches had already seriously delayed unloading operations and now there would be the additional
burden of getting ashore the XXIV Corps Artillery and the 27th
Division with all its supplies. He could not clear the area, could not
even spare room for a single seaplane tender and its brood. (It takes
an immense amount of space in calm water for the big patrol planes
to get off.) The best solution would be to push operations ashore
more rapidly forward, win Magicienne Bay and use it as a seaplane
anchorage. Under some persuasion from Spruance he did a little
more figuring and finally permitted the small tender *Ballard* to come
in. The six-plane squadron she served was ordered to fly out from
Eniwetok and the conference broke up.

<h1 style="text-align:center">V</h1>

At 0330 Captain Claude G. Rollen of B Company, 6th Marines,
called on the field telephone to report the first Japanese tank attack
of the war was bearing down on him. The duty destroyers were immediately alerted, moved closer in and began to fire spreads of
star shell; Colonel Jim Risely ordered up the half-tracks of Regimental Special Weapons. But before even the first star shells began
to burst a wave of tanks rushed out of the dark at B Company, with
riflemen and machine gunners howling from the backs of the tanks
and more infantry coming from behind.

The tanks rolled right over the company's first line and began to
cruise up and down, the 57-mm. guns in their turrets questing in-
quisitively for targets as the men on their backs dropped off and
began to spread. The whole position became a jumble of light and
sound, bazookas, grenades, machine guns, 37-mm. going off in all
directions, with the star shells hanging broodingly overhead. No one
got any clear picture of that combat, though someone saw enough

of it to make certain that Private Robert S. Reed received a Navy Cross for hitting four separate tanks with his bazooka and when he had run out of ammunition, climbing on another to toss an incendiary grenade inside. The incident was typical; these were veterans of Tarawa. They never budged from their deep foxholes but let the clanking machines roll past and went for them in the weak rear while the 37s fired at tracks and bogies.

The fight went on for hours though its main weight was broken by 0420, wave after wave of tanks coming through in groups of four or five. The company's heavy machine guns mowed their supporting infantry down, nor could the tanks get rid of those guns. Indeed, the tank commanders seemed to be possessed of some peculiar mania or to be waiting for the foot troops that never joined them. Instead of seeking to exploit to right or left what penetration they did achieve, they cruised back and forth aimlessly, then would "halt, jump out of their tanks, sing songs and wave swords. Finally one of them would blow a bugle and jump back in the tank if they hadn't been hit already. Then we would let them have it with a bazooka." As the hours went by, the Marines learned that there was nothing very grim or invulnerable about a Jap medium tank; then the half-tracks came into action and every time one of them hit a machine it burned.

Colonel Riseley sat on a stump smoking a cigar through the whole action; as a Jap tank approached he knocked off the ashes and said easily to his regimental clerk, "Son, get a bazooka." At 0630 with dawn breaking Company K came up to relieve and found little to do beyond mopping up and chasing Japanese survivors.

There were not many of them; one battalion of the 135th had been practically wiped out and twenty-nine tanks destroyed. At the Japanese headquarters conference that morning there was no effort to conceal the general pessimism and disgust over the inefficiency with which the attack had been made. Colonel Goto of the tank regiment was killed, but his surviving subordinates heard no little about their failure to keep up their communications with the rear and to co-operate properly with the infantry. The over-all result had been a great weakening of the position and the Americans were reported infiltrating under the growing light, both up the coast toward Garapan and along the slopes of Mt. Tapotchau. No communication at all could be obtained with the Oka command, though observers on high ground reported it also seemed to be giving way. General Saito reluctantly determined to shorten his lines by withdrawing to a position across the island from Garapan to Laulau on Magicienne Bay and sent out the orders. Admiral Nagumo did not think it possible or desirable for the southern wing of his naval personnel to attempt to retire up the eastern side of the island, and ordered them to withdraw across Aslito Field in the direction of Nafutan Point, where there were good prepared cave positions.

On our side, the 2nd Regiment along the shore toward Garapan and the 6th, next in line, made good progress up steep slopes. The enemy had constant observation and both regiments had to halt about noon to tighten up their lines and improve rear communications. The 8th Regiment, moving eastward, kept pace with the 6th on one wing, but on the other there was an extensive and unexpected swamp north and south of Lake Susupe with a wooded nose of hill projecting over it from the east. The next regiment in line was the 23rd of the 4th Division, the one which had had its left battalion so cut up on the first night. Coming round the swamp it had to present its right flank to the hill massif while it worked northeast along a steep side hill toward the nose where a group of Japs had impacted. The 8th Regiment similarly had to work round the north end of this swamp, then down with its back toward Tapotchau and the fire coming from there. The result was a wide gap between the two divisions, growling from both regimental commanders, Japs continually firing from the hill and seeping down through the swamp into our rear areas and Charan Kanoa town. Two were pulled from under the shack where General Holland Smith had his headquarters, days later.

Things were better that day on the right. Both the 24th and 25th Regiments reached their phase line without difficulty and with only light loss, while the 165th Infantry of the 27th Division relieved along the shore east of Agingan Point. When night of 17 June came down the 25th was close up to Aslito Field; the 105th of the 27th was coming ashore and most of the corps artillery was in. Out in the anchorages they had a lively time as Jocko Clark's pressure on Iwo let up and the second echelon of Jap air reinforcements came through to go for the shipping. Six several attacks are counted that evening, all by formations. Our people knocked down nineteen planes, mostly by gunfire, which shows how little skilled their pilots could have been; but an LST was torpedoed and the escort carrier *Fanshaw Bay* got a bomb hit on the elevator that put her right out of the campaign.

The next day, 18 June, was one of expectations and rumors all along the front lines, the gathering of civilians who were now surrendering in numbers, and of minor movements except on the right flank. The 23rd Regiment came up against the Japanese pocket on the nose of high ground and had a hard fight all day long. The 25th Regiment and 165th burst through across Aslito Field in a sweep. The 24th touched Magicienne Bay and wheeled left, facing north. Behind it the 105th swung in with the 165th and both began to move

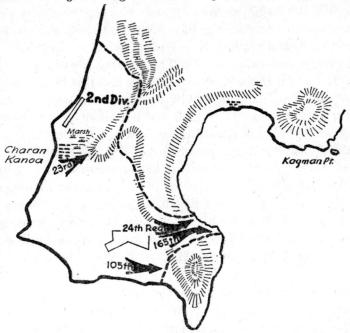

toward Nafutan Point, where more Japanese seemed to have holed up. Marine staff officers thought from the map that the 27th (the division's command was now ashore) was making rather slow progress. The Army men reported they were up against a well-organized series of cave positions, some of which contained guns behind armored shutters.

Chapter 15

Saipan: "Hell is on Us"

O N THE 16TH THE DESTROYERS MELVIN AND WADLEIGH had disposed of *Ro-114* down to the west of Guam in a manner almost incidental, and the next day *Newcomb* and *Chandler* eliminated *I-185* north of Saipan as she tried to run in, apparently with messages and urgent supplies. There were several other efforts on the part of the Japanese outside to communicate with the garrison on the days following D, usually beaten off by the minesweeps and PCs of the inshore patrol. Meanwhile there were Jap planes around the fast fleet like bats at dawn and twilight of the 17th and 18th, and on the latter day the situation as viewed from Admiral Spruance's flag cabin on *Indianapolis* became complicated.

The first new report came from the submarine *Cavalla*, out on her first patrol of the war. At 2000 on the 17th from her low deck lookouts spied a numerous Japanese fleet making high speed in the direction of Saipan in latitude 12-23 north, longitude 130-120 east, which is approximately 1,000 miles from the invaded island and 600 from San Bernardino Strait on a line a little south of the direct one between the two. The submarine was in an admirable position for attack, but information was more important at the moment. She went down, counted screws by sound and, when the enemy were well clear, surfaced and sent in a report. This reached Spruance before dawn of the 18th; *Cavalla*'s count showed fewer ships than *Flying Fish* had reported from San Bernardino, and if they were the same enemy group that had come through there, a speed of less than 10 knots had been made good in the intervening time, a fact which accorded ill with the news from both submarines about the high speeds the Japs had been making when seen.

Admiral Spruance had been fighting the Japanese for some time now and had learned that when they seemed most simple and obvious it usually meant they had an ace up the sleeve. He doubted whether they were going to accept a stand-up battle, as it seemed. Far more likely the main body of the fleet would seek to draw him into an action west of the Marianas while a force, possibly the one spotted by *Cavalla,* made an end run around by the south against the beachheads. At noon on the 18th, Clark and Harrill fell in on the main body from their Iwo Jima expedition, the whole fleet steamed out southwestward and flew searches. No result; they turned back in the twilight and after dark the patrol planes from *Ballard* went out on their long-range radar search.

That night the information previously so scarce began to come in in a flood. First was a dispatch from Honolulu reporting another radio fix on something Japanese in latitude 13 north, longitude 136 east; then one from the submarine *Stingray,* so badly jammed by the Japs that only her position came through—latitude 12-20 north, longitude 137 east. Both positions were well to the northeast of *Cavalla*'s sight. Next was a midnight dispatch from another submarine, *Finback,* which had seen numerous searchlights at 14-25 north, 135-45 east, still farther north of the other sightings but somewhat to west of them. Finally at dawn the most reliable report of all, from one of the patrol planes on radar search. During the night she had picked up two groups, one of thirty ships, one of ten, well separated, the ships headed toward Saipan, position 13-20 north 137 east. Add all these together; we have a picture of a Japanese fleet scattered into independently operating groups as at Midway, the eastern Solomons, and Santa Cruz, apparently bent on trying an air-sea battle combined with some kind of trick play. Spruance turned down a request from Admiral Mitscher to take the fleet west and attack the group sighted by the patrol plane; canceled a previously ordered heavy strike to tear up the airfields and demolish the shops on Guam and Rota, and steamed slowly out southwest of Guam with the battleships screening his carriers and a heavy combat air patrol above him.

Those Guam and Rota strikes had now been delayed nearly a

246

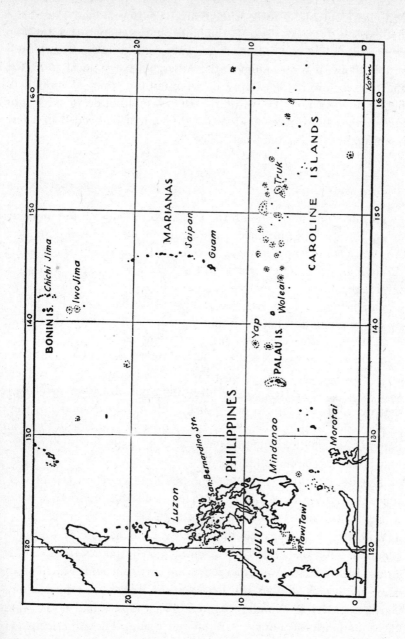

247

week for a reason dating back to that Jap snooper who had sighted Mitscher's onrushing force a day early. That event had caused the fast carriers to use an extra day's bombs against Saipan and it will be remembered that these carriers were an oceanic distance from a fresh supply. Now, it is an axiom in the American Navy never to let the ships get below battle supply in ammunition—that is, enough to fight a major action. The Admiral felt it would not do to use bombs against the Guam-Rota fields when they might be needed in a few hours against the Japanese battle fleet.

II

This decision, not to bomb the Guam-Rota fields on the morning of 19 June, had an important result. It removed from the mind of Admiral Ozawa (now in tactical command) any doubt about going through with his major attack on the American forces. There were several reasons why he would otherwise have doubted. He knew the Tinian field could not receive his planes, it had been badly dug up by bombing and naval gunfire, and the bomb storage depot had gone up in a titanic explosion on the night of the 15th. The situation on Saipan was "obscure"; he had intercepted a dispatch from General Saito to Tokyo saying "the neutralization of Aslito Field will have to be carried out by infiltration patrols as our artillery is destroyed," which looked very much as though the Americans were in possession of the place. As for the smaller strip at Marpi Point on Saipan, Banaderu Field, there was another Saito intercept, saying only it was "becoming usable again."

The Rota Field and the big one at Orote Point on Guam were the only refuges open, little damaged; and the question of fields ashore had assumed a sudden importance because the big air attack against the Americans could not now be delivered as originally planned. That plan had been essentially to fly planes from so close to the islands that in an emergency the carriers could pick them up after the attack. But as the fleet worked eastward from San Bernardino, traveling in well-separated task groups, it had no less than three submarine contacts in rapid succession. The Americans evidently had a strong force of submarines in the neighborhood of the

Ozawa's fleet and transmit information of his approach to their own fleet. Ozawa expected the Americans to counterattack him by air in such a case; it would be in line with the aggressive character of their moves. He did not want to be counterattacked, his whole plan rested upon putting an absolutely overwhelming force of planes over the American fleet, and if he had to hold out machines for the heavy combat patrols to beat off such a counterattack his striking force would be far from overwhelming—particularly since his approach a day and a half early meant that his carrier planes could count on no assistance from the land-based units of the Empire until they had actually reached the Mariana Gunto.

He changed the detail of his plan without (he thought) altering its essential features. He would fly his planes to the fields in the Mariana Gunto and they would strike the American fleet in passing as in the earlier version; but they would fly off from a point 300 miles west of the spot originally intended, that is, too far out for the American carriers to strike back. The Japanese planes would rearm in the Marianas on the night of the 19th, make a second strike on the American fleet on the morning of the 20th. Not till they had delivered this second blow and severely damaged the American ships would his own run toward the Mariana Gunto, pick up their aircraft, and rearm them for a third strike, which would be followed closely by the attack of the land-based planes and the gunnery ships running in.

In accordance with this scheme the Combined Fleet turned west then during most of the 18th; before dawn on the 19th it turned east into the wind to launch a great wave of 300 aircraft as sailors lined the flight decks, lifting their arms and cheering for the rebirth of the Imperial Naval Air Service.

Those turns, those shiftings in which he had indulged to lose the extra day he gained when he ran away from *Harder* and his anchorage, had brought him once more into the area where *Cavalla* was on patrol. Now, when that submarine had reported, Pearl Harbor ordered another undersea craft, the veteran *Albacore,* to close toward the area. At 0750 that morning *Albacore* sighted from periscope depth two carriers, two cruisers and eight destroyers, with the tops of more ships far on the horizon. She closed the nearest carrier,

249

which happened to be the new *Taiho,* and fired six torpedoes, going to deep submergence from whence she presently "heard an explosion that was definitely not a depth charge." The depth charges came soon after, fierce and persistent, and *Albacore* had too much to do avoiding them to learn that by one of the chances of war one torpedo had caught *Taiho* just after she launched her first wave of planes and while the hangar deck was full of machines being readied for the second wave, with all the gas lines running and spare fuel washing around. The fuel caught; there was an explosion followed by two others which turned the largest carrier in the world into a mass of flames quenched only by her sinking.

III

At 1005 that same morning southwest of Guam a big bogie was picked up coming in from a little south of east at 24,000, about 125 miles away. Admiral Mitscher got all his fighters into the air at once and followed by sending off his bombers, all armed, to clear the ships of planes and of as many explosives as possible. Within the next ten minutes seven Japanese air groups were counted, the smallest of them 40 planes strong, some 300 machines in all. These were the carrier air groups who had not yet trained in night landings and presumably in some other things; they were still in cruising formation, high up, for they had been briefed that they would have surprise, encountering our ships close to the islands engaged in supporting the Marines ashore, essentially unready. Here were the American fighters nearly 100 miles farther at sea than they expected, already at the same level as the Japs, and to crown all, there were more of these fighters than there were planes in the Japanese force, fighters and bombers together.

The action was that incredible slaughter which has become known as "The Turkey Shoot of Saipan." A *Cabot* pilot counted fifteen enemies streaking down the sky at once. A *Lexington* man noted that the Jap fighters made no effort to break formation and aid their doomed bombers. He broadcast the information, the Grummans hung right on the tails of the enemy bomber groups, shooting down plane after plane, instead of diving through. On the antiaircraft cruisers they complained bitterly they had nothing to do, and of all those 300 planes only 18 did break through the air patrols, all shot down and for the sacrifice of all getting exactly one bomb hit, on the armor of *South Dakota.*

What of the Jap survivors? They made for Rota and Orote Point, as instructed. But in the midst of the boiling aerial battle Admiral Mitscher had made another, very rapid, command decision. It was then evident the enemy air groups were not going to hurt him very badly this day and by the number of planes they were losing their capacities for battle would be seriously reduced. He could spare some bombs; and ordered the bombers already up to go for Rota and Orote Point. Planes were already thickening like flies below as the dive bombers went in and red funnels of flak came up, but here were the bombing squadrons of four major carrier groups, and in a matter of minutes they reduced both fields to craters and rubble. Some Japs landed, crashed and burned; some dumped in the water and some flew around till shot down. None escaped; and when Admiral Ozawa's second wave of attack came in between 1315 and 1500 it met with the same fate for a total of Jap planes shot down which our commanders conservatively estimated at 353, but which turned out to be 404, the largest single-day bag made at any time in the war, anywhere. Our losses were 21 planes and from some of these the pilots were rescued.

That second wave of attack was weak, not only from the lack of *Taiho*'s planes, but also because in escaping from the region of her disaster the Japanese had again stumbled on *Cavalla.* Shortly after 1100 that submarine's sound stack reported once more the noise of many screws. She put up her periscope in a choppy sea and sighted two heavy cruisers and three destroyers circling around the big *Shokaku.* The Jap was taking in the fighters of her normal day patrol and her flight deck had almost a complete load of bombers for the second attack wave, with more just coming up in the elevator. *Cavalla* worked in and fired six torpedoes; three of them hit. The big carrier that had come through nearly every Pacific battle canted over amid frightful explosions, spilling planes from her flight deck, and before all the men could be taken out of her was on her way to the bottom of the sea.

While the great air battle was being fought and the Jap carriers were going down operations ashore dwindled except on the front of the 27th Division near Nafutan and that of the 23rd Marine Regiment opposite the pocket on the hill behind Lake Susupe. The latter formation, with a battalion of the 24th and some tanks, attacked the pocket after a heavy rocket concentration and broke it up. The 4th Division was straightening up its rear areas and getting supply lines organized, a difficult job across the keel of mountains, as it moved up to a line slanting from south of Garapan to the middle of Magicienne Bay. The 2nd Division could hardly advance without support from its flank and Merritt Edson fretted, telling one of the correspondents that now the Japs were being given time to dig in and the place would turn into another Guadalcanal.

The 27th had its 165th Regiment in line on the left facing south, its 105th Regiment on the right. Their progress was distinctly slow, a fact partly explicable because out here on the high rising point the terrain suddenly becomes jungle. But a good many Army men around corps headquarters were inclined to agree with Marine suspicions that at least part of the difficulty was internal. The men of the 27th were brave enough, fought sharply and took considerable casualties, but seemed to lack military know-how and to be not well led, especially in the higher echelons.

On the next day, the 20th, the 4th Division swung forward again close up to Tapotchau and the Kagman Peninsula that juts eastward from Saipan, the right flank of the 2nd Division keeping pace. The Japs still had a lot of guns and good observation posts on that mountain; it would be a tough place to take. The 4th got a rather weak counterattack that day, supported by a handful of tanks.

Holland Smith perceived he would probably have to use the 27th in storming Tapotchau and established an area for it in the hills east of Charan Kanoa, picking the 165th out of line and adding to it the 106th, which had been held afloat till the fleet beat off the great Jap air effort.

These troops would be under division command and would be pushed into the center between the two Marine divisions, of which the 4th at least was pretty tired. The 105th Regiment would continue against Nafutan Point, operating directly under corps. In fact, the original order was for only one battalion of this regiment to be left there, but General Ralph Smith protested that a single battalion could hardly cover the assignment that two regiments had been carrying. A Jap civilian cut the throats of his wife and two children, boasting "this is what we'll do when we get to the Empire," and one of the staff officers went up to the Nafutan Point front to see what was holding up the Army men. He found Colonel Gerard Kelley of the 165th with his regimental CP in what had been the ammunition dump for the airfield, a mile and a half from the front. The battalion command posts were not much farther forward, over a mile from the fighting, in fact, but presumably the Army had its own methods. It was nearly evening when he reached the front; one company of the 105th had just attacked and taken the position it desired. Its dead lay on the slopes and the Captain who had conducted the attack almost tearfully exhibited an order just received from battalion to withdraw even behind the former front line and dig in for the night. "They don't know what's going on up here."

V

Late on the afternoon of the 19th *Cavalla* emerged from beneath the blanket of water she had drawn over herself and reported. *Albacore* made a report also and got an acknowledge for it, but it turned out later that this came from a Japanese station. As twilight came in Admiral Spruance knew only that one Japanese carrier had been torpedoed; no knowledge that any had been sunk. The enemy were quite evidently pretty bare of planes and no longer in any shape for end runs; they would probably be detained trying to get their crippled carrier home. He stepped up fleet speed to 20 knots, running steadily westward through the night and morning, much hampered by the fact that the wind held in the east and every time a search flew off the involved carrier had to turn back. Toward noon another difficulty developed: the destroyers were very low on fuel.—What shall we do?

"Send them back one by one as soon as it becomes dangerous for them to continue," said the iron Admiral. "We will go on without destroyers if necessary. I am going to strike that fleet and I will not be distracted by details."

As a matter of fact "that fleet" was now running for Okinawa in a state bordering on the disorderly. Admiral Ozawa received an ambiguous dispatch the night before to the effect that some of his planes, number not specified, had landed on Guam. He now had fewer than 60 left in the whole fleet and in the morning, when the refueling operation was attempted, American search planes began to buzz around instead of his own fighters and bombers back from the Marianas. He assigned a fueling area a little farther westward, but before the ships had reached it there was a radio dispatch from Tokyo saying the whole operation had been abandoned, he was to return to base. Ozawa could only know that something had gone dreadfully wrong and he put on speed toward the northwest.

At 1545 Lieutenant Robert Nelson of *Enterprise* found that outliers of the flying Japanese fleet at 15 north and 135 east, running fast, 290 miles from the position of Task Force 58, which meant, as one pilot put it over his plane phone when he took the air, "Well, suh, we have just fifty per cent chance of getting back to those carriers."

For night was coming fast, it was already 1647 when the last planes took the air with the ships forced to run eastward again to get them off, which brought the distance the fliers had to make before they could reach the Japs up to 340 miles. A near thing, one of the riskiest of the calculated risks in the whole campaign. Many a plane dropped into the water or crashed on the carrier decks that night, when after 2100 they came slanting down through the fleet's uplifted searchlight beams with their last drops of fuel running out, the pilots overwrought and shot up, unutterably weary: 95 of the planes were lost, 49 of their crews, but those who returned, returned victorious. Destroyers of the fleet, running out to pick up survivors on the morning of the 21st, found two who had been shot down in the middle of the Japanese Navy and had lain in rubber boats all night, watching the carrier *Hitaka* burn and burn, throwing out pieces from her sides like a volcano until she sank. *Hayataka* had bomb hits so bad she would never fight in the war again; *Ryuho* a bomb hole in her decks and her structure so wrecked that she would fight no more either; *Zuikaku* had bad fires; *Haruna's* shaft brackets were loose and her propellers out of line; the destroyer *Shiratsuyu* was gone, two tankers had burned up and been abandoned, and of the carrier pilots so painfully assembled during the last year and a half not one was left.

Jocko Clark jubilantly asked permission to run down for a raid on Manila, but Spruance was not satisfied yet that danger was over. It seemed to him the number of planes staged down through the Bonins thus far was altogether incommensurate with the scale of the Japanese effort. He switched Clark's and Harrill's carrier groups back to Iwo Jima and himself steamed for the anchorages off Saipan, arriving on 23 June, just in time to step into the hottest controversy of the war.

VI

It was the slow progress of the 27th Division. Napoleon said once, "There are no bad regiments, only bad colonels." Now General Ralph Smith of the division was very popular with his men and was later considered a satisfactory officer, but it seems indisputable that he did not during the two years in Hawaii exercise that tight rein on his National Guard officers that was, for instance, exercised by General Omar Bradley in another division. An observer at an amphibious night exercise in the islands reported that as soon as they got ashore several of the 27th's officers went to a hotel for the night. Nothing happened.

Some of the bad habits that were a product of this laxity had already become evident. On 21 June, General Ralph Smith added to these difficulties by an overt act. From his divisional CP north of Aslito Field he issued an order on that date that the 105th Regiment would hold its present front line at Nafutan: "The battalion in reserve will not be committed to action without authority from the divisional commander." At the time the order was issued the 105th was not under his command at all; it had been detached and belonged to Corps and Corps had ordered it not to hold but to attack. There was some excuse, to be sure, in the fact that General Smith had already protested using a single battalion for the Nafutan task that had engaged the attention of two regiments; and in the confusion incident to the relief of the 165th, whose positions the 105th had taken over. But an efficient divisional commander and an efficient staff do not allow such confusions to arise. The practical effect was that Division countermanded the orders of Corps to troops over which Division had no authority. That's a hell of a way to run a war.

For the moment, however, it did not matter in an operational sense and was important only in establishing an atmosphere. On the morning of 22 June the attack northward jumped off at 0600, its main mission to sweep the refused right flank forward and gain the eastward slopes of Tapotchau while the center climbed that object. On the right, where the 4th Division was, this called for a 4,000-yard advance, with the 24th Regiment working along the Magicienne Bay shore toward Laulau, the 25th between it and the 8th Regiment, which was the rightmost element of the 2nd Division. The artillery support was extraordinarily heavy, a 75 and a 105 battalion for each infantry battalion, with more in general support. Extra guns were obtained by placing the 27th's divisional artillery under XXIV Corps artillery command, an arrangement that worked very well, as the gunners attached to the Army troops were unquestionably good.

The attack started off at a good pace, and by noon the 4th Division had made some 2,000 yards. At this point it encountered a system of defenses in some depth along the line south Garapan-Tapotchau-Laulau, a rough, irregular line, but in fact that along which General Saito had "decided to make a showdown fight," as he informed Tokyo. Directly ahead of the left elements of the 4th Division was a plateau running north and south that later became known as Purple Heart Plateau, separated from the main mass of Tapotchau by a valley which both Japanese and Americans called the Valley of Hell. The 25th Regiment got heavy fire from the Tapotchau slopes into its left flank as it tried to move against this objective. The 8th Regiment had made good progress against the main mass of Tapotchau and had demolished one well-populated strongpoint, but now that formation was on steep slopes cut by cliffs and overgrown with tropical jungle. It was impossible to see more than a few feet; it was impossible for units to keep in contact with those adjacent to them; it was next to impossible to bring up supplies, and the attack stalled.

256

The 23rd Regiment passed through the 24th and tried to get things going again near the Magicienne Bay shore in the afternoon, but supply and communication difficulties delayed the start and little progress was made anywhere. After all had dug in for the night it became clear from the activity of Jap patrols that we had reached a main battle position. General Holland Smith ordered the 27th up into line against the Purple Heart Plateau and Valley of Hell, with the 106th and 165th Regiments abreast. It was a difficult move and instead of the usual early hour for attack the assault was to be made at 1000 to provide light and time.

The 23rd and 25th Regiments, now much reduced, were to

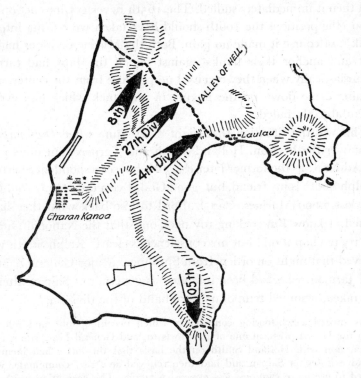

squeeze rightward into less space, and as the attack moved onward, swing out eastward to clear Kagman Peninsula. The 6th and 8th Regiments were to go straight forward up the western flank of Tapotchau. Nafutan Point still held out sternly in its cave positions;

257

the single battalion of the 105th which was now there would attack at dawn.

Everything that possibly could go wrong went wrong. General Army Smith or someone on his staff, apparently under the impression that he was still in control of the battalion of Nafutan, gave it an attack order but for 0800, not for dawn. In the northern sector the 106th was late reaching position and apparently mistook some Marine support elements who were not moving for front-line troops. It was 1055 before that regiment's attack began and then it was only a single battalion, which was halted almost at once against the caves and rugged grounds of General Saito's battle position. The rest of the regiment did not go forward till 1115, an hour and a quarter late, and then it immediately stalled. The 165th never got into action till 1300 (the positions the 106th should have taken were firing into its flank); of course it made no gain. Both the Marine divisions had to halt and anchor their flanks against which the Japs had turned enthusiastically when they received no pressure from the center, and evening came down on the picture of an attack which had everywhere abjectly failed.

This was the situation that night of 23 June when *Indianapolis* hove over the horizon. Holland Smith and Turner went out to see the Admiral; as the former later explained to correspondent Sherrod, "Ralph Smith is my friend, but, good God, I've a duty to my country. I've lost 7,000 Marines. Can I afford to lose back what they have gained? I know I'm sticking my neck out, that the National Guard will try to chop it off! but my conscience is clear." Ralph Smith was relieved that night on orders from Spruance. Major General Sandeford Jarman, who had been intended as governor of Saipan after it was taken, assumed temporary command of the division. [1]

[1] This started a whispering controversy which became public and red hot when the Hearst press, in one of its efforts to laud General MacArthur, contrasted him with Holland Smith on the basis that the latter had incurred excessive losses on Saipan and had then relieved an Army commander who wished to use more cautious, less expensive tactics. The accusation produced a not-unjustifiable outburst of anger in Marine circles. By this time General Richardson, in command of Army troops throughout the Pacific, had come to Saipan, where he showed a disposition to support Ralph Smith; it thus became an interservice controversy in which even some Army men who had originally been highly critical of the 27th Division's performance rapidly reversed their

That night General Saito reported that there remained to him five and one-half battalions of infantry, 13 field artillery pieces, and two companies of tanks. Colonel Oka had been killed. "We have lost not less than 50 per cent of our troops, but the personnel within the division is comparatively strong. There are about 6,000 of other units, but their fighting ability is reduced by lack of weapons." He radioed orders for the Tinian and Guam garrisons to send troops by barge to land in the rear of the American lines.

Down near Charan Kanoa a mop-up squad captured a Jap who said fiercely, "You may have a little part of this island, but back there is the Empire."

VII

During the night Jap tanks poked their noses out at the joint where the 165th Regiment abutted on the 4th Marine Division and a Jap battery dropped a sudden concentration on the CP of the 10th Marine Artillery that killed the exec of that regiment and broke up its communications. Their tank attack failed, the Marines getting two and the soldiers five with their bazookas; and the next morning, 24 June, the attack that should have been delivered the previous day went forward all along the line.

It was everywhere a savage fight. On the left at Garapan seven tanks tried a counterattack but gave it up after five of them had been smashed by an opportune half-track. The burden on the left center was carried by the 1st Battalion, 29th, which had to scale an almost vertical cliff toward the crest of Tapotchau, where a tangle of tree-ferns was overgrown with stinging vines. The heat was ex-

---

field in order to stand by opinion from on high. In the Army's Court of Inquiry on Ralph Smith there was no cross-examination, only four witnesses were called, and they testified only to facts with regard to the general movement of troops. Later still an official Army historian produced an Army official version of the whole affair, which pointed to Ralph Smith's acquittal by the Court of Inquiry as though it answered everything and declared that Holland Smith "made no effort to find out the true situation." Actually both the situation with regard to Japanese defenses and the question of whether Marine tactics were expensive in lives are beside the point. General Ralph Smith was clearly removed because of the complete lack of co-ordination in the movements of his division on 23 June, with formations attacking late and not together; because this sacrificed lives not only in his own units but also among the Marines on the flanks; and because Ralph Smith had assumed an authority (over part of the 105th) that did not belong to him.

hausting and the maps made from photo reconnaissance were almost meaningless. They got 800 yards.

The 27th Division in the center carried the ball against Purple Heart Plateau that day and fought well through opposition so severe that 14 of its 16 medium tanks were disabled and one company of the 106th lost 40 per cent of its men. The 165th was twice counterattacked, once with light tanks, lost some ground, recovered it, dug in for the night with precipices on both flanks, but with a considerable gap still between it and the flank of the 4th Marine Division, which was now spreading out across Kagman. That night the Japanese High Command knew the jig was about up. Saito to Tokyo:

"Having lost the influence of the Emperor due to the weakness of our representatives, we are not able to work at our best here. Please apologize deeply to the Emperor that we cannot do better than we are doing. The Army will defend its positions to the very end though it be death to guard the Treasure. However, because of the units sunk at sea there is no hope for victory in places where we do not have control of the air and we are still hoping for aerial reinforcements."

Those reinforcements were on the way, the squadrons from the Empire. Their first outriders had slipped down the Saipan coast on the night of the 22nd and one low-flying plane caused the most spectacular naval damage of the campaign by blowing off part of the battleship *Maryland*'s bows with a torpedo. The rest had reached Iwo Jima and were just airborne, forming for the run down, when Jocko Clark's strike groups ran in on them. It was mutual surprise: "I never saw so many meatballs in my life," said one pilot of our forces. There was a long dogfight in the skies during which many of our bombers had to return to their decks with racks still loaded. During the night Jap snoopers tracked Clark and at dawn they attacked him with 12 torpedo planes—all shot down. The following morning, morning of the 24th, Clark's fliers went back and this time there was no surprise on either side. But these Japs were the student pilots, no match at all for the veteran American carrier men. We lost 5 planes, the enemy 114 plus the 12 torpedo planes, and now the job begun in the great battle was complete; the Japanese naval air force wiped out except for those few squadrons now isolated down in the South Seas Development Area.

The campaign settled down from event to difficult and arduous incident, accompanied by a drizzle of small casualties as Japs popped up from various hide-outs or tried to infiltrate the northern lines by night. There were still snipers in the swamp around Lake Susupe; they would hide in the water with only their heads up, like frogs, and fire one shot. Colonel Evans Carlson, now operations officer of the 4th Division, was badly wounded by one such. There were still Jap guns in the hills; they would fire little groups of shells at some spot that looked possible to them and then move. A plane or two occasionally came down from the north; two of them attacked the escort carriers on the night of 26-27 June and two more bombed Aslito Field ineffectively that same night.

It was a night of alarms and excursions in other respects. The Japs on Nafutan Point slipped through the lines of the 105th and went on the war path. At 0430, a couple of hours after Aslito had recovered from its air raid and tucked itself in for the night, it was roused again by streaks of machine-gun fire and the crash of a 20-mm. cannon, which set fire to a P-47 (Army planes had begun to arrive on the 22nd) and burned it up. Marine engineers and Sea-bees turned out, weapons in hand, and perceiving the attack was not in force, started a series of patrols that knocked off some 25 Japs up to 0740. The main body of the Nafutan refugees drifted north up the trails leading to the rear areas of the 4th Division where they succeeded in pinning the divisional artillery into its emplacements and halting all supply traffic to the front. Fortunately the 25th Regiment had lately been taken out of line for reorganization preparatory to a new attack northward, and was assembled on a hill in the center of the island due east of Afetna Point. They killed some 200 of the Japs in a sharp little fight that lasted till about 1000; then, with the corps Reconnaissance Battalion, went after the rest in the area eastward toward Magicienne Bay and got rid of another 100 or more.

This brought about that the attack of the 4th Division, which had now cleared Kagman, did not get off the next morning till an hour after the 2nd and 27th had moved. It was not a tactical drawback as the 4th's left flank was already ahead of the 27th. That division lost men and lost officers—seven of the rank of major and up in seventy-two hours—but those remaining found it difficult to deal with the cave positions on Purple Heart Plateau. "We've put I don't know how much mortar and artillery fire on those caves, but it takes men with rifles and satchel charges"—the old refrain of the Pacific islands. The 4th Division slashed well ahead that day and the next and then had to mark time while the 27th moved up to clear its flank at the rate of 400 or 500 yards a day. The Army men had to do a good deal of maneuvering on a small scale.

Under these conditions, in this type of fighting, with snipers being constantly dug up all over the island the three divisions struck the northeastern shore on 4 July. On that date in the early morning 100 Japs charged slowly against the 165th Regiment, singing as they marched, and most of them were killed. The enemy was clearly beginning to break up and the 2nd Division was now pinched out of line. The orders for the following day contemplated a swing toward the northeastern peninsula which completes Saipan, with the 27th and 4th moving down it abreast. At 0700 on 5 July the two divisions attacked. The 4th made good progress at once, but Major General George W. Griner, who had come out to take over the 27th, was obliged to report after two hours that his command had made no perceptible gains. There was a good reason for this. The ground ahead to Tanapag Point was low-lying and rather flat. The enemy had studded it with vast numbers of mines, well covered by fire from concreted pillboxes and with a good many mortars and antitank guns. Two tanks which attempted to lead home an advance were knocked out by bangalore torpedoes and three more were put out by gunfire. The two regiments in line had made no more than 200 yards into this maze by evening.

General Smith accordingly changed his plan for the next day. The 4th Division was to drive ahead against its relatively light opposition from Marpi Point, while the 27th cleared that angle of resistance as far as the village of Makinsha. Nine destroyers were told off to furnish call fire for the operation and planes with rockets to give close support. The attack was set for dawn of the next morning, 7 July.

262

There was nothing either in air observation or frontline intelligence to indicate it, but the 27th Division had penned nearly all the surviving Japs, to the number of 5,000, in that fortified pocket, including one of those two big fish, General Saito and Admiral Nagumo. Of the latter nothing more was ever heard. He had decorously committed suicide on one of those last days without letting the General know about it; an impolite action. There had been a fierce naval bombardment during the day of 2 July, which seemed likely to burst in the headquarters cave. General Saito was slightly wounded and in any case feeling very poorly, having neither eaten nor slept well. His beard had grown quite long and ragged (there was a desperate shortage of water and none could be spared for shaving); tears came into the eyes of his staff at the pitiful sight.

They discussed things that night. There were only two possible courses: stay there and be starved to death or make a last attack and fight to the finish. Of course the latter alternative was chosen, though many of the troops had no weapons and there were only a few tanks left. The orders were written out and distributed for the attack to take place on the morning of the 7th, the date being set so far forward because all communications were gone and it would take four days for officer messengers to distribute the orders to all units. On the night of the 6th the task was finished and obviously there was now nothing more for headquarters to do. As General Saito, because of his age and the exhausted condition of his body, could not take part in the final attack, he decided to commit *seppuku* in the traditional fashion. The headquarters cook kindly prepared as much of a farewell feast as he could, but there was nothing but sake and canned crab meat.

After they had all eaten and drunk, the General himself cleaned a spot on the rock and, sitting down, bared his belly. "It makes no difference whether I die today or tomorrow," he said, "so I will die first. I will meet my staff at the Yasukuni Shrine!" Then he drew his own blood with his sword, but he was too weak to get the guts out as required by ceremonial, so the adjutant kindly shot the old man in the back of the head. The brave officers and men now went out to join their comrades; it was 0330 in the morning and the time of attack had been set for one hour later.

X

The position of the 27th Division was this: the 2nd Battalion, 105th, only a couple of days back from Nafutan, where in the attack and mop-up it disposed of some 900 Japs, had its flank on the shore just east of Tanapag Point. Next it, with its right thrust forward on a little rise, was the 1st Battalion, 105th, then the 1st and 2nd Battalions, 165th, these facing north. Two battalions of the 106th were in reserve behind the left flank of the 165th; the 3rd Battalion, 105th, was echeloned a little behind the 1st. The CP of this last

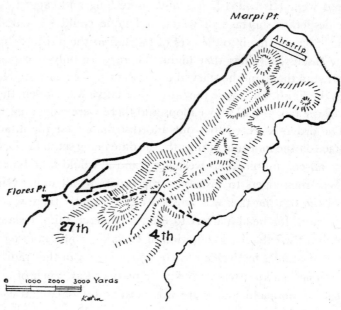

regiment was about 1,300 yards to the rear, which is a little farther back than a Marine CP would have been, but this is not itself a reason for criticism here. It is more difficult to justify the fact that neither battalion had patrols out, though the justification is that there had been minor, sporadic Jap attacks all night, they were in too close contact with the enemy to need patrols. The fact that the two battalions of the 105th in line lacked physical contact by a matter of 200 yards cannot be justified at all.

264

The attack came as a surprise and thus in one small area met no defenders. The Japanese were in mass formation, some with guns, but many with only a couple of grenades, a bayonet on a long wooden pole, or even with clubs. They were well loaded with sake, singing and screaming as they rushed, perfectly careless of death, so that they kept right on coming over piles of their own killed in front of machine guns and again piling up till the guns could not fire, then climbing over the piles to attack the gunners. Both the infantry battalions were swept right away, the 2nd into a pocket against the beach not over 50 by 100 yards in extent, where the Japs besieged it, throwing in mortar shells at a terrific rate. The rest of the attackers poured through, swept away the regimental CP and in no time at all were attacking the gun positions of the 10th Marine Artillery, which was in position to fire support for the 4th Division farther down the peninsula.

The Marines fired away all their ammunition, the last of it in airbursts fused for four-tenths of a second, so close were the enemy upon them, then took the locks out of their guns and made their defense with pistol and carbine. The mad charge rolled right over them, and then it began to peter out. Its tanks had all been burned by this time and as it moved mainly along the shore the 106th was put in on its flank in a sharp counterattack. A battalion of the 6th Marines which was near the area also was hastily committed and by afternoon the Japs were beginning to flow in the other direction. Destroyers worked into fire at them and to pick up 135 men of the 2nd Battalion, 105 who had used up all their ammunition in the pocket and waded out along the reef.

By evening most of the guns were again in our hands and the position was pretty well re-established after quite the most desperate banzai charge of the war, which had cost the 105th over 1,000 men. The following morning the 8th and the remainder of the 6th Marines came up to help the Army men squeeze the Jap pocket into the sea. The enemy had been squealing all night and on that morning they did their banzai stunt in small groups all over the place, but there were no break-throughs nor anything approaching them. On that day also the 4th Division reached Marpi Point and the island was declared secure. It had cost the invaders 3,214 killed, 13,084 wounded; it cost the Japs all the nearly 30,000 they had, though many of these by slow erosion, for nine months later patrols on the island were still killing Japs at the rate of ten a day.

But the casualties are by no means all the story or even the most important part of the story. On our side there was a residue of bitterness of *l'affaire Smith* and Marines were a little inclined to point to the banzai charge as justifying everything they could say about the 27th. In truth there is some, but not much reason to believe they would have come better out of an attack of such weight and sacrificial intent. The Japanese dead buried in the area over which it had passed were 4,211 in number; and it is probable that when anyone in a war is willing to give that many lives to inflict some 600 killed and 800 wounded upon the enemy, there is no very easy way of preventing it.

In addition there was a residue of horror. When Marpi Point fell some of the Japanese civilians beat out their children's brains on the rocks and jumped into the water to drown in hand-linked chains. The correspondents saw it and the report came through to the papers in the U.S. simultaneously with those of the banzai charge. They were magnified in the popular imagination to a general belief that the conquest of Saipan left very few Japanese alive on the island. This was not true; more than 90 per cent of Saipan's population survived as a problem for our civilian government people. But the idea had an impact on American imaginations that not even the blood of Tarawa had been able to produce and its ultimate effects are still not fully visible.

It also tended to overlay the true results of the campaign, still further obscured by lack of knowledge about the carriers sunk by submarines, the fact that Tinian and Guam remained to be captured if we were to have a really valid base among the islands of the west and space enough to use the B-29s. To most people the campaign and accompanying naval battle seemed an unfinished, unsatisfactory, indecisive business. They did not realize that the Japanese naval air force had been destroyed and their Navy would never again be able to operate beyond range of cover from the shore. They did not realize the importance of possessing at Saipan secure anchorages and staging areas for attacks on the other Marianas and the Empire. Only one of the Marines had remarked, "If we can land on Saipan we can land anywhere there are Japs."

266

Among our enemies the assessment of results was more accurate. When the news from Saipan came in everyone on the Navy Staff sat silent for a few minutes without looking at the others. Then someone said, "Hell is on us."

Not much else could be said. There were a good many visitings back and forth among various notables, a large consumption of tea, and various attempts at arrangement, but one result was inevitable— Shimada, Tojo's hand-picked admiral, resigned from the Navy Ministry, and no other naval officer would accept the uncomfortable place. Japan was an effective totalitarianism everywhere but at the topmost level, where one of its governmental peculiarities is that the ministries of the two fighting services must, by inviolable custom, be held by officers of those services. The lack of an admiral therefore meant that there was no Cabinet, no government. Even Tojo, the most powerful subject in six hundred years of history, dared not attempt to rule without one. On 15 July, five days after the fall of Saipan, he returned his enormous powers to the Son of Ten Thousand Years and retired to a position of the most despised obscurity it is possible to imagine. It was widely felt that he should have committed suicide.

The new premier was Kuniaki Koiso, a retired general from the fringes of the Manchuria Gang, who had been known chiefly as a penetrating critic of Tojo—but on the point of the latter's execution of the over-all schemes, not of his fundamental planning. Koiso's Cabinet was from the beginning an affair of torsions and tensions, including three main currents of opinion—a group who believed that the war was so nearly lost that Japan would benefit by asking the Allies for terms; what may be called the Takagi group, which agreed with the premise of the first, but believed Japan herself should offer terms so abject that the Allies could not refuse them in the face of home public opinion for acceptance; and those who considered Tojo a miserable bungler, wished to carry on the war, but more skillfully.

The Imperial rescript setting up the new government admonished Koiso to give Japan's position "a fundamental reconsideration looking toward the end of the war," which, so far as it means anything, would seem to mean that the Imperial mind was veering in the direction of the Takagi group. Koiso, himself the leader of the third

267

stream of thought, did not so interpret the document. He set up a new "Inner Cabinet" containing himself, Shigemitsu the Foreign Minister, with the Ministers and Chiefs of Staff of the Army and Navy. This body stood above the regular Cabinet and the pacificating members he had been forced to take into the latter were, of course, eliminated from the inner group. Theoretically this inner Cabinet's decisions were without force until ratified by the whole body, but it also possessed access to the Imperial ear, and in cases where the members of the Council of Six were unable to agree among themselves, it became the custom to submit matters to the Emperor for decision in the form of alternatives for his choice. Under these circumstances nothing was easier than for this Inner Cabinet to present any ideas from the surrender groups as though coming from themselves and to present them in so unattractive a form that their rejection was guaranteed.

In the technique of government the result was that Koiso was only symbolically a head; actually he was a member of a committee. In practical effect this committee accepted his critical view that Tojo had not waged the war hard enough. From this point on there streamed down through all operations as directed from Tokyo a darker, fiercer, more desperate tone difficult to put in precise terms but distinctly perceptible in its effects on the Marines who charged across the coral beaches, heads down into the level storm of bullets.

Chapter 16

Guam: A Campaign of Maneuver

T HE MEN OF THE III AMPHIB CORPS REMAINED ABOARD THEIR ships in the offing, not having a very good time, while the early Saipan fighting was going on. They were fulfilling the function of floating reserves for emergencies which had originally been that of the 27th Division. By 25 June two things were evident: the III Amphib would not be needed on Saipan since the enemy's Tapotchau position had been penetrated, and it would be some time before the Guam attack, to which the corps had been dedicated, could begin. That day the transports with the 3rd Division steamed back to Eniwetok to let the men stretch their legs ashore, and a week later the 1st Provisional Brigade followed.

In the meantime General Geiger and Admiral Connolly had begun a series of conferences with Turner and Holland Smith. The talks lasted for a week, going right up and down the ladder of everything that had happened and revising all plans in the light of the Saipan experience. Plans for the capture of Guam were nothing new in the Marine Corps, of course; it had been obvious for many years that the island must fall at once in the event of a Japanese war and the means of its recovery had long been a favorite operation in those imaginary conflicts which are fought across sheets of paper at the Marine Corps Schools. But all these older plans had been thrown out the window as early as April of 1944, when III Corps down at Guadalcanal began considering the reconquest of Guam as a practical proposition. The old plans had the fundamental defect of not being able to predict the progress of invention. That is, they provided only for landings from boats on the few and restricted sand beaches, whereas the appearance of amphitracs and DUKWs (the rubber tires of the latter had, to the surprise of many Marine officers, proved quite impervious to coral) made it possible to consider going right in over the reefs.[1]

The Saipan experience had shown the need of changes almost as basic in the April plan. It had been made in anticipation of a Japanese force of less than 10,000 men on Guam; that figure was now more than doubled in view of the underestimate at Saipan; and being doubled, it was clear that a force of one Marine division and a brigade was not enough, not even if the brigade lacked very little of being a division in size. General Geiger asked for the 77th Army Division (Major General A.D. Bruce) and got it, but as this division had no training in amphibious action, it was contemplated that the Marines would take the beaches and the Army men be brought in as soon as there was enough room to maneuver. On Saipan neither air nor naval bombardment had eliminated anything like the proportion of fixed defenses they should, considering how incomplete those defenses turned out to be after we got hold of them. Aerial reconnaissance showed that, while the long fighting for the more northerly island was going on, the Japs had been working like mad on their Guam positions. The bombardment plans were stepped up as radically as they had been between Tarawa and the Marshalls, and stepped up not only in quantity but also in deliberation, which is to say that instead of firing at general areas the ships were to take their time and go for exact targets, individual gun positions and pillboxes.

The matter of getting quicker unloading of the supplies received a good deal of attention, most of the bulk cargo going aboard LSTs, with large numbers of DUKWs to serve them, and tractor cranes at the top of the load to handle packages as soon as the beach was touched. Finally there was a major change in the artillery ashore. Always before, the Marine guns had come late to the landing because it was necessary for them to wait till the infantry had passed the minimum limit of howitzer range before opening fire—a matter of anywhere from 300 to 750 yards, depending on elevation. This left

[1] Indeed, it was the obvious tactical difficulties of making a Guam landing without such vehicles, as developed in the mimic wars, that led the Marines to insist upon the invention of the amphitrac, which they described in advance as "the strategic surprise of the next war."

an ugly gap through what was normally the toughest part of a defense system which the Marines must cross without help from their guns, the gap in which the 23rd Regiment had had its trouble on Saipan. General Del Valle, who had the artillery, worked out the scheme of putting in guns early, letting those of formation A fire to the flank in front of formation B, while B's cannon similarly obtained range enough to cover A's advance by also firing off at an angle.

This was carried so far, indeed, that the 155s of II Corps Artillery were scheduled to land behind the 1st Provisional Brigade at the more southerly of the two sets of beaches and open fire forthwith, 12,000 yards across the angle of the island into the rear of the positions opposing the advance of the 3rd Division between Adelup and Asan Points in the north. The Brigade itself would go ashore between Bangi Point and the little town of Agat, facing the tall hill mass of Mt. Alifan.

Between the two beaches lies Apra Harbor, formed by a pair of rocky fingers projecting from the western coast of Guam. The southern finger is Orote Point with its big airfield, the town of Sumay and the area where the old Marine garrison used to be. General Turnage's 3rd Division would anchor its left flank defensively toward the interior island and General L.C. Shepherd's brigade its right flank. The two would then work toward each other to clear the harbor and Orote. In all probability the 77th would be landed to cover the brigade's rear since Orote was a strong position. The northern point around the harbor is not really a point at all, but an island named Cabras. Intelligence did not think it was or could be heavily fortified. Except for small elements to take that island the 3rd Division, like the 77th, would be facing inland in preparation for whatever operation could be undertaken there.

General Geiger was by no means sure about these future operations and had made no specific plans for them. In fact, even the plan given was not hard and fast beyond the point of getting the division and the brigade ashore before the 77th came in. He wanted everything as flexible as possible, a trick he had learned as an air officer. He remarked that he could establish a beachhead all right but whether he could break out of it was somewhat problematical.

Of course that did not matter in the early stages. Apra Harbor

271

and Orote Field were the essential points. East of the latter, at the center of the island, tall Mt. Tenjo rises and from its slopes on to the southern coast Guam is one mass of wild cliff-strewn high jungle country, while to the north Tenjo falls away into elevated, rolling plateau, not very rough. A good deal of the future of the operation would depend on which of these areas the Japanese chose for their stand. Late photos from Saipan-based planes showed that the enemy had obstructed both sets of beaches with obstacles quite as formidable as those at Tarawa and much more numerous.

II

The officer in charge of the Guam defenses was Lieutenant General Sho Takashina, nominally commander of the 29th Division, one of those formations organized in 1941, when war with the United States had been decided upon. It had received field training in Manchuria for three years before being ordered down to island defense in the early part of 1944. In a practical sense the division now amounted to the 38th Infantry Regiment and some headquarters troops. Its tanks, most of its artillery, the transport unit and nearly all the 18th Infantry Regiment, which formed the remainder of the division, had all fallen sacrifices to American submarines on the way down. The 50th Infantry also belonged to the division and had also suffered losses; what was left of it was on Tinian. There was also an Independent Mixed Brigade, the 48th, of Major General Shigematsu, theoretically containing four battalions, but it was really made up of scraps and patches of formations that either had been diverted during the spring command troubles or had been partly lost at sea. It amounted to 2,811 men, which is about the force of a good regiment. There was also an Independent Mixed Regiment, the 10th, likewise understrength, with a variety of small units partly or wholly rescued after torpedoings, which brought the total force of Army troops on the island up to some 13,000. There had been more, but a couple of battalions had attempted to obey General Saito's orders to reinforce him on Saipan in the fading days of June, had been caught on the sea by American planes, badly shot up and marooned on Rota.

272

The naval personnel were about 5,500 strong, mainly one of the normal naval defense units. Its commander was only a captain, so much outranked by General Takashina that the command question did not arise and the naval men co-operated almost as fully as though they had been soldiers. Their primary interest in any case was the defense of Orote Point and the installations covering Apra Harbor. They manned several batteries of excellent naval 6-inch in the area and had good concreted positions around the airfield and the former U. S. Marine reservation. Along the western shore of the island to the south of Orote the defenses were in the hands of two battalions of the 38th Regiment, which could call on the 10th Independent Mixed, stationed among the mountains to the rear. With it were three-gun batteries of 6.1-inch, well emplaced, and a variety of smaller pieces all along the beaches. Time and materials were lacking to build a proper series of beach defenses as ordered by General Saito, but each individual unit prepared its own positions, digging in under tree roots or in cliff faces. The labor troops both here and farther north did excellent work in setting up anti-boat obstructions below the waterline, mostly in the form of barbed-wire and coconut-log cradles filled with crude coral lumps. A continuous line of trenches paralleled the beach from Agat to Facpi Point with communication trenches leading back to cave positions. At Gaan Point at the center of this area the 38th had managed to build into a hill an excellent concrete blockhouse holding two 75s and a 37 and with a roof four feet thick.

North of Apra Harbor and including the main town of Agaña, General Takashina took his own station with the remainder of the 38th Regiment, the 48th Independent Mixed Brigade, and the various scattered formations. It seemed to him that this was the place where the Americans were most likely to land. He had another good battery of 6.1-inch concealed in the face of Chonito Cliff where it would bear right down the coast line. The beaches down the shore were defended not only with obstacles but also by small mines, of which there was a good supply. Land mines unfortunately were short, but after the air battle of 19 June construction was stopped on the new field in the plain east of Agaña and the supply of aerial bombs and torpedoes were emplaced along roads and in various defense positions, fused as mines. The General issued careful instructions that the artillery was not to reply to naval gunners but to reserve its fire for good infantry targets.

On 7 July, Takashina's fortifications officer returned from a wide trip of inspection and expressed himself to the General in terms of high dissatisfaction.[1] The positions, except in the area of the naval troops, had been constructed without proper materials or engineering supervision. Although they were mutually supporting to a certain extent, the main reliance of the defense must be placed in infantry action and in the heavier guns. The soldiers who had built most of the positions appeared to be more interested in concealing themselves than in placing their weapons where they would do the maximum damage to the attackers, and as a result the apertures were small and the fields of fire very restricted. The fortifications man recommended that the whole system be revised; but the very next morning the Americans began to bombard so earnestly that there was no time.

III

Early on the morning of 8 July the cruisers *Wichita, Minneapolis,* and *St. Louis* ran past the northern beaches, shelling points ashore, while planes from *Corregidor* and *Coral Sea* began work on the fortifications between Agat and Facpi Point. That afternoon Close-in Connolly, in general charge of the operation, fixed the 21st as W day, while ships and planes knocked off bombarding so the air photographers could make comparison shots to see what had been hit. This was the daily program for the next two weeks, with the number of firing ships increasing steadily: three battleships on the 12th, two more carriers on the 13th, another battleship, a carrier and destroyers for the next day, and so on up. Connolly lived up to his name; had them closing in till the reefs became dangerous and they were firing from the 40-mm. It was all aimed shooting with batteries being checked off as they were destroyed. Three big coast defense guns were thus knocked out on the 16th, four antiaircraft guns on the 18th, eight more defense guns and an anti-boat battery on the 19th. The five towns in the area, Agaña, Piti, Tepungan, Asan, Agat,

---

[1] We do not know his name; it was obliterated on the only surviving copy of the Japanese records.

were systematically razed with heavy shells, which was too bad for the Chamorros of the island, but there was no point in letting the Japs make fortresses of the buildings, as they were sure to do.

On W minus 3 underwater demolition teams moved in in broad daylight, not only against the chosen beaches but enough others to make the enemy do some guessing. They had destroyers and LCI rocket gunboats in close support. As soon as so much as a machine gun opened up against the divers these ships plastered it with projectiles of every caliber in the book. Only one man of these demolition teams was killed; they took out 640 obstacles at the north (Asan) beach and over 300 at Agat in the area of the southern landing, with 377 mines at the two beaches together. That night the ships fired star shell all through the dark to keep the Japs from planting new obstructions.

H hour was 0830; at both beaches the troops went ashore exactly on schedule. The earliest report that reached the flag was that the strafing P-47s had shifted targets 1,000 yards inland and that the Marines were moving toward the vegetation line standing up and walking. It was not quite as easy as that sounded; there was still a good deal of fire left in the enemy at the Asan beaches, where the 3rd, 21st, and 9th Regiments had gone in abreast. The two latter landed with one battalion at a time as their beaches were restricted; the 3rd had two battalions in the initial wave. The fire came from the latter's flank, the left, where Adelup Point juts out beyond the landing area to form Chonito Cliff and the sheer steep headland of Fonte overlooks all from the south. The Japs remanned a couple of pretty heavy guns in Chonito face; used machine guns from the point; and had a lot of mortars in the rugged reverse folds of Fonte.

Asan, completely pulverized and empty even of dead Japs, lies as it were at the bottom of the bowl, of which Fonte Hill forms the outer lip. The mortar fire arched over to the beach line, pounding both the 3rd and 21st Regiments there, and most especially their reserve battalions. The assault formations had worked through the danger area while the Japs were still numb from the effects of the preliminary shelling and the 4,500 rockets that had been dumped on the position. Now these assault formations sifted through a region of rice paddies and up the inside of the bowl.

275

By night the right wing of the 21st was well forward on the rugged face of Fonte, linking up with Colonel E. A. Craig's 9th Marines, who had early reached their phase line against insignificant resistance. From this point the line of the 21st bent back to its left at a right angle to connect with the 3rd, which had nowhere been able to reach the assigned positions and all afternoon had been locked in a close flame-thrower and grenade fight with mortar shells coming down continually. The Japs beyond the Fonte crest were so close that during the night the men of the 21st could hear the click as they dropped mortar shells in their pieces, but there was no way to get at them, since Fonte faces the attackers with verticals that nothing but a cockroach could climb. Yet on the whole General Turnage could be satisfied with his day. His over-all casualties were light, the new unloading method was working in a pleasing manner, and in the direction of Apra Harbor, which was the critical flank, it looked as though he could progress readily enough.

The 1st Provisional Brigade was made up of the 22nd Regiment that had been at Eniwetok and a new 4th Regiment built from the Raider battalions and parachutists after the old 4th was removed from the lists on Bataan. The brigade went across the beaches with two battalions of the 4th abreast on the right, two battalions of the 22nd abreast on the left, the boundary between the two being that Gaan Point where the Jap 38th Regiment's big blockhouse was. The structure had been well hidden, not spotted by the photo interpreters nor bombed. Farther back in the rising ground there were a number of enemy's 70-mm. battalion guns, with a single big piece still alive on Orote Point and another on Bangi. All these guns opened up as the amphitracs rushed in and the pieces on the projecting points enfiladed the beach from both directions. Ten of the vehicles were hit and there was blood on the sand, but the destroyers and planes took care of the guns at Orote and Bangi as soon as they showed their positions, the 70-mm. cannon had but narrow fields of fire and only the big blockhouse was a serious nuisance.

The Marines found an excellent Jap trench system, but unmanned, the naval guns and 4,500 rockets having driven the enemy back to his holes. Machine-gun and mortar fire from those holes could be legitimately described as heavy. Neither could the amphitracs work 1,000 yards inland before discharging (the Marines were always trying this idea throughout the Pacific and it never worked); the ground inland from the beach was pediculous with mines, anti-tank ditches and obstacles. But the attack was so heavy and in such expert hands that, notwithstanding all difficulties, it broke through the beach lines with hardly a check. By 1034 the assault troops were 1,000 yards inland, the reserve battalion of the 4th was already ashore and working on the by-passed bunkers, and tanks were in. Three hours later the Gaan Point blockhouse had been taken and brigade command was on the beach.

It would seem to have been very nearly this early in the game that General Geiger decided to put the 305th Regiment from the 77th Division in here and to follow it with the remainder of the Army division as soon as the unloading areas could stand the pressure. The attack on this southern flank was definitely moving and by twilight had already taken one of the peaks of Alifan. It is a good principle of tactics to throw one's weight behind the thrust that promises a break-through, and an additional reason in this case was that Guam was large enough for a war of maneuver so it was important to fix the enemy in position.

Most of the 305th landed, then, before dig-in for the night was ordered. Of course the Japs counterattacked around midnight—in the north against the 3rd Regiment's line, not very vigorously, but with the greatest energy all round the perimeter of the southern beachhead. The main thrusts were along the beach from Agat and down a pass from Alifan, where the Jap 38th Regiment came against the 4th Marines behind six tanks. The tanks were all destroyed and the beachhead attackers broken up, but in the rough ground at the center of the 4th Regiment's line the enemy infiltrated as deeply as the regimental CP. There was a lot of shooting till day broke and local reserves linked up the lines again, made everything secure, and collected about 600 Jap bodies. The enemy's attack had been quite incoherent. They would walk a line of mortar bursts along till it almost reached a target, then cease fire for no reason at all. On the front of the 22nd a Jap post that had held off three attacks by a full company was abandoned during the night, the enemy carrying their machine guns into our lines as though there were no Americans there at all and getting themselves all shot down for no return.

On both fronts the next three days were a period of adjustment, probing, and preparation. On the south the Provisional Brigade gained the full line of the Alifan crests and the ridges that run southward from them, working into the valley lying to the east. In general the brigade's right flank was pegged toward the wild mountainous southern part of the island, the advance was by the left, toward the other beachhead. Agat was engulfed and the base of Orote fairly well cut off while patrols fanned out to the east without finding much of anything. The 77th Division's troops were being assembled toward the right and by 25 July had taken over all the extensions of the old beach line. The 4th Marines had been pulled out of position to be put in with the 22nd against Orote and the latter regiment was making slow, rather painful advances through an area of rice paddies too soft to offer approaches for tanks and defended by prepared positions on its far side.

In the north beachhead the 3rd Regiment was unable to gain an inch against Adelup Point and the Chonito Cliff. It was counterattacked every night. All the remainder of the division pivoted on this regiment in an enormous left wheel. On the extreme right flank the 9th worked rapidly along the shores of Apra Harbor, seizing Cabras Island (where few Japs were found but an immense number of air bombs buried as mines) on 23 July, then working along the shore through the ruins of Piti Town into the rough country behind.

Colonel A.H. Butler's 21st Marines found a pair of ravines leading to the crest of the flat-top Fonte elevation and began working upward. Both gullies turned out to be simply packed with Japs, no progress was made in the first assault and the Colonel asked for a close air strike on the morning of 24 July. It was so close that there were some casualties from it in the Marine line, but the Japs in the most useful ravine were all killed to the number of 200. The 9th Marines had put out patrols to link up with its own beachhead but fire from Orote turned them back along the shores of Apra Harbor.

The result of all this was that on the morning of 25 July Guam had settled down to a war on three fronts. The Provisional Brigade had Orote blocked off and was preparing to attack it the following morning. It was already clear that this would be one of those drives by inches so common in island warfare. The Japs in there were the naval garrison force. They had been granted time to fortify every inch of the ground with pillboxes, mine fields, and mortar positions

and they had by no means neglected their opportunity. It was a question of attacking and reducing each fortress in a separate operation—handwork.

A patrol from the brigade worked along the beach this day, the 25th, and made the first contact with General Turnage's division, but it was only a contact for the record, not a true liaison. With their backs toward the Orote Point operation and their faces toward the

279

rugged south central island, the 77th Division was consolidating positions and sending patrols out among the mountains. The 3rd Division had one regiment (3rd) still trying to work in against Adelup Point. One battalion of the regiment had been badly battered and was being withdrawn, having taken a good part of the division's casualties; the regimental commander was relieved after showing signs of overstrain, and replaced by Colonel James A. Stuart. Butler's 21st Regiment had been pulled toward its own left on Fonte Height and was concentrated in that direction, its right trailing off to the southwest in the direction of the 9th Marines. This regiment, out on the rim of the wheel, was swinging to get in position, facing east, trying to engulf the high mass of Mt. Tenjo in the process. The wide swing of the night had produced numerous gaps in the line, one of them of 1,500 yards between the 21st and the 9th. Colonel Butler covered this gap with a couple of outposts on the most likely routes, similar to those frequently used in the Guadalcanal jungles.

There was abundant enemy artillery still active around Adelup and Agaña. The Japs seemed to be reinforcing constantly from a central reserve somewhere in the rough triangular region Mt. Tenjo-Pago Bay-Toggha Bay. General Geiger believed the enemy main body lay in this triangle with the Adelup-Fonte fortified position anchoring its right wing on the north. His over-all plan was now to bring the 77th and 3rd Divisions into line with each other and break through the center of this enemy main body to Pago Bay. He rather expected them to make a try at getting into the southern mountains to conduct a guerrilla fight there, but as usual he kept his plans flexible. The operation order for the 26th provided only for the continuation of movements already begun except that the 14th Defense Battalion was to set up its guns on Cabras Island and support the attack of the Provisional Brigade by firing across the harbor, while the 77th Division's artillery helped from its area.

Actually, the estimate was in error as to both the positions and the intentions of the enemy. General Takashina's main body was far forward, close up to the Fonte-Adelup position, and he had no intention whatever of retiring to the southward if driven from there. He possessed a taste for maneuver and far more flexibility of mind than the average Jap commander. When the beachhead defense prescribed by his doctrine became impossible, he clung to the one position he could hold, at Adelup, pulled all the troops in the northern area together under his own hand and prepared for a counterattack. This took time; the terrible violence of the American shelling and air attacks had so thoroughly destroyed communications that all messages had to be taken by a runner and usually at night. It was thus 25 July before he could get his orders out and his troops arranged. In the meanwhile the naval forces had been sealed up on Orote, the two battalions of the 38th Regiment at Agat had been practically destroyed, and it proved impossible for the 10th Independent Mixed Regiment to join from its position among the southern mountains even by the 25th. But he dared no longer delay his attack. His scouts reported the Americans closing in on Mt. Tenjo from both sides and there were so many of them that they would outflank him once they got beyond that height. The attack was accordingly set for that night. It would move down the steep ridges into the northern of the two American beachheads and large bundles of demolition charges were prepared to be rolled down the slopes ahead of it. The orders were to destroy artillery particularly. Large quantities of sake were distributed and the company officers took a unanimous oath to kill as many Americans as they could before they died, then announced themselves as very happy. The naval troops on Orote were to attack their opponents at the same hour.

They were in no very good position to do so on the southern flank of that peninsula, where the 4th Marines had just come into line, but on the Apra Harbor side the defense positions terminated in an extensive mangrove swamp, in which about a battalion of the Naval Defense men gathered as darkness fell. Sake was served; as it warmed the men they began to sing and to encourage each other with speeches. The proceedings were somewhat noisy and attracted the attention of observers among the 22nd Marines, who realized at once that an exhibition of spiritual power would soon be forthcoming and tried to get an artillery concentration into the mangroves Unfortunately the wires were out and all the radio frequencies were full of Jap gabble and jamming. A brave sergeant managed to get some of the lines pieced together under fire and an intelligent captain secured momentary silences in the jamming by using French and German, which the Japs took for a new kind of code. The amount of time necessary for them to finish the sake did the rest; just as the attackers came pouring out of their swamp the shells landed crash on their heads.

They were cut to pieces, but enough survived that steel rain to reach the Marine positions and engage in a fight so close that knives, grenades, and pistols were the only weapons. The fire ran out of fuel toward dawn; as our support elements moved up they found Marine and Jap dead in many of the same foxholes, with over 300 enemy bodies and our losses only about a quarter of that. That day the brigade swung forward by the left.

On the 3rd Division's front the case was different and a lot tougher, since the attack was made in much greater weight and to a degree came as a surprise. Part of it swept through the 1,500-yard gap between the 21st and the 9th Marines, wiping out the outposts before they had a chance to report. This swing rushed right down into the beach area, attacking the hospital and division CP, where clerks and orderlies grabbed guns and Japs were seen within 100 yards of the beach. But this river of battle had a long distance to flow, got split up among ridges, was illuminated by star shells from the ships, and by time it reached the area where it might have done real damage was only a kind of leakage of staggering, drunken Japs who could not co-ordinate with each other.

Part of the attack struck the 1st Battalion, 21st, right in the center, part of it the 3rd Battalion of the same regiment. In the 1st Battalion area the attackers broke right through and the company that bore the brunt of the thrust could muster only eighteen men the following morning. This stream of Japs went screaming down into the hollow where the battalion mortar platoon was, wiped that out also and flowed up against the regimental command post, where Colonel Butler was summoning shore parties from the beach and any troops he could find to form a line. The 3rd Battalion held, but with both flanks bent back into a horseshoe, and the battalion commander sent a message soon after dawn that he was burying his ciphers as he expected to be carried away. But as elsewhere, distance, the late start imposed upon the enemy by their lack of good communications, and the fact that the defenders were panicproof veterans, solved all difficulties. In the morning it was found no positions had been lost, the 9th Regiment closed onto the 21st, the divisional reserve and whatever other troops could be found at the beachhead turned to in a grand mop-up operation, and by night of 26 July, General Takashina's effort had cost him 3,500 men without gaining him an inch of ground.

V

In a tactical sense that was the war on Guam. General Takashina's command and the naval forces on Orote had alike been so badly hurt as to be deprived of the power to strike. The campaign turned into another of the fossorial operations that had been seen on Tarawa, Saipan, and Eniwetok. Yet even so it retained that curious character of maneuver, rare in the Pacific war. Orote, for example:

Nothing had happened to alter General Geiger's view that the first essential was to gain the airfield and the harbor. The Provisional Brigade jumped off at the scheduled hour of 0700 on 26 July, supported not only by its own artillery and that of the corps but also by some of the guns from the 77th and 3rd Divisions. It had priority on all air missions. The 4th Regiment was on the left, the 22nd on the right.

As soon as the drive started the latter regiment began to get heavy artillery fire, the men thought it was coming from their own guns and a pause for reorganization was necessary, as this is the most demoralizing of all beliefs that soldiers can have. Colonel Shapley of the 4th and Colonel Schneider of the 22nd had a brief consultation, secured General Shepherd's permission for the former regiment to extend its lines a little into the latter's area and the attack went on. By 1245 the day's objectives had been reached all along the line and the troops pushed ahead toward what had been foreseen as the objective line for the following day. The pace slowed during the afternoon, both regiments having trouble—the 22nd with mangrove swamps, the 4th with emplacements well dug in and so heavily mined along their approaches that tanks could not be used. But they were still well ahead of schedule by night, when there occurred a little incident that well illustrates the character of the Guam fighting.

At midnight shells began to drop in the southern beachhead area where the tractor cranes were working.—From where? An Army flash and sound ranging team, "the flash-bang boys", on Alifan

283

looked across the crests and picked out a spot near Sumay, too close to the forward lines for our own rear artillery to do counterbattery without hitting the 22nd. The word was passed up to the front; the Provisional Brigade's artillery and a couple of close-in mortar squads took the annoying guns under fire and silenced them in fifteen minutes.

Next morning the Orote attack moved on again. Now the terrain had dense undergrowth on both flanks, interspersed with swamps. All through this thorny tangle there were pillboxes covered by mines. The only real avenue of approach was along the road from Agat to Sumay, the boundary between the two regiments, and along both sides of this were the strongest Jap positions. Toward noon advance elements of both regiments were pinned down there and casualties began to pile up. General Shepherd ordered the tanks forward and called for more from the Army division. The latter's mediums were not yet ashore and some of their lights had been damaged in crossing the reef, but what they had they sent, though too late to help that day. In the meanwhile, after a halt for reorganization and a call for air support, the 22nd had held with its left and swung forward by the right, slugging through a network of positions and gaining some high ground south of the Sumay road. Here the Japs broke and ran, the only time they did it on Orote, but this single rout turned out to be decisive, though the 22nd was now far ahead of the network of positions still detaining the 4th.

For the result was that next morning, 28 July, we had observation posts on that high ground, a great help to our artillery. The Army light tanks joined the Marine mediums; each machine had 50 yards of front to cover as they led the advance, working so close in that they were firing from 10 to 15 yards' range right into the slits of pillboxes. Japs who tried to get out with grenades or satchel charges were cut down by the infantry and by twilight of this day all the positions south of the airfield were taken with 250 pillboxes knocked out.

29 July saw more fighting, not heavy, around the airfield, where the remaining Japs stayed in their dugouts to die, and at 1530, with smoke rolling over the fields and occasional bullets still peening past, the Star-Spangled Banner was broken out over the ruins of the old Marine barracks, while a musician tooted colors on a captured Jap bugle and General Shepherd stood at salute.

The brigade had 2,000 casualties; it had disposed of the 5,000 Jap naval troops besides destroying the two battalions of the 38th Regiment that met it at the beaches.

VI

After Takashina's attack General Geiger ordered a battalion from the 77th up under control of the 9th Marines and changed the division boundaries to give the army men a much broader front, including all of Mt. Tenjo. The movement to positions took most of the day of this flank, while at the center the 9th came forward, and the indomitable 21st, so far from being slowed by the Jap counterattack, pressed on to grip the ridge line south of Fonte. These were preliminaries for the main assault; it went ahead rapidly on 28 July with Tenjo falling on the southern flank and long-contested Adelup on the north, Mt. Chachao behind it and several ridges in between. The Japs seemed mostly concentrated in these northern positions, but now they stayed in caves. The typical incident was that of the flamethrower team which saw a single enemy soldier duck into a hole and sent an interpreter to yell for surrender.

"Go to hell," the Jap replied. Three grenades were tossed in, but when the sound had died voices were still audible in there so the team used its flame throwers, then a couple of blocks of TNT. When they finally worked in there were 63 dead Japs in the cave.

Even as late as this General Geiger seemed still to have believed that there were considerable Jap forces beyond Tenjo in a southeasterly direction, an error for which he can hardly be blamed, since nearly every questioned prisoner said 3,000 men were in that area. Actually this was past-tense information; but not even the Japanese High Command knew it or knew where all the troops remaining to it were. General Takashina had been killed during the attack of the 28th as he tried to leave his Fonte CP, and the senior Jap officer was now Lieutenant General Obata. That commander's communications had collapsed so completely that hardly any messengers were getting through and a good many minor units, like those in the 63-man cave, were being isolated and mopped up simply because they received no word to move.

Under such circumstances it is difficult to see what Obata could have done, but what he did do was stick to the Takashina plan of fighting a war of maneuver. He ordered a general retreat across the rolling plateau of the northern island to the region of Mt. Santa Rosa, with the intention of setting up a holding position, splitting the advance, and striking into a vulnerable flank. The 29th Division celebrated the anniversary of its organization while the move was in progress: "In an environment how different from last year," wrote one of its officers. "I was deeply moved. There was only a little sake to drink each other's health. The American mortar shelling is awful and a wounded man, Corporal Nakaji, committed suicide."

Our attack renewed on 30 July and punched right through to the island's eastern coast by night of the 31st, meeting almost no resistance. The 3rd Division went through Agaña and a tangle of wild ravines and draws where regiments and companies were often out of touch with each other, finding Japs chiefly in the form of rear-guard detachments in spider holes, like those on Kwajalein. General Geiger assigned the Provisional Brigade to the southern portion of the island and drove his other troops hard on the track of the enemy in the north.

The advance was three or four thousand yards a day and this high country is nearly all close-knit jungle, in which little scattered knots of the enemy were encountered in fights of an endless variety. Thus the 9th Marines ran into a spider-hole position beyond Agaña with tank traps scattered all through it. The Japs let their vehicles and the accompanying infantry through one line without firing, then opened simultaneously from front and rear, and it was quite a savage little fight until reinforcements came. On the 77th's front a single Jap would walk slowly toward our lines at night, tempting fire so his concealed companions could shoot back at the revealed positions of our men. At another place a whole group of the enemy attacked the Army men by night with hatchets.

By 3 August it was clear that no serious enemy forces were in the south; the Provisional Brigade was brought north and put in on the left of the 3rd Division, which had encountered very tangled country and what looked like the beginnings of an organized position west of Mt. Santa Rosa. The 77th had been forced to narrow its front along the direct approaches to the same objective. In reality both divisions were approaching what General Obata considered his battle position. He was apparently expecting to let the right flank of the 77th ad-

vance up the lower slopes of the mountain along the coast, then cut
into that wing. The messages for the counterattack never reached his
men and in any case both Army and Marine divisions hit the Japanese position too fast for a counterattack to move. Obata's drive
turned into a series of what the 77th described as small local counterattacks, Santa Rosa was overrun in a single day, and on 10 August
our soldiers looked out across the Pacific from the north capes and
the island was declared secure. It cost us 7,032 casualties all told,
five-sixths of them wounded, 900 of them Army men.

VII

"Secure" was of course only a somewhat inaccurate metaphor
for the actual conditions on Guam as of 10 August, and its use seems
to have been at least partly dictated by the fact that General Vandegrift was to visit the island, so the commanders wished to get their
achievement on record. For a week after the secure date it was still
impossible to have lights at night in the 3rd Division's command post
and down to June, 1945, there were scattered groups and single
Japs all over the place, doing the peculiar things those people do in
emergencies. In that month a dignified Japanese major stepped out
of the bush with two orderlies who took turns mopping his forehead
while he sat down in the sun to talk over surrendering "the Japanese
forces on Guam" with Colonel Howard M. Stent, a Marine language
officer. The Major wanted to be sure that he was surrendering to
someone of properly exalted rank so that he would not lose face. Re-
assured on that point, he whistled 33 men from the coverts and the
fighting on Guam was over.

They were the last remnants of the 13,000, but in reality of course
the back of the Japanese resistance was broken when Takashina's
counterattack failed at the end of the fifth day. This means that the
heart of the defense was broken before that. The reason the counterattack failed, in spite of achieving strategic surprise and being made
from a particularly favorable tactical position, was that it was made
too late in the game. The reason for this was that the Jap communications were gone.

In fact there is no factor in the whole Pacific war more striking
than this repeated pattern on islands of all shapes and sizes, of the

287

destruction of enemy communications by naval gunfire and bombing. It happened at Tarawa and prevented the first-night counterattack; it happened at Eniwetok and turned that operation into an exaggerated mop-up; it happened on Saipan and deprived Saito's counterattack of all weight. The general effect was to restrict enemy mobility while giving the Marines great mobility, and this is one of the basic reasons why, in spite of the most carefully prepared positions and in spite of resistance genuinely carried to the last man, there was so enormous a disparity between the enemy's casualties and ours. Whatever the over-all numbers in the field, the Marines generally had numerical superiority at the points of contact where it counts.

The Japanese defense plan, viewed in the large, gives the impression of woodenness and stupidity, but this is really factitious; the case was that without communications no plan but the purest passive defense can be made to work. Guam presents perhaps the most visible single case of the value of the mobility conferred by naval fire. General Geiger's estimate of the position and the intentions of his opponent was wrong, but it made not the slightest difference in the campaign. Takashina might as well have had no plans at all and the plans he did have only made matters easier for the Americans. Of course, General Geiger rates good marks for keeping his own plan flexible and his troops balanced for a jump in any direction; but without the mobility conferred by his extraneous support, he could hardly have drawn the advantages he did even from this.

It is not clear that the Marines were at this time fully sensible of what they were getting out of naval gunfire. They tended to think that its main value was in area firing, to drive the enemy away from the open positions where he could have made the most effective resistance, and in its effect on his morale and nervous system during the first critical half hour on the beaches. They even thought so in the case of Guam, where the shelling was strikingly effective and got rid of perhaps as many as 50 per cent of the defending guns before the landing was made. These ideas, held by many Marines, were based on inspection of the Jap artillery positions after they were taken. Few of the guns were actually dismounted and few of the pillboxes blown apart. The view is a trifle narrow. A fixed gun can be put out of action quite as effectively by destroying its connection with an observation post or disposing of all its trained artillerists as by a direct hit.

288

One other feature of the Guam operation deserves comment for the backlight it throws on the controversy about Saipan. The 77th Division was completely green when it went into action, and on the first three nights there was a good deal of confusion in its lines from trigger-happy soldiers letting off at shadows. These soldiers learned not much less rapidly than the 3rd Marine Division had on Bougainville and by time they reached Mt. Santa Rosa the Army men were behaving as though they wore the world-and-anchor badge. The only regimental commander relieved during the campaign was a Marine. The 77th was simply a well-led division as some Army divisions were not.

Chapter 17

Tinian: Perfection

TINIAN IS SHAPED LIKE A FLAT FOOTBALL, 21,000 YARDS FROM tip to tip. It is a high plateau, rising sheer from the sea with a 500-foot hill in the south and another near the northern tip, Mt. Lasso. The island is extensively planted to sugar cane; the inhabitants live on rice and pickled beef. Northeast of Mt. Lasso lies the airfield and another had been begun, but only carried so far as a little grading, halfway down the western side. We had to have the place for two reasons—Saipan could be seen from it, so that while the enemy held it they could look across and report everything that went on at what was to be one of our most important bases; and the island itself offered sites for no fewer than six 8,500-foot runways, which would be needed if B-29s were to be used against Japan in the anticipated quantities.

The commander of the island was Colonel Ogata of the 50th Infantry Regiment from the 29th Division. He had that regiment, which had been one of the submarine sufferers but was now built up to strength by reinforcements from other units; about a battalion of the 135th Regiment; the 56th Naval Defense Force, and some scattering troops, making up a total of 4,700 Army and 4,110 Navy personnel. The major artillery consisted of a battery of three fine British 6-inch; six 140-mm.; ten 120-mm. dual-purpose; five 76.2 mm. dual-purpose (this was a lot of experimental guns); and thirteen 75s. There were a variety of 47- and 25-mm. cannon.

A great many of the small guns, the British 6-inch, two of the 75s, and four of the 120s were mounted around Tinian Town, down near the southern tip of the island where the excellent beaches made it most likely the Americans would attempt to land.

There is another series of beaches in Asiga Bay, near the northeast tip and south of the airfield. Here Colonel Ogata had mounted seven of his 140s to enfilade the beach areas, six 75s and three of the 76.2s to fire into the beaches from the rear. Many of the smaller guns were disposed in a system of pillboxes just behind the water's edge on the system that worked so well at Tarawa. Most of the remaining guns, three 140s, three 120s, two 76.2s, two 75s, were on the flanks of the small narrow beaches in the Hagoi area on the northwest coast, where there is a steep shelf and an abrupt rise toward the northern projection of Mt. Lasso. Three of the 75s were on a spur of this mountain, mounted so they could cover either Hagoi or Asiga Beach. All the rest of the island shoots steeply up from the water into terraces and there is great depth offshore so anyone debarking from a boat would be over his head at once.

All the guns had long since been dug back deep into the cliff faces and camouflaged, after which rapid-growing tropical vines had been trained over, which effectively hid them from view. They were so deep in as to be immune to air attack. The 140s on the northern point, the 120s covering Hagoi, and the whole battery of 75s near the airfield had opened fire on *Tennessee* and the cruisers when they were bombarding Saipan and every single one of them had been wrecked by 14-inch shell. On 25 June it became clear that Saipan was going and the Combined Fleet would be unable to come to the relief of the Mariana Gunto, so Colonel Ogata issued his final battle plan.

He divided his forces into three sector commands. The Southern Sector Force consisted of a battalion of the 50th, with most of the naval forces and scattering formations. It covered an area comprising about half the island on a line running across it just south of Asiga Bay; that is, this force was to defend the most likely landing spot at Tinian Town. The Northern Sector Force was to defend Asiga Bay; it had the 2nd Battalion, 50th, reinforced by a couple of platoons from other formations and a good many naval artillerists. The Western Sector Force was to protect the inferior beaches at Hagoi and consisted of a single company of infantry with an antitank gun squad. The remaining troops were in reserve south of Mt. Lasso, ready to turn to Asiga or Tinian Town as called for. The Colonel's

291

orders were to "counterattack to the water and annihilate the enemy but be prepared to shift two-thirds of the force elsewhere."

II

The original plan for Tinian had been drawn up in April, along with the other plans for the Marianas, by Holland Smith's Corps Staff and submitted to Holland Smith as head of troops, an in-one-pocket-and-out-the-other arrangement. It was changed during early July, when it became time to descend from the general to the specific. Marc Mitscher in the meanwhile had gone back to the Marshalls with a good many of the fast carriers to investigate why the new SB2C dive bombers had such frequent deck crashes and Jap planes had almost ceased to come from the north. Tinian was to be an amphibious campaign with no naval element except that furnished by the occasional submarines with which the enemy still sought to maintain a kind of communication to his doomed sea fortresses. The new command plan elevated Major General Harry Schmidt from the 4th Division to the V Amphib Corps; Clifton Cates, who had done so very well on Guadalcanal, now a major general, was brought out to head Schmidt's old division on 12 July.

On that date the V Corps Reconnaissance Battalion had already twice been in at night along the two practicable beaches of northern Tinian, Asiga and Hagoi, getting out without casualties and with sketches as well as samples of the vegetation for study. The beaches down at Tinian Town were the best, of course, but General Smith never even considered them; persistent photos from air and sea showed them to be heavily defended by fortifications which could be effectively turned by an overland campaign from the north. The Reconnaissance Battalion's report showed Asiga to be nearly as well defended and it had the additional disadvantage of being dominated by Mt. Lasso, which would mean a steep climb out of the beachhead against fire after landing. The Hagoi beaches were excessively narrow and with a bad shelf, but General Smith was a firm believer in the Napoleonic principle that no geographical opposition is half as serious as that which an active enemy can offer. He decided on Hagoi; and he had to argue with Admiral Turner to get it approved.

This decision was partly based on captured Jap documents and interrogations, a major named Yoshida from General Saito's staff being particularly useful. There had been a little communication between Tinian and Saipan during the fighting on the latter island and we had a good count on the Jap forces (the preliminary estimate said 8,350) as well as a copy of Colonel Ogata's battle plan. Such information is not as reliable as that from observation—the enemy might change—but when confirmed by observation has extra weight.

The 4th Division would make the assault, supported by a mixed artillery component, partly from the 10th Marines, partly from its own 14th. They would go in from LSTs in a shore-to-shore movement from Saipan, and it was expected to get all three infantry regiments and their guns onto the beach the first day, then drive directly forward to seize Mt. Lasso. The wastage of war had brought this division down to 65 per cent of its infantry complement, but neither General Schmidt nor General Cates believed the Japs could assemble enough troops for serious opposition in time to prevent a rapid extension of the beachhead, given that the enemy would have trouble making daylight movements in the face of our bombing and naval gunnery.

The date, called J day, was set for 24 July. As early as the 15th all the XXIV Corps Artillery and all the V Amphib Corps guns were assembled in southern Saipan to fire on Tinian. The heavier pieces could cover nearly the whole island. As the assault waves went in they would be covered by the battleships *Tennessee* and *California* and the cruiser *Louisville,* whose principal mission was to fire counterbattery against any Jap guns that might open up. There were destroyers in the plan too, and a scheme of fire had been worked out so that one ship would be specifically on call to each battalion of the two regiments in the first wave. Thus *Conway* would support the 1st Battalion, 24th, *Tennessee* the 2nd Battalion, *Eaton* the 3rd; of the 25th *Pringle* would support the 1st Battalion, *Waller* the 2nd, *California* the 3rd. *Birmingham* would take care of the western slope of Mt. Lasso; *Montpelier* and *New Orleans* the eastern slope and the Asiga Bay positions; *Indianapolis* would cover anything that showed at the point south of Hagoi beaches, Point Fabius San Hilo.

Meanwhile the 2nd Marine Division (now up to 85 per cent of its nominal strength, having received replacements) was put afloat in regular transports. Convoyed by *Colorado, Cleveland,* and the destroyers *Remey, Wadleigh, Norman Scott,* and *Monssen,* this division was to appear off Tinian Town and make a bluff at forcing a landing there and being beaten off. As soon as the Hagoi beachhead was secure the transports and the 2nd would move up thither, landing the division across the same beaches that had served the assault wave. The 2nd was to operate on the north, the left flank, sweeping across the airfield to the east coast of the island, then down on the Asiga defenses from their flank while the 4th Division took them in the rear. Both divisions would then move abreast toward the southern island. Air support for the operation would come from five escort carriers, *Midway, Nehenta Bay, Gambier Bay, Kitkun Bay, White Plains,* three combat carriers, *Essex, Langley, Princeton,* three Army fighter squadrons and one Army bomber squadron from Saipan and a Marine night-fighter squadron. The 27th Division was on four hours' notice to land in support; Harry Hill was the Amphib Force commander.

H hour of J day was 0745. Before that time the whole northern end of Tinian had been plastered by the fire of no less than 156 pieces from Corps Artillery in addition to the ships. They eliminated all the guns near the airfield and practically all those on the western slope of Lasso. The battleships had been working on the pieces Colonel Ogata had dug into the cliff near Fabius San Hilo Point, and got rid of the 140s by firing armor piercers into the cliff face above them, which brought down the whole structure in an avalanche of rubble. A Marine observer (his name was Boyneston) came aboard *Waller* to get acquainted and to direct fire; the men of the destroyer, who had themselves been through all the hard fighting and the wild nights up the Slot of the Solomons, stared in something like awe at his haggard, hungry face and worn uniform. "When we saw him we knew who was fighting the war." Aboard *Pringle* they had some Jap aviator prisoners who had been picked out of the water; the skipper was so impressed by the hard-bitten appearance of the Marines who wanted to guard them that he said no, he'd turn them over to a Navy Shore Patrol.

III

At Hagoi everything ticked off like a close order drill. The beaches were so narrow that only a single battalion could be landed on any one at a time, but this caused no trouble at all and the succeeding battalions poured in rapidly. Some of the amphitracs with the 24th were carried by tidal currents to land on rocks a little north of the true position, but this turned out to be no drawback and both assault

TINIAN

Scale   Yards

0   1000 2000 3000 4000

Tinian
Town

AIRSTRIP

Kotin

regiments were already 500 yards inland by 1000, with the 23rd coming ashore. The main opposition was from mines; two amphitracs were blown up and Marine engineers had to dig something like twenty mines out of the beaches where the Japs had cleverly planted them between low- and high-water lines. Colonel M. J. Batchelder's 25th reported a few pillboxes on its right, but not much was coming out of them, casualties were light.

At about 1100 aviation spotted four tanks pushing rapidly along the main road west of Mt. Lasso. Corps Artillery from Saipan put them under fire, blew one up with a direct hit and sent the others back, one with smoke streaming from its vitals. By 1335 two battalions of artillery were in position to fire from the beachhead; half an hour later the 23rd Regiment was all on the beach on the right flank working toward Fabius San Hilo. The 25th had the center now, the 24th the left flank toward the airfield, and all made such rapid progress that by night they had a beachhead 4,000 yards wide, 2,000 yards deep. The artillery was all ashore and one battalion from the 2nd Division.

The weather had been fine, with almost a complete absence of swells, but that condition could not be expected to endure, and preparations had been made to meet a change. Two big ponton causeway piers, built on Saipan, were under tow for the beachhead and reached it before morning. The casualties were 15 killed (mainly in the mined amphitracs), 225 wounded, the lightest for any landing yet. Surprise had paid off.

Surprise paid off down at Tinian Town also, but the Japs gained the surprise, where *Colorado* and her attendant destroyers supported the fake landing. The Higgins boats formed up as though for attack and rushed for the beach, at which the Jap anti-boat guns all blazed out. Just as the landing craft reached a position where they effectively blocked any attempt the old battleship might make to maneuver (she had a reef behind her and could not turn) Colonel Ogata's English 6-inch let her have it. They were shooting over open sights and could not miss. In ten minutes *Colorado* had 150 casualties, a fuel tank penetrated, and two 5-inch mounts knocked out, her upper works cut to pieces. *Norman Scott* beside her got seven hits and was a wreck with 22 killed, 47 wounded. The battleship had to take it like a sitting duck; but battleships are built to take it; her 16-inch imperturbably fired back right down the throats of the Japanese and, aided by *Cleveland,* silenced the brief flurry and destroyed all the Jap guns.

Colonel Ogata also tried to get surprise by bringing concealed forces into play against the beachhead which had established itself in the north. A pair of his 75s in casemate mounts near Fabius San Hilo had survived undetected and his communications, mainly by field radio, were very much better than Japanese usually had after the gunfire haircut. He ordered a double counterattack to drive in the American lines, his naval troops attacking westward across the north end of the island, his army men straight north up the island's main road past the outer spurs of Mt. Lasso, with the support of his single company of tanks. The difficulty was getting troops into position for this operation. All afternoon, after the *Colorado* attack had been "beaten off," he kept trying to move men up from the Southern Sector Force in small parties. The American airplanes spotted them every time and brought down so much fire that the formations had to disperse. It was hard to keep organization or tactical control, the soldiers tended to duck into cover and stay there. It was as bad with the tanks; two were disabled by American gunfire and most of the rest could not move. When the hour had reached 0200, which Ogata had concerted with the naval men as that of the attack, only six tanks, the battalion of the 135th from the reserve area, and about a company of the 50th were available for the main drive.

But the Colonel was a Japanese officer; that is, he permitted no difficulties to interfere with putting into effect a plan already drawn. At 0300 he tired of waiting for more troops, and attacked, his surprise guns of Fabius San Hilo furnishing covering fire.

As soon as the tropical night shut down under a sky that had grown more and more overcast through the day, Japanese activity began to be noticed both by the 24th on the left flank and by the 23rd on the right. General Cates, who was still controlling from an LST out in the water (the narrow beaches were too congested to put anything more ashore at once), ordered beach patrols set up; outposts were established 30 yards in front of the lines.

At 0200 the show started on the 24th's front—the usual Jap hullabaloo, men running forward in small groups, screaming and throwing grenades. At the same time artillery fire began to fall on the beachhead from some unidentifiable point. It was a wild night, but the 24th was a little more closely formed on a little better ground than the other two regiments. The Japs never got an entrance into its lines.

At 0300 a second attack developed against the joint of the 23rd and 25th Regiments, led by tanks with Japs yelling and beating rifle

297

butts on their tops. Just where the blow struck there was a little lake surrounded by soft ground from which rise quite a few draws to the outer slopes of Lasso, so that it was difficult to keep liaison along the front. In spite of illuminating star shells quickly put up by the ships several hundred of the Japs got through to the rear areas and attacked the artillery positions. But that was the limit. The Jap tanks had the usual luck against our bazookas, that is, none at all, five of the six being knocked out at once. 37 mm. canister and rifles had taken so heavy a toll of the attackers that they were reduced to little groups who merely sought cover, and as soon as morning came the mop-up squads got busy and cleaned them all out. By 0930 on the morning of 25 July the division was ready to go forward again and found 1,241 Jap bodies along its lines. The enemy artillery fire was never really serious; something seemed to be wrong with the traverse of their guns and all the shells fell into the narrowest of areas.

IV

That night attack was in fact the effective conclusion of the campaign, as the night attack on Guam, just twenty-four hours later, effectively concluded the campaign on that island. During the night the gunners of the 10th and 14th Marines had supported the troops in line not only with call fire but also with shoots in the rear of the enemy lines at points where activity had been noted by daylight. One of these shoots hit the jackpot, landing right on Colonel Ogata's CP and killing him with his whole staff.

No one in the Jap lines knew who was to take over or that anyone was to take over, since headquarters had no survivors. Some units, from a squad to a platoon in size, simply dug in and stayed where they were, waiting for orders that never came. Some, from a company to a battalion, obeyed that vague sentence in the battle plan which bade them shift two-thirds of their forces elsewhere. Thus on the afternoon of the 25th, two companies of the 50th Regiment who had tried and failed to reach the front for Ogata's counterattack began to march back south again. They were spotted by advance patrols from the 25th Regiment and were cut to pieces by the sudden artillery concentration.

On our side the morning attack had been set for 0900 but it had been delayed an hour to finish the mop-up operation. Nothing was lost; when the drive started it at once made a big heave forward all round the perimeter, carrying the 24th Regiment halfway across the airfield and the 25th well up the slope of Lasso. Resistance was nowhere more than "moderate," which meant that machine-gun bullets frequently ripped across open spaces, there were occasional bursts from mortars and constant sniping, so that men had to advance cautiously, using cover. But there was no appearance of really well-organized resistance and of counterstrokes none.

The whole 2nd Division landed that day and CP of the 4th. That night the 24th Regiment was picked out of line and placed in reserve while the 2nd Division took over its positions. The following morning both divisions attacked, the 2nd successfully going through with its right wheel around the foot of Mt. Lasso while the 4th took the summits. One wing of the latter pushed forward to capture the positions from which the 75s had fired during the Japanese night attack and it was revealed that the reason these guns failed to accomplish more was that they had been so deeply dug in that they had an arc of fire of only about 15 degrees. From this point on, the daily journal was one of 3,000-4,000 yard advances till 1 August, when the Marines of the three divisions could look from the southern shore and General Schmidt could announce in the classic phrase that "all organized resistance had ceased."

The island cost us 1,727 casualties, of whom 290 were killed. It cost the Japs everything they had and it was the easiest conquest the Marines had made to date. Of course part of this was due to the overwhelming force developed—two full divisions and the fire power of a fleet against the unfortunate Colonel Ogata's scrap and patch command. But another and very big reason for the light loss and heavy gain was full information as to the enemy dispositions and smart tactics in making use of this information. At Tarawa, Kwajalein, Eniwetok, Parry, nearly 50 per cent of the casualties had come at the beaches where the Japs elected to make their main defense; at Saipan and Guam the beach casualties were the heaviest of all. At Tinian the relative figures were reversed. General Schmidt's men landed where there were no beach defenses and thus turned the campaign into a pushover.

299

Tinian was also remarkable for another feature—the tryout of the Napalm fire bombs. Only a few of them were received in time for use there and they were employed just behind the beach areas, where they proved so effective in burning out vegetation and camouflage that much wider employment was immediately recommended. They were referred to by correspondents as a new and very terrible secret weapon, no hint of whose nature was allowed to escape by the censors. As a result everyone back in the States began to imagine that the problems of amphibious warfare had been solved and the rest would come easy.

As a matter of fact, most of the problems had been solved as against any system of defense encountered to date. Covering fire, air support, co-operation, beach parties, landing craft—all the techniques were essentially worked out by time the Marianas fell. It was not quite apparent at the time, nor even later, when different methods of resistance began to be encountered; but August 10, 1944, when Guam was declared secure, marks a historic date—the date when the U. S. Marines and the Navy carrying it to the beaches arrived at the answer to a question that had perplexed all history and had not infrequently been pronounced as beyond solution. The question was that of how to land on a hostile and defended beach.

Chapter 18

Marines under MacArthur:
Cape Gloucester

W AR IS A BUSINESS IN WHICH THERE IS NEVER TOO MUCH of anything, nor indeed enough to make things go as rapidly and decisively as a commander could wish. Down in Australia they were, at the close of 1942, still nervous about being invaded in spite of the fully appreciated air and naval victories off Guadalcanal, the fact that one Jap point had been blunted at Milne Bay and another turned round in the opposite direction on the Kokoda Trail. The Australians wanted a division for security purposes; specifically their own 9th Division, which was serving with Montgomery in Egypt. That officer had just broken Rommel's front in the truly decisive clash of Alamein. In fact, the battle had not yet been fought when the first request for the 9th came through. The British were in no mood to spare the men who might make the Egyptian victory permanent by a thundering pursuit. The matter went to the Combined Chiefs of Staff, who made decisions in that vague domain where strategy and politics are one. Ruled: that the Australians could not have their 9th Division back but would receive an American division instead. That division was the 1st Marine, just out of the Guadalcanal fighting and (thus things are dovetailed) sent down to Melbourne for "reorganization, re-equipment and recreation."

Of all three the division stood much in need. Replacements reached it in Australia and were shaken down into the organization; there were some changes of command by the natural process of promoting officers out. One of them brought Major General William H. Rupertus to the head of the division with Colonel Amor Sims as his chief of staff and Brigadier General L. C. Shepherd as assistant divi-

301

sion commander. The really important feature of this Melbourne idyll, however, is that the division was now in the Southwest Pacific, the MacArthur command area, and at a time when MacArthur was permitting the press to make public complaint for him that his theater of the war was starved for troops. He determined to use the 1st Marine Division as his own; and he wished to use it specifically in an operation against New Britain Island, at the northern end of which stands Rabaul, the center of the Southwest Pacific war.

The planning stage began in June at Brisbane but it was not until the last day of August (this is 1943) that the first operations orders were issued. They made the 1st Marine Division a part of the "Alamo" Force, the U. S. Sixth Army, under Lieutenant General Walter Krueger; and they looked forward to the capture of all western New Britain up to a line running from Gasmata across to Talasea. Airfields would be set up in this area "for operations against Rabaul," a somewhat vague statement which reflects a similar vagueness in the minds of our high commanders at the time. At this date it was not certain that the great Jap base could be neutralized from air and sea; an overland campaign might be necessary. In any case the airfield at Cape Gloucester on the western end of New

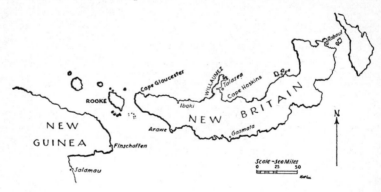

Britain was needed before the move to the Philippines along the coast of New Guinea could go ahead.

This August plan looked forward to a landing at Gasmata on the southern coast, followed shortly after by one on the north coast, and made the date November. The information as to enemy strength was exceedingly good and quite plentiful, the Australians having excellent coast-watchers on New Britain and General MacArthur's

5th Air Force being very active in getting photos. Cape Gloucester held an old commercial airstrip, not in very good shape, and a quite good new one built by the Japs, with something between 1,200 and 1,500 troops. Gasmata had a small strip and 800 to 1,000 of the enemy; Talasea, a partly developed strip and about a battalion. All these places might as well have been on little separate islands, since central New Britain is the fiercest kind of jungle country, as bad as Bougainville.

As September deepened into October and more information was accumulated the Gasmata landing was dropped from the plan. The strip there was not in use and the land on which it lay was so impossible that to make it suitable for our airplanes would involve both more time and more men than MacArthur was willing to spend on a field not very near the scene of anticipated future action. The Marine division, which was to carry the ball, had meanwhile moved up to staging areas at the eastern end of New Guinea—the 5th Regiment to Milne Bay, the 7th to Oro Bay, and the remainder to Goodenough Island. It was doing advance jungle training.

At the last of these places there was another and more detailed staff conference in early November. The original date for the landing would be upon them in a very few days and it was clear that such a date could not be met for two reasons. One was the transport situation. The only two big transports available were Australian ships equipped with nothing but the normal ships' boats. It was held necessary to use U. S. APDs, which could get around fast under air attack and which carried their own landing boats, since it was a virtual certainty that the landing would be strongly opposed by enemy planes. (At that date Sherman and Montgomery's big carrier strikes on Rabaul were just being delivered and were finding plenty of Jap aviation.) All the APDs in the area were, and would be for some time, supporting the 3rd Marines and 37th Army Divisions on Bougainville.

The other detaining factor was a shortage of cruisers for supporting fire. Rear Admiral Kinkaid, who commanded the 7th Fleet under MacArthur's orders, had available at the moment only that veteran of the Southwest Pacific, the light cruiser *Phoenix*. He had been promised *Nashville* and *Boise,* now back in the States for repairs, but they could not arrive much before the middle of December, which date was itself no good, since it meant making the approach under a full "bombers' moon." There were a pair of Australian heavy cruisers, but they had so much draft it was not certain they could close in enough for effective support. All the other ships were wanted up in the Gilberts, where it was not unlikely that our advance would be opposed by the main Jap fleet. There was certainly something to MacArthur's complaint about running his war on a shoestring.

The delay to late December had the inconvenience that it would throw the landing date into the monsoon season, when rain to the extent of 20 inches a day falls on New Britain; and also it gave the Japs time to reinforce those outposts over which the shadows were gathering. At the November conference, Colonel E. A. Pollock, the old Guadalcanal hand and now divisional G-3, said frankly that the allotment of troops for Operation Backhander (the Cape Gloucester attack) was quite insufficient. That allotment had not in fact been changed from the August plan which embraced a double landing. The arrangement then was to land one battalion west of the airfield on the cape, the other two of the same regiment east of it. This was very well as against 1,200 Japs, but there was a new, late report from MacArthur's headquarters that the number of enemies in there had shot up to nearly 8,000. A single regimental combat team would have rough going against so many. "You will have to speak to your unit commander about that," said General MacArthur, but it was quite evident that he agreed, and though General Krueger was at first annoyed at this going over the head of his Sixth Army Staff, he was a just man and reasonable, and the plan was revised.

It now called for Lt.-Col. James M. Masters's 2nd Battalion, 1st Marines, to land west of the airfield with some guns and block the coastal trail which was the only practical method of movement either for reinforcements or for the retreat in that direction of the airfield garrison. The 7th, under Colonel Julian Frisbie, would land about five air-line miles east of the airfield on the shores of Borgen Bay, followed closely by the remainder of Colonel William J. Whaling's 1st Regiment. Colonel John T. Selden's 5th Regiment would be the reserve afloat and the 32nd Army Division in distant reserve behind. Part of the latter's units would land at Arawe on the southern coast on 15 December to give us a *pied-à-terre* there, but were expected to have no great difficulty as Arawe held but few Japs.

There are some wide fields of kōnai grass just south of the Cape Gloucester airfield. General Krueger planned to drop a battalion of Army parachutists there, the 503rd, still further to confuse the enemy's counsels and split his forces. But this feature was cut from the plan by General MacArthur himself. The ground for the purpose was very rough, the kōnai grass taller than a man, and there had been some casualties from fire in similar country during the big drop that preceded the pinching out of Salamaua in New Guinea. A detachment of Australians, familiar with the country and the peculiar natives who live in it, accompanied the expedition. From their information and elaborate photos, plaster relief maps were built. Down at Goodenough every man of the expeditionary force went over them till the details of the terrain were fixed in his mind and it is enough to say now that this part of the plan worked out perfectly. When the landing was made nobody got lost and everybody steered by geographical features he could recognize at once.

The new table of organization provided that the regiment of engineers formerly attached to each Marine division should become a battalion, but a great deal of difficulty was anticipated in moving through the roadless jungle, so that the 1st kept its 17th Marines, the engineers, and even augmented them for this operation by attaching the 19th Battalion of Seabees. The expedition would lack close air support normal in Marine operations, since the only cooperation planes in the area were Army A-20s, whose pilots had not trained with Marines.

D day was finally set for 26 December; the total strength of the division was 18,877.

II

The Japanese Army uses all sorts of oddly designated formations with meaningless numbers and the command at Cape Gloucester was one of these, the 65th Brigade, apparently so called because there were not sixty-four others like it, nor even one. The commander was Major General Iwao Matsuda, who was directly under General Hitoshi Imamura at Rabaul, an officer whose exalted rank had somewhat dimmed General Hyakutate's luster when the former came down to set up shop as head of the 8th Army Group at Rabaul. This command included Hyakutate's 17th Army and the 18th Army as well as Matsuda's brigade.

The brigade had been organized in 1941; Matsuda had seen it through a period of special jungle training before taking it down for the campaign on Bataan, where it had won a citation. So did nearly every other Bataan formation; the special distinction of the 65th was that it managed to keep its medical casualties down.

The brigade originally had three infantry regiments like a division, but each of them contained only two battalions; and things were still further muddled in the winter of '42, when one of the regiments was taken from the brigade to be sent up into the Mandates, being replaced by two artillery and two antiaircraft artillery battalions. Most of another regiment, the 142nd, was still in the Philippines at the date of which we speak and the elements of that formation which had reached New Britain were at Talasea.

The garrison at Cape Gloucester thus consisted of the remaining regiment, the 141st, the four artillery battalions, an extra mountain artillery battalion, and a strong Shipping Engineer unit, say 6,600 men all told, with another 500 out on Rooke Island. The 53rd Regiment of Hyakutate's command was spread along the eastern shore of New Britain in remote support. Matsuda expected to be attacked, but in the enervating heat and the frightful jungle conditions there had not been time to dig proper positions. There were good stocks of food and medical supplies, but malaria and dysentery had already set in in spite of the brigade's precautions, and nearly a quarter of the men were incapacitated. The over-all plan of General Matsuda's defense was to hold the beach and coast trails with relatively light forces. His artillery was partly on a 450-foot elevation just behind Silimati Point where it juts into Borgen Bay, partly on a taller hill farther south, and partly in the jungle-covered draws close behind the airfield. Beginning on 19 December, as many as fifty heavy bombers of the land type began coming over every day and General Matsuda knew that the hour of destiny could not be far distant, especially as these big craft were followed by flights of light B-25s at low level which demolished all the buildings not concealed under jungle.

306

Christmas Day, clear and windless, found the invasion convoy running steadily up through Vitiaz Strait. For the men below it was paralyzingly hot. Besides *Nashville, Boise,* and *Phoenix,* Rear Admiral D. E. Barbey, in command of the attack force, had three Australian cruisers, *Australia, Shropshire, Hobart,* with destroyers *Shaw, Drayton, Mugford, Bagley, Lamson, Hutchins, Beale, Daly, Brownson.* Other destroyers *Flusser, Mahan, Reid,* and *Smith* were to, and did, furnish close support. The monsoon still held off, but that night its forerunner arrived in the form of clouds that slid in to hide the moon. This was considered a good augury; it might permit the convoy to escape observation from Japanese outposts on islands in the straits—a hope which proved vain, incidentally, for Rooke Island had marked the dark silhouettes and warned Matsuda.

As it happened this did the Japanese no good, nor did the fact that the ships carrying the troops and furnishing fire cover had to work so slowly through almost totally uncharted reefs running to 7,000 yards off the coast (*Flusser* and *Mahan* had to use radar to find breaks in it) that there was no surprise. The previous air attacks had been heavy; our cruisers were the 15-gunned ships that get off nearly ten salvos a minute. Just after they opened fire no fewer than 65 B-24s and 50 B-25s came over to drop 215 tons of bombs, the largest concentration yet seen in the Southwest Pacific.

A hill reaches up out of the jungle southwest of the beaches, where some Jap artillery had been located. Our people called it Target Hill; it was so drenched with white phosphorus as to be completely invisible and to all that firing as landing craft came in the enemy replied with a single shot from a single gun. The B-25s made strafing runs till the first wave was only 500 yards from the beach; the Japs were too much hurt and stunned to offer any opposition at all as the assault wave of Battalions 1 and 3, 7th, went in from their Higgins boats, standing up at 0745 to find themselves in a jungle worse than Bougainville. A tall man could lie with his head under the cover of the vegetation line and his feet out in the water; that was how wide the beach was. Those who penetrated that jungle line had to do it by cutting their way in with machetes, and when they did so found themselves on ground which the map (perhaps in a strained effort at humor) called "damp flat." The intermittent rains of what New Britain considered its dry season had reduced the ground to ankle-deep sludge; from ankle level to far overhead was the abatis of tangled stinging vegetation. This had been foreseen; amphitracs and bulldozers followed close on the heels of the combat infantry and began to cut lanes toward the areas where dumps were to be established.

Meanwhile the troops were being poured rapidly ashore and were spreading into the "damp flat" behind. By 1015 all three battalions of the 7th were in with their supporting elements and the 3rd Battalion, 1st; General Rupertus had set up his CP ashore and the gap between the two beachheads had been closed, incidentally engulfing a small Jap supply dump. During the morning the 1st Battalion, 7th, pushed southwest and made contact with some of the enemy on Target Hill, where they rapidly beat down resistance from a couple of Jap battalion guns and anchored the southern front of the beachhead. The fact is that most of the enemy positions on the hill were unoccupied; the Marines had reached them before the Japs who had left under the bombing could return. Next in line northward was the 2nd Battalion, 7th; they met some resistance and took some casualties in the green gloom but smashed through, took a big supply dump full of food, ammunition, and medical supplies and dug in for the night 900 yards from the water. The 3rd Battalion, 7th, carried the perimeter on around its northern rim. The 3rd Battalion, 1st, attacked to the northwest along the coast trail; ran into a small group of pillboxes, reduced them rapidly and also dug in.

The 1st Battalion, 1st, landed during the afternoon, along with a supply echelon, and while that was going on the Japs came down from Kavieng with a passionate air attack. They ran into four flights of P-38s from Dobodura in New Guinea which were furnishing the afternoon air cover. Now, these Japs were the "relic" air groups of the 24th and 25th Air Flotillas, which had been so badly battered in the fighting for Bougainville and the aborted attack on Montgomery's carriers—a few survivors who had survived because they kept out of harm's way and a lot of bold but badly trained new pilots. They lost no fewer than 59 planes to 4 of ours. A few broke through to rush the unloading LSTs from low altitude; here we lost a couple of planes, for a flight of B-25s was just going over at low

308

level in the opposite direction and two of them got caught in the barrage our ships put up. Bombs jarred the bay and water sprayed on all the ships, but no cigar.

At twilight the Japs sent down another attack and that might have been serious since the hour was so late our fighters had gone home to tuck themselves in for the night; but with their usual skill in choosing the wrong objective the enemy let the piled supplies on the beach alone and fell on the retreating convoy. A torpedo damaged the destroyer *Brownson* so badly she foundered during the night and a hole was knocked in the side of one LST, paid for with two planes.

Landing successful, then, supplies coming in according to plan, divisional casualties for this first day 21 killed, 23 wounded. The proportion of killed for wounded was high; it shows the damage was mostly by sniper fire and that these Japs were good shots.

IV

During the night the enemy counterattacked of course, especially at the weak joint of the 2nd and 3rd Battalions, 7th, where a battery of special weapons men arrived just in time to plug the gap, fighting with small arms. The enemy got nothing but casualties for his trouble; but as the last wave of his attack turned squealing back into the jungle cover, the monsoon broke overhead and water came down in thick straight lines, a drench that was to continue uninterrupted for five days and nights. This must be remembered as the background to all the rest of the operation. The division could use none of its numerous trucks in mud where even jeeps foundered and had to be hauled out with winches; where artillery pieces were in above the wheelhubs; where amphitracs were the only means of supply, and where Marines in their spotted jungle clothing were wet to the skin the first night and did not dry out for weeks. The little streams were all torrents, Engineers and Seabees no sooner set up a bridge than it went out, cooks at the galleys stood in water to their knees and it was hot, hot, hot. A sergeant gazed at a B-25 running past beneath the streaming skies and said, "If I was flying one of those things I'd be just halfway from a private to a general. I don't know how I got into this business."

309

Under the rains the attack picked up again on 27 December, Colonel Whaling's 1st and 3rd Battalions, 1st Regiment, moving northwestward along the coastal trail while the 7th dug in a perimeter engulfing Silimati Point and inched toward the jungle slopes inland. It had been intended that the rightmost elements of this regiment, from the 1st Battalion, should support the flank of Whaling's advance, but during the morning there were constant tappings and attempts at infiltration along the 7th's whole front. The regiment had to stay where it was. Whaling pushed ahead anyway, finding along the shore a mess of wrecked barges, some positions for 75s, and finally some pillboxes flanking the trail, which were disposed of by the tanks. Night found the 1st well ahead of schedule; it set up a little separate perimeter of its own and the artillery had reached position to fire supports by dark.

28 December was spent by the 7th in merely improving positions and in patrols—particularly on the front of the 2nd Battalion in the

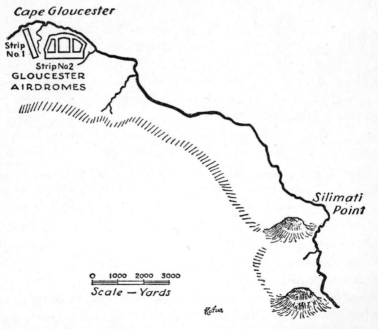

center, where Japs in about company strength were discovered in a pretty well-built position behind a small stream. There was a little fire fight with this gang. The 1st Regiment pushed on toward the

310

airfield; it met one really formidable road block with a lot of bunkers and artillery positions and carried it with a rush and the help of tanks. Most of the guns were captured unmanned, a fact which caused a good deal of speculation in our lines at the time, but the explanation was really simple. The original landing and quick, deep penetration in the Target Hill area had cut off many of the Jap artillerists from the pieces they were supposed to serve and they were now down on the 7th's front, unable to get back save by an impossible circuit through mountain jungle.

These, really the bulk of the Jap force, were keeping the 7th fully occupied, not because they were so very active but because it was necessary to maintain long and tight lines in blind country to keep the enemy from infiltrating into the vital supply area of the original beachhead. There were thus only the two battalions of Whaling's regiment for the attack on the airfield on which it was now closing. General Rupertus had already decided that he would have to use his reserve regiment, the 5th, to capture the field, and had secured from Sixth Army the release of one of its battalions, originally intended to clear out the Jap nest on Rooke Island. The first two battalions of the fresh regiment reached the beachhead early on the morning of 29 December and were immediately dispatched to join the airfield front, partly by road and partly by Higgins boats along the shore.

The attack on the field had originally been scheduled for noon of that day, with the 5th sliding leftward past the rear of the 1st in the kōnai grass area south of the field where it had originally been intended to set down the parachutists, both regiments together then to conduct an envelopment. In the morning the artillery fired preparations for such an attack, giving special attention to the wooded ravines leading from the field southward up to the high mass of Mt. Talawe, where the main Jap positions were supposed to be. But the rain had not ceased; the 5th simply could not reach its jump-off line in time and after one postponement and another the hour for the attack was carried over to 1500.

Dark was already close as the four battalions swung forward. The combination of late hour, jungle, rain, and the ridges made it a big left wheel instead of the right wheel and envelopment that had been planned. The two battalions of the 1st with their accompanying tanks rushed rapidly through light resistance across fairly good

311

ground on their flank, had both airstrips in their possession, and were digging in, facing south, when operations were called off for the night. The 2nd Battalion, 5th, linked up with them and also dug in facing the ravines southward, where patrols had found a number of unoccupied Jap positions. The 1st Battalion, 5th, lost contact with the rest and set up its own little perimeter on a ridge south and some-- what east of the airfield. All expected to be counterattacked during the night but nothing of the kind happened.

What had happened was this: a second artillery preparation had been fired when the attack was postponed and the double rain of shells had produced something like a panic among the defenders of the two airstrips. The Jap colonel in command emerged from an elegantly appointed dugout just in time to catch a shell with the back of his neck and most of his men fled away up the draws of Mt. Talawe. During the night, as they were let alone, they began to re- member Bushido and to crawl back toward the airfield. As they did so they encountered other crawlers among the range of positions at the outlets of the draws.

When Colonel Selden sent out a patrol in the morning to find his 1st Battalion, it found instead the Japs in their positions and a fire fight started. He supported the patrol with a platoon and then with a company. It was not enough; he asked for help from the other regiment, which also sent a company, and that was not enough either but in the meanwhile Lieutenant Colonel Joseph F. Hankins of the 3rd Battalion, 1st, had gone forward for a look, and seeing what the front was up against, drew most of his battalion and a platoon of tanks into the fight. At the same time the 1st Battalion, 5th, had of course moved toward the sound of fighting and the direc- tion of its move brought it on the rear of the Jap positions. Before noon they were all taken; at 1300 General Rupertus could report to General Krueger that point and airfield were secure. The next day the moves began that brought the 5th and 1st Regiments with the 12th Defense Battalion into the perimeter of our new airfield. The engineers and Seabees incredibly carried a passable two-lane road from the old perimeter to the new that same day, 31 December.

All this time the 2nd Battalion, 1st, had remained within the small perimeter that set up along the ends of ravines running steeply to the sea on the western coast of the peninsula. Patrols went out

312

daily and had a good many minor contacts with the enemy, catching one or two prisoners who belonged to the 53rd Regiment of the 17th Jap Division. The only thing remarkable about these contacts was that the Japs shuttling around in the jungle never seemed to have any security. Again and again our patrols found a whole platoon asleep or marching along a trail with their rifles slung and no scouts. On the night of 30 December enough of the Japs assembled to try an attack on the battalion's perimeter. It was beaten off with a loss of 83 dead to the enemy, who carried away his wounded to the south and bothered the battalion no more, so that in the early days of January it was withdrawn to its parent regiment around the airfield.

V

The invaluable native scouts reported that in spite of the ominous appearance of the Jap 53rd Regiment, which had not been counted on, not much was to be expected from the west of the airfield perimeter, where the few enemies remaining were pulling back in a state of disorganization. At the eastern end around Borgen Bay toward Natamo Point, things were different; General Matsuda had pulled his men well together, organized a position, and prepared to hold on. This position was centered around the hill rising sharply from the flats of the shore some two miles south of Silimati Point. It was called by us Hill 660 because of its measured height, and by the Japs, Manju Yamma, which is to say "Sweet Cookie Hill." It is not like Target Hill a bald-top, but heavily overgrown with tall jungle trees; and it was within artillery range of the newly captured airfield, so the strips would not be of much use to us till it was taken.

On 29 December, when it was clear that the airfield would soon be captured, General Rupertus assigned the job of clearing this southern flank to General Shepherd, with a separate command consisting of the 7th Regiment, the 3rd Battalion, 5th, two battalions of artillery and one of engineers. His battalions in line were in order from south to north the 1, 2, 3, of 7, then the 3rd of the 5th, with the stream (nameless) running from north to south across the front of the 2nd and 3rd Battalions, 7th, and the enemy fixed position facing the former battalion.

The general planned to advance by the right flank, sending the 3rd Battalion, 5th (Lieutenant Colonel D. S. MacDougal), well

313

inland to sweep round, passing the front of the 3rd Battalion, 7th (Lieutenant Colonel William R. Williams) to let it across the river, and both abreast coming down the west bank till the front of the 2nd Battalion, 7th (Lieutenant Colonel Odell M. Conoley), was cleared and the position facing it taken. That battalion would then be available as a reserve and the other two would be linked up with Battalion 1, 7th (Lieutenant Colonel John E. Weber). A direct attack southward would be carried forward by all three till the next obstacle was met, when the reserve battalion could be used for a second end run. The forces involved were small, the weapons wholly different, but it is worth remarking that here was an approximation amounting to an identity with that most famous of all campaigns in which superior numbers were used against fortified lines—William Tecumseh Sherman's drive through the hills to Atlanta.

As in that classic of the soldier's art, the numbers were not so very superior either (General Matsuda still had practically all his 141st Regiment and some scattering), the enemy both determined and alert to the possibilities of counterattack, and the geography far from favorable. On the first day, 2 January, MacDougal's 3rd Battalion, 5th, got into trouble with the tall, knife-edged kōnai grass, did not enter the jungle rim till noon and at 1545, when it began to get intense sniper fire, was out of touch with the 3rd Battalion, 7th. The latter had not yet crossed the stream when it was time to dig in for the night, and during the night Matsuda lashed back in a violent counterattack against Target Hill, with a covering attack across the stream against Conoley's 2nd Battalion, 7th. The Japs spent most of the night cutting steps in the face of Target Hill and toward dawn came right up, every gun they had pounding the summit from the rear. It was hot work for a while, but the Marine artillery silenced the Japanese, then turned to on their infantry, and the nearest "the monkeys" got to our lines was 20 yards. When the patrols went out to count the enemy dead they found a document on one of them:

"In today's battle, the Abe Company, as the leading company in the attack, succeeded in breaking through and taking Target Hill. However, the enemy, with fierce artillery fire and fierce bombing, counterattacked but nothing can induce us to give up our positions." It was a carbon copy, for the original had gone to higher echelons, and it was a lie.

On the attack front Colonel MacDougal gained only a few hundred yards through the jungle, most on his right; the 3rd Battalion, 7th, gained nothing at all beyond getting partly across the stream to link with MacDougal. This left the front at nightfall of 3 January a U; the series of Jap strongpoints was in the cup. At this point the resemblance to Sherman's famous campaign increases; the engineers became the determining factor. All of both days they had labored to put a corduroy road through swamp and jungle to what had now been dubbed "Suicide Creek"; on the evening of 3 January a bulldozer pushed forward to cut down the bank so tanks could cross. The operator was promptly shot. A volunteer replaced him while a platoon of Pioneers took on the Jap snipers who were holding matters up, and by the hour for digging in a practicable passage had been made.

That was the pay-off. Next morning, 4 January, three big tanks stuck their ugly snouts into the middle of the Jap position, blew up its bunkers one after the other, and flushed their remaining defenders for MacDougal's men to shoot down. By night the line was as General Shepherd planned it, across the stream and well south of Target Hill. The 2nd Battalion, 7th, had already swung wide to prolong the western flank of the 3rd Battalion, 5th.

5 January was a day of patrolling and preparation for the next jump. Just ahead of the left center of the line was a hill called Hill 150, and between it and the coastal trail a swamp even more gelatinous than most of the Cape Gloucester ground. One of the captured documents was an order that "Aogiri Ridge" must be held at all costs, with a sketch map that seemed to identify Hill 150 as the ridge in question. General Shepherd planned an attack on it by the 1st Battalion, 7th, and 3rd Battalion, 5th, converging, while the 2nd Battalion, 7th, swept in from the flank and the 3rd Battalion, 7th, was pinched out of line. One company from the 1st Battalion, 7th, was to move along the coastal trail outside the swamp, with tank support.

It turned out that the information was everywhere wrong or incomplete. Hill 150 was not Aogiri Ridge, in fact it was not occupied at all, and was taken with ease by the rightmost elements of Battalion 1, 7th, and the left of Battalion 3, 5th. But south of it was a heavily wooded bottom with another hill behind, and in this bottom

315

the Japs had established themselves in so great strength that neither the right of 3/5 nor all the efforts of 2/7 could make them budge an inch. Colonel MacDougal was badly wounded and had to be replaced by Lieutenant Colonel Lewis Walt from the 5th.

The left of 1st Battalion, 7th, found a heavy and well-defended road block on the sandspit along the shore with a stream in front of it that was too much for the tanks. Here again a bulldozer solved the problem under fire, but the bottom ground at the center of the line was still not cleaned out by the evening of the next day. Only the engineers made progress; they had discovered Hill 150 was just what they wanted and were taking its red cinder ash apart bit by bit as fill for their corduroy.

On 8 January the 3rd Battalion, 5th, managed an advance through its sector of the bottom ground and found itself on the lower slopes of a high ridge missing from the map, the one terrain feature intelligence had failed to mark. It was the real Aogiri and the fire that came from it was terrific, for there was nothing fake about Matsuda's order that it must be held at any cost. It covered the route to his one remaining and very slender supply dump in the rear, and the men who had escaped the shock at the landing beaches had only a couple of days' rice besides what was in that dump.

All that day the battalion moved forward by inches, taking heavy casualties. "We were five days in the swamp," says one private who was there. "You could hardly walk. If you'd try to watch where you were stepping the vines would cut your face. We got to a swollen stream and tried to cross. When we were waist-deep in water they let us have it. Some of us ducked behind logs, and some got hit and went under. I began to pray. I prayed to keep awake when I was on watch. I prayed most of the time, I guess, except when I was thinking. I'd lie there with my face as deep in the ground as I could get it, and I'd fix my eyes on something. Once it was an ant. I wanted more than anything else to be an ant. Once it was a blade of grass. It started me thinking about all sorts of things. I was in a daze, forgot where I was. All of a sudden I'd be in Forest Park, St. Louis, lying in the grass like I used to. Then a machine gun would open up, and you couldn't make up your mind where you were—in St. Louis or out in this beat-up jungle. When the order came to get up

316

and charge you'd just go ahead—half of you in Forest Park and half on Hill 660."

Colonel Walt practically carried the battalion in on his shoulders, himself lugging forward a 37 to the edges of the ridge where he could open fire. On the night of 9 January, with the lines only 10 yards apart in some places, General Matsuda decided it was time for a counterattack on the exhausted men who had settled on his ridge, in order to knock out the troops there before our tanks could come up. It was touch and go all night; the enemy had made five formal assaults, once ammunition almost ran out, and once our artillery was firing only 50 yards in front of the lines, but the place was held. That seemed to break the hearts of the enemy; when the tanks came up on the 10th the line everywhere pushed ahead and Aogiri was ours.

All was now ready for the final job, the capture of Hill 660 itself. On the right the 2nd Battalion, 7th, had reached a position which General Shepherd considered valid for the permanent perimeter. He ordered that battalion to dig and wire in where it stood. On the left center the 3rd Battalion, 7th, now under command of Lieutenant Colonel Henry W. Buse, was ordered to make a direct assault on the hill while the 1st Battalion, 7th, swung to its own right and covered the flank of the advance. Meanwhile a patrol scouting the base of 660 found nobody holding the coastal track running down it. General Shepherd set up an odd little task force consisting of a weapons company, two light tanks, a rocket DUKW and some Pioneers with bulldozers; they were to work along the track and set up their own little perimeter at the base of the tall eminence to keep the enemy from escaping. This force, under Captain Joseph E. Buckley, was in position by the night of the 12th and on the morning of the 13th Colonel Buse tried his direct assault.

It failed; the fire was too heavy. He dug in for the night in possession of the lower slopes and next morning tried a different tack, directing his main effort toward working around the west face of the hill, past some ravines where the tanks could not follow, till he reached the south slope. Hill 660 is almost sheer cliff at this point, but he sent the men up it, climbing by handholds. It was the decisive event, for the Japs did not wake up till the Marines had already reached the crest of Sweet Cookie and began to plaster them with

317

close-in mortar fire. Some of them died at their guns, more fled toward Buckley or scattered down the slope, and the campaign was over in a practical sense, though twice in the succeeding few days small groups of the enemy did assemble for banzai charges. It was also the end of Matsuda's command, for if any of his men reached Rabaul by the impossible jungle trails it was an accident, since they were without food, medical supplies, or transportation. The 5th Air Force had its new field, and the campaign had cost the 1st Division 296 killed, 1,036 wounded. Strategically, the operation was very nearly useless.

Chapter 19

Marines under MacArthur:
Willaumez

E ARLY IN FEBRUARY OF 1944 THE CAPE GLOUCESTER AIRFIELD
went into operation. At this time the over-all situation was
that new Army divisions were beginning to come out from
the States and up from Australia (the Aussies got their 9th back
from Africa after all), and MacArthur's leapfrog offensive along
the New Guinea coast was in full swing. There was no particular
place in it for the 1st Marine Division, which was in effect con-
demned to garrison duty among the rots and stinks of the New
Britain jungle. Garrison is not good for the physique or morale of
any troops, particularly if they are to be employed later in assault,
as every Marine knows. The question of finding employment to pre-
serve the fighting edge of the 1st began to exercise General Rupertus
and his staff.

To be sure, there was some employment. After the Battle of Hill
660 the whole of western New Britain was full of small straggling
groups of Japs, drifting, drifting toward Rabaul like filings toward a
magnet; hungry, footsore, and dangerous. From Cape Gloucester
the division sent out patrols of a company or more in strength
through the mountains to round up these stragglers and to batter
them into fragments again every time they tried to coalesce. But this
was hardly divisional or even regimental employment. Neither was
the operation along the north coast of the island to complete the
rout of Matsuda's command, which even in its broken and disorganized state represented the most considerable body of enemies in the
area. The operation was conducted by sending platoon patrols along
the coastal track till a suitable *point d'appui* was secured, then
landing a company from LCMs and organizing a little forward base,
from which a new patrol would move on. The main objective was

319

to get Jap supply caches. The 5th Regiment handled this job; by the end of February a place named Iboki had been reached, on Rein Bay, some 60 miles to the east of Cape Gloucester.

In the meanwhile General Rupertus had come back from a Sixth Army conference with a plan for employing the division—to take Rabaul, by landing on the southwest coast of the peninsula that holds that base, and a march across, while an Army combat team landed near the place for direct assault. The 1st Marine Division staff took a dim view of the proposal. It involved a trek across a trackless mountain range through jungle into the teeth of what Intelligence estimated as 40,000 Japs. (Intelligence was wrong, as it found out at the end of the war; there were nearly 80,000 of them in there.) The staff prepared an alternate plan for a landing on the north coast of the peninsula with not less than two full divisions in assault and more in reserve, supported by a major fleet with battleships and carriers. When General Rupertus took this back to Sixth Army the whole idea was dropped as too expensive; then he partly solved his unemployment problem in a flash of inspiration by deciding to take the Talasea airfield and Willaumez Peninsula. The only operation order was a one-paragraph letter from Sixth Army; the date was now 1 March. The high command appears to have considered that the capture of Willaumez would look good on the map.

The peninsula in question juts out from the north coast of New Britain, in shape resembling a blunted banana. Colonel O. P. Smith, now commanding the 5th Marines, would have the job (Selden had moved up to be Rupertus' chief of staff) supported by a company of engineers, one of Pioneers, a few tanks, and a battalion of artillery. It was strictly a shoestring operation, with no ships to fire support, and it was more or less a dive into a dark pool, since there was no good photographic or map coverage of the area. Estimates of how many Japs were in there varied all the way from that of Intelligence, which thought they might have 4,985, to that of General Rupertus himself, who believed there were none at all. If Intelligence were right the place was altogether too heavily held for attack by a single regiment, so the first thing Colonel Smith did was to send a two-man patrol by a PT boat, one of the two being an Australian lieutenant named Rodney Marsland, who had once owned a plantation in the area.

320

Marsland was back by 4 March with word from the native headman as to where the Japs were established and information indicated their number as 150; but he warned that the figure was not very reliable since the New Britain native can count only as far as his fingers before taking refuge in "many-many." Down toward Cape Hoskins, 40 miles southeast of Talasea, the enemy had installations which might contain a considerable garrison. There was a possibility they would interfere and there was some chance of the arrival of their group from Gasmata, 3,500, who had quitted their station and were wandering around somewhere in the interior of the island. The expedition was thus not without its perils, but both the General and the Colonel believed the Japs of New Britain were too interested in getting into cozy at Rabaul to be doing much thinking about counterattacks. Most of the Willaumez Peninsula is surrounded by bad reefs, but Marsland said there was a narrow channel and a practicable beach at Volupai Plantation on the peninsula's narrowest neck, with a trail leading across to Talasea. The landing would be at Volupai; to reach the place the regiment would have to voyage 57 miles across water in the forty LCMs and seventeen Higgins boats of an Army shore and boat regiment commanded by Lieutenant Colonel Amory. The only naval support available consisted of five PTs, which could do no more than furnish escort. The possibility that the enemy might have guns at the shore line would be partly cared for by bombing from two squadrons of Beauforts on each of the three days before D, with more aviation in close support of the landing; partly by an ingenious scheme the division staff thought up for using tanks while still afloat in their LCMs. A Sherman medium is an overload for this type of LCM, but these were braced in position with 8 x 8s and firing tests from the water were conducted at a little island down near Iboki. They turned out satisfactorily. The channel through which these craft were to approach the beach would only permit one to pass at a time, which would not do for the assault wave, so amphitracs were taken along aboard five LCTs, to be launched directly into deep water and move in across the reefs, also an innovation at this time. There were only enough boats to land one battalion at a jump.

321

D day was 6 March and H hour 0800. The trip up was uneventful though nervous; all the boats were so overloaded that they had only a foot or so of freeboard and clouds began to climb the horizon, with lightning flashes during the night, but the weather did not break.

The first fly in the ointment was that the air support never showed up; it was weathered in at its base back in New Guinea as a matter of fact, and no planes arrived till three days later when they came so close to strafing our own troops that Colonel Smith asked them to go bombard Cape Hoskins and not bother him any more. At the time he waited a while and then sent the boats in without air cover, but it was all right, there were only snipers at the beach and the tanks did not have to fire till they landed. Two companies of the 1st Battalion got in and established themselves at once, flushing the Japs from a single machine-gun nest on the slopes of Little Mt. Worri. A company landing on the left found itself up against a big swamp of the

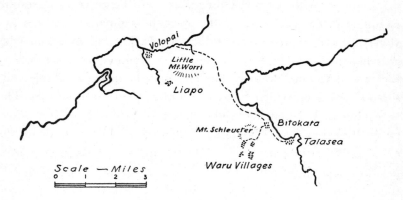

usual tropical type, was crowded rightward toward the trail, knocked out one little pocket of Japs and drove some more into a series of prepared positions among the coconuts of the plantation. The company commander at the front wanted to assault these positions and asked for reinforcements, but Colonel Smith told him merely to hold on; the 1st Battalion now had a perimeter and the 2nd would pass through it in assault as soon as it came ashore.

That battalion was now landing by boat through the narrow and tortuous channel, quite slowly. About the time it began to move forward and the boats carrying artillery were working in, some Jap 90-mm. mortars, well back, got the range of the beachhead and raised havoc by dropping one shell right into the midst of a group manhandling a gun and others into the boats for a total of casualties that made our loss for the day 13 killed and 71 wounded, or twice as many as there had been in the divisional landing at Cape Glouces-ter two months before. There was nothing that could be done about it except to capture the mortar positions and these were too far back to be taken that night, though the 2nd Battalion managed to work 2,000 yards forward. It captured a small range of positions, consisting mostly of individual trenches, at a cost of one tank knocked out by a magnetic mine and an antitank gun. There was a piece of luck in this fight. One of the dead Japs was an officer with a fine map on him, showing all the undercover trails paralleling the main route from Volupai to Talasea, with the dispositions of the enemy.

The map was translated and reproduced at once and from it Colo-nel Smith made his plan. He had a small group of positions in the coconut grove directly opposing his front, but the enemy's main strength (incidentally, four times as great as the natives had re-ported) was concentrated at the four Waru Villages on the south-facing shoulder of Mt. Schleuchter at the opposite side of the penin-sula. The Jap map showed a secret trail leading to this area by way of Liapo, a far more direct route than that of the main trail marked on the air maps, which led to Bitokara on the east coast of the penin-sula and then struck back inland. The boats had gone back to Iboki for the regiment's 3rd Battalion; when it arrived the 1st would move on the Waru Villages by the secret trail, while the 2nd took the trail through Bitokara.

As usual in military operations there were slips between cup and lip. The boats did not get back with the 3rd Battalion till late in the afternoon of 7 March, and the 1st Battalion's secret trail faded out into nothing a little way beyond Volupai, so the men had to work their way through the toughest kind of jungle on compass, aided by fierce-looking native scouts who jabbered in pidgin. On the front of the 2nd Battalion there was action, with our artillery firing sup-port, giving special attention to the trails by which the Japs might retreat. The mortar positions that had caused all the casualties on the previous day were taken together with one of the mortars. Mines slowed the advance but it reached the northern slope of Mt. Schleuchter by evening and beat off an attempt to turn its flank, then dug in around the perimeter for the night. The Colonel noticed that his Marines were a little careless about planting their Japs; they had folded one up in his own foxhole and then thrown dirt over him, but a pair of oddly inverted feet still projected.

Next day, 8 March, the 1st Battalion made Liapo, found no Japs, and pushed on toward the Waru Villages along a trail now somewhat better. The 2nd reached Bitokara during the morning, after the artillery had fired search shoots along the trails thither. They found any number of hastily scooped out foxholes, as hastily abandoned, which shows what the guns can do for you in a case like this. At Bitokara the battalion split, one patrol toward the airfield, one toward the Waru Villages. The airfield proved a total washout, nothing but a rough plain overgrown with tall grass getting taller; it was doubtful whether it had been used in months if ever. The Waru patrol ran into fire, developed the facts that there were Japs there and that they had at least one battalion gun and a mortar; then withdrew.

The artillery fired all night on the four Waru Villages and in the morning the 1st and 2nd Battalions together attacked, quickly overrunning the place with the capture of gun, mortar, and two prisoners, one of whom said the Japs had pulled out during the night, leaving a hundred-man rear guard. Patrols followed them along the coastal trail and there was a brief contact on the 16th, but the real fighting was over and the Japs only did their vanishing act again, still moving toward Rabaul. They left somewhere between 150 and 200 dead behind; the little campaign had cost us 18 killed, 122 wounded.

III

It was not a campaign of great strategic significance, any more than Cape Gloucester. Both are remarkable chiefly as examples of what can be accomplished by amphibious operations against country sparsely settled but fairly strongly held. In point of actual numbers on the island of New Britain the Japs possessed force enough to have eaten up the 1st Marine Division as that division ate up Matsuda's

65th Brigade. But the enemy had no thoughts beyond that of getting down underground of Rabaul and staying there. Partly this was because of their command morale; both Hyakutate and his successor had been reduced to a state of funk by repeated defeats. But mainly it was control of the sea and command, though not absolute control, of the air. We had the lines of communication, a fact abundantly evidenced in the Willaumez Peninsula operation, 57 miles across open water with nothing but PT boats for escort.

In reality, of course, all this traces back to the Guadalcanal operation and grew out of it. There ought to be, but there probably is not, a method of graphically expressing the relation among the various parts of the strategic complex that was set in motion on August 7, 1942, and was terminated on March 16, 1944, when the last Japs toddled off into the jungle from the direction of the Waru Villages. The amphibious landing of Guadalcanal forced the Japanese Navy and its air force to give battle; through the defeats on the sea their own amphibious counteroperation failed, fundamentally for lack of communications; it then became possible for the American forces still further to extend their field of amphibious operation and these further landings exercised a progressively restrictive influence upon Japanese naval and air movements—with the final result at the Willaumez Peninsula, where a landing could be made across open water and the enemy had no thought but retreat.

In the meanwhile the Army 40th Division relieved the Marines on New Britain toward the end of April and the 1st Division went back to Pavuvu in the Russell Islands to be reorganized according to the new table of organization. The veterans were pretty disgusted with the place. "If they give us a battle star for Cape Gloucester," remarked one, "they ought to give us a couple for this dump."

Chapter 20

Peleliu: The Hardest Battle

OUR CARRIER AIR STRENGTH HAD SO GROWN BY THE END OF August, 1944, that an operation in any direction could be contemplated, even if that expedition had to meet at its point of impact the combined land- and sea-based air forces of the Empire, covering the counterattack of their Combined Fleet. We had the techniques for making good a landing on any hostile shore and we had (one of the little-noted but most important developments of the war) discovered how to support amphibious operations at an oceanic distance from base by means of logistic echelons afloat. We had the Marianas, which are almost equidistant from the whole circle of key points in the enemy's rackrent empire—metropolitan Japan on the north, the Ryukyus and Formosa to the northwest, the Philippines directly west, Celebes, Helmahera and the outer tip of New Guinea to the southwest—which is to say we had interior lines and could hurl the massive force of the Pacific Fleet against any one of those points before it could be reinforced from the others.

The question was where to strike. Admiral Nimitz, Spruance the strategic brain, McMorris the memory and logician, all would have undoubtedly preferred the direct thrust west to cut among the Ryukyus the dangling life cord to the southward. But the days of island hopping in the old sense were now past. All the points open to attack shared two characteristics—they were within mutually supporting distances of one another, that is, none could be isolated by fleet operations alone, as the Marianas had been isolated; and they consisted of land masses larger than any the Marines had yet attacked.[1]

[1] New Britain excepted; but as indicated above, the interior communications of New Britain were so bad that in effect it was not so much a large land mass as a series of small islands.

Both characteristics, and the combination of the two, placed a requirement on the attack: it must contemplate a land campaign of continental dimensions after the beachhead had been secured. The pure amphibious phase of the war was ended; from Guam forth every major campaign must bear the stamp of Guam, with a beachhead force securing the beachhead and troops who need not be specialists in such work pouring through their perimeter for inland operations.

The requirement was for troops. Now, of the Navy's private army, the 2nd, 3rd, and 4th Marine Divisions had been in action among the Marianas and would not be ready, except in emergency, for another campaign till several months had passed. In the same state was the Provisional Brigade, now being erected into a new 6th Division down on Guadalcanal, with its organization still incomplete. The 5th had been organized, but was in Hawaii, still incompletely trained; the 1st was under MacArthur's command and he was showing no disposition to release it save for purposes that served his own strategic ends. Of the Army divisions that were operating under Central Pacific, that is, Navy command, the 27th and 77th, like the Marine divisions, needed rest and recruitment; the 96th was green and Admiral Nimitz could hardly look forward to making a major expedition with the 7th Division, the only one at the moment both experienced and available.

All the other soldiers of the Army of the United States were either busy beating out the Germans' brains in France or under the command of General Douglas MacArthur. Troop availability thus formed a limiting condition which practically imposed a Navy operation conjointly with that able, strong-minded and difficult officer. This meant that the operation would only be the return to the Philippines toward which MacArthur had bent every effort during three years of war. Nimitz brought Halsey up to command the major sea forces, giving them the name 3rd Fleet (though they were the same ships that had sailed under Spruance as 5th Fleet) and the staffs began to look at their maps.

The moment they did that it was clear we would need an air base and an anchorage nearer to the Philippines than Saipan. The islands to be attacked are an oceanic distance from the Marianas (Manila-Guam, 1,500 sea miles, reads the track chart) and however efficient

327

our floating docks had become, one could not expect to tow a battle-damaged ship that distance. There was also the question of getting some land-based air over the Philippines, and a forward strip, or a couple of them, were needed for light bombers. Finally there was the question of the western Carolines themselves.

CINCPOA and MacArthur headquarters knew a good deal about Japanese bases by that time, thanks to the enemy's incurable habit of leaving documents around for our people to mull over after they had taken one of those islands, and his equally incurable failure to devise ciphers that would amuse our cryptographers for more than a couple of hours. Yap was a major base, and strongly held—8,000 men—which in its much smaller area made it a bigger Tarawa. Ulithi had only about a battalion, could be taken nearly as easily as Majuro in the Marshalls, and like that atoll would serve admirably as an anchorage for the units of the train. Palau is a queer formation, a series of volcanic islands inside a coral reef, 77 miles long, 20 wide, the most important being the island of Babelthuap, economically valuable for its phosphates and aluminum ore; the natives had the quaint habit of eating their grandmothers. It was the strongest of all, fortified to the eyeteeth, a much more powerful base in reputation and in fact than mysterious Truk. Intelligence estimated (it may be said now, correctly) that there were not many fewer than 40,000 troops to hold the place, and for a long time after Spruance's big raid on Truk it had been the favorite anchorage of the Japanese fleet.

The plan was to take all three—Yap, Ulithi and Palau. The reason for including the last was that no one on our side yet knew how badly the Japanese fleet had been hit in the June battles. *Shokaku* and *Taiho* had not been seen to go down. It was expected that *Hayataka* would be repaired as well as *Ryuho* and at least one, maybe two, of the six new Japanese carriers would be ready. That is, interference from a Japanese fleet with eight combat carriers could be counted upon. Halsey's own fleet contained sixteen (eight of them light carriers), but the proportion was less important than the existence of a Japanese fleet capable of conducting ocean operations. Such a fleet could strike a dangerous blow, especially if they woke up to the fact that they could damage an amphibious expedition more by hitting its supply ships than by going for the fighting vessels.

328

While they still had the well-protected anchorage in the Palaus it would be possible for them to emerge from some point on the circle of Empire, hit our train, then lodge in security at the Palau base, as they could not at Ulithi. In military terms Palau was too well fortified a base to leave in our rear.

It would not be necessary to take the whole atoll or to deal with all the 40,000 troops it held in order to neutralize the place. A fairly small island, Angaur, lies outside the reef at its southern end and had a garrison of only 2,000-odd. Just inside the atoll Peleliu Island possessed a big airfield and a garrison variously stated as 4,500 and 10,000. Take these two, set up a fighter strip on Anguar, sweep out the mines in Kossol Passage which led to the anchorage at the north end of the atoll, and it would be unnecessary to touch Babelthuap or its 26,000-30,000 men.

This was the plan, with the Army 81st Division to take Anguar and Rupertus' 1st Marine Division Peleliu, while other forces of the MacArthur command fell on Morotai Island, north of Helmahera. From these, air cover for the Philippines invasion could be provided, while to cover our rear the 7th and 96th Divisions would seize Yap. Target date for these preliminary island invasions was 15 September; that for the big campaign, the return to the Philippines, was early spring of 1945.

The fleet movements that accompanied this plan were intricate. Halsey was to come down from the north with Mitscher's fast carriers and Lee's fast battleships for a strike at Ulithi, Yap, and Palau in order, then push on to cover against a possible emergence from the Philippines of the Japanese fleet the advance of MacArthur's convoy to Morotai. Kinkaid's 7th Fleet would take over the protection of the Morotai operation while Halsey swung north along the range of the Philippines, putting heavy carrier strikes on the fields there to keep Jap air from interfering with operations at Morotai or Palau, then run farther north to catch whatever aerial reinforcements would be staging down the Ryukyus. Behind Halsey the old battleships and escort carriers under Admiral Oldendorf would meanwhile have convoyed the attack units to Peleliu and Angaur and covered their advance across the beaches. The two divisions for Yap would come in a later convoy, Halsey's run to the north interposing between them and any source of Japanese interference. By time they reached that island Oldendorf's force should be through with the Palaus and would furnish support.[1]

II

When, after the fall of the Marshalls, it was decided that the Palaus were the most likely objective of the next major American attack, the Imperial General Staff granted them top priority on construction material and troops. Both Field Marshal Terauchi, who commanded the whole Southern Area from the Philippines, and Admiral Toyoda (who will be remembered as Koga's successor at the head of the Combined Fleet) were very much concerned about the place, which represented for the one his surest bastion against an American movement on the Philippines, and for the other his best

[1] Halsey's fleet—it was the one which fought the battle for Leyte Gulf, so deserves recording—consisted of Task Force 38.1, Rear Admiral J. J. McCain —carriers *Wasp, Hornet, Cowpens, Monterey;* heavy cruisers *Wichita, Boston, Canberra;* destroyers *Izard, Charrette, Conner, Bell, Burns, Boyd, Bradford, Brown, Cowell, Farenholt, McCalla, Grayson;* Task Group 38.2, Rear Admiral G. F. Bogan—carriers *Bunker Hill, Intrepid, Cabot, Independence;* battleships *Iowa, New Jersey;* light cruisers *Vincennes, Houston, Miami, San Diego, Oakland;* destroyers *Owens, Miller, The Sullivans, Stephen Potter, Tingey, Hickox, Hunt, Lewis Hancock, Marshall, Cushing, Colahan, Halsey Powell Uhlmann, Yarnall, Twining, Stockham, Wedderburn, Benham;* Task Group 38.3, Rear Admiral F. C. Sherman—carriers *Essex, Enterprise, Langley, Princeton;* battleships *Washington, Massachusetts, Indiana, South Dakota, Alabama;* light cruisers *Santa Fe, Birmingham, Mobile, Reno;* destroyers *Clarence Bronson, Cotten, Dortch, Gatling, Healey, Cogswell, Caperton, Ingersoll, Knapp, Porterfield, Callaghan, Cassin Young, Irvin, Preston, Longshaw, Morrison, Prichett;* Task Group 38.4, Rear Admiral R. E. Davison— carriers *Lexington, Franklin, Belleau Wood, San Jacinto;* heavy cruiser *New Orleans;* light cruiser *Biloxi;* destroyers *Maury, Craven, Gridley, Helm, McCall, Mugford, Ralph Talbot, Patterson, Bagley, Wilkes, Nicholson, Swanson.* Oldendorf's command had the battleships *Maryland, Pennsylvania, Tennessee, Idaho, Mississippi;* the heavy cruisers *Indianapolis, Portland, Minneapolis, Louisville;* light cruisers *Cleveland, Columbia, Denver, Honolulu;* destroyers *A. W. Grant, Bennett, Bennion, Bryant, Fullam, Guest, Halford, Hudson, H. L. Edwards, Leutze, Newcomb, Robinson, Ross, R. F. Leary;* with the escort carrier group of Rear Admiral Oftsie containing the escort carriers *Marcus Island, Kadashan Bay, Savo Island, Ommaney Bay;* destroyers *McCord, Trathen, Heerman, Hoel, Thorne;* escort carriers *Sargent Bay, Petroff Bay, Kalinin Bay, Saginaw Bay, Gambier Bay, Kitkun Bay, White Plains;* and destroyers *Haggard, Hailey, Johnston, Welles, Claxton, Aulick, Cony, Sigourney.*

forward fleet base. They saw that the priorities were actually carried out in spite of difficulties from American submarines. In charge of Palau-Yap-Ulithi, together named "The Palau Sector Group," they placed Lieutenant General Sadae Inoue, one of their very best men.

He seems to have arrived in the Palaus during March, while the command question was being settled. When the attack on Saipan and the Battle of the Philippine Sea made it improbable that Palau would be used by the fleet in the immediate future, he could and did make his defensive dispositions without reference to the Navy. The General perceived his problem as that of arranging a defense which would inflict crippling losses on the American forces, leave them incapable, even if they took the islands, of undertaking another major operation for months, during which months the Japanese fleet and air force could recover. That is, it was a case of trading an island or two for time, fortifications for blood, a small command for the shattering of a great one.

The Saipan reports, which were very detailed since Navy Captain Sawaguchi and a couple of Army observers had escaped by submarine during the last days, gave General Inoue a basis on which to proceed. His first step was withdrawal from Ulithi, an atoll of featureless flat islands, where adequate defensive installations against the violent American gunfire could not be constructed. The next was to draw up a document entitled "Palau Sector Group Training for Victory." The title is rather flamboyant and "spiritual discipline" was placed first on the list of requirements with the remark that "we must first resolutely penetrate to the enemy and then we shall display our short swords and slash to the very marrow of his bones." But from this point on the paper demonstrates why Inoue was considered one of the major officers of his service.

All personnel, all tanks, all guns, the General prescribed, must be kept underground in positions of "absolute security" during the American bombardment, with special attention given to communications equipment, whose wires were to be well dug in. Units must be prepared to act independently in support of the general plan should communications fail. It would be most advantageous to repel landing craft before their arrival at the beach by means of strongly prepared beach positions, but we cannot hope to accomplish this. Therefore we must not open fire prematurely on his boats, but wait till his first wave has reached the beach and then counterattack, firing at the same time on the boats of the enemy's support wave, not allowing him to organize his formations ashore. A major counterattack must be launched the very first night with all reserve units and troops from sectors not under immediate attack, to take advantage of the enemy's insecure bridgehead. At the same time a counterlanding force in boats must boldly tail the enemy's boats and going ashore in his rear, attack his command and communications centers.

"Without concerning ourselves with the great explosive bursts or the strong local effect of naval firing, the destructive power wrought upon personnel is not so very great against men who are advancing at a crawl, utilizing natural objects and shell holes, especially when we consider that originally the object of naval guns was to sink ships and that their shells possess the special quality of traveling in a low line. Aerial bombardment is almost identical. By observing very carefully the activity of enemy planes and the bombs while they are falling, thereby avoiding instantaneous explosions, and by taking advantage of gaps in bombardment in order to advance, it can cause no great damage. The only fearful thing is the psychological effects upon ignorant personnel. This must be impressed upon the minds of everyone.

"Daring penetration by counterattack forces must utilize surprising power developed by instant concentration of all types of ordnance. It is certain that if we repay the Americans (who rely solely on material power) with material power it will shock them beyond imagination. It is most urgent that we prepare secretly and take the enemy by surprise by concentrating all material power against one sector.

"If the situation becomes bad we will maintain a firm hold on the high ground and prevent the enemy from establishing or using an air base by a daring guerrilla warfare with our ordnance weapons."

In implementing this program of defense, so different from the usual Japanese doctrine of save the beach line and you save all, General Inoue made the error of placing his strongest forces on Babelthuap under the impression that the Americans must sooner or later attack it, but this was almost the only mistake he did make. Angaur was outside the atoll, flat and not very rugged; it received

332

a single battalion of infantry, four tanks, and a battery of artillery—
2,100 men all told. Peleliu, which is what chiefly concerns us, had
a major general, Kenjiro Murai, commanding a force that totaled
close to 11,000, the most important elements being the 2nd Infantry
Regiment, a battalion of the 15th Infantry, a battalion of the 54th
Independent Mixed Brigade, a Naval Guard Force, and a battalion
of tanks. The majority of these belonged to the 14th Division, of
which Inoue was the unit commander. It was a good, old division,
formed at the time of the Russian War and with a tradition of continuous service; it made the Hankow campaign and spent four years
in Manchuria. It was thoroughly trained, even at crawling forward
under bombing, the General having used the casual American air
raids on his islands during the summer for this purpose. He placed
an urgent requisition with Marshal Terauchi for three hundred
collapsible rubber boats for his counterlanding force, but there do
not seem to have been that many available in the Philippine command and a ship bringing down more from Japan unfortunately ran
afoul of an American submarine.

The big airfield lies at the southern end of Peleliu and had been
erected out of what was essentially jungle swamp. All along the
western face of the beach below it, to a lesser extent along the eastern
shore, the most likely places for an American landing, coconut log
cradles, concrete tetrahedrons, and barbed-wire systems were strewn
from the reef-edge, intermingled with mines, of both controlled and
contact types. There were more mines on the beach itself, below high-
water mark. Inland, the roads were all mined with 100-pound aerial
bombs, and so were all the defiles in the old coral worn to limestone
which constitutes the structural bulk of the island. The only direct
antiboat defenses were on Ngaramoked Island off the southern tip
of Peleliu, on a little island just north of it, and on a point just before
the west coast turns northeast—in each case 37s or 75s in concrete
pillboxes heavy enough to be impervious to bombing.

The General regarded it as of the greatest importance to keep
the American tanks from forming and advancing with the help of
their infantry. All his beaches had therefore been extensively tank-
trapped with systems of ditches and mined obstacles two or three
deep. In view of the tactics Americans had used against such obstacles
on Saipan (which were for their infantry to work through the ob-

stacle system while the tanks covered them with fire) the General placed machine-gun pillboxes in the flanks of the tank traps themselves, where they could not be hit except by a tank actually in the trap.

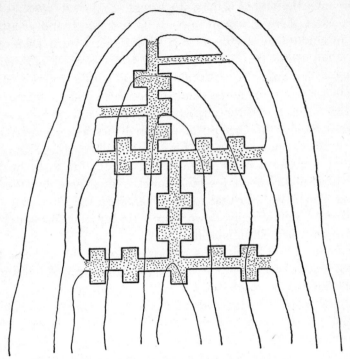

Peleliu Cave System —— Top-Section.

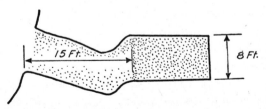

Cave Entrance —Cross Section

The most original feature of the defense system was with relation to the ridge running the length of the northeast-southwest peninsula of the island, which the Japs called Momiji Plateau. It had a system of natural caves and crevices; from the hour of his arrival General Inoue worked at extending and developing them. In them he placed all his artillery except his beach guns, all his heavy mortars, and the launchers for the new 200-mm. rockets recently received from the Empire. By the end of August there were over five hundred such caves. Most of them were connected by interior tunnels; nearly all had entrances on more than one level and on both sides of the plateau. Many had up to five or six stories, dipping and winding from the entrances to keep gunfire from coming in, with living quarters branching off and another set of exits branching off from these, so that if the top of the ridge had been removed they would be in the shape of an H lying down, or several E's back to back and end to end.

In the mouths of these caves the guns had protected firing positions; whenever time and material could be had these were fitted with sliding armored doors, opening semiautomatically for long enough to permit the gun to shoot. All the caves had along their side passages rifle slits that might be natural crevices, very hard to locate from outside. The bulk of the artillery in them was arranged to keep constant fire on both the main airfield and the minor airfield on Ngesebus to the north, connected to Peleliu by a causeway. The guns were not arranged in battery but individually; each was assigned a specific type target of an area on which to fire and all were carefully calibrated for that type of firing.

The General issued seven separate counterattack plans, the one to be used depending upon where the Americans landed. All the men were carefully trained in each plan; unit commanders were examined upon them to make certain they knew precisely where they were to employ their troops in each. A system of flag and flare signals was arranged so that even if the normal methods of communication were destroyed, all would be advised of the proper moment for counterattack and of which plan would be used.

On 13 August a report came in from Guam that the seriously wounded had been disposed of and only one last battle remained to be fought there. A lieutenant in a machine-cannon company wrote that he could not help feeling the same fate was closing in on those in the Palau Sector. It was one month later, 12 September, when in the darkness before dawn the roar of American airplane motors was

335

heard and the antiaircraft men went to their positions as a pale moon rode down the sky. No sooner were the guns ready than a naval bombardment from the south began. All hands were ordered under concrete; the firing continued so fiercely until 1800 that no one could even lift up his head. Word was passed through the caves that the enemy had planned landing. As it happened General Murai was visiting Babelthuap for a conference; Colonel Nakagawa of the 2nd Regiment assumed command.

III

The 1st Marine Division contained 17,490 men and had the support of four Marine and two Army amphitrac formations, with 2,352 more, plus a couple of independent artillery battalions, 1,222 more. The plan was to land the three infantry regiments abreast on the western face of the island, fronting the airfield. The 7th Regiment of Colonel H. H. Hanneken (we met him on Guadal) was to go in across the southernmost beach on a one-battalion front, swing right, clear out Ngaramoked and the southern tip of Peleliu, holding one battalion in division reserve. This assignment should be complete by the night of D day. The 5th (Colonel H. D. Harris) on a two-battalion front to push right across the airfield and beyond to clean out everything in the low ground of the main body of the island. It should be all around the airfield by twilight of D day and push across in the next morning. The 1st, two battalions abreast, should take the most northerly beach, capture the outlying points from which the beachhead might be swept by fire, anchoring the flank for the first night, then left wheel and ascend from two directions the ridge on the island's long peninsula. D plus 1 should find it on the ridge. This was Colonel Puller's regiment.

There had been growling at Pavuvu about shortages, the eternal cry of war—not enough water, spare parts, amphitracs, flame throwers for proper training; but all that was now past and forgotten as the LSTs lined up off Peleliu on the morning of 15 September with amphitracs spewing from their jaws. Out beyond, other ships stretched away as far as the eye could follow; battleships and cruisers out in the dim, a sight which had rendered the Japanese lieutenant of machine cannon "so furious I could feel the blood pounding in my veins throughout my body." Overhead arched the fire of the big

336

ships; the concussion of their guns shook the landing craft in the water as though by an undersea earthquake and gusts of heat rushed past. Ashore their missiles burst in bright red balls of flame from which smoke ran up in swift spirals to form little question-mark-shaped clouds. Nearly all the vegetation was down or damaged, there had been no fire from the shore in three days of shooting and ten of bombing, and how could anyone live under that?

The Navy men said it would be another Roi-Namur; Admiral Oldendorf actually reported all important installations had been destroyed and one of the transport commanders remarked to Colonel Puller as the latter went over the side, "Coming back for supper?"

The Colonel paused. "Why?"

"Everything's done over there. You'll walk in."

"If you think it's that easy why don't you come on the beach at five o'clock, have supper with me, and pick up a few souvenirs?" replied Puller a trifle grimly.

He did not believe that many Japs were dead and the lieutenant of machine cannon agreed with him, noting meticulously in his diary that although the scenery of Peleliu was completely altered only one man in his company had been slightly injured. It was probably not much different in the other caves, as the Marines discovered when they got across the reef line 700 yards out under a clear, bright day. The first wave of amphitracs hit the beach at 0832 through small-arms fire; as though its arrival were a signal the guns on point and island opened, many of those back in the ridge, and a mortar barrage so heavy that those who lived through it said it was the worst they had ever seen. Amphitracs and DUKWs were hit across the shelf area and sank or drifted burning while Marines strove to wade ashore. The guns on the island north from Ngaramoked were particularly deadly with their enfilade, cut up the right flank of the 7th badly, and produced confusion among platoons and companies reaching the beach.

Out in the offing on the heavy cruiser *Portland* they watched through glasses as a steel shutter in the limestone ridge opened to let a gun fire down on the beach; threw in five full salvos of 8-inch fire and after each saw the gun fire again. "You can put all the steel in Pittsburgh on to that thing and not get it," said the cruiser's gunnery officer.

337

Down on the beach of the 1st Marines one platoon got involved in a tank trap with fire coming from three sides and had to be evacuated. Company K became isolated from the regiment, took the blockhouse on the point at the cost of more than half its personnel, and was nearly out of ammunition, food, and water by noon, with prospects of

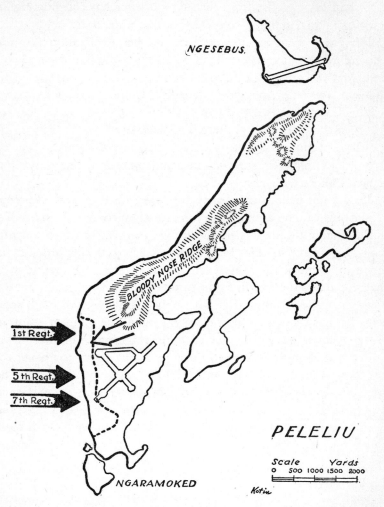

a counterattack coming up. By 1000 the lines were nowhere much deeper than 50 yards, though the reserve battalions had been committed earlier. Shells, continued to drop on the beaches where men were trying to unload supplies—unpredictably, infuriatingly, without

338

rhyme or reason, though it might have been a good deal worse had the Japs concentrated their fires.

Nor must it be imagined that the 50-yard gain before noon was won against artillery alone. Japanese infantry was everywhere; Company K of the 1st killed more of them than the number of men lost at the blockhouse on the point. The odd thing, the new thing, was that these Japs were all attacking, coming forward. They were as yet only the local efforts of local garrisons at our beachhead lines; but about noon one of the Jap guns fired a series of the flares they called Red Dragons and air observers noted signs of movement in the interior of the island. The Red Dragons were in fact the signal for putting into effect General Inoue's counterattack plan Number One, which prescribed that all troops should be withdrawn from Ngesebus and from positions east of the airfield, these forces being added to the mobile reserve via the tunnels through Momiji Plateau for a major counterattack. It was ready to move at 1630 and Colonel Nakagawa must have thought highly of its chances, for at this hour the 1st Division's line was nowhere more than 200 yards in, had many gaps, and was far short of the airfield. The attack had in it all the tanks the Japs could muster, about thirteen; two infantrymen rode behind each in a curious drum lashed to its rear, and more swarmed over the ground behind, leaping and crawling.

The point of impact could not have been better chosen had the Japs been furnished with our operations orders, for the spearhead of the thrust fell exactly on the joint between 1st and 5th Regiments, where there had already been difficulties about liaison. Many of the riding and following infantry were cut down by small-arms fire but the tanks broke right through and turned south to the beachhead where one was blown up by a bazooka just as it opened fire on the evacuation station for wounded. Fortunately for our side, five of the eight tanks that had reached the beach in this area were still intact, waiting in defilade for the infantry to move on with them. They turned on these mechanical enemies with appreciation, and the Jap "medium" tank is only a rather underarmored light by comparison with a Sherman. There was a sharp, crashing tank-to-tank fight over the heads of the Marines cowering in their foxholes, the only one of its kind in the war. Jap 37-mm. tore the treads from one of ours and bent out of shape the gun of another; but every time the American

75s hit a Jap they made a 12-inch hole and the second shell burned them out. The crippled American got no fewer than six; when the fight was over, all thirteen Japs were destroyed and all the men in Nakagawa's attack wave were dead.

That was the crisis; hearts lifted all along the line, the beachhead that had half an hour before seemed so precarious was made good. By twilight the division had reached a line 3,000 yards long and some 300 yards deep, except south of the airfield, where the 7th had run deeper. Most of the Japs had withdrawn toward their ridge, which the Marines were already calling "Bloody Nose." The casualties in our lines were 1,298, over 10 per cent of the troops ashore, for of the artillery it had been possible to land only one battalion of 105s and one and a half of 75s, which were firing from the midst of the infantry, their gunners much troubled by snipers. Everything was far behind schedule. The Jap lieutenant of machine cannon was dead and his diary being read at our headquarters.

IV

All night the Japs tried infiltrations under the flares and star shells, according to plan, but these attacks did not come off very well, Nakagawa had lost too many men in the tank attack and did not wish to jeopardize his ridge position by committing all his reserves to mobile warfare. Moreover, it had developed that the plan for counterattack Number One had a defect. It had been based on the assumption that a landing on the western beaches would be accompanied by one on Ngaramoked and the southern tip of Peleliu. Thus, though the troops from other unattacked sectors had been drawn into Momiji Plateau those in the southern area (a couple of battalions) had remained where they were. They were now isolated, out of communication and with no plan.

This brought it about that on 16 September, D plus 1, there were no more counterattacks and the 5th was able to heave right across the airfield. They had to do it fast because mortar and artillery shells from the ridge kept dropping on them. The 7th had hard, slow going against the isolated battalions, who were well underground; the 1st gained almost nothing along the approaches to Bloody Nose. It had come on very hot that morning; between the weather, water

340

shortage, the sleepless night and constant fire, all the men were suffering much from exhaustion, but they found time to laugh at a Jap propaganda leaflet, which is worth reproducing as an example of what the Oriental mind thinks American minds are like:

"American brave soldiers!

"We think you much pity since landing on this ileland. In spite of your pitiful battle we are sorry that we can present only fire, not even good water. We soon will attack strongly your Army. You have done bravely your duty.

"Now, Abandon your guns, and come in Japanese military with white flag (or handkerchief), so we will be glad to see you and welcome you comfortably as we can well."

That day also was a key date out on the ocean, far from the struggling Marines. "Bull" Halsey had run his great sweep up the flank of the Philippines and had discovered the fact (till then concealed) of Japanese weakness in land-based air. Messages flashed to Pearl Harbor; Halsey flew down to see MacArthur, who had found Morotai a pushover. It had been intended that one of the fast carrier groups should go on to cover the Yap attack after Peleliu, but it was already evident that the Marines on the latter island would need more support. What if the Yap landing were canceled? What if the two divisions for it were loaned to the MacArthur command? Would he not be willing to move on the Philippines immediately instead of after the turn of the year? Yes, said MacArthur.

That was the 16th; then, by digging-in time that night, it was already clear that it had been something of a mistake to adopt a tactical plan which threw the weight of two regimental combat teams against the flat ground on the right while leaving only one for the ridge that would render the rest of the island useless until it was taken. Still there was nothing to do now but make the best of the plan as it stood, and the artillery being now in a position to fire support, a general assault was launched next morning. The 1st gained 500 yards, right up to the slope of Bloody Nose; the 5th got a little town north of the airfield, and the 7th all its southern peninsula and most of Ngaramoked. The last regiment completed its business on the following day, 18 September, though not until one battalion of 155s just going into position was forced to reverse direction and fire at 300-500 yards, while a 105 battery lost all its guns to mortar fire and had to fight as infantry. The 18th also saw the 5th complete its job of overrunning the low ground beyond the airfield and the small islands that lie offshore on that side.

The rest of the Battle of Peleliu was all Bloody Nose and a bloody business it proved. There was no room for maneuver, there was no story to tell but that of men climbing up vertical faces and working on those cave mouths by hand with flame-thrower and satchel charge while the Japs sniped from their rifle slits. Tanks were used freely but they got hit too—twenty-five of them lost all told, about half to mines or rather to the combination of mines and mortars, for as soon as the Japs saw a tank in trouble they put a mortar barrage on it. Artillery afloat and ashore was used; planes bombed and strafed, but it was only by accident that any of these weapons achieved the necessary direct hit. The heat was sweltering, the water supply short; 1st Marines lost 56 per cent of their numbers (more than that in the combat infantry) before they were pulled out on 23 September with the advance at a standstill. [1] By that date the whole of the 7th Regiment had fed into the battle for Bloody Nose, one battalion at a time. It was up against a cleft a hundred feet deep, with the opposite wall full of Japs. Some 1st Division officers wished to put the 5th in also, but General Geiger of III Corps brought over instead the 321st Army Regiment of the 81st Division from Angaur, which had been easily conquered.

That night, the 23rd, General Inoue from Babelthuap tried his counterlanding as a reinforcement from the inside of the lagoon, with a little fleet of barges. On the previous night three such barges had come down alone, were seen and driven ashore by artillery fire, so the larger move was not altogether a surprise. Destroyers from the offing fired star shell, under which Marine artillery took the barges under fire while armored amphitracs from the 5th Regiment's area charged into the water in direct counterattack. All the barges were sooner or later sunk or wrecked on the beach, but the low-lying craft made uncertain targets in poor light and several hundred Japs got ashore on the rocky northern tip of the island, immediately disappearing into the cave system.

[1] They had taken 10 defended coral ridges, 3 large blockhouses with 3 guns or more apiece and shellproof coverings, 144 caves, 22 pillboxes, 13 antitank guns—or about a third of the island's armament. It took over 4 regiments to take the rest.

The 321st were put on the left along the coast road, did a right wheel toward the ridge, and came up against it on a broad front, gaining perhaps 200 or 300 yards up the north slopes before being halted, still short of the crests, on the evening of 24 September. The airfield was in operation by this time, but dangerous to operate; the Japs had it under occasional artillery fire from their ridge and mechanics on the field were being hit by snipers. The same kind of fire in another direction made it difficult to keep the 321st supplied along the coast road.

This brought about a recast of strategy at a headquarters conference on the morning of 25 September. The new plan was to pass Colonel Harris's 5th Marines through the rear areas of the 321st along the beach, cut easterly along the northern ridges of Bloody Nose, and come back south on the rear of the enemy while sending a detachment to clear Ngesebus. The order was issued telephonically at 0945; Colonel Harris did a nice feat of marching and by noon was already pouring his troops into line. The drive of the 5th proved the key move; the regiment got heavy mortar fire in its lines from Ngesebus during the night and had quite a few casualties but, attacking at dawn of 26 September, slammed right across the ridges at the north end of the island, while the Army men reached the crest line. The 5th had, in fact, moved so rapidly that the now faltering Japanese organization lacked time to register its fires on them, and by night they had rounded the whole upper tip of the island. The enemy reacted with what were doubtless supposed to be local counterattacks but which were in effect banzai charges, poorly made and costly to them.

Ngesebus remained; the 3rd Battalion, 5th, took it on the 28th in a shore-to-shore operation with sixteen tanks leading across the reefs. There was now only one group of Japs remaining, but it was a big group, still well established in that middle section of Bloody Nose which overlooked the airfield, and still well led by Nakagawa, whose CP was very deep in. Clearing it out was a process of advance by inches over the precipitous ridges, sealing up the entrances of caves, from which the Japs occasionally escaped later. On the night of 1 February, 1945 in fact, five of them dug themselves out of one entrance and went on the warpath, which gives an idea.

On 12 October the island was declared secure, mainly in order to draw a line, but fighting was still going on, a whole month later an Army colonel was instantly killed by a sniper as he stepped from a transport on the airfield. There was still cave sealing for the men of the 81st to do when they relieved the last of the 1st Marine Division troops on 26 October. The show had been worth Presidential Unit Citations to both 1st and 5th Regiments.

V

By this time General Rupertus' command was pretty well worn out, with 6,265 casualties, or more than one man in every three of the division, after what was undoubtedly the hardest single fight of the war, harder than Tarawa and more prolonged. Whether it needed to have been quite so hard is something of a question. Certainly Inoue was by far the best Japanese commander the Marines had yet encountered. His plan of defense was admirably adapted to the ground and to his means, and he had been granted time to set it up as he wished, which is something Saito on Saipan did not have.

There were defects in the plan, to be sure. The guns and mortars in his positions fired continually on the thoroughly bad system of special assignments for each piece. An American tank group, for instance, would be ignored by a gun that had been assigned to fire on planes or infantry. Even when the Jap guns did shoot, they never thought of putting down a concentration in our sense of the term, but would fire three or four shots and then quit, which amounts to harassment rather than employing artillery for effect. The error in assuming that the Americans must assault the southern tip of Peleliu has been mentioned. The counterattack to the beach on the afternoon of the landing, though the most serious our men had to face since the Battle of Edson's Ridge on Guadalcanal, really stood very little chance of success—partly because of the military shortcomings of the outnumbered Japanese tanks, to be sure, but even more because it was a violation of the very principles Inoue had laid down in the "Palau Sector Group Training for Victory." It was delivered into the teeth of fire from sea and shore, not by small groups crawling forward, but concentrated bodies of men running, who made admirable targets.

344

But to say that there were flaws in their arrangements is no more than to say that no military plan is perfect and that under the fierce pressure of such a battle any mistakes in arrangements previously made will be laid bare. On the whole, Inoue planned soundly and flexibly, fought the kind of battle he wanted to and presented our forces with the worst problem they had yet encountered. It is also to be noted that the problem was solved: the Marines had 1,241 dead, the Japs had 11,000 and lost their island.

But the question does remain whether there might not have been fewer Marine dead, whether the place might have been taken more quickly by the expenditure of more intelligence and less muscle. It is very hard to justify the use of two full regimental combat teams to sweep out the airfield and the low ground around it, while the Japanese held the dominating ridge.

Of course, there was not enough muscle for the operation in any case, regardless of how it was employed. The 1st Marine Division contained 9,000 combat infantry and, given the conditions under which the Japanese fought, they had well over 10,000 effective infantrymen, which left our forces with nowhere near the necessary superiority against fortifications. There is also the fact that the naval gunfire was nowhere near sufficient quantitatively, nor had it done the damage the naval officers thought, and there was some Marine indignation about this later.

The final footnote to the desperate, mismanaged campaign was furnished just the day before the tired Marines re-embarked for Pavuvu—under a red twilight far to the west, where the remnants of the Imperial Japanese Navy were fleeing from the fatal waters from Cape Engano to Surigao, where three-quarters of the national sea forces had gone down. That Navy was done; the landings on Leyte were secure; and it would not have been necessary to take Peleliu after all. But of course no one could know that beforehand.

345

Chapter 21

The Sands of Iwo Jima

ON NOVEMBER 24, 1944, THE JAPANESE ON IWO JIMA ISLAND were roused by the far-distant growl of airplane engines and poured to their positions to meet one of those attacks which had grown disgustingly frequent of late. Their error; the plane sounds diminished and died away and some hours later bombs began falling on the streets of Tokyo. The 21st Bomber Command had been born and from its home in the Marianas would thenceforward deliver its loads of death to the sacred homeland in a measure increasing to the date when Hiroshima was wiped from the world in a flash of almost soundless light.

Yet the operation had inconveniences which would ultimately become insupportable in a military sense. Only the B-29s could use fields so distant as those on Saipan and Tinian, and a B-29 is so very expensive an instrument (not in money alone, but in man-hours, which are the true specie of war) that a percentage of loss which could easily be supported by an air force using smaller craft would be unendurable for them. General Le May, the new bomber commander, thought that the 21st had achieved more publicity than results and under the conditions did not see how results could be much improved.

Not only would it be essential sooner or later to provide the B-29s with fighter cover, but it was desirable to the edge of necessity to have a way station on the route where planes damaged in battle could descend. The Japanese interception station on Iwo could be and was fairly well kept out of business by persistent shelling and bombing, but early in the game the enemy fell upon the plan of staging small numbers of light bombers from the Bonins to Iwo, then counter-

346

attacking our big machines on the ground at Saipan both with bombs and by crash landings on our fields. On 27 November two Jap bombers surprised Iseley Field by night, destroyed one B-29 and shot up nine more; next noon they came back, burned up three more of the big bombers and sent half a squadron to the repair shop.

Iwo Jima was the key of the air war against Japan, the necessary way station, the essential fighter base. It would have to be taken.

The possibility had been foreseen as early as August while the last fighting was still going on on Guam, and instructions to prepare a plan for the capture had gone from the top echelons to General Holland Smith's staff and from there to the new V Amphib Corps Staff of Major General Harry Schmidt. To the latter it was evident at once that they had a very tough proposition. Iwo Jima is one of the most revolting pieces of real estate in the whole Pacific, pear-shaped, $2\frac{1}{2}$ miles wide by 5 long, with a quiescent volcano at its southern tip and the whole island so recently under active eruptions as to be built entirely of lava, slag, and ashes. The trees are few and stunted; the ground grows nothing but a little sugar, gets all its water from rain, and by August, 1944, the whole island was a fort. Its strength was clearly being increased rapidly at that date; frequent aerial photos showed the Japs burrowing like moles and there was an abundance of fresh concrete.

Early in October the Joint Chiefs of Staff in Washington issued the decision to take Iwo and the plans moved into another stage. The expedition was to include the veteran 4th Marine Division of General Cates and the 5th Marine Division of Major General Keller E. Rockey which, in spite of its newness, could be looked upon as not altogether an inexperienced outfit, since it had been built round a higher proportion of battle-trained cadres than any other Marine division. The 3rd, now under Major General Graves B. Erskine, would form the reserve afloat. The fleet would be under Spruance again, as 5th Fleet commander, with Richmond Kelly Turner as his chief of amphibs and Holland Smith head of expeditionary troops. D day was set for middle February.

Here was the strategic background after Leyte Gulf. 5th Fleet would have comparatively little interference from the Japanese Navy to worry about, for they were now down to three battleships and a possible but not probable operational force of three carriers. But the

Japs could be expected to react strongly from the air and the same Leyte Gulf Battle that had destroyed their surface forces had brought the first appearance of that Kamikaze system which made even single planes dangerous. Spruance and his staff planned a great distraction and destruction raid on the Tokyo area for the date of the landing, with special attention to aircraft factories and the fields from which the suicide fliers might come forth.

On Iwo the October intelligence figures placed something like 12,000 Japs, a figure raised to 13,500 in January. Photos and captured documents showed the island well fortified, not at the beach line but all over, like Peleliu. The water was deep and the shore steep all round the two dominating terrain features, Mt. Suribachi on the south and the high plateau that filled the round northern half of the pear. The landing would therefore have to be made on low ground at the neck between the two and the troops work uphill in both directions. This made the question of getting rid of the guns on these slopes by means of preliminary bombardment and later supporting fires a matter of capital importance. V Amphib thought that, in view of the beach losses at Saipan where there had been two days' preliminary bombardment, and at Tarawa where there had been none, and the lack of loss at the places where it had really been crushing (Roi-Namur, Tinian), they wanted not fewer than ten days of naval gunnery against Iwo Jima.

Their plan came back from 5th Fleet amended to three days' bombardment. General Smith protested; instead of a change in plans he got an explanation. A warship firing bombardment at the usual pace shoots away her ammunition in approximately three days. Iwo lies in open ocean with no anchorage near where ammunition could be taken aboard, even were it possible to trust ammunition ships so near enemy air bases. A bombardment of over three days would have to be a serial operation, with ship replacing ship, while those firing first went back to the Marianas for more shells. Now there simply were not enough ships to provide for such an attack in relays.

The plans for the attack on Okinawa were already well advanced and the latter was a truly vital strategic operation, one which might well lead to the starvation of Japan. It would have to be begun by strikes on Okinawa itself and on the fields in Kyushu from which the Kamikaze would come down to interfere. These strikes must be

348

begun by 18 March and therefore no ships scheduled for the Okinawa operation could be allowed an involvement at Iwo—that is, the fast battleships could not be used there. For several reasons— Iwo might be prolonged beyond the date when the Okinawa operation was to begin and it would not do to take any ship off that job once she was on it; there was a fairish chance that a ship off Iwo might be hit by Kamikaze and have to go back to dock.

For the same reasons the cruisers that normally wait on and cover the fast carriers could not be used at Iwo. As to the older battleships, there were six available, enough for a three-day initial bombardment but no more; and three of these had come from the Atlantic. Where were the rest? Two had picked up Kamikaze and were under repair. Six had been attached to 7th Fleet for MacArthur's Luzon campaign and they were still in the MacArthur area. The General would not release them, nor would he let go the older cruisers serving with them.

This explanation was somewhat fancy, but Holland Smith's staff were forced to take it as it stood and make their plans on a three-day bombardment basis. The more they tried to do so the less they liked it. The upshot was a second and more strongly worded protest, pointing out that photos showed the defense installations on Iwo being pushed forward rapidly; the three-day bombardment was simply not enough and they wanted four as an irreducible minimum. It was unfortunate that just at this time Holland Smith should be ill in the hospital; his eupeptic personality might have made the protest stick. As it was, Admiral Turner put an endorsement on the protest saying he "had no objection to an extra day of shelling providing it did not interfere with the great strike against Tokyo." This passed the buck to 5th Fleet Staff. Fifth Fleet had been getting plans from other staffs involved and it was much felicitated to observe that Army Air from Saipan proposed sending B-24s and B-29s to bombard the target island with great weight for ten days preceding the landing. To the second protest they replied that aerial bombardment would replace the fourth day of shelling. There the matter rested, though it was allowed that two of the fast battleships (*North Carolina* and *Washington*) should load their magazines at least partly with bombardment ammunition and do some shooting on D day when they came back from Tokyo.

The Navy men undoubtedly believed, as they said they did, that the Iwo Jima concrete was so heavy as to be impervious to shelling, so that the positions would have to be taken by assault; but the fact is that they had let themselves fall into a formalization instead of judging the case purely within its own terms. Three days' bombardment was enough for an island; if shelling could not reduce it in that time, then some other means was necessary.

Normally this was not the way Navy minds operated, but in this case they had become more than a little fascinated by that Tokyo operation, scheduled for exactly the anniversary of the great blow at Truk. This would be the first time American warships had run up to the shores of metropolitan Japan and there was a disposition, less a reasoned belief than an incalculable feeling, to imagine that equally sensational results would be produced. Insensibly 5th Fleet permitted the tail of the diversionary attack on the Japanese homeland to wag the dog of the operation against Iwo.[1]

II

The commander on Iwo Jima was Lieutenant General Tadamachi Kuribayashi, who fulfilled the dual functions of head of the Ogasawara Defense Sector (which included the Bonins) and commander of the 109th Division, the chief military unit involved. He was an officer of the cavalry, which in the Japanese, as in so many armies, is socially the top sirloin cut of the service; had commanded the

[1] The actual bombardment thus fell to Task Force 54 under Rear Admiral Bertram Rodgers, comprising the battleships *Tennessee, Idaho, Texas, New York, Nevada, Arkansas;* heavy cruisers *Tuscaloosa, Salt Lake City, Chester, Pensacola;* light cruiser *Vicksburg;* destroyers *Leutze, Newcomb, H. L. Edwards, R. P. Leary, Bennion, Twiggs, Halligan, Hall, Stembel, J. D. Henley, Bryant, Evans, D. W. Taylor, Terry, Capps,* and fast minesweeper *Hamilton.* At the last minute MacArthur released the battleship *West Virginia* and she was ordered direct to Iwo, but arrived too late and low on ammunition. It is worth noting that the force compared very poorly with that which threw shells into Saipan and even (considering how much larger, steeper, and more built up Iwo was) that for the Kwajalein Islands. One improvement in command was made; as a result of the comparative gunfire failure at Peleliu a new command was instituted including Rodgers's ships and such craft as the rocket LCIs. It was in charge of Rear Admiral W. H. P. Blandy, whose specific duty it was to see that the fire delivered was sufficient—or at least as near sufficient as the ships available could make it.

picked guards of the Imperial Palace, directed the Censorship Office, and had finally received the inexpressible honor of a personal audience with the Emperor, a privilege which is usually reserved to members of the Divine Family, or ministers in moments of grave emergency. Our Intelligence had placed his headquarters on Chichi Jima, but he was really on Iwo and the fact that all his headquarters troops were with him was one of the sources of error in advance estimates of Japanese strength.

His forces were rather a strange mixture of units and types of units, owing partly to the fact that in the hasty reinforcement of the island barrier during June, when it appeared Saipan might go, all sorts of troops were shipped there as most available in Japan; and partly to the American submarine attacks in the spring, which had caused many rescued survivors to be brought to Iwo as the nearest land, there being reorganized to the new special formations. The backbone of the infantry strength was the 2nd Mixed Brigade, a Manchuria formation with much experience, 5,200 strong; and the 145th Independent Mixed Regiment, 2,400 men. There was a tank regiment which had lost half its vehicles to a submarine but still had thirty mediums and ten lights; there were three independent mortar battalions, equipped with very big mortars—155s and 240s and some with a new piece, 320s. The General himself had requested these units for his island because of its small area and high ground. He had also brought down from the Bonins five Independent Antitank Battalions with their weapons because he believed that Iwo would be the next point of attack and that the Americans would be certain to try forcing his positions by means of tanks.

The commander of naval forces on the island was Rear Admiral Ichimaru, who had 7,020 men under his jurisdiction. The island command difficulties of early 1944 had not directly affected the Ogasawara Sector, but had left their mark in the refusal of the General and the Admiral each to recognize the other's superior rank. However, they had worked out one of those co-operation agreements so incomprehensible to Westerners, and in this case the co-operation was something more than a word spoken across a steaming teacup. The reason for this was that the bulk of the naval personnel belonged, not to one of the naval guard units, but to a naval construction group and the ground force of the Southern Air Group. After

351

the Battle of the Philippine Sea and the loss of Saipan, Japanese ships came no more to Iwo and its function as an air station was merely to provide a staging area for planes from the Empire moving down to attack the Americans farther south. The naval men had nothing to do in their specialties and w^{e}re accordingly retrained as infantry and artillerists; retrained in haste, since Kuribayashi and Ichimaru were quite agreed that their island would be attacked by November of 1944 at the latest.

They drew their battle plan early in September, like Inoue, on the basis of the reports from Saipan; and like Inoue's plan, theirs recognized that a defense at the water's edge was brittle. The general outline of the Iwo plan was an intensely organized passive defense everywhere but at the beaches. That is, the Americans were to be permitted to land but not to expand; cut to pieces by fire as they piled up in the narrow areas at the neck of the pear. Main positions were dug in in the northern plateau, around the two more northerly airstrips (Motoyama No. 2 and No. 3), and on Suribachi quite early, gradually expanded and connected by caves, tunnels, and defiladed trenches. They had this central purpose in view—all major weapons were sited to fire on the beaches and the roads leading out of the beaches, while machine guns and the lighter type of mortar were arranged to cover the heavier pieces and each other. A wide belt of main defensive positions ran across the ball of the pear and there was another up the inner slopes of Suribachi. A narrow belt of positions connected these two between No. 1 airfield and the beach line on either side of the island.

General Kuribayashi regarded it as of the greatest importance to stop the American tanks, which would be the enemy's main means of escape from the trap he was laying at the beaches. Tanks as targets were to receive priority on all artillery firing. He issued a strict order against any counterattacks except those on the smallest scale and for purposes of securing information, demanding that his men "make maximum use of their defensive works"; but there was an exception in the case of tanks. All personnel were trained in the use of anti-tank mines and grenades, and unit commanders were authorized to counterattack tanks at discretion. Units were directed to stay where they had been placed and die in position unless specifically ordered to move by high command. Quite a large reserve (three infantry battalions and most of the naval troops) was held out of the original positions, but only with the design of feeding them into the fighting areas as needed, the over-all plan of the defense being gunfire from cover.

The total of troops was 22,000, within an error of a few hundred.[1] Of the outsize mortars there were twelve; of 155 guns four, of 140s four; there were 14 120s, six 90-mm. mortars, 10 88-mm. guns, 17 75s, 30 70-mm, guns or howitzers, 36 antitank guns, 54 of the 25-mm. machine cannon, and 478 machine guns were later counted, though it cannot be said that this is all there were. General Kuribayashi reported the morale of his troops extremely good, and described his men as filled with dauntless, courageous fighting spirit. This was doubtless true within the limits of the morale necessary to fight the kind of battle he had outlined, and the men gave many expressions of their desire to make the Americans pay for all they had done to destroy the very life of the Empire, but there was a good deal of grumbling and goldbricking in the Iwo Jima garrison. Candy and tobacco had been short ever since the submarine attacks in early 1944 and by the turn of 1945 had altogether disappeared except from officers' pockets. Mail did not come and there was nothing to do but this continuous job of improving the fortifications, digging away at hard rock. The men felt they were rather exiled to some kind of penal colony than proud defenders on the frontiers of the Empire. There were incidents like that of Superior Private Nakamura, who dug himself a fine shelter only to have it usurped by the company commander. He told his platoon leader that he "could not die with such a brutal guy" and asked to be ordered to some other formation.

At the beginning of February information was circulated that Iwo was to be attacked by one battleship, eighteen destroyers and cruisers, and the 3rd, 4th and 5th Marine Divisions, which had left Hawaii aboard forty transports and would arrive in four days.

III

Nobody in the fleet moving up to Iwo Jima thought it would be easy. General Holland Smith expected 15,000 casualties; Kelly

[1] For a few units no muster rolls were found, but on nearly all our intelligence obtained accurate figures after the battle from ration returns and similar documents.

Turner thought the figure might run higher than that. On this island there would be no question or possibility of tactical maneuver, no surprise or any of the other devices by which losses are kept lower. It would have to be a straight slugging match; and as the force approached the island the prospects that a good many people would get hurt were increased, for word ran in through the ships that the Army bombardiers had not been very accurate—"laid a lot of their eggs in the water"—and part of one day's firing from the supporting ships was missed, because the weather turned heavy, with low-riding clouds, which so interfered with air spot that Admiral Blandy called off the bombardment.

There were other indications also. On 17 February, as Spruance and Mitscher were giving Tokyo its taste of carrier war (the weather turned foul and they achieved more damage to planes than factories), the ships moved in on Iwo to cover the underwater demolition teams. *Pensacola* came close enough for the 155s on the north slope to draw a bead on her. At 0938 the other ships saw splashes go up beside her, masthead high; the next shells went right in, clouds of brown smoke came out, and a plane on her catapult began to burn. The big cruiser was one of the "Treaty tinclads" and ill-protected against such treatment. She had to haul out with six bad hits and 137 casualties and though she came back later (ceasing fire while the medics operated and gave blood transfusions) it was clear that the shore guns were not knocked out, only ceasing fire because they wanted to.

An hour later off the eastern beaches a group of twelve LCI rocket gunboats, covering underwater demolition teams, got into an argument with a big battery at the base of Suribachi, into which the machine cannon were drawn as the heavier guns began to score hits. All twelve gunboats were hit, LCI 474 capsized, the destroyers had to come in and cover them with a white phosphorus smoke screen, and of these last *Leutze* was hit also. During this flare-up a four-gun battery nowhere noted in the preliminary surveys opened from above the east boat basin, a position from which it could enfilade the intended landing beaches. It was in *Idaho's* area of fire; she poured in 14-inch all around it, but there was no sure evidence that the battery was out.

354

The general gunfire plan had been to smash all the main battery positions on the island. The revelation that there were more of them and better concealed than any preliminary intelligence had indicated caused a revision that night. For D minus 1 the fire of four battleships was concentrated along the eastern beaches while the cruisers did what they could against the high ground to the north. That night the naval gunfire men were satisfied they had eliminated the four-gun battery discovered by *Idaho* and had pretty well crippled everything in the neck of the pear that might directly oppose the landing, but they warned they had not been able to do much about the mortar positions—too easy to camouflage, with too small openings, and they had not shown their location by firing. The most Navy could do was set the Marines on the beach in fairly good shape; they must handle the rest themselves.

They reached the beaches to do it a few minutes after 0900 on 19 February, with the 4th Division on the right of the eastern beaches, the 5th Division on the left. Each had two regiments in the assault wave, reading from left to right, the 28th (Colonel Harry Liversedge, the old Raider), the 27th (Colonel Thomas A. Wornham)—these being of the 5th; the 23rd (Colonel W. W. Wensinger), the 25th (Colonel L. J. Lanigan). The 24th (Colonel W. L. Jordan) was in reserve behind the 4th Division; as soon as the beachhead was secure it would be shoved in between the other two regiments and the three abreast were to do a right wheel up against the line of the cliff and quarry that marked the edge of the high ground to the north. On the extreme outside of this wheel would be the 26th Regiment (Lieutenant Colonel Chester B. Graham) of the 5th Division, landing after the assault regiments and cutting across the island at its narrowest point, with the 27th on its right. The 28th was to swing south against the defenses of Suribachi; the 0-1 line, or objective for the day, was to have the No. 1 airfield in our possession, with the troops everywhere on the first steep ground. Each battalion was to have a 500-yard front on landing.

There was a break from the weather, which turned fine, no swells, and Secretary Forrestal was watching from the command ship *Eldorado*. Off to seaward *North Carolina* and *Washington*, with the cruisers *Biloxi* and *Birmingham*, had come from 5th Fleet and were firing with the rest, the boats were in admirable order, and at least

355

one Marine was swearing because he had just seen on the deck of his landing craft a discarded copy of *A Tree Grows in Brooklyn,* which he had been trying for months to get hold of.

As the boats touched shore, the line of shellbursts moved inland in an original artillery performance, a rolling barrage fired from the sea. Under this fire the armored amphitracs moved through the first terrace level of obstacles by gaps that bombing and gunfire had cut and the Marines hopped out of their personnel carriers without difficulty. There was only a scattering of fire from mortars and light weapons; the main trouble was the coarse gray sliding volcanic sand, which from the start paralyzed every vehicle we had. Wheels would not turn at all, even treads halted, the infantry had to climb the steep volcanic slope alone in short rushes. "Light opposition," "Light machine-gun and mortar fire" came the radio reports back to the flag and in the first hour 150 yards were made, with the 27th hitting deepest. They were finding some mines, and bulldozers were getting ashore. The 23rd reported the ground practicable for tanks and General Cates sent in those that were to support this regiment.

By the time the LSMs carrying them had reached the beach, at 0945, the rolling barrage had rolled deeper and the picture changed. As naval fire and the strafing planes could no longer work on the first areas of their attack because the Marines were too close to them, the Jap guns and mortars one by one came to life. The arrival of succeeding waves warned Kuribayashi that this was the real thing, not a feint preliminary to a landing on the western beaches as he had first thought. He began to feed his reserves into the gun caves. Fire, especially mortar fire of such calibers as no Marine had seen, built up gradually and remorselessly. Four of the six LSMs behind the 23rd were hit, two of them badly, one so badly she could not get her tanks ashore. Every moment and from every direction the fire increased, new types of weapons joined in down to machine guns. The 25th found itself up against a system of blockhouses only partly destroyed by shells, most of their guns still active, the blockhouses protected from direct assault by machine-gun pillboxes buried in sand and not damaged at all. The regiment was getting a dreadful fire from the flank; so was the 28th from Suribachi down on the other wing; so was the 23rd from the terraces up to the airfield; in the

356

27th John Basilone was killed, the Medal of Honor man who had disposed of thirty-eight Japs on Guadal.

At 1100 mortar fire was officially "heavy" which, with Marines using the term, means very heavy indeed. Worst of all were the conditions right at the beaches, where the severest fire was falling. Tanks churned helplessly in the volcanic sand and were hit; at the water's edge amphitracs, LCMs, Higgins boats were hit, burned, broached, capsized, and added to the confusion of a number of old Jap wrecks that had lain there. The beaches were speedily jammed with this debris. It was almost impossible to bring in more craft and those that did come in were being knocked out with dismaying regularity. Shore and beach parties were taking heavy losses, especially among their officers, and were not getting their equipment in.

The division artillery officer of the 4th, Colonel De Haven, recommended that his guns not be landed till the reserve battalions had reached the shore and deployed; there was no room. At 1315 General Cates, with a worried frown, told correspondent Sherrod, "I wish we had six more hours of daylight. I'd compromise for two." The 25th's assault battalions had 25 per cent casualties and their dressing stations were being shelled; the 23rd had 20 per cent and was calling for more air support. Colonel Wensinger, via radio: "The gunfire spotters have got to get down low and locate those mortars. We can't see them. They're buried in six-foot holes."

Sum it up this way: General Kuribayashi's defense system was achieving a success sensational because he had found for this island a method against which the tactical knowledge gained in three years of beachhead war was not of much use. The only thing that remained to our side was Marine determination, guts, forcing the solution of an insoluble problem. Late in the afternoon the reserve regiments of both divisions went in and the artillery, whether it had cover or not. They had an extremely hard time with the guns; had to be taken out of their DUKWs just at the waterline and hauled to position by bulldozers. Other DUKWs with supply were pulled up the sand terraces by tractors—and all this time the mortar and artillery shells kept coming at such a rate that the frightful experience of Lieutenant Benjamin F. Roselle of the 1st Joint Assault Signal Company was not exceptional but typical.

He had a six-man naval gunfire liaison team. They got 200 yards in, to the second row of terraces. One man was hit; Roselle picked up his gear and they went on. A mortar shell knocked three of them down, almost cutting off one of Roselle's feet. The others put a tourniquet on his leg while the wounded tried to crawl away. A moment later another mortar shell hit two of the unwounded and threw splinters into the Lieutenant's other leg. He could neither move nor be moved; an hour and a half later as he and the surviving member of his team lay under the dust and acrid smoke, another shell landed on them, tore off the right leg of his remaining man and again wounded Roselle in the shoulder. A fourth shell wounded both his thighs, a fifth his left arm, and it was night when a medical party got him out—to live, amazingly.

IV

During that night, fitfully lit by star shell over the inner island, fitfully lit by bursts of Jap harassing fire along the beach line, the two divisions had nowhere reached anything like their objective lines. The 27th Regiment was nearest; had jagged across the southern tip of No. 1 airstrip almost to the western beaches. Most of the artillery was in position ready to fire such guns as had not been hit. The 28th was facing the lower ledges of Suribachi, but had not begun to mount. Three tanks of the 4th had been knocked out by mines and more by gunfire. Their flame throwers had disposed of a number of pillboxes but only one tank had reached the level of the airfield and that one was unable to stay. The 23rd had gained little beyond the 200-yard line; the 25th still less, and had taken the heaviest casualties, with more fire coming down all the time from front and flank. Indeed, the regiment was in such shape that it was the opinion of some officers a Jap counterattack on that flank would have broken through. To climax all, the beach and shore parties were having little luck clearing out the wrecked craft and the weather prediction for the morrow was gales and heavy surf along the water.

The Suribachi command, now cut off from the main Japanese body, did try one silly little counterattack by means of a barge containing twenty-five men, who were all killed by the 28th Marines. But on the main part of the island General Kuribayashi, instead of counterattacking, sent a radio message to Tokyo saying that he was

358

going to die on the island. His defense system, which had so many advantages, had the disadvantage of conceding all movement to others than himself. The Japanese forces out in the beyond could not move because the tall gray forms of Task Force 58 were walking the sea; and when the Marines moved in the great dawn redolent of

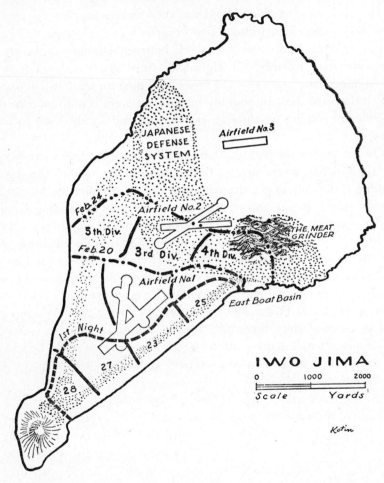

coming storm, they coalesced, refined their communication lines, brought up the guns, and went forward in a general assault.

It began at 0830 on 20 February and it moved in both directions, the 28th against Suribachi with two battalions in line, the remainder of the two divisions toward the o-1 line in the north as originally planned, pivoting on the 25th. The Suribachi assault was as tough as it was expected to be. All round the base of that volcano was a network of mutually supporting concrete positions; from the cliffs above, the Japs poured every kind of fire into the faces of the attackers, and from the north end of the island more into their backs. The tanks could not accompany the first assault. Their maintenance section had not been able to land and they had no juice or ammunition. When they did get into action progress was made, especially by flame-throwing tanks and teamwork between gunnery tanks and flame-throwing infantry. But the night closed down with only 200 yards gained here and Colonel Liversedge's men found that pillboxes which they had most thoroughly burned out were being reoccupied by enemies coming up through the tunnels and would have to be gone over again.

Out on the sea the bad weather did develop, still further hampering the beaches, where fire continued steadily throughout the day, making it difficult to get the wounded out or supplies in. Admiral Blandy finally issued an order to use LSMs only in landing fresh troops or equipment and the UDT boys, who had thought they were all through with this island, had to come back to blast out some of the wrecks. It was already clear both to Holland Smith and to General Schmidt that they would have to use the 3rd Division, and one regiment of it, Colonel Hartnell Withers's 21st, was under orders to land on D plus 2. This made the matter of clearing those beaches a first emergency, since furnishing food and ammunition for 50,000 fighting men would require all the beach facilities that could be had. As it was, the 28th had twice been held up that day by shortages of mortar ammunition.

On the big northern front D plus 1 saw a battalion of the 26th and one of the 27th swing up the western side of the island for close to a thousand yards, taking that side of the airfield but also taking heavy casualties, especially on the left flank, where the 26th's battalion had to work through the zone with which Kuribayashi had intended to defend the western beaches. Nineteen of the fifty tanks with the division were knocked out; mortar fire fell constantly and early in the afternoon a fine rain began to fall which turned the ash to a pasty mud that effectively clogged everything movable, especially the parts of weapons.

At about the same time as the arrival of the rain (1330) the 27th began to experience difficulty from persistent shelling of its CP and discovered that its right flank on the airfield was open.

The 4th Division, in fact, had thus far been able to gain little. All its moves were under observation from the heights, on its right it was up against a perfect maze of positions below the ridge of the quarry, and on its left was crossing the open airfield into a zone where tanks were almost useless because the whole terrain was filled with elaborate mine fields swept by the fire of 47-mm. antitank guns. The 5th Division put another battalion of the 27th in, took over 400 yards of the 4th's front, and with a heave the lines were carried beyond the north end of airfield No. 1. They were still short of the original 0-1 line when they dug in for the night with total casualties 3,055. The beach congestion was as serious as ever and the 25th lost most of its ammunition dump when a Jap shell set fire to it.

D plus 2, 21 February, was more of the same, with the main improvement at the beaches. In spite of intermittent fire from the enemy's big mortars and the pounding surf that did not decrease, some LSTs worked in to discharge direct and some matting was laid across the sand permitting vehicles to reach the upper terraces. On the northern front both divisions attacked. Their gain was an average 100 yards, but most of this was made on the extreme left, where the 5th Division troops worked up to the foot of the hill line and into the outer edge of Kuribayashi's main position, already reached by the 4th. Twelve destroyers were firing support; they worked in so close they were laying salvos of 5-inch 50 yards in front of our lines, but they were to get closer yet before the war on Iwo was over. Against Suribachi, Liversedge made 400 yards this day, reaching the base of the vertical slopes, while two companies seeking a way to the top worked around a ledge 50 feet above the water. It rained all day, cold and drizzling; food was short, the 28th reported its combat efficiency down to 75 per cent.

Out on the ocean the Japs came down from the Empire that evening with a storm of fifty Kamikazes through low clouds that prevented a proper combat patrol. They fell on the supporting carrier group; the escort carrier *Bismarck Sea* was hit in the stern by one which set fire to her torpedo stock, she burned and capsized with 318 casualties. *Lunga Point* had holes all along her sides from an-

361

other that exploded close aboard, and the veteran *Saratoga* was hit by no fewer than four, going back to Pearl Harbor with (oddly enough) 318 casualties also, and "more kinds of damage than I ever saw aboard a single ship," as reported by the dockmaster.

V

There is an hour of crisis in every battle in which something takes place that determines whether it will move forward or back. At that moment the worst and best have become known; the problem has been grasped and everyone in the fighting organization from the rear-rank enlisted to the top brass has become aware, on different levels of comprehension, of what is to be done and how the resources available compare with the difficulties to be overcome. It is ebb tide, the time when victory is determined in the minds of the men. This awareness is often inaccurately described as the state of morale. It is something more than that, for it is a feeling which underlies even command decisions—as such a feeling underlay Admiral Fletcher's decision to take the carriers out of range on the second night of Guadalcanal.

This hour of crisis on Iwo was not the first desperate night when the beaches were under fire and jammed with wrecked landing craft. That was merely the height of the conflict, when the irresistible force was still in clash with the immovable obstacle and neither side was as yet fully aware of the determination and resources of the other. The true spiritual crisis of Iwo Jima came on the night of 21 February; and it came simultaneously to both sides. On ours one carrier had been lost and another badly wrecked at sea—how long could this be borne? Ashore one airfield had been taken but it was as useless as that on Peleliu had been while still dominated by the guns in the overmastering ridge. No way of ascending Suribachi had been discovered. Against the belt of defenses in the north only the barest early penetrations had been made. The 23rd and 25th Regiments had been beaten to pieces, the men were in low spirits under the rain, and short of food. Not many more than half the tanks of either assault division were still in action. That night a Jap shell blew up an ammunition dump with all the 4th Division's 81-mm. mortar

362

supply and most of its gasoline, and the 23rd had to deal with a nasty infiltration counterattack toward morning.

And the Japanese? They had not succeeded in holding the Americans in their beach trap, the losses were unreasonably heavy, and one of their officers wrote in his diary: "Today is the most important day. Today we must annihilate those who have landed. There are no reinforcements for us. Are we not losing the battle at this moment? I feel keenly the need of increasing the production of airplanes."

The battle was at a standstill that night; but next morning the pendulum swung delicately in the direction of the attacking Marines. On the ocean Admiral Spruance calmly detached *Enterprise* to take the damaged *Saratoga*'s place and went back to soak the Empire's airfields again. On Iwo men who now knew what they were up against began to take the situation with the grim insouciant humor of Americans in a long battle. They laughed to see a Marine go past, prodding with his bayonet the behind of a Jap he had flushed from a pillbox, and roared when an auto-rifle man cut the runner down before the bayonetist could catch him. On Suribachi Colonel Liversedge, finding that all the trails to the crest had been destroyed by gunfire or by the Japanese themselves, surrounded the base of the mountain. On the following day, 23 February, the weather smiled once more as he attacked for the crests. His 1st Battalion found the cliffs impassable in that area; the 2nd by foothold and handhold worked a patrol up to the lip of the crater. They found a row of machine guns with ammunition but no Japs, and at 1100, three men—Lieutenant Schrier, Sergeant A. L. Thomas, Sergeant Henry O. Hansen—raised an American flag affixed to an old piece of Japanese pipe.

The word passed through the line in the north and eyes were wet as men turned from the battle to look. But Suribachi itself was not yet taken, there were still hundreds of Japs in caves who used to come out at night in breechclouts with demolition charges tied around their waists, looking for CPs and artillery positions. It was 25 February before that sulphur-stinking volcano was declared secure and for two weeks later the engineers were still blowing up caves from which Japs occasionally scurried, a total of 380 caves in that small area alone.

War on the northern front also turned statistical. On the morning of 22 February the 21st Regiment relieved the 23rd and next day the 24th relieved the 25th; all the front-line formations worked forward into Kuriyabashi's defense system at a pace that did not exceed 50 yards a day. Correspondent Sherrod went over one of the blockhouses around which lay eight dead Marines. Its outer walls were forty inches of reinforced concrete, it had three chambers with 12-inch concrete baffles between, the vent opened only toward the heights in the rear, it had a 120-mm. in its gunport and a heavy machine-gun pillbox atop, the whole business covered with sand and smoothed down to look like a dune. It had taken a flame thrower to get that one and all the rest were as bad. There were no tactics in such a battle but the tactics of the squad and the three-man fire team; nothing to chronicle but the continual daily combat made up of a series of smaller battles.

In this kind of fighting, with heavy naval gunnery and aerial preparations each morning before the day's attack, the center worked up to Motoyama No. 2 by the night of 24 February. A reorganization brought the 3rd Division into the center of the line as an entity, its 9th Regiment passing through the 21st. The ground all round the airfield was mined and the runways afforded perfect fields of fire for Jap guns mounted on the other side; we lost nine tanks there on 25 February and eleven more the following day.

To the right of the 3rd, the 4th Division pushed slowly up Quarry Ridge into a hill formation known as "The Amphitheater" and Hill 382, too rough for the use of tanks. By 26 February the division was down to 55 per cent combat efficiency. It kept on against the network of positions east of the airfield which earned the unenviable name of "The Meatgrinder." On 28 February, D plus 9, all but this one position were broken through, the Marines gained the high crest and part of the unfinished No. 3 airstrip.

It took another eight days to cover the thousand yards to the rear of the defenses facing outward at the northeast flank of the island, but it must not be assumed that this rear position brought any tactical advantage. General Kuribayashi had sited his holes for all-around defense; the advance hung there until 16 March, when another big thrust carried it to the sea and the island was declared secure. Even at that date it was not really secure, of course. There were remnants of the pocket above Quarry Ridge and there was a very real pocket of some 200 by 300 yards among the gorges at the north end of the island which occupied the entire attention of the 5th Division for nine days more. The infantry had to work in while tank-dozers cleared the way for tank support. The men had been without relief for over a month of fighting and they were tired to death before the business was done on 25 March. Supply was all this time a continual ache. DUKWs and weasels were the only vehicles that could negotiate the sliding sand and food had to be flown in from Saipan with air-drops at the end of the line. The procedure worked very well toward the end of the campaign; an inspecting officer found one battalion CP a few hundred yards from the fire line where they were frying fresh beefsteak and onions with Jap bullets passing overhead.

By the terminal date the casualty count showed 21,972 for the island, 8,324 of them in the 4th Division, 8,262 in the 5th, which means that each of these units had lost nearly half its men in the bloodiest battle the Marine Corps had ever seen. It was the one battle in which the final casualties were approximately equal or even a little in favor of the enemy, though it must be remembered that only 4,644 of the Marines were dead and of the wounded three-quarters recovered sufficiently for return to duty, while the Japs were all killed but an insignificant handful of prisoners.

One comment on the casualties was furnished by General Le May's B-29s. On 9 March, while the fighting on Iwo was still going on, they made the first of the great low-level, fire-bomb raids. A third of the city of Tokyo burned up and with it all the little backyard shops where airplane parts were fabricated, so that this was the first month in which Japanese plane production showed an actual decline. No Jap planes took off from the Jimas to intercept; the raid came as a surprise. Two of the million-dollar ships landed on Motoyama No. 1 with damage that would otherwise have forced them down at sea, and were saved, planes and crews.

A second comment was offered (on 10 March) by General Douglas MacArthur or by his indefatigable publicity man:

"Our method of attack consisted in preliminary saturation bombardments to confine the enemy within the tunnels. When this has been accomplished a small demolition group from the infantry moves in with white phosphorus grenades and flame throwers, and demolitions of several hundred pounds of explosives are placed inside the entrance and blown to close the opening. When trapped in this way the enemy are suffocated to death and destroyed without taking any compensating toll from our troops. Slow progress of the attack is allowed by these methods but an enormous saving in life and materials is effected."

Yes: but slow progress of the attack was precisely the thing that could not be allowed on Iwo. The Navy wanted its ships for Okinawa, and the air force had to have its way station today. As for saturation bombardment, it is more than probable that the ten days' gunfire requested by the Marines in the beginning would have reduced both the casualties and the amount of time necessary to take the island, and comment about the desirability of more bombardment does not come very gracefully from the officer whose insistence upon retaining the battleships in his own area was one of the fundamental reasons why there was not more fire on Iwo Jima.

On the other hand, it is not likely that any amount of gunfire could have disposed of such installations as the 40-inch blockhouse found by Sherrod; not even certain that a direct hit by a 14-inch armor-piercer would have put it out of business. Late in the operation supporting destroyers, which had by this time refined their fire control systems to the point where they were laying 5-inch only 20 yards ahead of the Marine lines, poured approximately a thousand tons of steel into the Meatgrinder area, and it still had to be taken by hand.

What naval gunfire could have done and did not do, except in the narrow defense belts running down both sides of the airfield between Suribachi and the main position, was to get rid of the minor positions—machine guns and small pillboxes, covering the approaches to the heavier and better protected installations. A careful survey afterward and consultation of all the documents the Japs left behind showed that not over a couple of hundred of them were killed in all the preliminary bombardment. If General Kuribayashi's men had not been very low on morale themselves they might have done us even more damage.

The same remarks go for air bombing support. There were complaints from all the commanders on the island that the close air support was seldom adequate—or, to sum matters up, because of strategic commitments elsewhere, there was simply not enough fire power available properly to cover the Iwo Jima attack. The high command, the very highest level of command, the Joint Chiefs, were trying to do too many things at once and had abandoned that wise principle of concentrating all the forces in the Pacific for a single operation, the principle that produced such spectacular results in the Marshalls and at Guam-Tinian.

There is also the point, with relation to the MacArthur comment (which refers to the hill positions east of Manila city), that no amount of saturation and no amount of time could have prevented considerable casualties during the assault phase on Iwo. Saturating one cave entrance with fire, while the infantry lay the demolition charges or use flame throwers, was precisely what the Marines did on the island after the first three days and they had losses all the same. There were no covered avenues of approach and a good many of their casualties occurred out on the beach, where mortar shells continued to drop in the unloading areas to the very last. Farther in, the place was too concentrated, too intricately organized within a narrow area for MacArthur tactics to have accomplished any more than Marine tactics did. It was not possible to attack any cave without coming under fire from several more; heavy fire from heavy weapons, as the losses in tanks testify.

But now it was over; Iwo Jima was ours and the fleet swept its great circle to the south and toward Okinawa.

Chapter 22

Okinawa: The Coming of the Kamikaze

THE THIRTY-SECOND ARMY WAS ORGANIZED ON OKINAWA early in April, 1944, under a Lieutenant General Watanabe. In August, when the fall of the Marianas placed the island under direct threat, Watanabe fell ill and Lieutenant General Mitsuru Ushijima was sent down from Tokyo to take command. He brought a new chief of staff, Major General Isamu Cho, an engineer. Both men had recently been closeted with the head of the Imperial General Staff and were fresh from the earliest arguments at headquarters about the manner of island defense. In those discussions there had been general agreement that the log-type pillbox afforded insufficient protection against naval gunfire and air strikes and that it must be abandoned for a system based on caves and concrete. The agreement as to where the new type of structure should be placed was less general. The Imperial Staff contained a number of conservative old officers who were diehards for the idea of defending at the beach line, making counterattacks early and in great force. Ushijima and Cho belonged to the other camp, like Kuribayashi of Iwo Jima, but the contest between the two viewpoints resulted, as such arguments often did among Japanese officers, in a set of orders that embraced the ideas of both factions. That is, Ushijima and Cho were to hold at the beaches and make counterattacks but also to conduct a passive defense in the interior.

The forces assigned to the Thirty-second Army were not so large as to fill its commander with any great confidence in the value of this double defense. The area under his charge included the whole of the Okinawa Gunto, and he must provide for the defense of numerous out-islands—the Kerama Retto to the southwest, Ie Shima and Iheya Shima to the northwest—as well as Okinawa itself, which is the most important of all the Ryukyu chain that stretches in a great semicircle from Kyushu to Formosa, screening off the East China Sea. The main island is 67 miles long, very irregular in shape, from 3 to 10 miles wide, and has a native population of origins so curiously mixed that anthropologists have long since given up trying to separate its elements and are content simply to call the people Okinawans. There were some 450,000 of them, mostly engaged in subsistence farming with a few vegetables for export and nearly all living in the southwestern third of the island, all the rest of which rises sharply from the sea into wooded hills and ravines so steep as to resist cultivation. General Ushijima promptly conscripted all the able-bodied males to work on his fortifications, while the women carried baskets of earth for their men or were established in comfort houses for the troops.

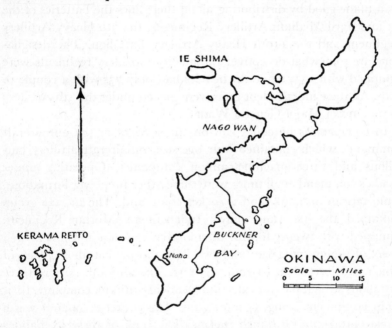

Of these troops he had three divisions plus a number of independent formations. The 9th, a very good and experienced division, with a history dating back to 1895, was assigned to the southern end of the island south of a line from the capital at Naha east to Yonabaru, the portion which General Cho considered the most defensible under the new system. This division was to be the center of the defense. In the zone north of Naha was placed the 62nd Division of Lieutenant General Takeo Fujioka, covering the Hagushi beaches, where it was most likely the Americans would land. It was a veteran formation, which had made the Keikan campaign in early 1944 and had since been built up via reinforcements. North of this, up to the island's narrowest part, was installed the 24th Division, commanded by Lieutenant General Tatsumi Amamiya, whose organization dated only from 1939; it had spent most of the intervening time in Manchuria but had never been in combat and was considered untried. As with most formations from China, where guns are normally more hindrance than help, the 62nd was without organizational artillery and the 24th had only a single regiment aside from the antitank company in each infantry formation. But this deficiency was more than made good by distributing along their lines the batteries of the 1st and 23rd Medium Artillery Regiments, the 7th Heavy Artillery Regiment and the 110th Heavy Artillery Battalion. The designations are somewhat deceptive; the medium artillery regiments were equipped with 155s while the heavies had only 75s with a couple of 120s. All these independent guns were placed under the 5th Artillery Command of Major General Wada.

In emergencies he could call on the services of the antiaircraft command, which contained four oversize antiaircraft artillery battalions and three machine-cannon companies. Operating under Wada's command at all times were three other firepower formations, a mortar, an antitank, and a rocket command. The mortar group contained the 1st (and only) Independent Mortar Regiment, equipped with twenty-four of the monster 320-mm. mortars as well as six of the 90-mm. size; and two light-mortar battalions, each of which had forty-eight 81 mm. mortars. The antitankers were three battalions strong, plus an extra independent antitank company, their main equipment being 47-mm. guns. The rocket command was a single battalion with 9-inch rockets. The bulk of these formations were in the south, in the areas of the 9th and 62nd Divisions. There was also a tank regiment, the 27th, but the General seems to have counted on burying its vehicles to the turrets and using them as immobile artillery, as Kuribayashi had done on Iwo.

370

North of the 24th Division's area and covering most of the uninhabitable part of the island as well as Ie Shima, was the remaining main infantry formation, the 44th Independent Mixed Brigade of Major General Shigero Suzuki, known as the Bimbo Tai, "Have-Nothing Unit," or "The Poor Boys." This was the result of a tragedy that had overtaken them on their way down to Okinawa in June. An American sub[1] torpedoed the transport that was bringing them in; there was a seaway on and 5,400 of the 6,000 men in the brigade drowned, while all its equipment was lost. General Suzuki was indefatigable in reorganizing his poor boys; added some conscript Okinawans and casual replacements to the 600 survivors at once and in November had the 15th Independent Mixed Regiment flown in to bring the brigade up to strength again by the end of the year. Equipment was another matter; in December he was yelling for 294 rifles, 1,011 bayonets, 556 mess kits, and 64 machine guns.

The total picture of the defense at this date was thus that General Ushijima was going to hold the beaches and the northerly portion of the island with the less valid units, the weight and strength of the system increasing toward the south where, in the 9th Division's area, it became the full Iwo Jima type of passive defense. Outside this general scheme were some 3,500 Naval Guard troops defending the area of the midget submarine and motor torpedo base on Motobu Peninsula in the north part of the island. Oroku Peninsula in the south had more naval men and there were seven Sea Raiding squadrons based on the Kerama Retto. Each of these was equipped with sixty one-man suicide boats; they were to attack the American fleet as soon as it approached Okinawa. All told, including the personnel serving the Yontan, Machinato, and Katena Airfields, Ushijima commanded some 87,000 men.

This was only true down to December, however. In November the lines on Leyte had cracked disastrously and Marshal Terauchi fled from his Philippine command to South China. The Imperial General Staff issued a new appraisal of the over-all strategic situation. They believed that the American operations plan would now contain two phases, the first an advance from the Philippines to the area of Southeast China and southern Formosa, consisting of a landing in China by three Australian divisions, an American landing at Takao

[1] This was the famous *Tang,* which did so much damage on various occasions.

in Formosa by four divisions at the end of March—combined with an attack on Iwo Jima by three American divisions about 19 February. The second phase would be an attack on northern Formosa in March or April by four American divisions and one on Okinawa in May or June by five divisions.

Formosa was thus the focal point; and despite Ushijima's anguished protests, they took his 9th Division away from him and sent it to that island. This of course required a radical revision of the General's defense plans. He brought Suzuki's Have-Nothings of the 44th Independent Mixed down into the eastern peninsula of southern Okinawa except for a couple of companies left along the approaches to Motobu. The defense of the beaches was altogether abandoned (let the Imperial Staff make something of it, who had taken away his best troops) and the 24th Division was placed in the western end of the southern part of the island, its northern boundary a line from the mouth of the river Kokuba across to Yonabaru. The 62nd was pulled in slightly so its northern outpost line ran across the narrowest part of the island, its southern boundary being the northern limit of the 24th's responsibility.

All the troops were set to work fortifying their areas on the new system with the greatest intensity under General Cho's direction. The main battle position ran from a little north of Naha through Shuri Castle in the center of the island to Yonabaru. The bulk of the artillery, mortar, antitank, and machine-cannon commands were emplaced to fire in defense of this line. The heart of the defense was a system of caves through the ravined and rolling hill country where no elevation is over 500 feet. The process of making these caves was sensibly aided by the burial custom of the Okinawans, who dispose of their dead in vaults dug part way into the hills and built of stone or concrete slabs. These furnished valuable cave entrances and firing points but they were haphazard and General Cho was systematic.

In each sector of the area he appointed a separate commander who assigned specific hills to his units, the normal hill being of a size to make it a battalion position. The battalion commander would confer with adjacent commanders under the supervision of engineers, and arrange for the cave entrances and firing points to be mutually supporting. Under battalion each company did the work on the ground it would occupy, with the help of conscripted Okinawans. The scheme was to tunnel to the center of the hill, always with bends just inside the entrances to keep fire from coming in. At the center living and sleeping quarters and supply dumps were hollowed out as caves. From these caves tunnels radiated to entrances at front, rear and both sides of the hill. The heavier guns, if the battalion had any, were installed at the forward entrances. Just behind them other tunnels paralleled the base of the hill, running around to connect with the lateral tunnels just behind the side entrances. Off these circular tunnels were machine-gun rooms, facing outward, and smaller niches leading to rifle slits covered each machine-gun position. Two of each company's automatic weapons had fixed fields of fire, 30 degrees wide and intersecting; the remainder of its heavy weapons were to be mobile.

Outside the cave spider-pit foxholes were constructed with connecting trenches. Normally one-third of a battalion's men would be outside in these trenches, but the instructions were that the moment a bombardment began all but ten or twelve lookouts were to be pulled back into the caves. When an American infantry attack on the hill began the reserves within would immediately issue forth, always by means of the side exits, in order to take the attackers in flank. The same side exits were to be used for reinforcing neighboring hills; if withdrawal became necessary the rear exits would be employed, small suicide rear guards remaining behind to defend the forward face as long as possible.

The 9th Division, as was to be expected from its record, had made excellent progress with the work in the southern part of the island and it now went forward rapidly everywhere else. General Ushijima had several worries, however. The Okinawans were lazy and showed little interest in the defense of the Empire. The morale of his troops was not as high as it should have been. When the men of the 62nd moved into their new positions they expressed discouragement on finding Naha almost completely burned out by American bombing and there were complaints over the poor quality of the food. In fact these were justified; the conscription of the natives had brought it about that the normal crops of vegetables were not raised that fall and winter and the shortage had not been made good from outside sources.

"I cannot bear having just a cup of rice for a meal with no side dishes at all," wrote one of the men. "Our health will be ruined." The General issued orders that the troops should "display a more firm and resolute spirit, hold to the belief of positive victory, and always remember the spirit of martyrdom and of dying for the good of the country." As a practical step an issue of a pint and a half of sweet-potato brandy was made and everybody was allowed to get drunk without any courts martial or other penalties, another issue being promised for the Emperor's birthday. Pilgrimages to Shuri Castle were permitted (although it was Army headquarters) so the troops could visit the shrine there, which was of special military and philosophical interest. It had belonged to Minamoto Tametamo, the famous bowman of the heroic Gempei epoch, who had been banished thither with his arm tendons cut, after the rivals of his house had captured him, and he left the seed from which the later Okinawan kings were sprung. Official lecturers discoursed on the hero and how he had later returned to Japan to become the very representative of Hachiman Taro, the God of War, though reaching this island under so discouraging circumstances.

In early January, General Cho flew to Tokyo, where he explained the steps that had been taken on the island. There was some feeling that General Ushijima had exceeded his instructions by abandoning the beach lines in the central part of the island, which General Cho countered by pointing out they were prepared resolutely to defend the beaches of the southern shore. His course was in the main approved because it fitted into a new rationale of island defense which the High Command had worked out. They would be well satisfied if General Ushijima fought on Okinawa the kind of battle that would delay the Americans a long time, forcing them to bring many ships of supply and of war into the area of the Okinawa Gunto and keep them there. The reason for this was, of course, the unqualified success of the "glorious, incomparable young eagles" of the Special Attack Forces, Kamikaze (Navy) and Tokobetsu (Army), who had first come into action in the Philippines, making suicide dives on American ships. Already some 26 units of these fliers had attacked and General Cho was shown a report which specified the results as the instantaneous sinking of 1 battleship, 6 carriers, and 34 cruisers besides various transports and destroyers with the damaging of many more.

(Whether the General believed this report as written is uncertain. Likely he did; on returning to Okinawa he issued it as secret intelligence for the benefit of higher unit commanders, commenting: "The brave ruddy-faced warriors with white silken scarves tied about their heads, at peace in their favorite planes, dash out spiritedly to the attack. The skies are slowly brightening.")

Interlude—The Kamikaze. *A certain amount of mystery attaches to the origin and development of this most spectacular of Japanese innovations in the war, in spite of all the elaborate examination of enemy documents and questioning of their officers that have taken place since. It was, of course, the logical outcome of the Koiso government and the strains that went into its formation. The nearest one can come to the specific process is that after the aerial disaster in the Battle of the Philippine Sea, Vice-Admiral Takejiro Onishi, who had been in charge of a carrier group during that disaster, reported to Toyoda that he wished to organize a corps of suicide fliers and to lead them himself. The matter was discussed at the Imperial General Staff, and while no decision was reached there, its officers were in frequent communication with the Philippine command, and Onishi himself was transferred thither in August. The first Kamikazes seem to have been organized by him there purely as a local and nearly spontaneous affair. When Admiral Kurita led his fleet to the Battle for Leyte Gulf, he did not even know of the organization or that he would have its help in the action.*

Once launched, the thing so exactly met both the needs of the military situation and the desire to find a means of bolstering a morale beginning to weaken under defeat that every Jap leader took it up with enthusiasm, and the home government backed it by an intensive propaganda campaign. During the Philippine campaign the organization and use of Kamikazes remained more or less localized; that is, the commander at a given air station would call for volunteers and, as soon as he got enough to form a unit, equip them and send them out. 650 Kamikazes went out during the campaign and 26.8 per cent of them secured hits, mostly on small ships. Official Japanese statements were, of course, that the number of hits was 100 per cent; actually their high command knew very little about the number of hits, and their guesses ranged from 12 per cent to 50 per

375

cent, but they erred badly in thinking that nearly all the hits were on major warships, battleships and large carriers.

By time General Cho reached Tokyo for his conference, organization had set in, all up and down the line, and there was a Kamikaze command in Tokyo under Vice-Admiral Ugaki, who worked his strategy into the general plan of campaign. He would order a local air group command to furnish so many suicide units for a prospective operation, just as he might order out the same number of dive-bombers. The air group commander, if he had not enough volunteers, then detailed some of his fliers to volunteer for suicide duty. In general, the better pilots were not allowed to become Kamikaze; and while in the Philippines, the very best and fastest bombers had been used, Ugaki's organization regarded this as wasteful, and began to employ all sorts of obsolete and obsolescent plane types, stripped of their instruments. A suicide unit normally contained six planes, and was led to its target by a well-equipped twin-engined bomber. The Kamikaze always had as much fighter cover as could be provided.

The Imperial Staff estimated the strength of the American Fleet as 18 carriers and a total of 86 battleships and cruisers, with another 30 of the latter to be ready by June. Quite clearly not even American production could keep pace with the rate of loss indicated by the report on the Philippines, and Okinawa was so much nearer to so many more airfields that much greater damage to a fleet in its waters could be achieved. It was therefore made a formal order that none of Ushijima's guns should fire on ships at any time. His duty was to hold out on land while the Special Attack forces wrecked the American Fleet.

In the remainder of his mission General Cho was not quite so successful. He wanted more troops and an improvement of the food situation but was told that the shortage of shipping prohibited either being sent to the Okinawa Gunto at the time. When Cho returned, Ushijima took his own measures to supply the manpower deficiency by conscripting the 7,000 best Okinawans into the Army, distributing them among the various units so that their general lack of a sense of nation and spirit of Bushido would have less effect. This brought his total muster rolls up to 83,999. Another 20,000 were organized as Home Guard Units, Boei Tai, but these were expected to be hewers of wood and drawers of water for the fighting troops except in emergencies. They ought to have sense enough to fire a rifle from a hill-cave slot.

On 23 March another intelligence statement of the general situation was distributed among the upper levels of the Thirty-second Army. It pointed out that there were now seven American divisions in the Marianas and that two or three more could be withdrawn from Luzon; that air attacks on northern Formosa and on Okinawa had become very frequent; that American submarines had appeared in significant numbers off southern Kyushu, all down the waters of the Ryukyu chain and around Formosa, while submarine activity in the Ogasawara Gunto had decreased. The conclusion was that an attack on Okinawa or Formosa was imminent. Apparently the Americans wished to signalize the coming conference at San Francisco in a spectacular manner. At this date practically all the fighting formations on Okinawa were well dug into their positions and many had prepared alternate caves for use in case they were driven from their first lines of defense.

The battle plan Ushijima issued did not look with favor on major counterattacks but prescribed infiltrations by night on a considerable scale, spoke strongly on the necessity of units not under attack reinforcing those actually engaged, and remarked:[1]

"You cannot regard the enemy as on a par with you. You must realize that material power usually overcomes spiritual power in the present war. The enemy is clearly our superior in machines. Do not depend on your spirits overcoming this enemy. Devise combat method based on mathematical precision; then think about displaying your spiritual power."

II

The fleet was under Admiral Spruance again with Richmond Kelly Turner as his chief of amphibs. Holland Smith was probably the logical man for expeditionary troops, but that command went to a new organization, Tenth Army. Its inception goes back to the Joint Chiefs of Staff in Washington and has slight overtones of what

[1] The text was originally issued by the Japanese 26th Division in the Philippines, but Ushijima consulted with the commander there, and later put it out as his own, so it is fair to attribute it to him.

had become of the controversy about the relief of the 27th Division's commander on Saipan. There was a certain amount of feeling in the Army that Army troops ought not to be under Marine command; and also a belief that an operation which involved a force two corps strong fell more legitimately in the province of the Army, even though its operations involved the establishment and extension of a beachhead.

Admiral Nimitz, whose method was always that of securing co-operation by the most generous concessions, agreed that Army should have the top command ashore. Hence there was produced the rather odd arrangement of a Tenth Army Command and Staff, with no experience at all in amphibious operations, placed over two corps organizations which were very experienced indeed. The corps concerned were the Army XXIV of Major General John R. Hodge, comprising the 7th, 96th, 77th, and 27th Divisions; and the III Amphib Corps under General Geiger, with the 1st and 2nd and the new 6th Marine divisions. The Tenth Army Command went to Lieutenant General Simon Bolivar Buckner, Jr., who had led the Aleutian campaign, a big man, strong on physical conditioning, fair-minded, and very decisive in his attitudes. He was a product of the complete Army system, Leavenworth and Staff College. The Marines found him rather strangely formal in his approach to the question of planning, which he handled, not in their free and easy conversational manner, but exactly as the book prescribes. The staff officers would come before him with a "presentation" of the problem; when they reached a point where decision was necessary, he would say "I decide —" and nothing could budge him from the decision thus made. No discussion.

The decisions he made with regard to the Okinawa operation (which the Joint Chiefs had chosen in preference to that against Formosa) were to land the 77th Division in the Kerama Retto on 26 March, securing this group as a seaplane base and anchorage that would protect the ships against the typhoons which haunt this region; to use elements of the same division for seizing the pair of small Keise Islands just west of Naha on 31 March and emplace heavy artillery there; to land on Okinawa itself on 1 April. The landing would be across the Hagushi beaches about 20 miles from the southern end of the island, just where General Ushijima thought the

Americans would come in. There would be four divisions abreast, the 6th and 1st Marine Divisions on the left, the 7th and 96th Army Divisions on the right. The central pair of these four divisions would cut rapidly across the island, severing the Japanese forces into two unequal parts. The III Amphib Corps would secure the big Yontan Airfield, then wheel leftward and clear out the larger, rougher northern sector of the island; the XXIV would take Katena Airfield, then wheel rightward toward the more populated southern sector of Okinawa.

The 2nd Marine Division to conduct a feint at landing on the southern beaches and remain in reserve afloat; 27th also to be in reserve afloat, and as soon as it had completed its job in the Kerama Retto, the 77th would act as a reserve ashore. Some troops from this reserve to take Ie Shima and Iheya Shima.

Intelligence believed the Japs to have approximately 66,000 men on the island, including two divisions slightly understrength, an Independent Mixed Brigade, and some miscellaneous troops. They would most likely defend the out-islands and the northern part of Okinawa with the Independent Mixed Brigade, the remainder of the troops being in the southern part of the main island. In view of Japanese doctrine and what the photos showed, the enemy were expected to defend the beach area with approximately a regiment in fortified positions, holding the bulk of their troops in mobile reserve.

There had been time for them to acquire the latest German doctrine of beach defense. The landing areas were expected to be heavily mined and strewn with obstacles of the most formidable type. They would probably counterattack not later than the night of landing day (L day), the early seizure of the Kerama Retto allowing them time to move their troops into readiness positions near the Hagushi beaches, which were obviously the only ones on the whole island suitable for a major landing.[1] This counterattack would be very dangerous, probably made by a full division on either flank of our beachhead, since the Japanese believed in the German doctrine of double envelopment. They were supposed to have a Shipping Engineer regiment on the island and it was likely that their counterattack would be accompanied by a counterlanding in our rear. The Navy could be expected to take care of most of the boats in such a landing,

[1] This was not true; but Tenth Army thought it was at the time.

but some might infiltrate through, and it was important to provide for the security of command and communications centers on the beach. There were known to be considerable formations of parachutists in Kyushu and the Japanese would undoubtedly use them as

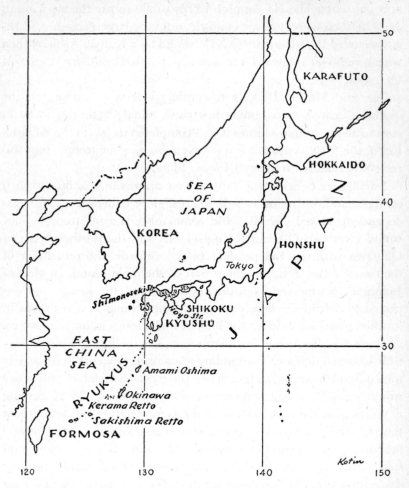

soon as they possibly could, being willing to sacrifice large numbers of planes to drop several thousand men behind our beachheads.

All four groups (each of four carriers) in Task Force 58 sortied from Ulithi on 14 March and stood up toward the Empire. They fueled on the 16th and on the morning of the 18th were near enough Kyushu to launch a strike mainly directed at the fields there, from whence might be expected the most serious opposition to the expedition, now that the Japanese were using Kamikaze in such numbers. During the night *Enterprise* launched out six planes on radar mission to simulate the appearance of a fleet 150 miles from the actual position of ours, but it failed to work: the Japanese found our ships and staged a heavy counterattack in which they made bomb hits on both *Intrepid* and *Enterprise*. The attacks on the field were a great success, though, with the claim, probably quite accurate, of 222 machines destroyed on the ground. In the air battles at sea and overland 306 more were shot down.

During the night the fleet pushed farther north and in the morning flew off strikes to take care of the remnant of the Jap Navy at Kure and Kobe. These attacks were not too successful, since Mitscher had to hold out so many planes for his combat patrols against Kamikaze. In the counterattack that day the ships took it hard—*Wasp* badly damaged by a bomb that went through her hangar deck and *Franklin* taking two terrible hits from a single plane that came through the clouds. Great sheets of flame swept through her hangar and across the flight deck, she had 1,102 casualties, her engine rooms had to be evacuated, she could not be steered, and steamed along masterless for hours. *Pittsburgh* and *Santa Fe* got her in tow and managed to save the ship and most of her people. The Marines at Ulithi saw her come in with the other damaged ships as they set out and wondered how such a wreck had been brought home.

It was not the only indication that the coming operation would be a rough one. The briefings on the way up were sober, to Army and Marines alike. All hands learned that they would have the support of the British Fleet for the first time in the Pacific war, two battleships and four of their armored-deck carriers going in against the Sakishima Islands which connect Formosa with Okinawa, while Spruance and 5th Fleet went back at the Kyushu fields and their supporting facilities. The men were told that for the first time we would be invading not Japanese-held ground, but genuine Japanese territory, where the natives would be as unfriendly as the country. That country was one of the less attractive islands of the world, not jungle indeed, but subject to torrential rains, overrun with insects, having most of the tropical diseases in endemic form, and one of the world's deadliest snakes, the habu. The last item caused as much

381

excitement as anything—unnecessarily as it turned out, since the only habu the Marines saw they caught, fried, and ate.

On 28 March news of battle began to come over the ships' radio. The 77th was ashore in the Kerama Retto, had swept out two of the islands and reduced opposition in the third to mop up. The seaplane base had been established, and among the coves of the islands the troops had found nearly four hundred suicide boats, little things about 20 feet long with built-in warheads. Most of them had been smashed in the air attacks that Mitscher's carriers had been putting on Okinawa and its vicinity ever since 23 March or in the heavy bombardment conducted by eight of the fast battleships[1] on the 24th. There was a cheering note in Mitscher's reports—air opposition was far less than anticipated, the strike of 18 March had evidently cut the Japs' aviation farther down than anyone had imagined at the time. The gunfire support ships of Admiral Blandy had arrived and were shooting, plenty of them this time, ten old battleships,[2] with eight heavy cruisers,[3] three light cruisers,[4] and twenty-four destroyers. The suicide boats had not bothered this armada in the least but Kamikazes coming out of the twilight had been a serious problem—*Nevada's* number 3 turret was knocked out, the minesweepers *Adams* and *Skirmish* were badly damaged, so was the destroyer *Kimberley.* Another destroyer, *Halligan,* and a minesweeper, *Skylark,* had run on mines and been blown all apart with heavy casualties. Rough work; and then Radio Tokyo came on the air with a "broadcast for you men standing off the shores of Okinawa, because many of you will never hear another program; here's some music to remind you of darlings, jazz, home, and mother."

That same day the fast carriers hit Kyushu and its fields once more, with fairish results. A hot little air fight accidentally developed when one of our pilots was shot down in Kagoshima Bay three miles from shore and a pair of our seaplanes came in to rescue him, each side feeding fighters in by small groups till it became a major opera-

[1] *New Jersey, Wisconsin, Missouri, Washington, North Carolina, South Dakota, Massachusetts, Indiana.*

[2] *Texas, Maryland, Arkansas, Colorado, Tennessee, Nevada, West Virginia, Idaho, New Mexico, New York.*

[3] *Tuscaloosa, San Francisco, Minneapolis, Wichita, Portland, Pensacola, Indianapolis, Salt Lake City.*

[4] *Birmingham, St. Louis, Biloxi.*

tion. Admiral Blandy expected suicide boats to become serious when the transports arrived, and set up "flycatcher" details of a cruiser and a destroyer each for night watch, with support from small gunboats, each detail having a section of coast under its care.

III

L day was Easter Sunday, also April Fools' Day—with a certain amount of appropriateness, since after all the ominous preliminaries and the eruptions of flame ashore, not a bullet nor a sound greeted

the amphitracs as they hit the beach at 0837. "There must be some mistake," wrote the correspondents getting reports aboard the flagship *Cambria*, and "This is hard to believe," wrote Sherrod ashore, when Yontan Airfield fell to the 4th Marines, with only a few shots from snipers and a casualty bill of two killed, nine wounded.

The correspondent found no one digging foxholes, the advancing troops everywhere standing up and talking; there were a few pitiful old Okinawans, undersized and emaciated. By afternoon the artillery was coming through and the divisional command posts with reserves, not because they were needed, but to clear the transports, since Kamikazes were expected with the twilight. By evening, when night guards were set, the lines were everywhere 4,000 yards deep, or at the point they had expected to reach by the third day, from which the men looked out to see the whole sky lit with antiaircraft fire above the rolling clouds of the smoke screen. The Kamikazes had arrived, not in great force, but one got through to crash *West Virginia,* another wrecked an LST, and that big burning flame was where the transport *Hinsdale* had been hit. Far to the south another group of suiciders had fallen on the British squadron, where they smashed up a destroyer, but when a second hit the armored flight deck of *Indefatigable,* the Britishers imperturbably swept the debris over the side and continued operations.

On the second day there was the same puzzling lack of strong centers of resistance ashore, the same sweeping advances everywhere, though now hampered by lack of roads across the ravines and razor-edged ridges of which central Okinawa is built. East of Yontan Airfield the 4th Regiment found a group of these ravines organized and defended. They had a hard little fight, for it was a puzzling problem how to get into the gullies with fire coming down from both sides and from the dominating massif above. Supply was already becoming a problem; no normal vehicle could negotiate the ground. The reconnaissance companies of all divisions were fanning out well ahead and reporting no serious contact. The 7th Division, which had a cross-island road, reached the east coast this day and on 3 April the 1st Marine Division was there also. The whole of the long Katchin Peninsula had been covered by the 1st's recon elements. The 6th was across the ridge line and working down the slopes with some elements, while others were sweeping up to the Isthmus of Ishikawa, which is the island's narrowest neck.

That day the XXIV Corps began to have casualties, and all the next three pushed slowly forward into the outer guards of Ushijima's line at 300-500 yards a day. The Army reserve of flame-thrower tanks was assigned to this corps on the 5th; on 7 April, General

Buckner gave them the III Corps Artillery and on the following day the heavy howitzers of the 1st Marine divisional artillery. The dog-faces were having a rough time down there. They had fought Japanese from the arctic to the tropics without finding any of them so well dug in, who used so much artillery with such accuracy.

All this while the 1st Marine Division was on duties mainly defensive in central Okinawa, the 6th was pushing north as fast as its supply trains would permit, and the main action was out on the rocking seas. The Imperial General Staff had launched the operation for which the Okinawa defense was planned—the great storm of Kamikazes to cripple the U.S. Navy. Combined with them was a naval attack, the last; since Leyte Gulf "there was no further use for surface ships except in special operations." The Kamikazes rendered this operation special; they were assembled in the Kyushu fields to the number of several hundred, six hundred, says one report, though the figure is not sure nor can be because the records are gone. The target of the naval Kamikaze was our major warships—"You will damage or sink twenty battleships and carriers" read the order from Vice-Admiral Ugaki, who had been placed in charge of both Navy and Army units "to produce a unified strategy."

Ugaki knew of the American weakness for escorting such damaged ships home instead of leaving them to their fate as the Japanese would do; calculated astutely that twenty damaged ships and their escort would so weaken our forces that the remnants of their own Navy could fight their way through and destroy the transports off Okinawa in co-operation with a second wave of suiciders, Army units. The date was to have been 8 April, but before that date, on the 4th, Admiral Spruance's snoopers had marked the assembly in Kyushu.

He looked at the air-strike reports; no B-29 had visited Japan's southern island for a fortnight, the last big air attack there had been Mitscher's strike of 18 March, so the enemy had been granted time to assemble. That night he turned prows north; at dawn on the 6th his planes were all over Kyushu, where they smashed up planes on the ground to a number estimated by the fliers as over two hundred, but considerably shaded from that by the Admiral, who knew how clever the Japs were at camouflage and building dummies.

The main feature was that there was an attack; of course the Jap

385

leaders had to launch their planes at once on local responsibility or have them killed on the ground, which brought it about that few of the Kamikazes had time for the farewell dinner and ceremonial drinking of sake. This also brought it about that, although they found our ships, the attacks were in succession and unco-ordinated, without the heavy fighter cover that had been counted upon to make them irresistible. Some 355 Kamikazes got off the ground; 248 planes were shot down, not all of them Kamikazes. Only four got near enough to do damage. Two of these exploded close aboard *San Jacinto* and the destroyer *Taussig.* The two direct hits were bad enough; the destroyer *Hainsworth* much wrecked, and the carrier *Hancock* taking one among parked planes on her flight deck that gave her eighty casualties, buckled her elevator, and holed the deck so badly she had to go back to Ulithi.

The Kamikaze for the beachhead ships had a longer distance to fly, therefore more time to form in the air, so they made their attack in better style. Admiral Turner had established destroyers equipped with special radar as warning pickets on 15 several stations, forming a circle of 35 to 75 miles with Bolo Cape as its center for reference purposes. The first news came from one of these, *Colhoun,* north-northeast of the island, at 1500. Forty to 50 planes were attacking *Bush,* the next destroyer in line westward, 10 to 12 attacking the destroyer next eastward, the whole air was full of bogies and the combat patrol in heavy action with another big group on its way south. *Colhoun* rushed to help *Bush,* but found her dead in the water and already sinking. The Japs came piling in on this new enemy uninterruptedly for twenty-five minutes. *Colhoun* shot down five but three more hit her and one penetrated so deep that the destroyer's back was broken and down she went.

The remaining Tokobetsu rushed on for Okinawa, losing heavily to our outnumbered fighters, reached the transport area about twilight, and raised pluperfect hell. Two big cargo ships were sunk with part of their loads and so was the fast minesweeper *Emmons.* The destroyers *Witter, Mullany,* and *Newcomb* were each hit by two suiciders and were just barely towed out. The destroyer escorts *Foreman* and *Fieberling,* the minesweepers *Defense, Devastator,* and *Recruit,* destroyers *Harrison, Howorth, Hutchins, Leutze, Morris,* and *Rodman* were all hit; *Hyman* was hit by one with a torpedo, and

386

another crashed through old *Maryland* so badly she had to be sent home for repairs. If half this damage had been distributed among the ships supporting the expedition there would have been difficulty ashore and there would have been a good deal more if Toyoda's naval attack had come off as planned, but the fact that Spruance had advanced the date on him did fatal damage to the scheme.

The battleships *Haruna* and *Nagato* and the cruiser *Oyodo*, which had suffered in the March raid, were not yet repaired enough to participate and American submarines and mines had closed Shimonoseki Strait, the western exit from the Inland Sea. The Japanese Admiral had only the giant battleship *Yamato*, the light cruiser *Yahagi*, and eight destroyers; and he had to come out through Hoyo Strait, south around Kyushu before turning west to run down the East China Sea. One of our submarines saw her; at 0300 Admiral Spruance was roused from sleep. "The *Yamato* is coming out, sir." He glanced at his chart; the carriers were nearest. "Tell Mitscher to go take 'em," and went back to his bunk.

The weather was bad and squally with low clouds, but strikes were launched from the task groups of Jocko Clark and F. C. Sherman [1] and about noon they fell on the Jap force, concentrating against the giant *Yamato*. When they took to the clouds again she had eight torpedoes in her and three heavy bombs; the accompanying destroyer *Kasumi* was gone. Half an hour later the planes from Radford's group [2] arrived; the largest battleship in the world took four more torpedoes and turned over. The cruiser *Yahagi* sank by the stern, the destroyers *Isokaze, Hamakaze, Asashimo* had disappeared, and the remaining destroyers of the attack force, all damaged, were hurrying back with what survivors they had picked up.

That night whatever Kamikaze could still be dredged from the Kyushu fields made one more effort, in which they managed to hit the destroyer *Gregory*, out on picket duty; but that was the end of the grand Kamikaze assault that was to break the American Fleet. It had done damage enough to appall people all the way up to the top story of our command and to bring down a censorship that was as stiff as anything used by the Japanese themselves for the conceal-

---

[1] Clark's group had the carriers *Hornet, Bennington, Belleau Wood,* and *San Jacinto;* Sherman's consisted of *Essex, Bunker Hill, Cabot,* and *Bataan.*

[2] *Yorktown, Intrepid, Langley.*

ment of losses. But planes and pilots were now gone, and so was all of the Japanese Navy that would ever take the sea under the Imperial standard.

Unfortunately our high command had no evidences that this was the major assault or that it would not be repeated indefinitely. How could we keep them from working up another like it? The Kyushu fields needed more attention. Representations were made to Pearl Harbor and back along the line; General Le May at Saipan somewhat reluctantly agreed to divert part of his B-29 force from their more important function of strategically bombing Japanese industry to that of keeping the Imperial kites in their nests. Those that did win free, 5th Fleet Staff decided, were making the old Jap error in attacking the radar picket line instead of ignoring them to come in on transports and cargo vessels. All the same, we would run out of destroyers in a hurry if the night of 6 April were often repeated. The picket stations must be strengthened. Admiral Turner assigned to each a pair of destroyers, with four LCS gunboats which, because of the heavy armament of light weapons these could carry and their low silhouette, made good close-in protectors.

Chapter 23

The Conquest of the North:
More Kamikaze

IT HAD BEEN INTENDED THAT THE 6TH DIVISION SHOULD PUSH north along the main bulk of Okinawa to the point where Motobu Peninsula juts northwestward, there securing artillery positions from which an attack on that mass could be supported. The 2nd Marine Division would then land, somewhere near the base of the peninsula, and clear it out. Three considerations interfered with this arrangement. The 6th had not yet sealed off the base of Motobu when the big drive of the Kamikaze pointed out the danger of keeping troops afloat (already on 3 April three transports bearing part of the 77th Division had been hit with the loss of a lot of equipment and one regimental staff nearly wiped out). The 6th itself had met far less opposition and had received far fewer casualties than expected. The country was so nearly roadless that it was doubtful whether the communications net would bear the weight of supporting two divisions in the north, which is to say that the Army did not want the 2nd Division ashore any more than the Navy wanted it on the water.

Accordingly on 9 April the 2nd Division was ordered back to Saipan to lie there in distant reserve and General Shepherd's troops of the 6th were ordered to finish off Motobu by themselves. Only the number of this division was new; we have met most of the troops before, its three infantry regiments being the 4th, made up of the old Raiders, the 22nd, which had been at Eniwetok and Guam, and the 29th, of which part had done time on Mt. Tapotchau of Saipan.

The commander of the peninsula was Colonel Takehiko Udo, nominally head of one of the infantry regiments of the 44th Independent Mixed. He had sited the best of his defenses to bear out-

389

ward against a landing from the direction of Ie Shima. He had a fairly strong group of Okinawan home guards and had organized them to conduct a guerrilla war among the ridges of the north, some in uniform, some without. The four midget submarines remaining at their base at Unten Ko he blew up; there seems to have been no fuel for them.

His defenses were concentrated on the 1,400-foot hill mass occupying the southern half of the peninsula (which is about as large as all Saipan) known as Mt. Yaetake. They were of the type designed by General Cho, with a command post very deep in, and one important addition not found in the south—corrals for horses, of which the Udo force possessed a considerable number, the best of all means of movement in that rough, rugged country. Yaetake is made up of a series of upthrust coral ridges, rising one above another to a pair of peaks. Just north of it a stream runs to the western shore to a place called Toguchi, with a small town, Itomi, near the headwaters of the stream and in shadow of Yaetake. Beyond Itomi and the stream another set of ridges occupies the northern part of the peninsula, curving slightly to the north at its center, so that a view from the stratosphere might show the general form of the mountains as a circle of a vast crater, with only the one break at Toguchi. It is heavily wooded with a species of pine; toward the main body of Okinawa a region of rice paddies runs down to the town of Nago, where there is an unimportant harbor.

Neither the disposition nor the strength of the Japs was known when the 6th pushed past Nago on 8 April, and not even the geography of the peninsula was known; nearly all of it had lain under cloud when the photos were taken from which our maps were made. General Shepherd planned to push tank-infantry groups of the 22nd Regiment up the western side of the main island to its tip, making short patrols inland; to bring the 4th similarly along the east coast, and with the 29th to wheel left against the hill mass of Motobu. The division Reconnaissance Company would feel around the edges of the peninsula to locate the main Jap concentration. The road situation was so bad that LSTs and amphitracs cruised along the shore to land supplies at every likely inlet. After Nago was taken it became a main base point.

The plan for the 29th was the 3rd Battalion to circle the south coast of the peninsula to Toguchi, while the 2nd Battalion moved north along the coast road to reach the northwest cape and the 1st Battalion waited in reserve near the center. The reconnaissance Company had been along the 3rd Battalion's road and found it clear except for mines, broken bridges, and gaps dug in the road where it circled the cliffs, which forced the company to leave its vehicles behind. The open character of the road was in fact an error; Colonel Udo's men had seen the scouts all the time, guessed what they were there for, and held their fire till bigger game came along.

By 8 April the 3rd Battalion had discovered that there were Japs in Yaetake; next night as it lay in bivouac around the deserted hamlet of Awa, heavy gunfire began to come down from the hills, but ceased when American artillery in the rear took up counterbattery. On the

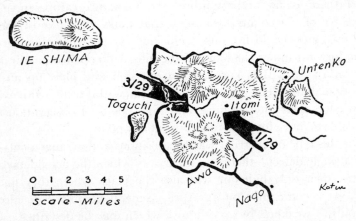

10th the battalion reached Toguchi in a pouring rain and tried to push into the hills eastward but was driven back by fire from the heights above whose exact source could not even be made out.

The discovery of Japs in the Yaetake mass brought the 1st Battalion, 29th, forward to Itomi on 9 April, with the tanks left behind because the bridges were all out, the road breached and covered with felled trees. The battalion encountered numerous little ambushes. Next day the two battalions tried to connect up via the Itomi-Toguchi road and stream valley, but the effort failed when both battalions encountered fields of fire from above to which they could

391

not even reply, and against which our artillery could give no help, since the guns had to shoot across a high hill mass toward our own troops. Another attempt to accomplish the same result, with a covering attack moving out of Toguchi into the hills, broke down under a vigorous counterattack on 12 April.

The estimate of Japanese strength at this time was 1,500 men, which we now know was far too low, but General Shepherd had a good picture of the character of the enemy he was facing and of the positions he occupied. Udo was in the Yaetake oval, with a few elements north of the Toguchi-Itomi road, exceedingly well supplied with mortars and automatic weapons, and he was a clever officer, making a passive defense, using his small force to pin down a much greater one, conduct guerrilla operations, complicate our supply problem, and hold ships in the offing for the Kamikaze to grind down. (Unless this matter of the Kamikaze be constantly kept in mind there is no understanding the Okinawa campaign.) The character of the country was such that tanks were almost useless. Our own guns could fire only from long range; when they tried to come forward under the loom of the hills, Udo opened counterfires, and on 13 April thus knocked out one gun and blew up an ammunition dump. The Japs thoroughly knew the trails, with which knowledge, their interior lines, and high points of observation they were able to move forces to meet ours at any point.

For this type of guerrilla war the positions and arrangements had only a single defect—there was no area to which the defenders could escape, their only hide-out was also the place where they had to fight. At a conference on 12 April, General Shepherd decided to exploit this weakness by an offensive which may be described as one of compression. A battalion of armored amphitracs was brought round by sea to Toguchi to give the battalion there some gunnery support. Two battalions of the 4th Regiment came over from the east coast of the island and worked round the southern shore of Motobu to hook up with 3/29 for an attack eastward toward the first of the rising ridges, while the other two battalions of Colonel V.F. Bleasdale's 29th Regiment were to move along the Itomi-Toguchi road, swing a little left into the ridges south of it, touch the Toguchi battalions, and drive the enemy into a narrowing V.

The attack was for the 14th; air support, artillery, and naval gun-

fire on call. The 4th Regiment crossed one ridge line before noon
without opposition. As they tackled the next rise they began to run
into small groups of machine gunners and riflemen beautifully disposed in pillbox and cave, supported by machine cannon and with

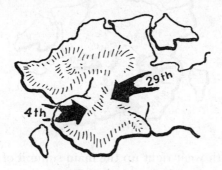

observation on every move our men made. Nevertheless the drive
went forward. By evening the 4th had gained its objective line and
was ensconced facing a deep valley. All would have been well had
the 29th made similar progress, but it had gained little and that
little off direction, to the southwest, with casualties the heaviest of
any day's fighting in the campaign. That night General Shepherd
replaced the 29th's command with Colonel W.J. Whaling, the scout-
sniper of Guadalcanal, who should be a good man among the continual ambushes of this mountain war.

For the following day the 29th was to cease trying to work along
the Itomi-Toguchi road, attacking southwest against the back slopes
of Yaetake, while the 4th, with its attached battalion of 29th, moved
against the summit of an eminence called Green Hill, just overlooked by the main Yaetake peak. 3/29 would move directly against
Green Hill; one battalion of the 4th slide rightward to get around
another crest, Hill 200, while the other assaulted it in front. The
fighting that day was as hard as any in the campaign and 3/29
stalled before Green Hill, where the Japs could fire on them from
reverse slopes, but the two battalions of the 4th gained the commanding ridge to the south of it and that night the Japs abandoned
Green Hill. General Shepherd sent the remaining battalion of the
4th up from Awa. The line was now a very deep horseshoe, with
the Yaetake crest in its center. Down underneath them the men of
393

3/29 could hear muffled explosions all night as Japs who had not been able to retreat from the caves blew themselves up with grenades.

On 16 April, 3/29 held position on Green Hill, while two bat-

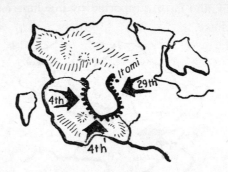

talions of the 4th went right up the main summit of Yaetake, across a slope of bare rock with mortar shells bursting on it, and gained the crest by twilight. The company up there had water but no food, was getting fire from several directions, and was forced to beat off a counterattack under the fading light, but it held. On the front of the 29th the advance went forward more slowly; there were still a good many pockets among the ravines by night. But the Jap position was now really broken; communication between the command and its units was lost and Colonel Udo was trying to set up a new head-quarters at Taira, north and east of the fighting area. One of his officers found him suffering from skin disease and quite weak. The remaining movements of the campaign have been described as the convulsions of a headless snake, but the figure is inaccurate; the fangs were still in the moving portion, and on 17 and 18 April (when Ernie Pyle was killed watching the 77th Division take Ie Shima) the 6th Division had casualties as heavy as any since they first began to encounter Udo.

Still, it was mop-up. The 17th saw the two regiments moving northward together to the Itomi-Toguchi road, the next day they crossed it and pushed through the rugged hills to the north coast, which was reached on the 23rd. The Marines had many strange encounters with groups of Japs organized and unorganized, found elaborate supply dumps in positions that might easily have held a division. The cost of the conquest had been 970 casualties to us; of the enemy 2,014 were found dead, a figure which does not include those who blew themselves up in caves, yet even so, fails to account for all the defenders of Motobu. The fact is that when the 29th's attack of 14 April failed to gain the road line and squeeze all the enemy into Yaetake, the way was left open for a considerable number of them to filter out like Udo and make for the northern island, where he expected to conduct guerrilla operations.

These did not turn out very well because Udo had either forgotten or had been unable to provide for the first necessity of guerrillas— that is, food. Getting something to eat became an overmastering necessity, groups could not hold together and the American patrols kept after them. After two little fights, one on the 22nd, when 100 of the enemy were killed, and one on the 26th, when 259 were knocked off, the whole affair sank to the level of beating out brigands who tried to get into our lines at night for a sample of "Roosevelt rations."

It had been a well-conducted little campaign, of a character as anomalous as anything in the larger operation which was made up of anomalies—mountain fighting by a force whose specialty was beach warfare. Some defects showed up in the process. The supply situation was never good, for instance, the Marines simply not being equipped to carry food and amunition into such country by any other means than on their backs. On the other hand, Marine drive again and again carried the men of the 6th to the crests of hills of which, once gained, all the elaborate system of entrances and exits only resulted in the enemy providing our riflemen with live targets; and every Japanese who survived remarked on the paralyzing violence of the Marine mortar fire.

II

Mimeographed sheet prepared at Colonel Udo's headquarters for distribution to American troops:

NEWS OF NEWS
No. I
Saturday, April 14

PRESIDENT ROOSEVELT DIED A SUDDEN DEATH

To the men of the 6th Marine Division!

We take it a great honor to speak to you for the first time.

We are awfully sorry to learn from the U.P. telegraph that the

395

*life of President Roosevelt has suddenly come to its end at 3.30 P.M.
on April 12. It seems to be an incredible story in spite of its actual
evidence.*

*Men of the 6th Marine Division, particularly men of the 15th and
29th Marines and the 3rd Amphibious Corps, we express our hearty
regret with you all over the death of the late President. What do you
think was the true cause of the late President's death? A miserable
defeat experienced by the U.S. forces in the sea around the island
of Okinawa! Were this not the direct cause leading him to death, we
could be quite relieved.*

*We do not think that the majority of you have exact knowledge
of the present operations being carried out by the U.S. forces although a very few member of you must have got a glympse of the
accurate situation.*

*An exceedingly great number of picked aircrafts carriers, battle-
ships, cruisers and destroyers held on her course to and near the sea
of Okinawa in order to protect you and carry out operations in con-
cert with you. The 90% of them have already been sunk and destroyed by Japanese Special Fighting Bodies, sea and air. In this way
a grand "U.S. Sea Bottom Fleet" numbering 500 has been brought
into existence around this little island.*

*Once you have seen a "Lizard" twitching about with its tail cut
off, we suppose this state of lizard is likened to you. Even a drop of
blood can be never expected from its own heart. As a result an
apopletic stroke comes to attack.*

*It is a sort of vice however to presure upon others unhappiness.
This is why we want to write nothing further.*

*It is time now for you, sagacieus and pradent, however, to look
over the whole situations of the present war and try to catch a chance
for reflection!!*

ARMY INFORMATION BUREAU OKINAWA

III

On the morning of 11 April an increase in the number of snoopers
around 5th Fleet, and the fact that it had been several days since the
Kyushu fields had a real going over, indicated another big Kamikaze
drive. The normal daily support missions over Okinawa were
dropped for the day and the fleet maneuvered at large, flying extra

combat patrols. Toward noon they began to come in, a few at first, dropping "window" to confuse our radar, then building up gradually, with heavy fighter cover. One just grazed *Enterprise,* the plane's bomb going off under the ship, with so much mining effect that the old veteran carrier had to return to dock; the destroyer *Kidd* was similarly mined by another near miss, and four more Kamikaze did some slight damage to *Essex, Missouri,* and the destroyers *Hank* and *Hale.* Twenty-nine were shot down; as night drew in more Kamikaze appeared, of which 18 were shot down in the Task Force.

It seems that Admiral Ugaki had had some difficulty mounting this attack, which was intended to fall simultaneously upon the fleet and the Okinawa anchorages. He had resorted to wide dispersion in Kyushu in order to keep away from our carrier-plane and B-29 counterstrokes, and this produced the result of so complicating the problem of fueling and arming the planes that not all the Special Attack units could leave together. It was accordingly the morning of the 12th before the remainder of the Kamikaze and 60 Tokobetsu of the Army force could shift the point of attack to Okinawa. There were a number of normal bombers in the sky, so the total force counted 165 suiciders with nearly as many of other types. They hit the picket line and fire-support group hard. The battleships *Idaho Tennessee,* and *New Mexico,* destroyers *Cassin Young, Purdee, Sigsbee, Stanly, Zellars,* minesweepers *Jeffers* and *Lindsey,* LCS 57, destroyer escorts *Whitehurst* and *Riddle,* all took suiciders aboard with damages described as major, which means that except in the case of battleships they had to go home and be practically rebuilt. Approaching the destroyer *M.L. Abele* a bomber launched from its underbody something like a winged torpedo which shot at the ship with a stream of smoke coming from its tail. It hit her amidships and blew up with a terrific explosion, breaking *Abele's* back so that she sank at once. Two of the LCS gunboats were sunk by Kamikazes, the minesweeper *Gladiator* and destroyer escort *S.S. Miles* were hurt, but less seriously. Normal bombers got hits on the cruiser *Oakland,* the destroyer escort *Wann,* and the destroyers *Brush, Conklin, D.W. Cummings,* and *Norman Scott,* but all these repaired their damage on station.

The failure of the Okinawa attack to co-ordinate with that against our fleet permitted heavy air patrols over the anchorage; 154 Jap planes were shot down. The thing that hit *Abele* was soon identified as a rocket-propelled winged bomb with a suicide rider; one was captured intact on Okinawa. It moved so fast as to be a singularly poor target for gunfire, but also so fast that the operator had only the slightest control and a well-handled ship could easily dodge; only one or two ships were hit after the first. The weight of the apparatus made its parent plane cold turkey for a fighter. Our people tagged the device, with a word borrowed from the Japs themselves, as the "baka"—foolishness bomb.

All scouting reports showed an amount of movement at the Japanese fields which indicated that this attack was only a first wave. Spruance took the fleet north again and on the 15th launched a heavy fighter sweep against Kyushu. It knocked down 29 airborne planes and the fliers claimed 51 grounded. The fighter sweep continued next morning, when 17 more Jap planes were shot down and another 54 destroyed on the ground, but that day Ugaki got this Special attack units away and this time really attacked both fleet and anchorage simultaneously. There were 155 Kamikaze and Tokobetsu together in the drive; they badly hurt the destroyer escort *Bowers,* the destroyers *Bryant* and *Laffey,* fast minesweepers *Harding* and *Hobson,* two LCS gunboats, and the oiler *Taluga.* The destroyer *Pringle* was sunk; the big carrier *Intrepid* got one through her flight deck that abolished everything in the hangar, smashed one of the elevators, and dished out the flight deck itself. She had to go home, but the Task Force considered the day a comparative success, having shot down 155 planes and destroyed 55 more on the ground. The landbased fighters from Yontan got 38 more.

Chapter 24

Sugar Loaf and Shuri: Hard Pounding

THERE SEEMS TO HAVE BEEN SOME QUESTION AT TOP COMMAND levels about this time as to whether it would not be better merely to run supply ships in for quick unloading and take them out again to avoid the Kamikazes which, if they were not whittling our fleet down as rapidly or as seriously as they hoped, were clearly beating up ships at a pace which the Navy could not support for long. One answer to this was that much of the damage was taking place on the picket line, without which there would be no radar warning for the forces ashore against attacks on their rear areas. Another, and the really operative objection, was that the demands of the Army on the ground were too nearly insatiable to be met by any program of touch-and-run supply, and somebody had to protect those cargo carriers moving in. By the third day of the invasion Yontan Field could take emergency landings, but it was a long way from this to the point where a self-sustaining air organization could be built up on the island, with shops, spare parts, dispersion areas for planes, and the planes themselves.

The first planes to reach the island were the fighters of Marine Air Group 31—94 day fighters and 15 night fighters, who came in on 7 April, and began to fly patrols at once. On the 9th, Marine Air Group 33 arrived with 96 more fighters. It was some weeks before Army fighters began to come in in numbers, and before there was any space to service their planes. This sounds like a lot of planes; but under the conditions of Okinawa, where air combat was almost continuous, with interludes of all-out battle, it meant that as many as 12 planes a day would be lost, either through mechanical action, accident, or mere deterioration. These would have to be replaced at

399

once, and with every replacement, every repair job, shopwork would become necessary. Normally the two Marine Air Groups together would be able to get about 66 operational fighters into the air for combat on short notice; and after every battle there would be a new replacement problem.

Air power, so very mobile tactically, is strategically one of the least mobile of forces unless it is based aboard a carrier. Even bringing in these limited aviation installations was a long and slow process while the Tenth Army was involved in a major campaign against what officers called "big Cassino" to indicate that the one in Italy had been only a comparatively minor affair. By 8 April the 7th and 96th Divisions were up against what they knew as the Machinato line, running east and west across the island from north of Machinato to the shore north of the town of Tomi, but which we now know was only the outer glacis of the great fortress whose citadel was Shuri. On 9 April the 27th, some of whose units had been conquering the out-islands to the east of Okinawa, began to move into line on the right, west, flank of the main island, with the 96th in the center of the 7th on the other wing.

The three divisions kept up steady pressure and by 15 April were ready to attack abreast except for one thing—not enough artillery ammunition, the final commentary on the necessity of keeping ships flowing into the landings, supplies across the beaches. Tenth Army, in fact, saw its problem as primarily one of artillery. On the front of the 96th they were finding it necessary to register individual guns on located machine-gun positions and fire enough rounds to get a direct hit. But when the infantry went forward they found all the guns in the flanks of the hills still alive and working, and were vigorously counterattacked from General Cho's lateral exits. There was later a 400-yard hill on this division's front, known as "the Conical"; two regiments would take two weeks to get past it. General R. O. Gard of the divisional artillery thought twenty-four hours of preparation fire would be too little against such a position, a figure like those from the trench-warfare front of Western Europe, 1916.

It was 19 April before the ammunition situation cleared up enough for the attack to be launched with artillery support not only from the XXIV Corps guns and those of Tenth Army, but all those of III Amphib Corps and the borrowed cannon of the 1st Marine Divi-

sion. By this date the third great Kamikaze attack had taken place
and Admiral Nimitz had come out in person, a good deal worried
over the way his fleet was being cut down. He, and not a few others,
would seem to have urged on General Buckner the desirability of another landing far enough south to get behind that ominous Shuri
system. The 2nd Marine Division was available, all the 77th Army
Division soon would be, and in a pinch the 1st Marine Division could
be used. Buckner said no; he had already examined the possibility
in that direction and had made his decision. There were practicable
beaches from Machinato down to Naha, but they were commanded
by the hills west of Shuri, where the Japs had abundant artillery of

every sort. General Bruce of the 77th had early suggested a landing
on the southeastern beaches, but Tenth Army found it could supply
food, but no ammunition, for such a move. True, that 2nd Marine
Division was available, but the best estimates showed that the beaches

at the southeastern tip would only handle a single division, there would be the same old problem of supplying it, the distance was too great for it to have any fire support from Corps Artillery north of Shuri, and (final argument) it would be facing all the Japanese 24th Division and most of the 44th Independent Mixed Brigade, since to date only their 62nd had been identified in the fighting. No; the extra landing was not practicable.

The attack went forward on the 19th then, the general plan being a double envelopment by the advance of the 7th and 27th on opposite flanks, while the 96th (which had come to the battle 1,000 men understrength and had already had 2,731 casualties) exerted lighter pressure in the center. There were twenty-seven battalions of artillery in support, in addition to the Navy ships off shore and a heavy preliminary bombardment, flown from the carriers; and the attack failed.

An abrupt ridge runs nearly across the island at this point, Kakazu. The left of the 27th and most of the 96th succeeded in gaining its crest, but it would take five days to clear it and the 7th Division could advance only 200 yards without having its flank fired into from this ridge. West of the ridge there was a fairly broad avenue of approach. Here a battalion of tanks led in the right wing of the 27th. Now, General Ushijima had issued, among other orders, one for concentration against tanks—"The enemy's power lies in its tanks. It has become obvious that a general battle against the American forces is a battle against their tanks." The Jap commanders at the front called down artillery fire on the infantry supporting the 27th's tanks and the foot was stopped cold. The crews of the tanks not hit abandoned their vehicles and ran. Ushijima, in close touch with the situation, promptly overruled his own rules to order a counterattack in so favorable a situation and every one of the tanks was captured and blown up, nearly sixty of them.

Later in the day the divisional infantry, under urgings from above, picked itself up and followed the retiring Japs into the town of Machinato, which looked good on the map but which really meant little, as this was ground undefended except by fire from the rear.[1]

[1] The episode produced a second 27th Division incident, with the relief of the only infantry regimental commander who had come through from Saipan, this time on Army, not Marine, inspiration. Most of the battalion com-

On the 21st, with everything at a standstill except the handwork on Kakazu, Tenth Army sent down an order to the III Amphib Corps to make available the tank battalion of the 1st Marine Division and the Japs began violently shelling our forward areas by night as a matter of practice. The order brought a protest from the Marines. The tank battalions in their organizations, they said, were not formations attached for a particular operation, but integral parts of the division, accustomed to working closely with a particular body of infantry, with whom they had developed those mutual understandings which so often render formal orders needless. To take these tankers away from the 1st would reduce the efficiency of both vehicles and infantry. In any case the need was not for tank crews, of whom the 27th still had plenty, but for tanks; could not the requirements be met from the corps reserve of spares and by salvage operations?

General Buckner agreed and the advance ground slowly forward —500, 400, 200 yards a day—into the outer Jap positions till 28 April when the 27th had flowed over most of Machinato Airfield, Kakazu Ridge was all ours, and the 7th Division had taken one of the most difficult cliff positions in the entire campaign. It had become clear several days before that any hope of a quick victory was gone; this would have to be an erosion attack. XXIV Corps now thought a landing in the rear of the Japs was possible and suggested using the two Marine divisions for the purpose, but General Buckner's staff still saw logistic difficulties in such an expedition. Moreover, the General wanted to get that 27th Division out of there and furnish relief for the 96th. Neither change could be accomplished if the Marines were used separately.

His plan was for a double envelopment of Shuri; on the 24th he had warned III Corps to make the 1st Marine Division available and had assembled Bruce's 77th in the rear areas. On the 30th the

---

manders were gone by now, too. It required a good deal of official butter over gaps of silence to render the matter palatable, including a statement from General Buckner that the 27th "have paid heavily and have shown lots of guts." So they did; but the loss of the tanks, the reliefs of officers, the fact that the 27th was in line less than two weeks tell the true story. True, the 27th had 618 dead; but the 7th had 1,500, was in line for over thirty days and did not have to be relieved; the 96th, a fighting division, had more dead than that, and after a very brief relief went right back in again.

1st Marine Division took over from the 27th and the 77th replaced the 96th, the relieved formations leaving their artillery in position. By this date XXIV Corps estimated the Jap dead as 15,865; there were 57 prisoners. Our casualties for the month, including those in the Navy and in the air, which the Japanese figures do not, were 34,279. Units of the Japanese 24th Division had been identified in line, opposite our 7th.

It was thus a new campaign, and in more than one sense, for although there had been a continual dribble of Kamikaze attacks, there were no more large efforts until Admiral Ugaki poured his suiciders down in an assault on a new system on the night of 27 April,[1] continuing till the morning of the 29th. He could only assemble 65 Kamikaze and 50 Tokobetsu. A cargo carrier was sunk; the transport *Pinckney,* the destroyers *Haggard* and *Hazlewood* and the APD *Rathburne* on the picket line received home-port damage from Kamikaze, as did the destroyers *Daly* and *Twiggs* with the fleet, while the destroyer *Ralph Talbot* was badly bombed and *Hutchins* holed by a suicide boat. Six destroyers—*Bennion, Brown, Butler, Hickox, Shannon, Wadsworth*—and a destroyer escort, *England,* had lesser hurts; but what chiefly excited indignation in American ranks was that a Kamikaze crashed into the side of the white-painted, brightly lighted hospital ship *Comfort* lying out at sea. This was all bad enough, but it now seemed evident that the conscientious work done in the air and on the Kyushu fields was beginning to bear fruit, for the whole attack did not count much over 200 planes, of which a number were patched-up old trainers, and there was a noticeable decline in the quality of the Jap piloting. The fleet shot down 118 in this bout; planes from the Okinawa fields got 35 more, and antiaircraft batteries around the fields another 5. For the month of April the fleet had 1,298 Japanese planes to its credit.

III

Since General Rupertus died the 1st Marine Division had been under Major General Pedro A. Del Valle, the artilleryman whose guns saved Guadalcanal. He was a Puerto Rican, who had been

---

[1] On the 18th *New York* took a Kamikaze aboard; on the 22nd the destroyer *Hudson* had been badly hurt by a bomb and *Isherwood* by a Kamikaze; the same day the minesweeper *Swallow* was sunk.

through Annapolis and worked his way up to this command on sheer furious drive; had been with the Italian Marshal Badoglio as an observer during the conquest of Ethiopia; was active, excitable, very quick of mind. His regimental commanders were Colonel K. B. Chappel for the 1st, which took over the right of the line close to the shore, Colonel John H. Griebel, whose 5th Regiment moved in next to the 77th, and Colonel E. W. Snedeker of the 7th, in reserve. The objective was the Asa Kawa, a stream which slants northwestward between bluffs from the nub of the island around Tametamo's Castle.

In its original position the division was well forward on the right along the southeast-facing slope of the low ridge that holds Machinato Airfield, just short of the Village of Nakanishi, which lies in a valley between the airfield and the next upthrust of the ground. The attack opened at 0930 on 2 May, the heaviest effort on the extreme right to get round that next ridge and work eastward up the north bank of the Asa. As soon as the turning point was reached heavy fire came down onto the flank from the south bank of the Asa and onto its front from Shuri Ridge; 200 or 300 yards was all that could be made this day. Next morning both regiments attacked again, with the 3rd Armored Amphitrac Battalion lying offshore to give fire support for the 1st Regiment's right. There was some gain here and the 5th in the center made all of 500 yards, but the left wing of the 1st was held up in a heavy street fight for Nakanishi Village. The veterans of the 1st were finding it the same kind of work as against Bloody Nose on Peleliu, with extra Japanese refinements, the chief of which was the enemy employment of artillery. Americans had never seen the Japanese use it on so large a scale or so effectively. They still avoided concentrating fires in our fashion, but their guns shot all the time and they had the ground thoroughly registered. They combed over all possible lines of approach and the rest areas where troops in reserve were waiting, so that the men in these positions took almost as many casualties from shells as those at the fighting front from mortars and small arms.

That night, 3 May, the Japanese bombardment rose in a crescendo and spread all along the line till XXIV Corps estimated the enemy had fired not less than 7,600 rounds. At the same time a night air battle broke out toward the north; planes began to drop bombs near Yontan Field and ships vaguely outlined by star shell began to move along the water, as our destroyers went into a perfect passion of firing. It was, in fact, a major counterattack, the first, last, and only one launched on Okinawa; ordered from and supported by Tokyo. The Empire's part was a big drive of Special Attack units, this time exclusively against the offshore shipping.

The air part had 75 Navy and 50 Army suiciders in it; there were almost as many fighters and bombers. On the picket line no fewer than six Kamikaze crashed *Aaron Ward;* it was a miracle she was not sunk. The destroyers *Little, Luce,* and *Morrison* were sunk, with three LSMs. More Kamikazes badly damaged the cruiser *Birmingham* and the destroyers *Ingraham, Macomb* and *Shea*; the escort carrier *Sangamon* was so much hurt she was found not worth repairing when they towed her home. Lesser damage was done to the minesweeper *Gayety,* the destroyers *Bache, Gwin, Hopkins,* and *Lowry,* and to the seaplane tender *St. George.* A suicide boat got one cargo carrier and for this the Japs paid with 98 planes shot down by our carrier patrols and 50 over the island.

Ushijima's part in the operation was ingeniously organized; it was intended to retake Katena Airfield and all the areas up to it. He had brought a good part of his undamaged 24th Division into line and launched it with tanks down the slopes against the right flank of our 7th Army Division, while nearly a battalion attempted a counterlanding in that division's rear. Along that eastern side of the island the barges were discovered early and cut to pieces by our ships. Only 20 men reached shore and these were shot down in a hurry, while the 7th beat off the inland attack with losses that amounted to about a third of the Japanese 22nd Regiment.

On the 1st Division's flank some 500 Japs did get ashore in another counterlanding at the Village Kuwan, just behind the 1st Regiment's front line. But these attackers had no luck at all, for they had reached ground just at the edge of the area where the 3rd Armored Amphitracs were bivouacked. The infantry companies at the beach formed line along the first high ground and held. The armored amphibs came in and pinned the Japs down with fire; General Del Valle sent a battalion from the 7th Marines to help and by noon the 500 were wiped out. A smaller band reached shore well back, near the division CP, but the ordinary security detachment took care of them, capturing several, who proved to be armed with demolition charges and instructions to blow up command and communications centers, but above all, tanks.

The morning of 4 May, Army had reached the decision to swing the 1st Division southeastward against the ground that was dominating the coastal flats and to insert the 6th Division on the right for a swing across the Asa Kawa, beyond which the island widens westward. The attack of that day was delayed only one hour by the hullabaloo during the night and did pretty well on the left flank, gaining the north bank of the Asa Kawa for a distance of some 1,000 yards. In the center both the 5th Marines and 77th Division were up against a system of ridges north of Dakeshi Town, the Army men astride the main keel of the island. The going was slow against extensively organized positions; the 1st Division could not take the ridges by up-and-over assault, but must pivot round each and work up the valleys between, against fire from both flanks and ahead.

Ushijima renewed his counterattack on the night of the 4th, striking hard both against the joint where the 77th met the 1st Marine Division and that where it bordered the 7th Army Division. The attacks were beaten off with losses so heavy that it now seemed even to General Buckner and his staff that the enemy were in a state of exhaustion that would permit a landing on the south coast.

It was, of course, impossible for another reason: that all our available troops had been committed. III Amphib Corps was assuming control of the west end of the line, the 6th Division moving on 6 May, leaving behind it road signs;

MARINES AND JAPS THIS WAY

——————————————————————→

27th DIVISION AND USO THIS WAY

←——————————————————————

All that day and the next were consumed in arranging the right flank while the 1st Marine Division and the 77th ground away slowly along the approaches to Dakeshi. It rained so hard on 8 May that tanks could not be used and the 1st did not actually take Dakeshi Town till the 12th, when it was a little ahead of the 77th, which was having trouble with the most difficult terrain of all. By this date the 96th had replaced the 7th Division and was making good gains east of Shuri. The 1st Marine Division lines were now somewhat in the form of an L, and with tunnel exits along flat and riser, this seemed to Ushijima favorable opportunity for counterattacks. He launched a whole series of them, in strength from a platoon to a company; got some of his ground back and inflicted fairly heavy casualties in exchange for we do not know how many of his own. Now the 7th Regiment had to attack leftward against the high ground flanking any further advance by the division, while the 77th worked along the main ridge of the island and the 96th attacked its Conical Hill west of Yonabaru Airfield.

The advance in the center was working into the main Shuri defenses and gains were measured in yards a day. The supply situation was bad in all units for lack of roads and the continual Jap artillery fire along possible routes. The terrain in the center was impassable to tanks; nothing could solve the problem of counterattacks from the tunnels but hand-to-hand fighting. By 17 May the 1st and 77th were at the foot of opposite sides of the ridge that rises to Shuri; but on the 20th, the 96th had taken Conical and was able to support the 77th with some fire from the flanks. A new scheme of maneuver was set up.

This was partly the result of the gains by the 96th, partly that of the work of the 6th Marine Division, which had been fighting its own private war along the western shore. When General Shepherd's troops went into line on 8 May it was already evident that Ushijima's positions consisted essentially of a series of spokes radiating both down and outward from the hub at Shuri. This was the reason General Buckner had adopted the double envelopment plan; any attempt to pierce the center would have come under converging fire from the spokes, impossible to bear. But it must always be remembered, with regard to the spoke-lopping operations of the 6th and 96th, that they were under distant observation from high ground at the center of the web as well as from the spoke directly in front of them at the moment. This observation was accompanied by accurate and persistent mortar and artillery fire which bore with special weight on the areas normally considered "safe"—command posts, communications centers, supply echelons. In addition the 6th had Machinato Airfield in its immediate rear, with good beaches; it was always necessary to provide guards against a renewed counter-landing.

These were the conditions under which the 6th prepared to cross the Asa Kawa on 10 May. The river and its drainage system form a bowl with one bite out of the lip at the sea. The stream itself was too deep for fording and patrols found the bottom too soft for heavy vehicles. Colonel Merlin M. Schneider's 22nd Regiment (the division had yet so narrow a front that only one regiment could operate) had the job of forcing the passage. The engineers set up a footbridge during the early night; the plan was to pass two battalions across it, send one to ford the upper part of the stream, seize the high ground on the south side of the bowl and set up a bridge that would bear heavy traffic. The movement started at 0330. Two companies only had passed the footbridge when a Jap suicide squad blew it and themselves up, but one of the bridge battalions took a detour to the fordable upper part of the stream and by daybreak six companies were in line and launching an attack on the southern hills.

They did not get far. There was an elevation on the sea face and from this, as well as from the high ground ahead and inland, artillery fire of all calibers increased steadily with the light. By noon the advance was only 150 yards; by twilight 350. There was a lack of fire from close supporting weapons, as tanks. During the night, with shells dropping all round them, the engineers got up a Bailey bridge. It was finished by 1000 of 11 May, the tanks poured across, and after a hard fight with the help of a cruiser in the offing the ridges round the Asa bowl were won.

IV

That day out on the ocean the Kamikazes came back. All night snoopers had been around both our fleet and the British down off the Sakishimas. With day the attack came screaming in, 70 Kamikaze and 80 Tokobetsu against our ships, about as many against His Majesty's. Of the latter the carriers *Victorious* and *Formidable* were hit; their own hard decks bore the shock well but plane operations were kept down to almost nothing. In our fleet two Kamikazes hit Mitscher's flagship *Bunker Hill*; she was a dreadful wreck, with over 400 killed. The destroyers *Evans, H. W. Hadley,* an LCS, and the battleship *New Mexico* (again—unlucky ship!) were also much damaged, but at the anchorages only one cargo carrier was hurt and she not badly. The carrier air patrols and those from Yontan worked well together that day, the former knocking down 72 planes, the latter 19 before any considerable number of suiciders could get in. Lieutenant General Sugawara, of the Army Special Attack units, complained bitterly that the efficiency of his planes was much reduced because he could not get gasoline for them; the railroads were being constantly bombed by the Americans. Admiral Ugaki, he said, must see to it at once that the American carriers were driven from the region.

The 22nd Regiment was now on high ground in the center with its right still held by the ridge near the sea and its left by a long upslope. It went forward on 12 May, slowly, for even the high flat ground was all eroded into little draws that held tombs which were the exits from tunnels. At 2000 that evening General Shepherd had decided to put in a battalion of the 29th on the left flank and make the main advance there. From the battalion commander a note arrived, saying that he had encountered a big hill, caved and tunneled, where three tanks had been lost.

V

The hill had no name at that time, but it would have a grim one not long later; for the 6th Division was up against the Sugar Loaf, main western anchorage of Shuri line, where there took place a combat not exceeded for closeness and desperation by that at the Conical or Shuri Castle itself or Iwo Jima or any other. The Japs had fed the 44th Independent Mixed in to help what was left of the 62nd Division in this area. They were fresh troops, and in this part of the brigade, unlike the elements encountered in the north, there were few or no Okinawan conscripts. Sugar Loaf itself was only the outer bastion of a general position which denied our forces not only access to the rear of Shuri, but also to the river Asato and the harbor and city of Naha; hence its careful organization.

About 300 yards long, it rose abruptly from the slightly tilted plain which lay completely open. 200 yards south and slightly east of Sugar Loaf was another hill, the Horseshoe, with its convex side toward Sugar Loaf, and east of both a third, much larger, and slightly higher eminence called the Half Moon, which is not really a half moon at all in trace, but more like a capital H with the left leg bent. All three had received the personal attention of General Cho and were more elaborately tunneled than most hills on Okinawa. It will be clear from any consideration of the supporting Horseshoe and Half Moon hills that their convolutions included reverse slopes from which mortars could bear on the Sugar Loaf without themselves being subject to any form of attack till Sugar Loaf itself were taken and our infantry could deal with them by grenade. Beyond Half Moon the ground rose rapidly leftward to Shuri in the 1st Division's zone.

Against this Sugar Loaf position the 22nd Regiment was launched

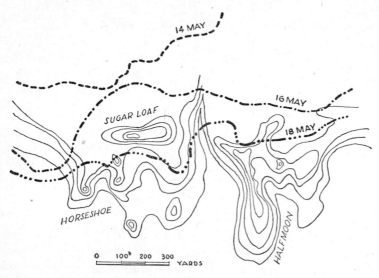

on the afternoon of 14 May, with tanks working around both flanks of the hill in support and one company each against the lower flanking eminences. The armor ran into heavy 47-mm. fire from Horseshoe and the Half Moon; part of it was disabled, the rest driven off. Three times one company reached the Sugar Loaf crest; three times they were beaten back by mortar fire from the supporting hills which the flanking companies could not approach. After dark Major H. A. Courtney, the battalion exec, detected signs of an imminent counterattack that would have been extremely hard to handle. He rallied the 20 remaining men of the company with 25 others from a supply echelon, rushed the summit once more, instructing his men to throw grenades as rapidly as possible and dig in under cover of the

411

explosions. They made it and held the crest all night; the Jap counter was completely broken up by their close-range grenading. Courtney was killed (they gave him a posthumous Medal of Honor); in the morning one officer and 19 exhausted men, all that were left of them, had to be withdrawn.

Colonel Schneider of the regiment nevertheless planned to drive home again next morning against Sugar Loaf, while General Shepherd of the division would take some pressure off him by putting in the 29th against the Half Moon on the extreme left of the divisional area. The 1st Division beyond was still held up by the broad, but high-rising gulch called Wana Draw, its sides fortified and overlooked by the guns of Shuri Castle.

The force of the Sugar Loaf position was now pretty well understood on our side, and the preliminary artillery fire for the 0800 attack, though scheduled for only fifteen minutes' duration, had not only the 6th Division's own guns in it, but also those of the Army 249th Artillery and some big pieces belonging to corps, emplaced farther back. This fire produced an unexpected dividend. General Ushijima, or Suzuki of the 44th Independent Mixed, had thought when the remnant of the Courtney command was driven down Sugar Loaf, that it was another chance like that offered by the 27th Division on 19 April and a strong local counterattack was ordered. The American artillery preparation caught these counterattackers just emerging from their holes, pinned them down, killed a good many, and took all the verve out of the movement.

With Japanese persistence the 44th Independent Mixed tried their attack anyway as soon as the fire let up, heaviest in the center against the exhausted 2nd Battalion, 22nd, but also spreading along the line to include part of the area where the 29th was working forward slowly under intense fire. The Japanese had withdrawn from some of the forward hill faces on that front to let their flanking guns fire in enfilade from the ridges the 1st Division had not yet succeeded in gaining. Attack and counterattack swayed back and forth till noon and later; by that time the 22nd had lost a couple of hundred yards, the 29th had gained maybe 700, and on both sides the men in the offensives were fought out. As soon as it grew dark enough to force our observation planes back to the fields, the Japs as usual opened up with all the guns and mortars they had, under

412

which fire 2/22 was relieved by 3/22. More companies of the 29th were moved in, and preparations were made for a general assault by the two regiments against the Sugar Loaf-Half Moon complex, in which Sugar Loaf was to be attacked simultaneously from front and both flanks.

That day, 16 May, was the toughest of the whole campaign; the attack failed and under appalling casualties. The encirclement from the west was stopped by the fire from Horseshoe where there were still antitank guns in force. At the center the crest of Sugar Loaf was reached and on the left the outer peaks of Half Moon, but from these points not an inch of progress could be made. General Suzuki had moved nearly all remaining of the 44th Independent Mixed into the firing positions and from them mortar shells fell continuously into the hilltop foxholes, while every minute down into the twilight, the guns of Shuri poured more shells from the left rear. By night all the advance elements had to be withdrawn with no real gain reported for the day.

What was now to be done? Renew the attack; this time with the 29th carrying the ball in an effort to win the Half Moon and flank out the heaviest of the firing positions supporting Sugar Loaf, while the exhausted 22nd held its lines. *Colorado, Mississippi,* and *New York* were moved in to fire support from their big guns; the carriers flew strikes with 1,000-pound bombs against Half Moon, and under cover of support fires closer than they had been since Iwo Jima, the regiment worked forward into the northern bowl of Half Moon and scaled the precipitous crest. The men were getting a lot of fire from Shuri behind them and more from the Horseshoe; and as soon as they were on the upper slope of Half Moon they were violently counterattacked from the lateral galleries and thrown off. They attacked again; were again counterattacked; and it was not until the fourth attack in the twilight that the Japs would let them stay.

By this time the ammunition of the spearheading company was exhausted and it had so many wounded that there were not enough whole men left to get them to the rear. The crest had to be abandoned; our men now held only that northern bowl of the Half Moon. But the Japanese positions had been in fact fatally shaken, for that bowl and its adjacent caves were the most effective of the firing positions from which Sugar Loaf had been supported, and in Sugar

Loaf itself the defending force was so cut down by casualties that the commander there doubted whether it could stand another day's fighting.

In this desperate case General Suzuki assembled what reserves he had behind Horseshoe and Half Moon and, as soon as dusk removed our observation planes, boldly launched them across the open to the rescue of Sugar Loaf. The inching advances had now given our forces enough points to permit ground observation, the Japs were detected forming and the fire of no fewer than twelve battalions of artillery came down redly on them in the early dark. This concentration blew the reinforcement attempt all to bits; it is doubtful whether more than a dozen men reached their destination. When the 29th attacked again on 18 May, tanks leading around both sides of Sugar Loaf, they broke through, and the long-contested hill was taken. It had cost the 6th Division 2,662 killed and wounded; the number of shells fired by the divisional artillery was 92,560.

VI

The height on which Shuri stands thrusts a long curved finger out to the northwest, on the north slope of which lay that Dakeshi Town for which the 1st Division had fought so hard. South of it stands another ridge, whose southern face bore the town of Wana with Wana Draw below it; and the ridge beyond, culminating eastward in Shuri itself, is that on whose outer tentacles the Sugar Loaf positions had been organized. It may be called Shuri Ridge. While the 6th had been engaged in its climactic struggle for Sugar Loaf, the 1st Division was attempting to negotiate this Wana-Northern Shuri position, with the 7th Regiment in line on the left, the 1st on the right. The battle was less desperate than that of the 6th Division only because the surrounding conditions did not permit it to have the same character. On the front before Sugar Loaf there was no cover; no matter how heavy the supporting fire, a moment arrived when men had to stand up and run across naked ground into a level stream of bullets. Where the 1st Division was fighting there was all too much cover except in Wana Draw itself. It was never quite possible to tell whether a given little depression in the almost-vertical rock wall was a good spot to take defilade from fire, or the outer slant of one of

414

General Cho's rifle slits, or merely a spot on which a gun above or to one side had been registered. The concerted rushes and stands against counterattack that marked the action of the 6th did not happen here. The whole battle was a series of individualistic bushwhacking encounters between units as small as a single fire team and Japanese who behaved in quite as independent a manner.

Technically the attack of the 7th Regiment was directed at first against the north face and crest of Wana Ridge. The 1st Regiment was trying to work eastward up Wana Draw to gain the north face of Shuri Ridge. Actually, both regimental commands operated chiefly as administrative organizations, which could do little more than assign a general direction of attack to their subordinate units. On 15 May the 5th Regiment passed through the 1st and took up the work against Wana Draw. Here tanks could be and were used, but slowly, every hundred feet of ground had to be combed over, the cave entrances sought and sealed—and all the while, fire came down from above.

In this type of fighting the western edges of Wana Draw were won by 17 May and the 7th Regiment gained the crest of the ridge above. Their presence there was one of the reasons why the 6th Division's assault out southwestward carried Sugar Loaf the next day; the defenders of Shuri had too much to do in their own front yard to think about helping units on their flanks, even with fire. On 18 May the whole line heaved forward again, the 7th capturing a regimental command post. On the 19th the Japs counterattacked the 7th all day long from their lateral tunnels, taking heavy casualties in the process, and that night the 1st Regiment went back into line to relieve the 7th. On 20 and 21 May the division cleared Wana Ridge, gained the little town that was the northern outpost of Shuri and came up against a narrow neck of high ridge. Beyond, Shuri Castle itself looked down. That day the division tried to work formations across Wana Draw onto Shuri Ridge, failed to do so, and was preparing for another try the following morning.

On the east side of the island the 7th Division had just broken through along the shore at Yonabaru; it was getting heavy resistance from the hills to the south of the break-through line, but only put out security detachments in that direction, wheeling the main force of its drive rightward, with the 96th Division on its own right, up against the main Shuri mass on that side. The design was to pinch out the 77th, which had been long in line, done much hard fighting, and needed relief; but that night it began to rain.

It is an open question whether Okinawa, Eritrea in Africa, or some place in the Belgian Congo has the highest humidity in the world over a year's run, but there is no doubt that the island of the Ryukyus can put on a spectacular rainfall performance over a brief space—as much as nine inches a day. The rainy season had now arrived; and all the other rains seen by Americans on Okinawa, though heavy enough, were reduced to the status of Scotch mist. In the ordinary fields mud became ankle deep; on the alleged roads it was up to the knee and even amphitracs had difficulty. Fires could not be kept up for coffee or hot food. On the eastern flank of the island, where supply lines for the Army troops had to run back across the made tracks through the vertical ridges, it became next to impossible to keep up with the ordinary logistic requirements for a static situation, to say nothing of handling the vast quantities of extra food, ammunition, and evacuations demanded by an all-out attack.

Only on the front of the 6th Division, which had the most direct supply lines, was there much action during the week of rains that supervened. During the night of 18-19 May Suzuki made repeated counterattacks in an effort to regain his Sugar Loaf. Next morning General Shepherd moved in the 4th Regiment, his last reserve, to the relief of the 29th. The main weight of the attack was against the western flank. It early won the western eminence of Horseshoe and the Marines could look down into the mortar positions that had beaten at them for so long.

This meant the jig was about up for the anchor position on the left flank of the Shuri line and no one was better aware of it than General Mitsuru Ushijima, for those protected fire positions on Horseshoe were the soul of his defense. If they were knocked out, our forces could get down into the Kokuba River valley, follow that corridor eastward to the rear of the Shuri positions, perhaps hook up with the 7th Division and surround the bulk of the Japs in their castle. The General issued preparatory orders for the evacuation of the Shuri position, but in the meanwhile called on the Naval Guard force covering the big Naha Airfield on Oroku Peninsula for a battalion to be used in a suicide attack. Rear Admiral Ota, in command

416

of the Naval Guards, did not take at all kindly to this idea, and went so far as to radio a protest to Tokyo, but Ushijima outranked him and there was nothing to be done about it.

The battalion marched then, and was launched in attack at 2130, small groups at first, building up to the crescendo of a full-scale assault under mortar cover. It was a true banzai and, like most of them, accomplished exactly nothing; in the morning there were nearly five hundred bodies on the ground before the 4th and the Japanese resistance was broken. All the next day was spent in reducing the tunnels of the Horseshoe and by twilight that ridge was ours. Over on the left flank of the attack the Half Moon still held out, nor could even the fresh regiment reach its crests because of the fire from Shuri falling onto our men's rear. That day, 21 May, General Shepherd made the command decision to set up a defensive flank on the outer, western slope of Half Moon, swing his weight rightward, across the Asato, and clear out Naha City, for whose northern flank the river formed a moat.

The next day was spent in closing up to the stream; on that night, under the first heavy rain, patrols pushed across. They found surprisingly little resistance among houses reduced to debris, and this gave General Shepherd the idea that the place might be taken without the help of tanks, which were in any case now too much mired down to be used.

By noon the 4th was wading the stream in the little groups of an infiltration attack. Within the city there were only snipers, but just east of the place is a ridge running north and south, separating the town from what an Okinawan would consider the elegant suburb of Machishi, and this ridge was tunneled in the usual fashion. A good deal of fire issued from it, and most of the 4th was gradually drawn into a contest that was not terminated in their favor till 25 May, for although the enemy were now too weak in manpower to use the elaborate positions with the greatest effect, General Mud stood their aid. In the meanwhile the 29th Regiment was brought into Naha and gradually cleared it out. By 29 May the town had fallen, the division was in line facing southeastward and pushing up the peninsula between the Asato and Kokuba.

On that same day both the 1st Division and XXIV Corps had planned to renew their assault on Shuri. For the last two or three

417

days there had been indications that the Japs were abandoning their castle under cover of poor flying weather and our inability to move tanks in rapid pursuit. Little groups of them appeared on the roads and were taken under fire; the shooting of their own guns showed a diminuendo. 29 May broke bright and clear for a wonder and at 0730 the 5th Marines jumped off in attack through mud only beginning to congeal. Now, during all those days of rain the 1st Division had been patrolling energetically, mainly in a southerly direction, and every patrol had taken fire from its left and rear, the eminence on which Tametamo's castle stood. The castle was in the 77th Division's zone, but the 1st Battalion, 1st, and its Reconnaissance Company pivoted round toward the place from a direction almost due south to get rid of that pestiferous fire. The head of the Reconnaissance Company got into a tunnel; its security detachment had just set up a machine gun above when down trail came marching sixty Japs who all fell down in three neat rows when the gun opened fire. They were the last organized group in Shuri; the 1st Battalion burst in and the long fight was won. The men of the 77th, whose attack was planned for later in the day, were more than a little annoyed.

Chapter 25

Last Stand

As early as 18 May when the fall of the Sugar Loaf and the Conical left his flanks substantially in air, Ushijima's staff had begun to draw operation plans for a general retreat and to move the service commands, with such items as files of correspondence and the Okinawan women who served the convenience of the officers, into the southern tip of the island. There is an escarpment there, a somewhat aberrant geological formation, jutting across Okinawa where it narrows toward a point after throwing off the Oroku Peninsula to the west and the Chinen Peninsula eastward. It rises just south of the town of Itoman on the west coast, the line of hills running through Yuza, just missing the town of Tomui and slanting down the east coast. All this area had been fortified by the 9th Division while it was still part of the Okinawa command, a job well done, like everything else by that division. In this area the Japanese General proposed to make his final stand.

The movement of troops and of such guns as could still be moved began on 26 May under cover of the rains and low clouds, and by the 29th there were nothing but the rear guards (one-fifth of each command) left north of the new line, except on Oroku Peninsula, where the Naval Guard troops remained to deny to the Americans the use of the big airfield, most important of all those on Okinawa.

The prospects of holding the new line for a long while cannot have looked hopeful to either Ushijima or Cho at this date. They had reorganized their formations, consolidating two of the regiments of the 24th into one (the remaining infantry regiment had but 800 men left), reducing the number of battalions in the 62nd by further consolidations, and bringing all such formations as engineers and transportation troops into the line as infantry. But the total strength now amounted to hardly as much as a division. This was insufficient for lines which, though well built, were nearly as extensive as those of Shuri, and the position was very weak in artillery, both in the effective large mortars and in machine cannon. The latter had borne the brunt of the American attacks and the former regrettably could not be moved through the mud. In fact, this mud made all progress so very slow that American spotting planes, which persisted in flying in spite of the weather, often found guns and troops on the road and called down artillery fire which destroyed them. One transport command started to march with 150 vehicles and arrived with less than 30 after being under salvos from an American battleship.[1]

Worst of all was the state of morale within the command. The Naval Guard troops on Oroku, who had not fought except for the single battalion that conducted the banzai at the Horseshoe, were in good shape.[2] The rest were tired out, badly beaten up and hungry, their uniforms ragged. The losses, as usual, had fallen most heavily on the best and boldest men, and in the formations remaining there was a larger proportion of the shiftless Okinawan home guards than the General cared to see. It had not been possible to make the promised issue of sweet-potato brandy on the Emperor's birthday on 29 April, and there was bitterness and whispering over this. General Ushijima had done his best to bolster the men's feelings by circulating on 20 May, just before the move to the south began, the story that an enormous landing of airborne troops had taken Yontan Airfield from the Americans and the latter's lines of communication were now gone. (As a matter of fact, this was a magnification of a radio dispatch from Tokyo which told General Ushijima that the landing would take place. It was not tried till the 24th and then there were only five planes in it. Four of them were knocked out by flak but the fifth reached ground and discharged ten Japs with demolition charges bound round their waists, who destroyed 7 planes and damaged 25 more. Yontan was out of commission for the day

[1] It was *New York;* nearly 500 Japs went.

[2] The state the Japanese command was in was illustrated by the movements of this formation. About 24 May they hastily retreated to Itoman in the south and had to be ordered back just as hastily before our troops began to tap at the roots of the peninsula. The change in plans undoubtedly represents some Japanese command argument of which we know nothing.

but this was not retaking the field.) After the troops were established in their new Yuza-Dake, Yaeju-Dake line another story was issued as an official bulletin. The troops on Okinawa had done well; they had now only to hold out till 20 June. On that date a great counter-invasion would take place near Katena Airfield, the old comrades of the 9th Division coming from Formosa and another fresh division from the China Coast under elaborate naval gunfire and air bombing cover, while a great force of parachutists struck behind the American lines and airborne troops landed to enlarge the holdings around Yontan Field.

How much of this fairy tale was believed is uncertain. Being an official order, it had almost the force of an Imperial rescript and no discussion of the matter was permissible. What Ushijima himself was really hoping for, of course, was a new series of Kamikaze attacks on the ships offshore. There had been a big one on 24-25 May in conjunction with the attempt at Yontan. Sixty-five Kamikaze and 100 Tokobetsu were in it, but their fighter cover was weak and most of the Army fliers engaged were conscripts rather than volunteers for suicide duty, a fact which caused Major General Miyoshi, commanding the units of Kyushu, to protest to Imperial headquarters that such procedures were not in accordance with the true Kamikaze spirit.

Most of them went for the picket line, the better to cover the Yontan attack. They sank the APD *Bates* and badly smashed up the APDs *Barry* and *Roper,* the destroyer escort *O'Neill* the minesweeper *Spectacle* and the destroyers *Bright, Butler,* and *Stormes,* with one LSM. The destroyers *W. C. Cole, Cowell,* and *Guest* received lesser injuries.[1]

[1] To keep the record for the campaign straight, there had been several other Kamikaze hits in less co-ordinated attacks since 11 May, when the last big effort took place. Thus on the 13th the destroyer *Bache* got it bad, and the next day the old veteran carrier *Enterprise,* which had seen nearly every battle of the war, was hit by a Kamikaze that came out of a small bombing formation making a normal attack during a squall. She was Mitscher's flag at the time, the second one he had shot from under him. On the 17th the destroyer *D. H. Fox* was much damaged and on the 20th the destroyer *Thatcher,* the destroyer escort *J. C. Butler,* and an LST, while the destroyer escort *Register* was less hurt. On the 18th the destroyer *Longshaw,* on flycatcher duty off the southern part of the island, ran aground; the Japs put one of their 320 mortar batteries on her and destroyed her.

The attack was thus a comparative failure and there seems to have been some heartburning in Tokyo about it, for Admiral Ugaki staged another under his personal supervision on the night of 27 May, partly to cover Ushijima's withdrawal southward and partly to demonstrate that the correct method was to throw a minor force against the American picket line while the bulk of the suiciders pushed on to the anchorages. He sent out 60 Navy and 50 Army Kamikaze this time, at night, with fairly good fighter coverage, and they did a lot of damage. The destroyer *Drexler* took two Kamikaze aboard and went down; the destroyer *Braine* also got two but survived; *Forrest* and *Shubrick* had major damage, so did the APDs *Rednour* and *Loy*, the cargo carrier *Josiah Snelling*, an LCS, a PSC, and the command ship *Dutton*; less hurt were two more transports, another PC and another LCS, the destroyer *Anthony* and the APD *Tatum*; the destroyer escort *Gilligan* was attacked by a torpedo plane that came with the Kamikaze, and was hit by a torpedo, but it failed to go off.

II

On our right flank the 6th Division was now north of the deep and wide Kokuba Estuary from Oroku Peninsula with its important airstrip and its control of Naha Harbor, which the Navy desperately wanted, for there were still supply problems at the front and the swinging advance that began in the last days of May gravely complicated them. As the 6th circled round Kokuba Estuary, it accordingly wheeled right to face the range of hills that runs almost north and south to seal Oroku from the main island. The 22nd Regiment was placed in line opposite these hills. The 1st Division slanted past the rear of the 22nd, reaching the coast of the East China Sea with its advance spearhead on 7 June. On the very next day it began to get supplies by water across the beaches and pushed on toward Itoman in good spirits.

Meanwhile, the question of taking Oroku had arisen all up and down the chain of command. Some time earlier it had been foreseen that such a question would ultimately come. The Marine commands concerned (III Corps and 6th Division) thought that once the land exits had been sealed off, the place should be assaulted in a regular Marine operation, from the sea, since the outer ground of the peninsula was flat and the beaches reasonably good. Tenth Army was rather of the opinion that an attack through the hills was preferable. There were hardly any amphitracs left (out of seven battalions whose normal equipment was 100 each, not one had as many as 25 in working shape), and those that were left were battered and broken. There would also be difficulties about shipping for the heavy equipment, and the Navy had enough to do with its picket line and Kamikazes without being called upon to furnish close supporting fire for a new beachhead. Still, said General Buckner, the area fell within III Corps's zone of action and if it could find the physical means, the decision as to the tactical means was one that corps could properly take. General Geiger of corps in similar fashion forward-passed the decision to General Shepherd of division, and while the discussions were going on, General Shepherd and his operations officer, the eupeptic Krulak, had been investigating possibilities. Patrols of the 22nd had found the routes into the hill mass before them intricate and subject to a good deal of the kind of fire usually encountered on Okinawa. On the other hand, our reconnaissance landing from the sea face on the night of 2 June achieved a miraculous success, getting back without losing a man to report that the beaches were not mined, everything in the northwest sector of the peninsula was lightly held or not held at all, but that the Japs were digging industriously down toward the land face and women had been moved into caves in that direction. There were enough amphitracs to carry a regiment and enough LSMs and LCMs to carry the equipment. Decision, then, for the seaborne landing—with the 4th Marines making it on the night of 3-4 June, on the tip at a place called Nishikoku.

A ridge thrown off from the island's central spine overlooks this landing spot from the south. The 4th should seize it rapidly to cover the landing of the 29th and the artillery behind. There is an island in the estuary, Ono Yama, where a two-span bridge from Naha City used to stand. The division Reconnaissance Company was to gain this simultaneously with the main landing to permit re-erection of the bridge and land transport down through Naha for purposes of subsequent supply. The remainder of the tactical plan was that as soon as the 29th landed it would work southwestward to clear the

423

Kokuba shore and seize the long high ridge that runs southeast from Kakibana, dominating the estuary, while the 4th pushed straight in from its ridge protecting the landing, cleared the airfield, wheeled left down the southwest coast of the peninsula till it touched our lines at the base, then wheeled left again, back toward the 29th, driving the Japanese before it into a narrowing sack.

The job of assembling the supplies and troops for a divisional move that was only thirty-six hours from planning to execution was something fantastic, but it was well and thoroughly done, and the landing went off like a clockwork, two battalions of the 4th striking the beaches almost exactly on schedule at 0551 on 4 June. One battalion pushed ahead to take the inland ridge, the other leftward to gain the nose of the big ridge below Kakibana. By midmorning both

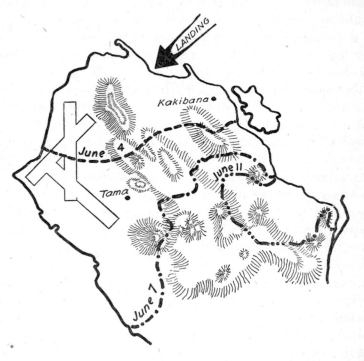

were well up the slopes against opposition that was everywhere insignificant till the crests were nearly reached, when some mortar fire began to come over. All the little outcrops of the main hill were found tunneled in the best Cho manner, but all vacant—Admiral

Ota had not enough men to hold both the beaches and the high ground in them where he had expected to be attacked. Ono Yama was ours by o600; by evening there was a Bailey bridge from Naha to the island, the 29th was ashore, the lines were nearly 1,500 yards inland enclosing nearly half the airfield, and casualties were few.

It was next morning when the advance for conquest started, a peculiar battle, for if this collection of Japs lacked the artillery support those on the Shuri line had had, and if they were far too few to man all the elaborate installations, they had, to balance these, two things not met with elsewhere—so many machine guns, salvaged from wrecked planes, that a fair estimate placed their number at one for every three defenders of Oroku; and a new type of rocket, jerry-built from an 8-inch shell. The thing sounded "like a locomotive from hell." Most of them soared out to sea with that noise which led the Marines to dub them "screaming meemies," but when one hit it exploded with an earth-shaking roar, usually after burying itself well in the ground, so that the physical damage was small. Very bad for the nerves, though.

That day the right flank of our lines swung forward to take all but the last corner of the airfield, while the 29th gained most of its Kokuba-dominating ridge. The night had given Admiral Ota time to recover a little from the surprise of finding Marines behind him and he had rushed a good many men out into the tunneled positions. One of these nests, at the Village of Toma, on the right-center, put up a long resistance to a battalion of the 4th. It was still nothing like Sugar Loaf, the enemy fire nearly all machine gun and mortar, and gains averaged 1,000 yards.

On 6 June the 4th ran rapidly forward down the southwest coast of the peninsula with its right and the 29th made some gains to its left, but along the axial ridge at the center of the peninsula where the Japs were evidently deciding to make their main defense, there was little advance. Tanks found the ground too rough or too muddy and when they did get into action, it was discovered that the Japs had brought up a lot of 20-mm. machine cannon, almost as hard to deal with as the machine guns, because their firing ports were so small.

The 7th and 8th were days of slow advance, even on the 4th Regiment's previously fast-moving right flank. Admiral Ota had shifted

425

some of his troops to hold off the menace of this drive, and everywhere mine fields and lack of roads made it hard to bring up armored support. On 9 June both the 29th and 4th broke through, the latter by the ingenious maneuver of using the Japs' own tunnel systems to work through bare hill crests when all the routes around and over them proved to be under fire from supporting positions. That day also the 22nd began to attack, and the squeeze was on.

It is not to be thought that the remaining four days of the fight were easy; they were days of the same crawling advance under machine gun and mortar fire, the same cave-sealing enterprises, that had marked all the rest of the Okinawa campaign. But the enemy's physical strength had been broken in the surprise and the hard fighting at the center of the peninsula (for he had lost heavily trying to move troops around and still more when the caves at the center were sealed); and on 12 June his morale broke also. Surrender flags began to appear along the line and the surviving Japs were forced out into a region of paddy fields and mudflats along the upper edge of Kokuba. Interpreters tried to get them to give up, but most answered that they requested permission from the kind Americans to commit suicide. The permission was granted as the Marines on the high ground watched, dropping their guns to applaud if the suicide were sufficiently spectacular, like that of the pair who seated themselves on a quadruple demolition charge and touched off the fuse. The peninsula had cost us 1,608 casualties for one of the most neatly performed operations on Okinawa; the Japanese loss would be not far from 5,000.

III

While this was going on, the Kamikazes came back in a new method of attack, beginning on 3 June. It was supposed to provide a steadily flowing stream of suicide planes, day and night on end for a long period, and wear out the nerves of the defenders, that old Japanese concept dating back to Guadalcanal. They lightly hit an LCI on the 3rd, a cargo vessel on the 4th; on the 5th the cruiser *Louisville,* the battleship *Mississippi,* and the destroyer *Anthony,* and did some damage to the minesweeper *Bauer.* On the 6th they crippled the latter's sister ship *Ditter* and on the 7th damaged the escort carrier *Natoma Bay.* Comparatively this was no success at all; his difficulties were beginning to catch up with Admiral Ugaki and for all this four-day attack he had been unable to get more than 20 Kamikaze and 30 Tokobetsu into the air. The Imperial Staff decided that Okinawa was now so nearly gone and the American air defense around the island had become so very civilized that it was no further use; the rest of the suicide fliers would be saved up for that invasion of the Japanese homeland which anyone with an ounce of prescience could see was in the cards.

However, the pressure was not yet off the American Fleet; on 5 June the heaviest typhoon any man in it had ever seen swept across the ships and damaged them far more than any Kamikaze attack. The heavy cruiser *Pittsburgh* had 100 feet of her bow bodily wrenched off; on the carriers *Hornet* and *Bennington* the forward ends of the flight decks were all bent down, and of other vessels the escort carriers *Salamaua* and *Windham Bay,* the cruisers *Baltimore* and *Duluth,* the destroyers *McKee* and *Conklin,* were all so much hurt as to require major dockyard jobs. A long list of other ships, headed by the big new battleships *Alabama, Indiana,* and *Massachusetts,* and ending with no fewer than eleven destroyers, were hurt enough to go into anchorage for tender repairs. It was perhaps just as well that the Japanese Navy had been eliminated before the storm struck.

On land the gale was represented by high winds and rain that did not seem much more than normal to Marines who had been under the May downpour. Under those rains the 1st Division was pressing on in its break to the coast, meeting in resistance only little pockets of Japs who made movement dangerous, the division so much hampered by problems of supply that air-drops were repeatedly asked for. By the evening of 7 June the division was in the upper end of Itoman (where a little airstrip was set up on a road so hospital planes could evacuate the wounded) and facing a small, muddy, sluggish stream called the Mukue Gawa, beyond which rose the steep outcrop of Kunishi Ridge, sheltering the town of the same name. The 7th Regiment was on the right next to the sea, with its zone of action including this ridge, which is flanked on the southwest within easy machine-gun range by another and larger ridge called the Mezado. The 1st Regiment was in line eastward, opposed to a hill bearing simply the number 69, the 5th in reserve. The

427

ground behind was so gelatinous that the 37-mms. had not been brought forward and neither had self-propelled guns; the tanks were well behind.

That day there was an attack; the infantry of both regiments worked across the Mukue and dug in on the slopes of their respective hills, but every patrol found this was a main Japanese battle position that could not be taken without supporting weapons. The 1st Regiment was also getting fire into its flank from Yuza Ridge, most of which lay in the zone of the 96th Division, next door. 9 June was accordingly spent in improving roads, getting tanks forward and providing means for them to cross the muddy Mukue. The main attack was for the 10th, with the 1st Regiment to take Hill 69 and the outer nose of Yuza, the 7th to assault Kunishi.

That assault was a brutal business. The 96th Division was in difficulties with a similar maze of hills and could give little help against Yuza, where one company of the 1st lost 75 men out of 175. Hill 69 was only scratched at, not taken, on this day. Both regiments were in fact not up to their old battle efficiency—full of new replacements, many of them not thoroughly trained; the officers had trouble. There was a good deal of Jap antitank artillery around which, with the mud, kept the tankers from giving effective support and the Japs had so much fire on the Mukue Gawa in the 7th Regiment's zone that the men who infiltrated across it could neither be supported nor supplied.

On 11 June the 1st Regiment gained its two hills and dug in, but was now so much ahead of the formations on both flanks that it must stand. That night came an odd incident which may be taken as the first real sign of Jap breakdown. A long file of Okinawan civilians wrapped round in dirty blankets began to come through the lines of the 1st. They had almost passed the fire positions when a sharp-eyed sergeant discovered that every fifth man in the line-up was a Japanese soldier with grenades under his blanket and a demolition charge around his middle. Of course they had to turn loose the machine guns.

At Kunishi the 7th could make no progress on either 10 or 11 June. On the second night Colonel Snedeker of the regiment turned the Japs' own tactics around on them with a night attack and succeeded in getting two companies onto Kunishi crest at 0300. But after daylight broke they might as well have been in Kamchatka, for all the avenues up to their post were covered by the most intense fire, they could not advance or retreat or be supported. Later in the day the somewhat desperate device of bringing small groups of men up the slope as passengers in tanks was hit upon. It succeeded so far as bringing in a handful of reinforcements but the men on the ridge were lying out on a hot coral rock that offered the most determined resistance to digging, under constant fire from Mezado and other ridges in the rear. Air supply was not much good, the Japs getting most of the drops, and an observer from our side might have thought the battle at a standstill. It was not really so; the driblets of reinforcement kept coming in by tank, and as they did so the party on the ridge expanded inch by inch down the sides, at each few yards' gain blowing a couple more tunnels or silencing another mortar. The result was that the Japs grew gradually weaker, and after a

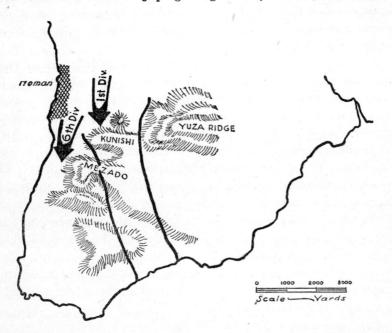

rough three-day battle the place could be called ours by the night of 16 June.

The capture of Kunishi brought about a new distribution of forces in III Corps. The 1st Division was understrength both in

429

numbers and in physical constitution, while Mezado loomed on its right flank, an obstacle as formidable as any yet faced. General Geiger sent the 6th Division back into battle to capture this ridge; the 5th Regiment relieved the 1st and the fresh 8th Regiment of the 2nd Division, which had been sent for as far back as the fall of Shuri, was brought into line between the 5th Regiment and the 6th Division. At the same time the boundaries of III Corps were somewhat expanded eastward to allow for the pinching out of the 96th Division, which had taken extremely heavy casualties, had fallen behind the other formations, and was also in much need of relief.

The 6th used its 22nd Regiment in the initial assault of 17 June, which reached the crest of Mezado; presently the other two regiments had to be put in, but now they and the revamped 1st Division drove forward rapidly against resistance that was everywhere crumbling into little unco-ordinated pockets. The 1st broke through to the coast on 19 June; the 6th cleared its area to the waters of the Pacific two days later, when it was announced that all organized resistance had ceased.

In those last days of Okinawa the final communication lines went out and Japanese morale, long on the teetering edge, collapsed. Surrenders, which began as a trickle, became a flood. A four-man patrol from the 6th Division captured over 150 after their officers had bowed politely, handed over their swords, shot the women with them and committed suicide. In the long run the number of prisoners came to 7,401, of whom about 4,000 turned out to be Okinawans in uniform. The counted enemy dead were 107,539; it was estimated that there were another 23,000 down in various caves. Tenth Army, after elaborately going over the Japanese records, concluded that 72,000 native Japanese troops had been killed in action with 20,000 Okinawan troops; the remaining 42,000 killed would be Okinawan civilians, though in this case and under the conditions of cave warfare it is extremely difficult to determine who is a soldier and who is not.

One of those killed on our side was Lieutenant General Simon Bolivar Buckner—in the very last act of the campaign, on 18 June, as he stood in an observation post near Mezado Ridge, when a shell dropped right on him. Of others the Army lost 4,379 killed, 17,558 wounded; the Marines, 2,834 killed, 13,523 wounded; and the

Navy offshore to Kamikaze and suicide boats, 4,907 killed, 4,824 wounded, for total casualties to our side of 48,025—about which it is to note that the Navy had more killed than either of the other services, despite all those caves and the hard fighting ashore. Since the Navy's casualties form part of the American losses at Okinawa, it is fair to include on the Japanese side of the balance the fact that they lost nearly 7,000 airplanes during the campaign with all their crews; and that the last seaworthy ships of their Navy went down.

IV

In war there is no fully typical combat or campaign, only individual cases. Yet the Okinawa campaign, last and largest of those involving the Marines in the Pacific, was atypical even among the compaigns of the Japanese war. It was the largest land operation undertaken against Japan. (MacArthur in the Philippines employed more American troops and had more Japanese to deal with, but in a series of operations, not any single one.) Yet in spite of this massiveness and the number of troops employed, it was a campaign in which there were no decisions of maneuver beyond those at the very beginning. After the 19 April attack broke down and General Buckner decided to encircle the Japanese fortress at Shuri by its two flanks, everything else became a matter of detail, a question of relieving troops or of logistics. He did succeed in breaking down those flanks and there is not, in the long view, very much that can be said against his conduct of the operation, unless criticism chooses to rest on the decision not to make a landing on the southern beaches early in the game. That decision was very severely criticized in the public prints at the time—so severely that Admiral Nimitz himself felt called upon to answer the strictures; but even in this case there is probably something in the oft-repeated contention of Tenth Army Staff that the supply difficulties of such an operation would have been insuperable.

The campaign throws an interesting backlight on the comments from General MacArthur's headquarters at the time of Iwo about "the slow progress of the attack" effecting "enormous savings of life and materials." The Okinawa campaign was fought under Army command, not that of the Marines, whom MacArthur's headquarters was criticizing. The Army men found that under the tactical and, above all, the strategic conditions, in and surrounding the war against fortified islands, it was necessary to employ the same "wasteful" methods Army officers had often criticized. At the approaches to the Conical, as at Sugar Loaf, there was no way to get into the complex of defense but by men standing up and running across open and fire-swept ground. Not even armor could do it; antitank guns and Jap suicide men emerging from the side hill entrances would stop tanks every time unless they had infantry close around them to protect them and engineers on foot to clear mine fields ahead.

The Marines have said that their methods are not in the long run really wasteful, even if the necessity for speed imposed by exterior strategic considerations were neglected; that when a formation is moving onward it suffers fewer casualties than when it remains in position and waits for artillery or weather or the J-factor to produce a break. It is true that on Okinawa the 96th Division, the most nearly static of those in line (let it be said, through no fault of its own, since the 96th was one of the best fighting divisions on the island), suffered the heaviest casualties. It is also true that the far more static Japs suffered greater casualties than we. But the statement as a whole has an air of specious generalization that requires it to be examined minutely.

Why should it be that an advance is less costly than holding a position? The moment the question is asked we are at the heart of the whole Okinawa matter, and indeed at the heart of the war in the Pacific. There is no logical physical reason why attack should be less costly. The difference, the change, lies in that field of morale with which military men are often reluctant to deal, because it contains no exact and ponderable factors. Yet it was in this field that the strategic decision of Okinawa was reached. One of the features that made the campaign an aberrant one was the fact that the high contending parties entered upon it with aims so divergent that only tactical decisions could be reached on the ground. Ushijima was deliberately fighting a non-decision battle. He could obtain a victory only by preventing one by our forces until the Kamikaze had whittled the American fleet down to where it could no longer support an operation so far from base.

432

For our forces to submit to slow progress was to play into the hands of the enemy's system, to save lives and materials ashore at the cost of losing far more at sea. The fact that the fleet did beat off the Kamikazes without being crippled is beside the point as far as the operations and obligations ashore were concerned. As a matter of fact, General Buckner did not submit to slow progress, in spite of having begun his campaign with a statement to the press that he intended to "kill the Japs gradually." He maintained constant close-in pressure which eventually broke their physical resources. Those resources were considerable, but Japanese acceptance of a passive role meant that sooner or later the active Americans would bring against every position enough force to overwhelm it; that the struggle was always hopeless. Most important feature of all in the campaign, knowledge of this ultimately broke even Japanese hearts.

Among all the abnormal features of the Okinawa campaign there is none more striking that the capture of 7,400 uniformed prisoners. This is more than were taken in all the rest of the Pacific war put together. One may make deductions for the fact that many of them were Okinawans; one may make more deductions for the fact that General Ushijima overplayed his hand in the propaganda department. At the end not even Japanese would swallow that story about the fleet and army of relief. The figure is still enormous; it still represents a genuine breakdown of morale.

Or perhaps it would be more accurate to say that it represents a seepage into the lower levels of the breakdown that had taken place at the Cabinet level as long ago as the invasion of Saipan and the Battle of the Philippine Sea. By time the Okinawa campaign began, indeed, the Koiso government was out of office, betrayed from within. In September of 1944, before the invasion of Peleliu and the Philippines, Admiral Yonai, the Navy Minister in that government, had bidden Admiral Takagi to resume his studies on how to get Japan out of the war. There was a difference in these new studies. The emphasis was now changed to rest on the point of how to persuade the Army heads to agree to ending the war on any terms that could be had. Nor did Yonai stop there. He held consultations, members of the Imperial Household became involved, and in February of 1945 the Emperor called in the Jushin and began se-

433

curing from them opinions that Japan was at the edge of defeat and must seek peace at once.

The strains thus set up were more than Koiso could stand when the landing on Okinawa came. Cabinet Ministers refused to serve under him; his government fell. The new one set up on 8 April, with Admiral Kentaro Suzuki at its head, found the pacifiers in the majority. They continued their pressures on the warmakers till that date in August when the appearance of the atom bomb offered a heaven-sent opportunity to save face. (Some other device would have been fine had there been no atom bomb.) There was a conference between high Cabinet members and the Emperor. One by one the Cabinet men spoke for accepting peace on any terms till General Korechika Anami was reached, the Army Minister and representative of the Manchuria Gang. He explained how many million undefeated soldiers were still ready to defend Japan, how excellent were the chances of wearing out American patience in an unending war. When he had finished the Divine Presence asked simply, "Are you lying to me again?" Anami made the obeisances without another word, went out and committed suicide—and Japan surrendered.

INDEXES

I—Battles and Campaigns, Place Names, Miscellaneous

A—Battles and Campaigns

B—Place Names

435

436

C—*Miscellaneous*

II—Our People

441

III—Our Forces

A—Units

446

B—Ships

449

IV—Enemy Staffs and Personnel

451

452

V—ENEMY FORCES
A—Units

B—Ships